NIETZSCHE AND MUSIC

Beginning and ending of *Tristan und Isolde,* connected and arranged by Richard Strauss. The original, in Strauss's own hand, is reproduced in Dieter Borchmeyer, *Richard Wagner: Theory and Theater* (Oxford: Clarendon Press, 1991).

NIETZSCHE AND MUSIC

GEORGES LIÉBERT

TRANSLATED BY

DAVID PELLAUER AND GRAHAM PARKES

THE UNIVERSITY OF CHICAGO PRESS
CHICAGO & LONDON

GEORGES LIÉBERT is *maître de conférence* at the Institut d'Études Politiques in Paris and a producer at France-Musique. He is the author of four other books.
DAVID PELLAUER is professor of philosophy at DePaul University.
GRAHAM PARKES is professor of philosophy at the University of Hawaii.

The University of Chicago Press, Chicago 60637
The University of Chicago Press, Ltd., London
© 2004 by The University of Chicago
All rights reserved. Published 2004
Printed in the United States of America

12 11 10 09 08 07 06 05 04 03   1 2 3 4 5
ISBN: 0-226-48087-9 (cloth)

The University of Chicago Press gratefully acknowledges a subvention from the government of France, through the French Ministry of Culture and Centre National du Livre, in support of the costs of translating this volume.

Originally published as *Nietzsche et la musique* © Presses Universitaires de France, 1995.

Library of Congress Cataloging-in-Publication Data

Liébert, Georges.
    [Nietzsche et la musique. English]
    Nietzsche and music / Georges Liébert ; translated by David Pellauer and Graham Parkes.
        p. cm.
Translation of: Nietzsche et la musique.
    ISBN 0-226-48087-9 (alk. paper)
    1. Nietzsche, Friedrich Wilhelm, 1844–1900—Criticism and interpretation. 2. Nietzsche, Friedrich Wilhelm, 1844–1900—Views on music. 3. Music—Philosophy and aesthetics. 4. Wagner, Richard, 1813–1993—Criticism and interpretation. I. Title.
ML423.N56 L5413 2004
780'.92—dc21
                                        2003012778

CONTENTS

"This small link with music and almost with composers, to which this hymn *does* testify, is something of inestimable value, considering the psychological problem which I am; and now it will make people *think*."[1] Thus wrote Nietzsche in 1887 regarding his last composition, the *Hymn to Life*, which he hoped people would sing posthumously in his memory. Yet the philosopher eclipsed the musician, especially while the musician's works were difficult to access. It was only in 1976, following seventeen years of research by Nietzsche biographer Curt Paul Janz, that the musical works were published.[2] Before that, though, a few of his musical works, including the *Hymn to Life* in a version for chorus and orchestra by Peter Gast, had been recorded by a number of different German and Swiss radio orchestras, as well as by ORTF (French Radio and Television). As for commercial recordings, until 1992 this consisted of only two lieder recorded by Dietrich Fischer-Dieskau, but since then almost all of Nietzsche's compositions have become available on compact disc.[3] While not masterpieces, these works are still worthy of attention. Beyond the fact that they sometimes are quite charming, they also cast light on the personality of Nietzsche, as he himself thought, and they also suggest illuminating comparisons between the composer and the writer.

But it is difficult to explain the silence about Nietzsche the composer that has extended to his many writings devoted to music. In reading most commentators on Nietzsche, one would hardly suspect that he had been a composer, or that he had ever even heard music. Yet it seems to me that if we are to understand Nietzsche, both him and his thought—which he believed were inseparable—it is at least as important to know *Tristan und Isolde, Parsifal*, and Wagner's principal theoretical writings as it is to know the complete works of Schopenhauer, Kant, or Heidegger.

To be sure, since three of Nietzsche's books—*The Birth of Tragedy, The Case of Wagner*, and *Nietzsche Contra Wagner*—have the composer as their subject, when his exegetes discuss them they do refer to the stormy relations Nietzsche had with Wagner. But treatments of their relationship do not generally acknowledge their full significance, even though the great number of "posthumous fragments" left by Nietzsche and his correspondence show, if it really needed to be shown, that this was the great affair of his life. More regrettably, they approach the subject with a haughty ignorance of Wagner's work and without ever allowing his voice to be heard. Commentators have been content to elaborate on the aesthetic, philosophical, and political case that Nietzsche made against Wagner without examining how well-founded his accusations might be. Wagner's old disciple would certainly have been the first to condemn this behavior, for Nietzsche did not want anyone "easily to appropriate" the judgment he brought to bear against Wagner. It is true that casting Wagner as the lone villain or bogeyman of an edifying history of music from Bach to Schoenberg in which only saints and martyrs are to be found—in which he is used as a foil—is an inexpensive way to gain a reputation as an enlightened mind and a friend of mankind. But drawing on a long study of Wagner's works and those of Nietzsche, I have departed from this tradition. Perhaps, in so doing, I have sinned against Nietzsche out of an excess of severity, but, as he wrote at the end of *The Case of Wagner*, "this essay is inspired, as you hear, by gratitude."[4]

I extend my thanks to Jacques Le Rider and my editor, Michel Prigent, who encouraged this undertaking, as well as Philippe Raynaud, Marcel Gauchet, Jean-François Revel, and Ivan Alexandre, for their advice, and Robert Kopp, for the help he gave me in carrying out my research; and above all, Pierre Manent, who was the first reader of this manuscript, and George Walden, who was the first reader of this English translation.

Georges Liébert

NOTE TO THE ENGLISH EDITION

In the original French edition of this book, the author was able to cite the French translations of the current standard fifteen-volume critical German edition of Nietzsche's works edited by Giorgio Colli and Mazzino Montinari. A multivolume English edition based on this material has finally begun to appear in the last few years. However, only four volumes have been published to date, only one of which readily applies to the material cited in this book. Hence, I have cited other existing English translations of Nietzsche's major works where available. These editions do not, however, include the posthumous material and the material from Nietzsche's notebooks found in the Colli-Montinari edition that Liébert draws on to support his argument. The decision was made, therefore, to cite the German rather than the French editions for material not currently available in English wherever possible. I am grateful to Professor Graham Parkes for undertaking the laborious task of locating the German references to replace the French citations in the endnotes wherever possible. He was also able in a number of cases to ensure that my English translation of this material conformed more closely to the German original than the French translation might sometimes suggest.

I am also grateful to Georges Liébert for his help in assisting me in the early stages of this translation with questions about some of the materials cited. His willingness to review an early draft of the translation was a great help in preventing errors and misreadings on my part. There are many books published on Nietzsche. I believe that readers of this translation will find that Georges Liébert has been able to bring a truly fresh and insightful perspective to our understanding of this important thinker, writer—and musician.

David Pellauer

"Without Music,
Life would be an Error"

I must appeal only to those who, immediately related to music, have in
it, as it were, their motherly womb, and are related to things almost
exclusively through unconscious musical relations.

Nietzsche, *The Birth of Tragedy*

This is how Nietzsche alerts the readers of *The Birth of Tragedy,* his first
work, whose original title when it appeared in 1872 was *The Birth of Tragedy
out of the Spirit of Music* and clearly announced his intentions. But his state-
ment holds as well for the books that were to follow. And it is significant that
this work was completed (or almost completed) as it had begun—in music,
if I may put it this way, with the pamphlet *Nietzsche contra Wagner,* thereby
closing the circle (or better, the ring), since both books have Wagner as their
protagonist, the composer of *The Ring of the Nibelungen,* who Nietzsche celebrated in 1872 but reviled sixteen years later.

Meanwhile, there is no work by Nietzsche in which music is not more
or less present. His works contain a sparkling selection of essays and aphorisms about music and musicians. Furthermore, there were numerous musicians among his shifting circle of friends and relations. "In the whole history of philosophy it would be impossible to find another philosopher who
frequented musicians to such an extent," notes André Schaeffner,[1] after
having listed more than forty of them: composers, orchestra conductors,
pianists, professors, musicologists, and music publishers—from Wagner, of
course, to Liszt and Brahms, and including Peter Gast, his faithful friend,

Hans von Bülow, Hermann Levi, and Arthur Nikisch—to cite only the best known among them and those who left a mark on his works or his correspondence.

Music, a Metaphor of Life

But music is not just present in Nietzsche's work in an explicit way, in the form of critical analyses and commentaries. Like that "golden thread" to which Marcel Proust compared it and that he said ran through *In Search of Lost Time,* it constitutes a constant reference as well as an invisible framework.

Like Schopenhauer, his principal "educator" to whom he owed so much, Nietzsche makes frequent recourse to musical metaphors: metaphors of the keyboard, of the vibrating string, of dissonance, of harmony, of melody. Their function is not simply to decorate his argument or to illustrate it. Music is the metaphor of life itself, of life as it ought to be if, from the harmonic jumble—the "ground, profound, disturbing bass," which at the origin are the individual and civilization—the melody emerges and asserts itself wherein we recognize, "freely and capriciously advancing," the will and "the plainly conscious desires of mankind." Then, when it reaches the peaks of its course, come those "great minds," the "strong individuals," for whose appearance humanity sometimes must pay a heavy price and who would not be possible without "the sustained chord" of all the elements that make up this melody.[2]

However, there are also contemplative natures:

There are people who repose so steadily within themselves and whose capacities are balanced with one another so harmoniously that any activity directed towards a goal is repugnant to them. They are like music that consists of nothing but long drawn out harmonious chords, without even the beginning of a moving, articulated melody making an appearance. Any movement from without serves only to settle the barque into a new equilibrium on the lake of harmonious euphony. Modern men usually grow extremely impatient when confronted by such natures, which *become* nothing without our being able to say that they *are* nothing. But in certain moods the sight of them prompts the unusual question: why melody at all? Why does the quiet reflection of life in a deep lake not suffice us?[3]

Just as Nietzsche regarded musical taste and its long apprenticeship as the model for the love of all things, similarly, musical discourse would be for him, except perhaps during his "positivist" period, his model for all discourse, even for philosophical discourse. To be sure, as a tireless writer, Nietzsche would not have authored so many memorable aphorisms if he had not loved words. Yet, as an heir of the German Romantics, he felt irritation for language that was too logical, too rational a language to translate lived experience without schematizing and mutilating it. To this was added the mistrust aroused in him by words that have acquired a life of their own, one made up of habits and prejudices, through a kind of instinctive fetishism, an abusive belief in grammar. Finally, this uncompromising individualist became impatient with the fact of belonging to the "herd" that language imposed upon him. Language, along with consciousness, was born out of need for communication and out of mutual aid extended to those humans who were incapable of confronting the necessities of life alone. He explains in *The Gay Science* that language does not belong to the individual nature of human beings but to what makes humans a gregarious animal. And it can only express from "the perspective of the herd" the thought that has become conscious, that is, the smallest part of it—"the most superficial and worst" part.[4]

> Our true experiences are not garrulous. They could not communicate themselves if they wanted to: they lack words. We have already grown beyond whatever words we have. In all talking there lies a grain of contempt.[5]

As Charles Andler will put it, this "anti-verbalism" was rooted in the intense experience Nietzsche had of music, both as a listener and a composer. And as Nietzsche himself will note in 1887, "*In comparison to music* all communication through *words* is shameless. The word diminishes and makes stupid; the word depersonalizes: the word makes what is uncommon common."[6] This resembles the narrator of *In Search of Lost Time* (another great reader of Schopenhauer), for whom music seemed to be "the unique example of what might have been—if the invention of language, the formation of words, the analysis of ideas had not intervened—the means of communication of souls."[7] We may think as well of Rousseau, one of Nietzsche's bêtes noires but, like him, a composer and writer, who gave the first humans "singing and passionate languages," which the growing hold of need and reason degraded into instruments for lying and duplicity.[8] "It should have *sung*," Nietzsche will say in 1886 about "the new soul" that "babbled" in *The Birth of Tragedy*.[9]

As a composer, Nietzsche will confide that "sounds allowed him to say certain things that words were incapable of expressing."[10] Yet unable to really communicate with sounds alone, it was to a musical treatment that he submitted those words to which his failures as an "unlucky musicaster" threw him back.[11] "One must write as one composes," Novalis had already said. Hence we find in Nietzsche a recurring aspiration to song, to speech that has been born of music, which does find free expression in *Thus Spoke Zarathustra* and in his poetry. Yet, with "an inexorable awareness" lodged in his ear, the prose writer shows himself to be no less attentive than is the poet to the music of words and their *tempo*—leading to uncommon charms in the writing of a philosopher, ones that have contributed a good bit to the seduction his words were to exercise. Paul Valéry, not very sensitive to Nietzsche's metaphysics and his "immoralist morality"—"for me, they are only combinations among other possible ones"—thought that "these would not have had such an effect except for the strong resonance that [Nietzsche] communicated to them and that do not necessarily belong to them. But in this way," he added, "Nietzsche has wonderfully resolved the difficult problem that the existence of great music has posed for almost a century to every writer who *thought about* it."[12] As Valéry himself, following Mallarmé, was to experience, this formidable rival could impose a model that could lead to despair. And it was both under its guidance and in resisting it that Nietzsche (like them) conquered his style. It was often necessary for him to struggle "before finding a phrase worthy of being printed, before being fully satisfied with its melody and its rhythm." Nostalgic for the way the ancients had read aloud, Nietzsche "would declaim it in order to experience its cadence, its accent, its tonality and metrical movement, also in order to test out the clarity and precision of the idea expressed."[13] This is a method that recalls that "test of reading aloud" to which the author of *Madame Bovary* submitted the fruits of his long torments. In this lies the musicality of numerous of Nietzsche's texts, even as regards their fastidious punctuation. One example is the dash, which, again like Flaubert, Nietzsche frequently made use of. However, whereas for Flaubert this sign did not break the continuity of the sentence but, like a short breath, helped lead up to the final falling off, the last backwash of the *adagio,* for Nietzsche (as for Laurence Sterne, whom he admired, or for Valéry), it breaks the cadence—something unforeseen springs forth, a surprising thought that, often, in a final rebound, *presto,* leaps "beyond," when it does not turn against itself. Or coming at the end of a sentence or verse (as in Sterne and Mallarmé), the dash prolongs the resonance in a suspension of sound and sense that elsewhere would be suggested by an ellipsis . . . Unless these dots evoke the leap of a dancing god, the impatience of a prophet, a euphoric haste to pull down idols, the implications of some "terrible audacity." Along with some imminent and definitive revelations, the late writings offer a premonition of the unfinished aspect in which madness will leave Nietzsche's oeuvre—if it were not its very nature to remain forever incomplete—the silence, finally, that such common, such superficial words had troubled for a moment: "For me, [in my writing] it always begins only after the dashes," Nietzsche would one day write to his sister.[14]

To Read Is to Listen

It would be a misunderstanding, therefore, to see mere coquetry or a dilettante's affectation when Nietzsche compares his writings to compositions, speaks of *The Genealogy of Morals* as a sonata in three movements, and especially when he speaks of *Thus Spoke Zarathustra* as a "symphony" and compares its first book to the first movement of Beethoven's Ninth Symphony.[15] "Perhaps my *Zarathustra* may be reckoned as music," he will write in *Ecce Homo*.[16] What is certain is that he presupposes a "regeneration of listening." And it is always with a reawakened ear that we have to read Nietzsche—and not just *Zarathustra*. For to read is first of all to listen:

> Just as the Italians *appropriate* a piece of music by incorporating it into
> their passion . . . this is how I read thinkers and sing after them their
> melodies: I know that behind all those cold words there stirs a soul of
> desire, and I hear it singing, for my own soul sings when it is moved.[17]

Both a metaphor and real, the musical kind of reading that Nietzsche practices and recommends is a privileged means of comprehension. A refined auditory awareness will easily perceive the inner movement of works, their *tempo* that conveys their key. "Upon closer acquaintance with the piece, the proper tempo will give the player almost of itself a clue to the proper rendering," said Wagner, whose teaching Nietzsche had meditated over.[18] But, alas, Germans do not read "with their ears, but only with their eyes: to read, they put their ears in a drawer." Whence the gauche, embarrassing style of so many of their books, which caused Nietzsche such displeasure:

> What torture books written in German are for anyone who has a *third*
> ear! How vexed one stands before the slowly revolving swamp of
> sounds that do not sound like anything and rhythms that do not dance,

called a "book" among Germans! Yet worse is the German who *reads* books! How lazily, how reluctantly, how badly he reads! How many Germans know, and demand of themselves what they should know, that there is *art* in every good sentence—art that must be figured out if the sentence is to be understood! A misunderstanding about its tempo, for example—and the sentence itself is misunderstood.

That one must not be in doubt about the rhythmically decisive syllables, that one experiences the break with any excessively severe symmetry as deliberate and attractive, that one lends a subtle and patient ear to every *staccato* and every *rubato*, that one figures out the meaning in the sequence of vowels and diphthongs and how delicately and richly they can be colored and change colors as they follow each other—who among book-reading Germans has enough good will to acknowledge such duties and demands and to listen to that much art and purpose in language? In the end one simply does not have "the ear for that"; and thus the strongest contrasts of style go unheard, and the subtlest artistry is *wasted* as on the deaf.[19]

To read is to listen, and to listen is already to think—without prejudging anything, freely. Instead of seeking to prove or refute; that is, to "*think* in terms of ends," the thinker must first "*listen*," just as one listens to a piece of music[20]—to resonate before reasoning. Thus it was guided by an aesthetic instinct more than by "a pure instinct for knowing" that Nietzsche studied the Hellenic world and made sense of the nature of ancient tragedy:

Listening to the overall sound that the ancient Greek philosophers produce, I imagined myself perceiving the tones that I was accustomed to hearing in Greek art, and above all, in tragedy. To what degree that depended on the Greeks, and to what degree simply on my ears, the ears of a man with a great need for art—I cannot to this day say with certainty.[21]

In fact, Nietzsche will never renounce his tonal intuition for Hellenism. Indeed, however things may turn out, we all should learn to listen, in two senses of the word: intellectually, of course, but also physically, without blushing that we trust our ears—no more, by the way, than we trust any of our other senses, for "we have the right to love our senses, we have made them spiritual and artistic to the highest degree." Above all, since "we possess scientific knowledge today to precisely the extent that we have decided to *accept* the evidence of the senses—to the extent that we have learned to sharpen and arm them and to think them through to their conclusions. The rest is abortion and not-yet-science: which is to say metaphysics, theology, psychology, epistemology. *Or* science of formulae, sign-systems: such as logic and that applied logic, mathematics."[22]

Now hearing sharpened by the practice of music, such as Nietzsche liked to think he possessed, will quickly reveal itself to be an incomparable instrument of evaluation. Using this yardstick of music, he noted in 1875, remembering Plato: if, for example, we compare it to gymnastics (which were very popular at that moment), "modern life appears as a repugnant form of barbarism."

> For anyone who lives in the rhythm of great music recognizes, in himself first of all and from there in all others, how he usually is incapable of matching that pure and elevated and yet strongly animated inner life of music with something that would belong to it as an image, an appearance: in such attempts, he usually has only the unpleasant impression of looking into a jumble of distortions and excesses. Now the impression that music itself produces is so powerful that the rhythm of gymnastics is not alone in having to justify itself before it: everything that has a rhythm, the whole life of individuals, the politics of peoples, relations among business interests, class conflicts, the opposition between citizens and noncitizens—involuntarily the man nourished by music will measure and judge it in terms of music: he will grasp what it means to found a state on music, something that the Greeks had not only grasped but also demanded. Nor is it a matter of the rhythmical alone; the soulful integrity of impersonal passion as well, and the *quiet* fire bursting forth that arises from unfathomable depths—all that will be for him the judge of his modern world.[23]

And thirteen years later, in calling for a "revaluation of all values," it will still be by his ear—his "third," his "wicked ear"—that, through Wagner, in whom the modern world "speaks its innermost language," Nietzsche will judge the world with a hammer—the hammer of the piano tuner—will "sound out" idols.

> For once to pose questions here with a *hammer* and perhaps to receive for answer that famous hollow sound which speaks of inflated bowels—what a delight for one who has ears behind his ears—for an old psychologist and pied piper like me, in presence of whom precisely that which would like to stay silent *has to become audible* . . .[24]

Nietzsche's reader is promised similar pleasures if he possesses a "subtle and patient ear." Aphorisms and fragments hang together like so many variations, sometimes barely sketched out: reductions in words, verbal vestiges of an ideal score whose incessant polyphony can only be evoked from their interesting echoes. Apparently discontinuous and even disparate, and throwing off the reader used to things laid out in chapters and paragraphs stitched together by the cadences of a linear causality, Nietzsche's work in fact obeys a principle of organization and coherence that is thematic in nature. It implies a *musical* attentiveness comparable to the one required by Wagner's works, for which it is in many ways the aggressive counterpoint. Ductile, dynamic, always underway, his themes, like Wagnerian leitmotifs, which do sometimes have the indiscrete insistence that he reproaches them for, overlap, interweave, change timbre and sense depending on the momentarily adopted perspective, then come together for a time in the provisory constructions that make up his books, each with its own tonality, before resuming their course—their chase, which he himself compared to that of a "Don Juan of knowledge."[25]

Philosopher Because Musician

In spite of such numerous and flagrant indications, Nietzsche's relationship with music—both as philosopher and composer—have solicited little reflection from commentators. This is true particularly in France; while across the Rhine it is not rare for a musician to hold a Ph.D., music does not enjoy such a welcoming or serious hearing in French universities.[26]

There has been a tendency therefore to consider the subject of Nietzsche and music as a biographical accident, a curiosity, a typically German craze—even as a somewhat doubtful acquaintance that had all too often turned the author of *The Gay Science* away from the honorable and silent company of ideas so that he cannot really be considered a genuine philosopher. Nietzsche's repeated avowal is often cited: "Without music, life would be an error,"[27] but almost as though it were a quip. Rarely is the decisive importance music, in fact, had for the economy of his thought recognized. What we actually have here is a key formula because of the twofold interpretation it is capable of receiving, an interpretation that Nietzsche never ceased to give it throughout his life and work.

That life without music would be an error may mean that music makes us forget life, that it constitutes a privileged means of "evading" it, as Flaubert said about work. A refuge, love potion, narcotic, or disguised religion, revealing a lack or insufficiency as regards existence and "dissatisfaction in the face of reality," it is a way of fleeing to another world that only justifies this world—or at least makes it bearable—by negating it.

Yet the same formula can, on the contrary, signify that life being understood only through music, music, far from being its negation, represents its immediate and irrefutable affirmation. The joy of being, the pleasure of existing reaches its culmination in musical experience and finds there its highest expression. The jubilation, the excitement of living that it provokes or enhances, expresses a full and complete acceptance of reality to the point of wishing for its permanence or its return. Just, as it turns out, like music itself where, once we have learned to listen to a figure, a melody, then to accept it despite its initial oddity, we wait for it and are so accustomed to it that it makes us "its humble and enraptured lovers who desire nothing better from the world than it and only it."[28]

With this twofold interpretation one senses that not just an aesthetic unfolds but a more general vision as well, a whole philosophy. Nietzsche moved back and forth throughout his life between these two senses within which music can be clothed. His role as herald of a revaluation of values, which dates to his break with Wagner, proceeded from a willingness to challenge the first sense, which he had initially cultivated with a kind of somber intoxication, in order to exalt the second one with all the more energy since physical suffering never ceased to torment him. For if, properly speaking, Nietzsche never *thinks* music—because it is unthinkable, happily unthinkable, he might have said—his thinking begins with music. It is the ultimate, sensible, physical ground of his reflections, where this latter plunges its roots into an initial, intensely felt experience of music. Rather than with philosophy, music begins with the body—which Nietzsche, who did not spare his own body, will be inclined toward the end to see as the hidden origin of all creation and all evaluation; for this reason we may sometimes be tempted to speak of a psychophysiolosophy.[29]

"I have always written my works with my whole body and life," he said. "I have no idea what 'purely intellectual' problems are."[30] Whence the reproach he addresses to traditional philosophers in *The Gay Science* that they have always mistrusted their senses, because these "might lure them away from their own world, from the cold realm of 'ideas.'" "Having 'wax in one's ears' was then almost a condition of philosophizing: a real philosopher no longer listened to life insofar as life is music; he *denied* the music of life."[31] Nietzsche, on the contrary, says he is a philosopher-musician—and a philosopher because a musician.

An Heir of the Reformation

In this, he who was so contemptuous of all things German shows himself to be wholly in conformity with his origins. One could not be more German, and the explosive product of a long gestation.

"The German even thinks of God as singing songs," he writes in *Twilight of the Idols*,[32] thereby recalling in an amusing way that it was to Luther's Reformation—the creator of the evangelical chorale—that Germany owed its musical vocation.[33] This was affirmed following the cataclysm of the Thirty Years' War with the multiplication of chorales, orchestras, and concert societies. Music, over time, became the food of a whole people: "It was as though, emanating from the sign of the celestial lyre, an immense Aeolian harp hovered over Germany, which ceaselessly spoke and answered to the genius of its inhabitants," said a French traveler at the end of the eighteenth century.[34] Reacting against the artifices of (French) "civilization" and tired of reasoning, Germans then discovered that if music was not their true national language, it was at least the only one that could truly translate the primordial innocence of *Kultur* and the Orphic depths of their obsessive and straightforwardly vertiginous inwardness.

If Kant took music to be a minor art having only to do with sensation and often lacking in urbanity, if it is absent from the works of Schiller and Kleist, and if Goethe at bottom distrusted it as something unclear, Herder, on the contrary—whose influence was considerable—glorified the "voice of Nature" in it. A "vital rhythm," pure becoming, it is that "magic" (*Zauberei*) that allows humankind to communicate directly with the occult forces of the world. It is the "language of the invisible."

Whereas France celebrates the consecration of the writer from Voltaire to Hugo,[35] Germany prepared for that of the musician, who, rather than the simple *Musiker* of the eighteenth century, now wanted to be a *Tonkünstler*, an "artist in tones." No composer across the Rhine after Beethoven failed to follow his example in hearing in music "the highest revelation of all wisdom and all philosophy,"[36] and as Schopenhauer would add, that of "the inner being of the world," with whom music acquired the dignity of a metaphysical status. To make or listen to music was therefore to do philosophy unconsciously, without knowing it. And "supposing we succeeded in giving a perfectly accurate and complete explanation of music which goes into detail, and thus a detailed repetition in concepts of what it expresses, this would also be at once a sufficient repetition and explanation of the world in concepts, or one wholly corresponding thereto, and hence true philosophy."[37]

In the words of Marcel Beaufils, henceforth "whoever says a German thinker says a seer informed by music."[38] Nietzsche was the heir of this tradition—which included equally Wackenroder, Jean Paul, Novalis, and Hoffmann—a rebel, divided within himself, but at bottom, he always remained faithful to it.

References to the plastic arts are quite rare in Nietzsche's writings and correspondence—as are visual metaphors, when compared with auditory ones, although the former are more numerous during the time Nietzsche lived in Italy and in Nice. The antiquity he dreamed of as a young philologist was not peopled with "harmonious statues" like the antiquity of a Goethe who, in his home at Weimar collected engravings and casts of the masterpieces of Greek art. *The Birth of Tragedy* presents an archaic Greece bathed in the sonorous effervescence of Dionysian mysteries, which opposes the ideal of visual beauty that classical Greece represented within the German Hellenistic tradition inherited from Winckelmann. And if Nietzsche shows that tragedy could not have seen the light of day without the intervention of Apollo, he does not conceal the fact that "the god of every plastic form" and of "beauty in appearance" plays only a mediating role. The priority and primacy in the creative process belongs to Dionysus, the god of intoxication and of ecstatic song, whom he names as the "true being," the "originary one." Having denounced Socrates in *The Birth of Tragedy* for having been the agent of the dissolution of Hellenism, Nietzsche will later add, "I think it was because he was the son of a sculptor. If these plastic arts were able to talk, they would seem superficial; in Socrates, the son of the sculptor, this superficial character revealed itself."[39]

As for drawing and painting, when in passing Nietzsche does mention specific works, it is without that grateful complicity that music nearly always evokes in him. They are images, examples meant to support an argument, not objects of delectation. With the exception of Dürer's celebrated engraving, *The Knight, Death, and the Devil,* which Nietzsche understands as a symbol of his own destiny, Claude Lorrain is the only painter for whom he shows a lively predilection the further he distances himself from Wagner and Germany and the more responsive he becomes to the "solar power of transfiguration" of the Mediterranean world. However, it is not the properly plastic quality of Lorrain's landscapes that attracted Nietzsche but, rather, their allegorical power. Their golden light revealed a dreamed-of South wherein "all the *bucolism* of the ancients" seems to be revivified, prefiguring the "heroic idyll" to which his soul aspires.[40] At least, he had seen three of Lorrain's paintings at Rome, just as he had seen some by Rubens and Van Dyck at Livorno, and quite probably at Dresden, *The Sistine Madonna* by Raphael—that icon of the Romantics and the obligatory reference of German aesthetics ever since Winckelmann—against which Nietzsche in *Human, All Too Human* throws himself into provocative and brilliant psycho-philosophical variations.[41] In general, though, he draws his quite superficial knowledge of painting from reproductions and lithographs. Museums are almost wholly absent in the notes and letters (from 1876 on) of this adopted Italian, and his myopia is a sufficient explanation for this. Like Wagner— who also did not frequent the museums during his long sojourns on the peninsula—Nietzsche could have said of the plastic arts and of painting in particular, "It is like a curtain one pulls to conceal the seriousness of things."[42] Translated into his own language, this means the veil of Maya of the Apollonian consciousness destined to conceal the horror and ecstasy of the Dionysian world.

When Nietzsche speaks of art, therefore, he is usually and almost exclusively referring to music. "Music as the *universal-unnational-atemporal* art is the *only flourishing* art," he noted in 1871.[43] "It represents for us art *as a whole* and the artistic world." In all this, notes Ernst Bertram, "Nietzsche is, in every way, the descendent of the Lutheran Reformation, which, even where it did not show itself in iconoclasm, nonetheless robbed the German of the serene joy of the eyes he had during the Middle Ages and gave him in exchange a nostalgic ear, the insatiable and metaphysical thirst for music."[44]

2

$\mathcal{A}$T THE $\mathcal{P}$IANO

In the beginning, then, was music. As a Saxon, and from that Saxon Thu-ringia that saw the births of Schütz, Bach, Handel, Schumann, and Wagner, Nietzsche was born into a family of pastors where music and theology tra-ditionally went together. From his birth in February 1844, Nietzsche lived in a world of sounds that he was quick to consider as "his most authentic world." "Let music, this most marvelous gift from God, remain forever my companion on the pathways of life," he will write at the age of fourteen. "One has to consider all those who despise it as soulless creatures similar to animals."[1]

His father "had acquired considerable facility at the piano; he was par-ticularly good at free variations."[2] When his father died when Nietzsche was barely five years old, his mother taught him, before a first teacher—"a choir director afflicted with all the loveable faults of his profession"—nearly asphyxiated this innate inclination. His progress at the piano was so rapid that after two years of lessons he was capable of playing several of Bee-thoven's sonatas and some transcriptions of Haydn's symphonies. These two composers, along with Mozart, Schubert, Mendelssohn, and Bach, formed "the pillars of German Music, the only foundation" he knew at this time.[3] Although it only had a few thousand inhabitants, Naumburg, where the family moved after the death of Pastor Nietzsche, possessed a rich and var-ied musical life. Public and private concerts, chamber music and vocal per-formances were common, and the young Nietzsche was soon to take part in them—notably at the home of his friend Gustav Krug, whose father was a magistrate and friend of Mendelssohn and also an excellent instrumentalist who had written numerous compositions, including sonatas and quartets. Autumn evenings would find the adolescent Nietzsche often attending the rehearsals of oratorios under the direction of a church music director who "excelled as much in composition as in the direction of an orchestra." "Seated in the solemn darkness of the cathedral," he wrote, "I listened attentively to the sublime melodies."[4] Starting in October 1858, as a boarding student at the well-known school at Pforta—an ancient monastery where a young elite was educated in classical languages and the history of antiquity—Nietzsche's correspondence is marked by requests for musical scores, at Christmastime, in particular, for he could not, he writes, "imagine Christmas presents without some musical score."

The Pleasure of Interpreting

Before the advent of radio or records, the piano, by way of transcriptions, constituted the principal means of coming to know music. It ordinarily provided a richer and more refined knowledge than does simply hearing a concert or a recording. The amateur, groping his way through a piece, finds himself reconstructing it so as to grasp its internal coherence. As a result, he gets closer to the composer who "hears" his score while he fills in the staves, more so than does the passive listener on whom it imposes itself as something self-contained, with the obviousness of something natural and miraculous.

"In the case of everything perfect we are accustomed to abstain from asking how it became: we rejoice in the present fact as though it came out of the ground by magic," Nietzsche will write in *Human, All Too Human*, imputing this transfiguration of human, all too human works to the persistent influence of "a primeval mythological invention" promoted by the artist's skill.[5] "The science of art has . . . to counter" this "illusion," he adds, by unveiling the calculations and tricks that enter into the genesis of such works and by thwarting "the sophistry and indulgences of the intellect that allow the artist to ensnare it." Having been rendered aggressively skeptical by his Wagnerian adventure, of which *Human, All Too Human* officially indicates the end, Nietzsche intended no longer to be misled by this magic of art and the cult of genius that it entailed. To produce masterpieces like so many miracles was itself a craft, a few of whose secrets he had learned by assiduous practice.

At the piano, the young Nietzsche above all taught himself to interpret, a notion that will occupy a central place in the thought of the philosopher. "No, there are no facts, only interpretations."[6] This well-known formula, which expresses what has been called Nietzsche's perspectivism, is first of all that of a musician. Indeed, music only exists as interpreted. However precise it may appear, any musical score only offers the work in a virtual state, which each performance, provided it is technically correct, transmutes into a different, unique, yet legitimate sonorous reality. An interpretation will be more or less seductive, or convincing, without our being able to qualify it as more or less "true."[7]

When we play old works, must we forbid ourselves, out of a concern for objectivity, from "placing our soul in them in order to give them life?" Not at all, Nietzsche will answer, anticipating current arguments about authenticity, "for it is only if we bestow upon them our soul that they can continue to live: it is only *our* blood that constrains them to speak *to us*. A truly 'historical' rendition would be ghostly speech before ghosts."[8]

But it is not just musical works, whether new or old, that call for interpretation. History, nature, customs, language must also be interpreted from the perspective proper to each of us, whereas too often these all too human constructions are offered or imposed as undeniable realities, as unconditional and universal givens. Against "the innate need to obey" that characterizes the herd, "free spirits" have the task of making their own interpretation of existence resonate loudly and clearly.[9]

The young Pforta student was certainly a "perspectivist" without knowing it, and although he attributed wondrous causes to all his activities, his fingers and memory were recording procedures and techniques that the author of *Human, All Too Human* will remember and use to forge the arms of his emancipation. Like Proust's narrator, who diverted himself while awaiting Albertine with a few pages of Vinteuil's sonata and a transcription of *Tristan*, the young Nietzsche, too, could say that, unlike the company of his fellow students, music helped him to reach into himself and discover something new. Undoubtedly it also helped him to overcome the deep division— a "civil war" between "wild factions"—that he discovered within himself each time he turned his attention inward.[10] And in being one with sounds, the musician at the same time experienced that "sense of distance," "of being different in every sense of the term," that constituted the most immediate sense of himself.[11] "To lay between himself and his neighbor his personal infinity": music above all had already allowed the future father of Zarathustra—the man apart, the dissembler par excellence—to do this.[12]

Apart from two close friends with whom he had founded Germania, a little society devoted to art and literature, it was the piano, the instrument of solitary intimacy, that was and that in the future would often be his principal confidant: "My regret is not being able to play," he wrote to his mother one day when he was ill and confined to the infirmary. "When I don't hear any music, everything seems dead to me." In February 1865, at Cologne, when he had mistakenly entered a bordello and suddenly found himself "surrounded by a half-dozen creatures clothed in gauze and sequins looking hopefully at him," he lost his voice for a moment—according to the account he gave to a friend the next day—then instinctively turned to the piano, "the only being endowed with a soul in this society," and played a few chords before slipping away.[13]

"The Medium of Superior Forces"

However, Nietzsche was not content just to interpret; already for some years he had been composing—generally in haste, with a "kind of frenzy,"[14] in the grip of that power Goethe calls the *demonic*, which, in music, "stands so high that no understanding can reach it."[15] "The demon of music took hold of me," he confided several times in his correspondence. This is not a mere image. Returning in 1888 to the Dionysian and the Apollonian, he will characterize them as "two states in which art manifests itself in the human being like a force of nature [Naturgewalt], making use of him whether he wishes it or not: in one case as compulsion to a vision; in another, as compulsion to an orgiastic state of mind."[16] Nietzsche spoke from experience. "If one had the slightest residue of superstition left in one's system, one could hardly reject altogether the idea that one is merely incarnation, merely mouthpiece, merely a medium of overpowering forces," he wrote during the same period in *Ecce Homo*, at the beginning of a superb evocation of the phenomenon of inspiration, regarding precisely *Zarathustra*, that new gospel born from the spirit of music: " One hears, one does not seek; one accepts, one does not ask who gives; like lightning, a thought flashes up, with necessity, without hesitation regarding its form—I never had any choice."[17]

No doubt this experience of inspiration—of something estranged from oneself—strongly colored Nietzsche's conception of the ego even if it did not determine it: this "alleged ego," this "phantom," this self-proclaimed sovereign instance that in reality is only a field of intersecting, antagonistic forces, each one battling to impose its unifying perspective; a mixture of drives, instincts, voracious appetites whose "motives always remain in the shadows." This will lead him to denounce the illusion, "the wondrous illusion" of free will and, as a consequence, to challenge the notions of causality, responsibility, and choice.[18]

To the "it thinks" in us that Nietzsche will launch in *Beyond Good and*

Evil against the prejudice of the subject so dear to philosophers, there was an early prelude: an "it composes in me," which must have aroused his suspicions concerning the supremacy of consciousness. As for the forces at work in the depths of the psyche—where his soundings did more than anticipate some of the "discoveries" of psychoanalysis—it was surely from music, often associated with tears, in "the emotional power of the tone,"[19] that he received the first and decisive intimation of them: a sudden discharge of energy comparable to a storm—that other "force of nature" to which he felt closely tied all his life: "How different the lightning, the wind, the hail, free powers, without ethics!" he wrote to a friend in 1866.[20] "How fortunate, how strong they are—pure will that in no way obscures the intellect!" "I want to disappear into the darkness of the storm; and in my last moments, I want to be both man and lightning," he notes while writing *Zarathustra*, that "symphony" whose hero proclaims himself to be the "prophet of thunder."

We can see that music for Nietzsche had that virtue that the ancients already had attributed to it "of discharging the emotions, of purifying the soul, of easing the *ferocia animi*."[21] Nietzsche will invoke this in October 1872 in a draft letter to Hans von Bülow, who had criticized one of his compositions in harsh terms. Nietzsche tried somewhat maladroitly to justify himself: "As for my music, I only know that it allows me to master a mood that, unsatisfied, would perhaps produce even more damage."[22] A lucid diagnosis. In Turin seventeen years later, in January 1889, on the edge of madness, Nietzsche sat at the piano improvising endlessly. What still remained "within the limits of an artistic activity, shortly thereafter was to express itself in brusque outbursts of frenzy."[23] Meanwhile, composing allowed both the philosopher and the psychologist to sharpen his comprehension of artistic creation: "If one wants to obtain some experience of *art*," he noted in 1877, "one must make a few works, there are no other means of arriving at aesthetic judgment."[24] "That is the advantage we draw from every false tendency," Goethe had already confided to Eckermann, alluding to the one that for several years drove him toward the plastic arts. "He who with inadequate talent devotes himself to music will never, indeed, become a master, but may learn to know and to value a masterly production."[25]

"The Premonition of the Divine"

However, before having recognized for himself this both cathartic and pedagogical virtue, the young Nietzsche had seen in music a means of testing and obtaining "presentiments of higher worlds," and above all "the presentiment of the divine," a prelude to the redemptive mission he will assign to it in *The Birth of Tragedy*. This began, in effect, by his prolonging and amplifying the inner experience of a God apparent to the heart, upon which the fideistic tradition of Christianity of his childhood simultaneously stressed that it prescribed a strict moralism meant to contain any effusions. Therefore it was quite natural that the son of the pastor from Röcken should associate it with religion—all the more so since his first strong musical impression probably dated from the death of his much revered father. He reported nine years later, in 1858:

> At one o'clock in the afternoon, the [funeral] ceremony began with a full ringing of bells. Oh, their hollow sounding knell will never leave my ears, never will I forget the somber melody of the chorale *Jesu meine Zuversicht* [Jesus, my refuge]! The organ resonated throughout the church.[26]

A short while after having recounted in his diary his memory of this mourning that haunted him, Nietzsche set out to write an arrangement for four voices of the hymn tune that remained closely associated with it. Several sketches of chorales and masses are also found among his first compositions. What is more, in 1854 it was after hearing an exultant performance of the "Halleluiah Chorus" from the *Messiah*—"I thought I was hearing the jubilation of the angels whose accents accompanied Jesus Christ on his ascent to heaven"—that he made "an earnest resolution to compose."[27] Four years later, the "thoughts on music" he consigned to his diary are most edifying:

> God has given us music so that *first of all* it might lead us upward.
> Music combines all qualities; it can exalt us, divert us, cheer us up, or break the hardest heart with the softness of its melancholy tones. But its principal purpose is to direct our thoughts toward higher things, to elevate and even to shake us. . . . But if music serves only as a diversion or as a kind of vain ostentation, it is sinful and harmful. Yet this fault is very frequent; all of modern music is filled with it.[28]

After the prophetic biblical exhortations of Zarathustra, the vehemence with which the author of *Ecce Homo* will assert his having been Christian "for only an hour of his life" can only confirm his profoundly religious nature. In his notebooks from 1878 we read, "Child, saw God in his Glory—Melancholic afternoon—service in the chapel at Pforta—distant sounds of the organ . . ." Early in the summer of 1860, when he was sixteen years old, he completes a miserere drawing on Palestrina, and not unskillfully at that. In 1861 he began a Christmas oratorio, which like many other pieces was never finished but from which he developed several themes for later use in subsequent compositions. The oratorio form at the time seemed to him clearly superior to opera, owing to its sacred character:

> Although until now the oratorio has always been believed to hold the same place in spiritual music as does opera in worldly music, this opinion seems wrong to me, and even a disparagement of the oratorio.
>
> In and of itself, the oratorio is already of an imposing simplicity, and indeed it must be so, as uplifting and, moreover, as strictly religious uplifting music. Hence the oratorio spurns all those other means that opera uses for effect; no one can take it for a kind of accompaniment, as operatic music is still for the masses. It excites no other sense than our hearing. Its content, too, is infinitely simpler and more sublime and, for the most part, is familiar and easily comprehensible to even an uneducated audience. This is why I believe that, in its musical genus, the oratorio stands at a higher level than opera. . . .
>
> The principal reason why the oratorio is not very popular is to be sought in the fact that its music often has in it an unholy mixture of profane elements. And this is the principal requirement: that it carry in all its parts the evident mark of the sacred, of the divine.[29]

Five years later, his mother will receive as a birthday present the piano version of a Kyrie for soloists, chorus, and orchestra, but at that moment Nietzsche already for some time had distanced himself from Christianity. Already in 1862 he saw nothing more in its principal dogmas than "symbols," and the idea of a supraterrestrial world seemed to him "an illusion," the "product of the infantile age of peoples."[30] Yet however ruthlessly, starting with *Human, All Too Human,* he will criticize this illusion and other worlds of any kind, he will never deny the benefits of the musical component of the Christian upbringing he had received. In 1878 he will comment: "It is the good fortune of our era that one can still grow up in a religion and for a while have, in music, a genuine access to art; times to come will not be so fortunate in this respect."[31]

Nor did his break with Christianity prevent him from continuing to appreciate religious music, all the more so because in this domain, too, he had experience as a performer. As a member of the choir at Pforta and during his university years in Bonn and Leipzig, he took part in numerous concerts. In 1865, during the Lower Rhine Festival at Cologne, he sang with much fervor in Handel's *Israel in Egypt*, and until the end of his conscious life he continued to admire its composer: "Handel, the most beautiful type we have of a *man* in the domain of art," he writes in 1885.[32] He adds two years later:

> Handel, Leibniz, Goethe, Bismarck—all characteristic of the *German strong species*. Living without second thoughts between contradictions, full of that supple strength that wards off convictions and doctrines by using the one against the other, keeping freedom for itself.[33]

Bach, of course, continues to figure in his pantheon. The same year as *Israel in Egypt* he took part in a performance of the *Passion according to St. John* in Leipzig. And in April 1870, as a young professor at Basel, he wrote to his friend Erwin Rohde:

> This week I attended *three* performances of the *St. Matthew Passion* by the divine Bach, with the same feeling each time of immense wonder. For someone who has totally given it up, Christianity here truly does sound like a gospel.[34]

A Great Improviser

It was to the piano, however, that Nietzsche owed his greatest joys. From his childhood he showed a pronounced taste for improvisations. And these free sonorous outpourings impressed all those who heard them. As his friend Gersdorff commented, "I do not believe Beethoven's improvisations could have been more poignant than those of Nietzsche, especially when a storm filled the sky."[35]

However lively and flattering the effect, Nietzsche nevertheless felt himself "too easily obtaining the admiration" of his listeners.[36] In 1877, "listing things according to the degree of pleasure they give" him, he placed "in the highest place, musical improvisation during some happy hour."[37] But in *Human, All Too Human,* which he was then working on, the aesthetic quality of this pleasure does not mislead him:

> In reality, the imagination of a good artist or thinker is productive continually, of good, mediocre and bad things, but his *power of judgement*, sharpened and practised to the highest degree, rejects, selects, knots together; as we can now see from Beethoven's notebooks how the most

glorious melodies were put together gradually and as it were culled out of many beginnings. He who selects less rigorously and likes to give himself up to his imitative memory can, under the right circumstances, become a great improviser; but artistic improvisation is something very inferior in relation to the serious and carefully fashioned artistic idea. All the great artists have been great workers, inexhaustible not only in invention but also in rejecting, sighting, transforming, ordering.[38]

Yet "the artist knows that his work produces its full effect when it excites a belief in improvisation, a belief that it came into being with a miraculous suddenness," he wrote in an earlier aphorism. Thus he will deliberately "introduce those elements of rapturous restlessness, of blindly groping disorder, of attentive reverie that attend the beginning of creation . . . as a means of deceiving the soul of the spectator or auditor into a mood in which he believes that the complete and perfect has suddenly emerged instantaneously."[39] The "good artist" therefore is one who, starting from an improvisation, succeeds, at the end of a patient elaboration whose traces he wipes away, in recreating it, or at least in giving the appearance of it in the completed work, at the same time that he imbues it with a sense of irresistible necessity.

If we perceive in Nietzsche's extant works for piano the echo of his talent as an improviser, and sometimes of that "orchestral sense" with which many of his friends credit him, these pieces equally reveal, as do so many others, a characteristic feature of his activity as a musician: excepting his short works, his imagination exceeded his capacities for composition.

Dionysus "took hold" of him, "constraining" him to express himself in sounds but to go beyond this to catharsis and to transform his improvisations into completed works. Yet all too often Nietzsche lacked "that freedom from wilder emotions, that calm of the sculptor god," Apollo.[40] Knowing his insufficiencies as a composer, we ought not be surprised that in *The Birth of Tragedy,* in which he opposes these two divinities, Nietzsche seems often to reduce music to the Dionysian alone, implicitly characterized by the absence of form and convention. Since Apollonian qualities are manifest in his writings, it may seem, therefore, that for him sounds, as the direct emanation of affectivity or of the "unconscious," only rarely attained—and at the price of a clear loss of energy—the level of organization at which language unfolds. When the improvisations erupted, which sometimes led him to "the perilous domain of the lunatic," Nietzsche experienced that chaos wherein he will see the truth of the world, "of all eternity," and against whose irresistible attraction he will never cease to struggle, before being engulfed by it.[41] Goethe had said, "music is the purely irrational, but words have only to do with reason." This is a formula Nietzsche appears to illustrate when in 1862, speaking of *Ermanarich*—a work that was supposed to combine words and music—he comments with clairvoyance:

> I was too deeply moved for poetry, I didn't have the necessary distance to produce an objective drama; it was in music that I thoroughly succeed in expressing the state of mind that the legend of *Ermanarich* plainly incarnated in me.[42]

Nietzsche the musician will not be a "good artist," or only rarely. Perhaps due to a lack of sufficient training that could have disciplined his talent, as austere philology was to do for his literary gift, the author of *Human, All Too Human* will remain, like Rousseau, a gifted amateur—for which he wrongly blamed Wagner, who had kindly let him know that. It is as a writer that he will reveal himself to be a good, and even a great, artist, where he will "know how to force chaos to take on form,"[43] transposing with an increasing mastery his talent as an improviser to the art of words, on themes that were often borrowed but upon which he will give a distinctive imprint. This was a conscious transposition, by the way, as testified by a letter from April 1867 to Gersdorff in which, after having announced that the desire to "write well" has taken hold of him, Nietzsche comments:

> Above all, a few gay spirits in my [writing] style must be unchained again; I must learn to play on them as on a keyboard, but not only pieces I have learned by heart but also free fantasias, as free as possible, yet still always logical and beautiful.[44]

A Rebel Nostalgic for Tradition

Logic and beauty also shaped the musical ideal of the young Nietzsche. Admiring only the "classics" as set by the then dominant opinion in Germany, he had begun by announcing an "inextinguishable hatred" for "modern music, the alleged 'music of the future' of Liszt and Berlioz," "impious and evil," which presupposed "a corrupted hearing," to which his friend Gustav Krug wanted to convert him.[45] If in *The Birth of Tragedy* Nietzsche will mock "the arithmetical counting board of fugue and contrapuntal dialectic,"[46] both incapable of compelling the Dionysian demon of German music "to speak," for the moment, with the help of a strict manual of counterpoint, the future eulogist of Dionysus was teaching himself to write fugues and chorales in a blithely anachronistic style, traces of which are evident in his first compositions. Their tonal uncertainty and weakness in development are counterbalanced by an evident "inflexibility and an intransigent linearity."[47] It is as though, by reproducing in music the ambivalence of his religious experience—where the strict moral rules counterbalanced an emotional adhesion to God's grace—Nietzsche needed external discipline to compensate for a deficient sense of form. The harmonic element that dominated his musical imagination threatened, under the effect of emotion, to degenerate into pure sonorous chaos, from which the melody emerged only rarely. After all, there were many people "who took pleasure in the strict form of the fugue and who saw it as the summit of music and even as the only genuine music," he noted in 1862, although by then he had been won over by the charm of Wagner's music. "And there is no shortage of people who will shake their heads and think you mad when they see you standing there as if struck down by the power of music, in the face of the passionate waves of *Tristan und Isolde*. Counterfugues by Albrechtsberger and Wagnerian love scenes are both music. They must have something in common, the essence of music. Feeling is no kind of measure of music."[48] Still, assisted by the spirit of the times, Krug's teaching would end by producing its effect as much on the composer as on the listener.

"I have written masses of fugues, and I am capable of a pure style—up to a certain degree of purity," Nietzsche will note in 1872 in the draft letter to von Bülow already cited.[49] "On the other hand, I have been sometimes seized by . . . a barbarous frenzy." This is a self-mocking and lucid allusion to his *Manfred-Meditation*, which the conductor had greeted with sarcasm. It also alludes to his two pieces for piano, composed a dozen years earlier, *Schmerz ist der Grundton der Natur* and *Ermanarich*, which marked a break with the conservatism of his earlier works.

The "music of the future" had overcome his resistance. And Nietzsche, leaving behind the forms he had learned, had abandoned himself to his inspiration in immediately switching over to the extreme forms of the new idiom—just as the philosopher would later do with ideas that took hold of him. "Always preoccupied with the most extreme expression"—in so defining Wagner's music, Nietzsche will better define the irresistible movement of his own thought, which always led him "beyond." In "Schmerz ist der Grundton der Natur," the introductory counterpoint quickly turns into a disorganized and quasi-expressionist succession of alterations, chromatic progressions, and sharp dissonances. He described how some of his music written when he was thirteen and fourteen years of age was "the blackest and most radical things I know in raven-black music,"[50] perhaps recalling that page in *Daybreak* where he offers an ironic praise of "interesting ugliness."[51] "Who has not experienced, who has not cursed," he will also write in 1887, "that wretched youth who tortures his piano to the point of drawing from it cries of despair, who with his own hands heaves up in front of himself the mire of the most dismal gray-brown harmonies? This is how one is *recognized*, as a pessimist."[52]

The second work, *Ermanarich*, is just as "dark." Originally conceived as a symphonic poem for large orchestra in the spirit of Liszt's *Hungaria* and on the model of his *Dante* symphony, it was to evoke the tragic legend of a Gothic king of the fourth century. And in the broad reading that he undertook in approaching his subject both poetically and musically, Nietzsche was fascinated to discover the heroic and bloody Nordic legends, which had inspired Wagner in *The Ring of the Nibelungen*, his then incomplete tetraology.

> This twilight of the gods, where the sun turns dark, where the sea engulfs the earth, where the swirling fire surrounds the world's tree of life, where the flames will lick the sky, is the most grandiose invention the mind of a man has ever dreamed, an invention that has never been surpassed in the literature of any time, an infinitely strong and terrible one, even though it resolves into enchanting harmonies.[53]

From 1861 to 1865, a period in which Nietzsche alternated between phases of writing and composing, Nietzsche will work on this "dramatic poem," with music that was supposed to illustrate the text and that was partly conceived before the text was begun. But the material did not find adequate form. Already in 1862 he was pointing out faults in the work, among them that his "characters lack the features and strong natures of primitive Germany: their feelings are too elaborate, too modern, too much reflection, not enough natural force."[54] Here we have an anticipation of the criticism that sixteen years later he will launch against Wagner's heroes, with Siegfried the incarnation of a new German paganism: "These superb monsters, with bodies from prehistory and nerves from the day after tomorrow," typical representatives of a modernity that seeks "the three great *stimulantia* of the exhausted: the *brutal*, the *artificial*, and the *innocent* (idiotic)."[55]

Only one piece for piano remains from this ambitious project. *Ermanarich*, although less "radical" than *Schmerz ist der Grundton der Natur*, still is filled with key changes and chromaticisms—and suffers from the same insurmountable weaknesses in its construction. Nietzsche was no longer able to organize his tonal material according to the rules of "classical style" or to match the subject matter, its poetic or dramatic content, like his model, Liszt's program music.

Following these two clumsy incursions into modern music, and while he was becoming familiar and enthused with *Tristan,* Nietzsche quickly returned to a traditional language and genres—album pieces, polonaises, lieder—just as twenty years later, at the end of his Wagnerian period, he would return to the "pure style" of the chorale to adapt Lou Salomé's "Hymn to Life" to one of his earlier compositions. It is as though he was never able to tame the "demon of music" except in regressing, because of the risk in giving it free rein, of ending up in a "barbarous frenzy" that he was incapable of mastering in an appropriate form: the Dionysian, freed of every Apollonian element. From *Tristan,* he keeps only the nocturnal intoxication, the exacerbated chromaticism of harmonic waves where every form seems to dissolve, without perhaps ever seeing the strict architecture of the work that underlay their spellbinding unfolding, and above all without being able to emulate the subtle art with which Wagner used and manipulated with virtuosity the frameworks, rules, and techniques of classical syntax. Having left behind his "classic" mold and early Romanticism, the composer in Nietzsche no longer corresponded with the listener. And when the former tried to fall into step with the latter, he composed beyond his means.

In *The Gay Science* Nietzsche comments:

> Don't we have to admit to ourselves, we artists, that there is an uncanny difference within us between our taste and our creative power? They stand oddly side by side, separately, and each grows in its own way. I mean, they have altogether different degrees and *tempi* of old, young, mature, mellow, and rotten. A musician, for example, might create his life long what is utterly at odds with what his refined listener's ear and listener's heart esteem, enjoy, and prefer—and he need not even be aware of this contradiction. As our almost painfully frequent experience shows, one's taste can easily grow far beyond the reach of the taste of one's powers, and this need not at all paralyze these powers and keep them from continued productivity.[56]

It is not surprising, therefore, if early in his Wagnerian adventure Nietzsche should have a particular affection for *Die Meistersinger von Nürnberg,* and that, still in 1886 in *Beyond Good and Evil,* the overture to that work should inspire his best artistic criticism. *Die Meistersinger* worked the tour de force of combining, not without humor, the harmonic writing of *Tristan* and a refined technique of the leitmotiv with the traditional forms of opera, Bach's language of counterpoint, and the Lutheran chorale. An art of "the day before yesterday and the day after tomorrow," Nietzsche will say, "it is magnificent, overcharged, heavy, late art that has the pride of presupposing two centuries of music as still living, if it is to be understood."[57]

This successful synthesis of the modern and the ancient could only satisfy the rebel nostalgic for tradition that would also appear in philosophy where, moreover, he was no less an autodidact than in music. "Beauty is no accident. Everything that is good is a heritage," Nietzsche, the always extreme "philosopher with a hammer," will claim in the second essay in his *Unfashionable Observations,* in which he denounced "historical sickness" because he was tempted to live in memory and to consecrate the past. Novelty disciplined by a long memory, an assimilated and surmounted past: such was the double lesson of *Der Meistersinger.* And in the alliance of Hans Sachs and the young Walter von Stolzing, wherein the conflict between imagination and form was resolved, the future author of *The Gay Science* saw his taste and his creative force reconciled.

Sounds or Words

While Wagner's harmonies were beginning to seduce him, having composed things that fell short of this new taste and that had led him to some aborted attempts, it was by returning to his first loves, whose works offered easier models to imitate, that Nietzsche sometimes showed himself to be a "good artist."

For example, in two Polish dances Nietzsche composed in 1862, which convey his lifelong admiration for Chopin and the Poles, "those French of the Slavic world" with whom he will identify himself, out of anti-Germanism, to the point of calling himself a "noble, pure-blooded Pole" descended—as a family legend claimed—from gentry named Nietzky. And, indeed, as the pages devoted to his mythical ancestors show, it was in brevity that Nietzsche was at his best: here his imagination fits nicely with the improviser's means. In a way, here again, the musician, from afar, announces the writer: the talent for aphorism that, starting with *Human, All Too Human,* will be the distinctive mark of his philosophical work, where, no more than in his music, will he be able to master the large scale, that large-scale form that he so will admire in Wagner; that, all evidence to the contrary, he will end up denying such mastery to him.

Brevity and concision equally characterize the lieder that Nietzsche composed between 1861 and 1864. Guided by the poems, the form here is less of a problem, and what is more, we find in them a melodic invention generally lacking in his works. Another striking fact is that whereas in his preceding compositions including vocal parts the words never worked very well, here word and music are united. But for one or two exceptions, the texts are not by Nietzsche. He borrowed them from poets, including Klaus Groth, Friedrich Rückert, Alexander Pushkin, Sandor Petófi, and Aldabert von Chamisso.

"I look for words for a melody that I have, and for a melody for words that I have," he writes to his mother in 1863, "and these two things I have don't go together, even though they come from the same soul. But such is my fate!"[58] And such it would remain. His musical and literary talents always competed with each other. This competition was all the more grueling as it was unequal: the writer rather quickly acquired that mastery of form that almost always eluded the musician's grasp. This leads to a double cleavage that the author of *The Birth of Tragedy* transposed into the Dionysus-Apollo pair in which Apollo symbolizes not only the world of images and concepts, but that of forms in general.

> Thus the intricate relation of the Apollinian and the Dionysian in tragedy may really be symbolized by a fraternal union of the two deities: Dionysus speaks the language of Apollo; and Apollo, finally the language of Dionysus; and so the highest goal of tragedy and of all art is attained.[59]

If this "fraternal union" was realized in tragedy, it was because in ancient Greece, "they took for granted the union, indeed the *identity,* of the *lyrist with the musician.*"[60] In this union, according to Nietzsche, the poet was inspired by the musician, a role that he believed at the time was restored by Wagner. Later, Nietzsche would instead reproach him for having reduced music to merely the servant of language since he was not an "instinctive musician." Whereas for Plato the melody and rhythm depended on the lyrics, and for Rousseau, in the beginning music and language were one, for Nietzsche music came first. In *The Birth of Tragedy,* the lyrical poem and the dramatic dithyramb both spring up, through Apollo's intervention, as "image sparks" of a primitive melody evocative of Dionysus's sufferings and ecstasies.

The word should only appear at the end of the creative process, Nietzsche will explain in 1883 to his friend Peter Gast, himself a composer. He said this upon reflection on the means required to bring together "a whole opera act in view of its symphonic unity," a "problem" that he considered "not resolved" by Wagner nor since:

> The musician should create a general movement, basing himself only
> on the most exact knowledge of the fragment of the drama he refers to
> (the emotions, the mutation and struggle of emotions); the whole scenic
> aspect must be *present* to him. But *not* the *word!* The *text,* properly speak-
> ing, of the poem should only be composed *after* the music has been com-
> pleted, in continual adaptation to the music: whereas, up to now, it was
> the word that dragged the music behind it. . . . In short, the musician
> must first guide the poet, and even more so *afterward,* when the music
> is completed![61]

Induced by the improvising, immediate nature of Nietzsche's musical talent and betraying, as we shall see, a misunderstanding of Wagner's composition style, the method this letter presents is, to say the least, unusual and difficult. It was however how Nietzsche must have composed his vocal works, with all the more difficulty, one presumes, since the words scarcely ever were his own. Evidence of this is a suggestion Gustav Krug made to him in November 1860 about his oratorio: "I believe it would be better to write a text in advance. It is too difficult, after the fact, to introduce a text that corresponds to the character of this piece."[62] Further indication includes the faults in prosody of several of his lieder, above all, the "Hymn to Life," first conceived in 1874 as a hymn to friendship for chorus and orchestra but that, left in the state of a piece for piano four hands, had to wait nine years for the addition of a text (from Lou Salomé). We can understand, therefore, that in 1865 after having composed, not without pain, a lied based on a poem that he himself authored—"Junge Fischerin"—Nietzsche renounced the genre and harbored serious doubts about his musical talents. "If it should be, honored Herr Professor," Hans von Bülow will write him in 1872, "you should have meant seriously your aberration into the realm of composition—something of which I still have my doubts—then at least limit yourself to vocal music and, in the craft that throws you in all directions on the wild ocean of sounds, allow yourself to be guided by the rudder of the word."[63]

Outside the framework provided by words, it is true that Nietzsche's short-lived musical inspiration almost always failed or got lost. But as distrustful of them as he was incapable of doing without them, no more did he succeed in producing such words himself or in combining them with sounds in a prolonged interaction. Composer, poet, philosopher, he seems unable to express himself completely either in music or, to a lesser degree, in language—and never in their union. Apollo and Dionysus were to remain separated, having only an intermittent relationship and then in one direction only: by way of poetry, words born from music. For Nietzsche, as for other poets such as Schiller, whom he cites as an example, "the poetical idea" always proceeds from a "musical mood."[64] It is "pursued" by "a melody of unspeakable melancholy" that in May 1883 in Rome—in a loggia looking on the Piazza Barberini, "where one hears the *fontana* singing at one's feet"[65]—the author of *Zarathustra* "composes" his "Night Song," "the loneliest song that was ever composed": "Night has come; only now all the songs of lovers awaken. And my soul too is the song of a lover."[66]

Yet if in *Zarathustra* and the *Dithyrambs of Dionysus* Nietzsche sometimes will know how to make Apollo speak the language of Dionysus, it was through experiencing through music the same "sublime jealousy" as did Mallarmé. This was a result of being unable to accomplish the converse movement, and doubly so: sonorous chaos rarely takes on a completed form. Word and music remain dissociated—except, in partial fashion; that is, with borrowed words, in a few lieder, which are the most charming and successful pieces Nietzsche composed. But this is a relative success, which ought not to surprise us—as a privileged means to express "inwardness," the lied, since Schubert, had become in a kind of national German sport. "In every German touched by music, there is an itch for the lied," notes Marcel Beaufils. "There is no small time musicaster who has not succeeded in putting together an album of lieder, sometimes quite well, where something of the music of Schubert or Schumann sings; for the lied, in a sense, is a German state of mind."[67]

ꟻROM SCHUMANN TO ꟻWAGNER

ꟻietzsche's lieder are reminiscent of Schubert and Schumann, especially Schumann, who died in 1856. He had so many affinities with Schumann that he must have seen in him a model in which, for some time, his taste and his creative force met. Like Nietzsche, Schumann presented that "double talent" that, from Weber to Wagner by way of Hoffmann and Berlioz, characterizes the Romantic artist.[1] But unlike Nietzsche, the composer of *Manfred* first seemed destined for literature more than for music. Torn between two vocations, Schumann attempted to escape this dilemma by resigning himself to the study of law to become a lawyer—just as Nietzsche will study philology and will be a professor for a time. A divided personality, playing with his different masks—Floristan, passionate and unstable; Eusebius, melancholic and fearful; Raro, meditative and placid—Schumann was another great improviser but he doubled as a great artist, the master of the short form, above all, of the lied, which reached its apogee with him. Schumann was successful, often even in his symphonies, in preserving the difficult equilibrium between formal requirements and subjectivity, which was always so fleeting and precarious for his emulator, at least as long as his genius was able to resist the madness into which he was to fall, like so many of the German Romantics, like the author of *Ecce Homo,* and at the same age.

Having recently arrived in Bonn in October 1864 to enroll in the university, Nietzsche paid his respects at Schumann's grave. And at Christmas a relative gave him "the best gift one can give him at that time": the piano redaction of *Manfred*. Weber's *Freischütz*, which he has seen at the opera, did not please him—the scene of the "gorge with wolves" even tempted him to laugh. Neither an opera nor an oratorio nor a cantata, this "musique de scène" in which the title role is taken by a narrator who does not sing, seems made to illustrate the impossible union of sounds and words that tormented him. He had himself given a striking illustration of this the preceding year in a "melodrama for narrator and piano," *Das zerbrochene Ringlein* [The Broken Ring] based on a poem by Eichendorff. Furthermore, *Manfred*, "the Romantic work par excellence," as Marcel Brion points out,[2] is not just by Schumann but also owes much to its inspiration, Byron, who at the time was one of Nietzsche's favorite poets. In the studious and austere atmosphere of Pforta, he had often pondered the words the English Romantic had put into his hero's mouth, the powerful magician who in vain seeks the repose of death that his art has conquered:

> Sorrow is Knowledge: they who know the most
> Must mourn the deepest o'er the fatal truth,
> The Tree of Knowledge is not that of Life.

"We have art so as not to die from truth," Nietzsche himself will cry some twenty-five years later. For the moment, Schumann and Byron appealed to his melancholic temper. For Nietzsche felt caught between contradictory aspirations. Having renounced theology, music tempted him more than ever, yet, even though he is flattered to pass for "an authority" on such things among his fellow students, he was aware of his shortcomings. "I am becoming a bit too critical to be able to deceive myself about my possible talent any longer," he writes to his friend Gersdorff in August 1865.[3] He threw himself into the "cold objectivity" of philology "to escape the sentimental waltz of his different artistic inclinations."[4] At first he was passionate about it and excelled at it, but if he owed an "exultant vision" of antiquity to philology, it was at the price of a constant struggle against a "heavy and asthmatic erudition." And the perspective of making a career of it, by becoming a "learned mole," of being tied to a "profession," all this repelled him, as though this would constitute a betrayal of a vocation more akin to his nature, albeit for the time being still as vague as it was imperious. The forces he was repressing made him all the more discontent with himself and the world.

The Return of Dionysus

In this mindset, the discovery of Schopenhauer was a revelation to Nietz-sche—just as it was for most of his friends, and as it had been, a dozen years earlier, for Richard Wagner, who found in Schopenhauer's philosophy "the true homeland of his soul."[5] In reading *The World as Will and Representation*, everything suddenly makes sense—but under the effect of a black sun.

> In this book, each line cried renouncement, negation, resignation. Here I
> found a mirror in which I could see reflected, with a terrible grandeur,
> the world, life, and my own heart. Here art looked at me from its disin-
> terested solar eye. I discovered there sickness and health, exile and
> refuge, hell and paradise.[6]

Will—a mute, blind, implacable, absurd, vital force that rules the uni-verse. Dividing itself to infinity among separated existences, it simulta-neously continued repeating itself just to assure its permanence. Bound to Ixion's wheel of desire, man is condemned to oscillate endlessly between suffering and boredom from the nostalgia for the primeval one. Thanks however to representation (*Vorstellung*), that is reflection, there are three means, which Schopenhauer presents as three stages, for man to liberate himself more or less enduringly from this tyranny: art, the morality of pity, and finally, asceticism, which leads to the pure and simple suppression of the will to live.

Instinctively, Nietzsche privileges the first of these, all the more so be-cause at the summit of his hierarchy of the arts, and even beyond it, is music, placed there by Schopenhauer. Totally independent of the phenomenal world, music reveals the very essence of the Will that it negates through con-templation. Therefore it allows man to free himself, provisionally, from the narrow limits of individuation, to transcend the suffering inherent in each separated existence.[7] This is why the effect it exercises is "so much more powerful and deeper than that of the other arts, which only speak of shad-ows, whereas it speaks of being."

> The inexpressible depth of all music, by virtue of which it floats past us
> as a paradise quite familiar and yet eternally remote, and is easy to
> understand and yet so inexplicable, is due to the fact that it reproduces
> all the emotions of our innermost being, but entirely without reality and
> remote from its pain.[8]

Nietzsche, more as a poet than a philologist, was quick to see Diony-sus in this mirror of universal will: the musician god torn to pieces by the Ti-tans, whose resurrection archaic Greece celebrated in the mysteries wherein Being as a whole revealed itself, completely irrational and terrifying. Op-posed to him stood Apollo, the "superb divine image" of individuation "whose gesture and look bespoke all the pleasure and wisdom of a beauti-ful appearance."

Tragedy was born from the mysterious union of the artistic drives fig-ured by these two divinities, the former, incarnated by the chorus, playing the impregnating role. With their scenic evocation of the great heroic myths, the ambition of Aeschylus and Sophocles was to ennoble their fellow citi-zens. This enterprise was ruined by the appearance of Socrates, the "des-potic logician," the "classic type of the theoretician"—in short, the non-musician.

Ever since, repressing myth and poetry, scientific optimism had not stopped pursuing its "unrelenting advance." But everything indicated it had reached its limits, Nietzsche concluded in 1870–1871, during the time when he was writing *The Birth of Tragedy,* which would assure him a thun-derous entry onto the literary and philosophical scene. For if ancient tragedy was not perhaps really born from the spirit of music, it was the spirit of music that gave birth to the writer Nietzsche and to his manifesto.

Modern Socratic-Alexandrine society was exhausted by labor, threat-ened by a revolt of its servile class in the very name of the happiness that served as its justification, and already dominated by the figure of the jour-nalist, "the paper slave of the day," and was devoted to the frivolous enter-tainment symbolized by opera, where "one takes facile pleasure in an idyl-lic reality." It had lost confidence in itself and in the validity of its grounds without being able to find the least help in its "pale, worn-out religions."

However a renaissance of tragedy was underway that ought to lead to a regeneration of culture, the young Nietzsche thought, momentarily carried away by patriotic enthusiasm for the war of 1870 in which he briefly participated. Socratic optimism was withdrawing, beaten in the breach by German philosophy—i.e., Schopenhauer—and above all, by the "sover-eign, solar march" of German music ever since Bach. The Dionysian spirit had reawakened, finding its most intense expression in Wagnerian musical drama. There, its formidable thrust "was reanimating tragic myth." For myth alone gives music "its highest liberty"—while protecting us against its "surge of life, suffering, and joy." Without the Apollonian illusion of drama, Nietzsche writes, how could the third act of *Tristan und Isolde*

33

"not fail to suffocate us under the convulsive tension of all the wings of the spirit"?

> How could he endure to perceive the echo of innumerable shouts of pleasure and woe in the "wide space of the world night," enclosed in the wretched glass capsule of the human individual, without inexorably fleeing toward his primordial home, as he hears this shepherd's dance of metaphysics?[9]

"From the moment when there was a piano redaction of *Tristan*, . . . I was a Wagnerian," Nietzsche will write in 1888 in *Ecce Homo*.[10] But this is one of those retrospective summaries that were then customary to him. Since it was in the springtime of 1861 that his friend Gustav Krug had first introduced him to the score, this conversion was undoubtedly a bit less rapid than he indicates. If the two pieces for piano he composed at that time, as we have seen, bear its traces, in October 1866 while still a student at Leipzig, it was with "quite mingled feelings" that he played the piano redaction of the *Die Walküre*, where, he writes, "the great beauties and virtues are balanced by as much ugliness and as many flaws."[11]

But two years later, the prelude to *Tristan* and the overture to *Die Meistersinger* heard at a concert set "each one of his fibers and all of his nerves aglow," especially the latter piece, which made him "besides himself with joy"[12] At Dresden in 1869, Nietzsche attended *Die Meistersinger*, his first performance of a complete Wagner opera. The musician's victory was then complete: "I had the liveliest impression of suddenly finding myself at home, in my element," he writes to a friend, "and my other activities seemed like a distant fog from which I have been redeemed."[13]

This was similar to the reaction, nine years earlier, of Baudelaire, who Nietzsche would one day see as a "Wagner without the music" and as a fraternal double of himself. "It seemed to me that this music was *mine*," the poet had written, "and I recognized it as every man recognizes the things he is destined to love."[14] Like Baudelaire and Nietzsche, many have had this reaction upon discovering Wagner's music, that same impression of recognition, of suddenly feeling at home in their "original homeland" from which until then, without knowing it, they had been exiled—and, at the same time, of discovering themselves. "We could let ourselves be swept away by the emotional vibrations of his music," Nietzsche writes to his friend Rhode in December 1868, "by this Schopenhauerian sea of sound the best of whose secret waves has such an impact that my listening to Wagnerian music is a jubilant intuition to the point of being an overwhelming discovery of myself."[15]

In June 1872, six months after the publication of *The Birth of Tragedy*, Nietzsche, "hungry for *Tristan*," finally attended two performances of that work under the baton of Hans von Bülow, who had directed its premiere in the same city seven years earlier. A few weeks later he will write to the conductor:

> You have given me access to the most sublime artistic impression of my
> life, and if I was unable to thank you immediately following the two per-
> formances, then please ascribe this to that total upheaval in which a man
> neither speaks nor thanks but hides himself away.[16]

The Archetype of the Artist

Under the spell of this music that the young Nietzsche described as Dionysian also unfolded the image of an ideal artist—at once, musician, poet, and thinker—in which seemed to sum up the rival aspirations at work in him.

Far from feeling that "prodigious versatility that is for all that the op-posite of chaos," which the author of *Ecce Homo* flattered himself as having acquired to be able to undertake "the immense task of a *revaluation of val-ues*," it was the scattered nature of his forces that disturbed Nietzsche at this time. Wagner, therefore—who, as Goethe had recommended, had known how to "preserve" and bind together his talents amidst an improbable suc-cession of shipwrecks and unexpected recoveries, following a debut that was apparently less than promising—could only fascinate him.

When we observe the childhood and youth of Wagner, Nietzsche will write in 1876, in the fourth of his *Unfashionable Obervations, Richard Wagner in Bayreuth*, "it seems as though he *himself* had not yet presented himself:

> those things that now, in retrospect, might be understood as heralds,
> prove upon closer inspection to be a desultory collection of traits that
> tend more to arouse misgivings than they do hopes: a restless, irritable
> spirit, a nervous haste in seizing upon a hundred different things, a pas-
> sionate pleasure in almost pathologically intense states of mind, abrupt
> swings from moments of most heartfelt serenity to states of turbulence
> and noise. He was not limited by any hereditary or family commitments
> to a particular artistic direction: he felt at home in painting, poetry, act-
> ing, and music as he did in being educated for a future career as a
> scholar; a superficial glance might lead one to believe that he was born to
> be a dilettante.

However,

> The dramatic quality in Wagner's development is wholly unmistakable
> from that moment in which the ruling passion attains self-awareness and
> takes possession of his entire being. From that moment on the groping
> and straying, the wild proliferation of secondary offshoots is at an end;
> the most tangled paths and transformations, the often quixotic trajectory
> of his plans, is now governed by a single inner law, a will that makes
> them explicable, however strange these explanations will often sound.[17]

Avoiding "traps and fetters," assimilating everything that he met on his way, "faithful to the highest that he bore within himself, which directed him to *express the extreme complexity of his nature by synthetic acts*," the "adventurer" succeeded in imposing himself as "one of the great forces of culture":

> He has mastered the arts, the religions, and the histories of various na-
> tions, and yet he is the opposite of a polyhistorian, of a spirit that merely
> pulls things together and organizes them, for he helps shape and breathe
> life into those things that he pulls together; he is a *simplifier of the world*.[18]

"Everywhere in *Wagner in Bayreuth*, where the text says 'Wagner,' one can without hesitation read my name," Nietzsche will proclaim in *Ecce Homo*. "Even from a psychological point of view, all the determining features of my own nature are attributed to Wagner." This book "is a prophetic vision of my future." And certainly, between Wagner and Nietzsche it is Nietzsche who "seemed a born dilettante." As an adolescent he was conscious of this danger, which for six years was warded off by the strict discipline at Pforta. In 1863, he had noted in his journal:

> I housed within myself the knowledge of several dictionaries, every pos-
> sible inclination had been awakened; I wrote horribly boring poems and
> tragedies; I went to much trouble to compose scores for orchestra and I
> was so deeply engaged in the task of acquiring a universal knowledge
> and competence that I ran the risk of turning myself into a muddle-
> headed dreamer.[19]

As for Wagner's dilettantism, this was a legend that Nietzsche will contribute to spreading, albeit involuntarily, for the most part, and with the assistance of its target, Wagner, who would regret it ("That bad person has taken everything from me, even the weapons with which he now attacks me," he will confide to Cosima in 1878).[20] As a sign of the confidence he placed in him, in November 1878 Wagner had charged Nietzsche to check the proofs of the autobiography that he had printed in a small edition destined for his close friends. There, he depicts himself, when young, as a sort of spontaneous genius who came to music by way of literature, having only the rudiments. This is a Romantic image contradicted by his adolescent works, including a skillful redaction of Beethoven's Ninth Symphony for piano and his first two operas, *Die Feen* (1833) and *Das Liebesverbot* (1836). But the composer chose henceforth to leave these in the shadows, and Nietzsche therefore could not be aware of them. Wagner had prosaically and very seriously learned his craft as a composer—much more seriously than how his future detractor had come to music or philosophy, for, as Karl Jaspers notes, he had "almost never studied the great philosophers thoroughly" and "relies upon secondary materials for most of his knowledge."[21] However that may be, what Nietzsche in 1888, anxious to give his existence the character of destiny, will interpret as harbingers, the Nietzsche of 1876 seemed hardly aware of, even if between the lines we can catch sight of an impatience to become what he obscurely felt himself to be.

Six years earlier, it is true, inspired and encouraged by Wagner, Nietzsche, who was bothered by the narrow specialization of philology, had developed the new ambition to "achieve wholeness."[22] "Scholarship, art, and philosophy are now growing into one another so much in me," he had written to Rhode in February 1870, "that I shall in any case give birth to centaurs one day."[23] This was *The Birth of Tragedy.* But with too much of the artistic and the philosophical at the expense of the philological, this book would offend scholars, who often saw in it the work of a dilettante, even as it conquered an audience of enlightened amateurs, those "free spirits," as Nietzsche will later call them and which he will be desperate to reach.[24]

It was necessary for him to at least "find a middle way" among his "three talents," if not to choose between them.[25] This was "his problem"— and the solution did not seem anywhere in sight. The morose confidences that, in the following years, he shared with his friends and the autobiographical notes in which he laments—"as a human being, musician, philologist, writer, philosopher"—always finding himself at the same point: "the same, always the same!" bear witness to this. "If I were ambitious, there would be perhaps no reason to despair of everything: but since I am hardly so, there is *almost* cause for despair."[26]

From this "almost," at the end of a crisis and convalescence marked by his bidding farewell to Bayreuth and to philology, a new philosopher-writer would be born with the publication of *Human, All Too Human*—without his renouncing music, however, nor even his becoming known as a musician. For never would Nietzsche—who "merely tinkered with self-domination," as his friend Rhode will say one day[27]—ever succeed in "becoming whole," in surmounting the incessant rivalry of his gifts and his instincts, with their "constant disquiet, jostling and tyrannizing,"[28] that state of "inner war," which, extrapolated to the history of civilizations, he will denounce as "decadence." "I who am nothing but a fragment and wandering misery," he wrote in 1881, "to whom it is rarely given, for a few 'beautiful minutes,' to cast a glance toward *the more beautiful land* where whole and complete natures travel."[29] From the consciousness of this failure will be born the *Übermensch* prefigured in the half-dreamed self-portrait from 1876: "The great *synthetic man*, in whom all various forces are yoked together without scruple for a single goal"; "the total man," inspired by Goethe and for which "the immense majority of men are only preludes and preliminary exercises."[30]

The composer of *Tristan* had given him a living image of such an individual. "I was indescribably happy in those days when I discovered Wagner!" he wrote his sister in February 1882. "I had sought so long for a man who was superior to me and who actually looked beyond me! I thought that I had found such a man in Wagner. I was wrong. Now I cannot even compare myself with him—I belong to another world."[31] Yet, even when the author of the *Case of Wagner* will level the accusation of dilettantism against his former idol, and diagnose the unhealthy discordance of instincts that were characteristic of the decadent behind the actor's mask, he will nonetheless salute the conqueror of Bayreuth as "the most grandiose example perhaps offered by the history of art of a man who does violence to himself." How could the young philologist of twenty years earlier, unsure of himself and of his vocation, not have seen in "this Wagner, who was only an implacable will to realize himself" and to impose the work that possessed him, what Mallarmé, Proust, the young Claudel, and Thomas Mann saw in him: the archetype of the artist, both a model and a challenge?[32]

In the Intimacy of Genius

Nietzsche's conversion to Wagner was the more ardent in that he was enthralled not only by the music and the artist but also by the man. This is a point that must be stressed because Wagner is commonly depicted as a monster: the villain, the bogeyman of an edifying history of music in which, from Bach to Schoenberg, only saints and martyrs figure but for him. Nietzsche writes to Carl von Gersdorff in August 1869 regarding in Wagner:

[Y]ou must not believe any judgments you find in the press or in the writings of musicologists, etc. *No one* knows him and can judge him, for the whole world lives on another basis and is not at home in his atmosphere. Such an unconditional ideality holds sway in him, such a profound and touching humanity, such a sublime seriousness about life, that when in his presence I feel as if in the presence of the divine.[33]

From their first meeting, in Leipzig in November 1868, Nietzsche (who speaks of it as being like a "fairy tale") was conquered by Wagner's vivacity, exuberance, and genius, his "bewitching charm."[34] For the first time, he was in the presence of genius: "The most evident incarnation of what Schopenhauer calls genius; yes, surely, to the smallest detail, the resemblance leaps to one's eyes."[35] Following Schopenhauer, who had immediately established a bond between them, here at last was a true living Master, in whom Nietzsche probably was also going to see a father, he who had barely known his own, born, as it turns out, the same year as the composer. "If we had not known you, what would I be other than a stillborn creature!" he confides in May 1873 to the one he calls "Pater Seraphicus." "I always tremble with fear when I think that I could well have remained apart from you: in that case life would truly not have been worth living, and I would have had no idea what to undertake in the next hour."[36]

His correspondence from this period overflows with a veneration filled with gratitude, an admiration "touching on the religious." "I understand why the Athenians erected sacrificial altars to their Aeschylus and their Sophocles," he writes to Cosima, "why they gave Sophocles the hero's name 'Dexion,' for having welcomed the gods into his house and taken care of them."[37] When the plan for Bayreuth began to take shape, Nietzsche devoted himself to it body and soul. He attended all the preparatory meetings, all the organizing committees, and if Wagner had not dissuaded him, he would have abandoned his university career to become a lecturer and fundraiser throughout Germany to gather funds destined to build "the theater of the future."[38]

Nietzsche could never really get over having left the Wagner he knew and loved (who appears so rarely in the words of his biographers), his "initiator into the mysterious secrets of art and life." In August 1880 he will confide to Peter Gast:

For me, nothing can compensate for the loss of Wagner's sympathy these last years. How often I dream of him and always in the style of our trusting intimacy of the past! Never was an angry word spoken between us, not even in my dreams, but many encouraging and cheerful words, and perhaps there is no one with whom I have laughed so much. All that is past—and what good is it to *be right against* him on several points? As if that could wipe this lost sympathy from memory![39]

Eight years later, in *Ecce Homo*, on the threshold of madness, referring to what in his life had "most profoundly and warmly distracted and fortified him," he will write, "were no doubt my intimate relations with Richard Wagner. . . . I would not exchange my days at Tribschen for anything, days of trust, gaiety, sublime chance—*deep* moments." In 1882 with Lou Salomé, revisiting those places where "he had spent unforgettable times with Wagner," she will report, "for a long while, he sat silent on the banks of the lake, and was deeply immersed in heavy memories; then, while, drawing in the moist sand with his cane, he softly spoke of times past. And when he looked up, he cried."[40] No doubt Nietzsche was thinking of this "happy isle," as he called it when he wrote the moving "Tomb Song" in *Thus Spoke Zarathustra*, that lament over "the isle of tombs, the silent isle where one finds the tombs of my youth."

At Tribschen, near Lucerne, between the lake and the mountains, with Cosima (the daughter of Liszt who had just left Hans von Bülow), Wagner completed his tetralogy and was preparing for the riskiest venture of his life: the construction at Bayreuth of a model theater devoted exclusively to the performance of his works. Starting in 1869, Nietzsche, who had just been named professor of philology at Basel, quickly had become a familiar visitor at the villa where his hosts kept a room available for him. It was there, through animated conversations with the composer, that the *Birth of Tragedy* took shape in the salon with its heavy draperies and decorated with portraits of Goethe, Schiller, Beethoven, and a watercolor by Genelli, *Dionysus Raised by the Muses of Apollo*, from which the young Wagner had received his "first lively conception of the Greek spirit and of beauty." This was a conception quite distant from the one filled with light and harmony that ever since Winckelmann had impregnated German classical culture. Even though it had lost its original impact, Wagner saw it too faithfully reflected in the music Mendelssohn had composed for Sophocles' tragedies.

The Birth of a Centaur

Indeed, Wagner had not had to wait to meet Nietzsche in order to discover Greek antiquity. As a child and adolescent it had been his passion: "People who learned nothing of the 'ancient Greeks' in their childhood have no eye for beauty," he told Cosima.[41] Having neglected its study during his hard years of apprenticeship as a conductor, Wagner returned to it when, as the *Kapellmeister* at Dresden, he began to think about opera and ways to reform it.

Herder had noted that in the absence of a Shakespeare or a "classical" theater like that of the French, Germans had to look to the model of the Greeks for a theater. Wagner, too, was persuaded of this, and it was not long before musical circles in Dresden were surprised to hear him "speak, often with animation, about Greek literature and history, but never about music," through which he wanted to "approach the real goal of his desires, the study of Old and Middle High German," seeing in it "the eternal elements of human culture."[42] German legends and myths often were only the "reworking" of perhaps universal, "purely human conceptions," which had already found a noteworthy formulation among the Greeks and which, as a result of their simplicity, lent themselves more easily than did historical subjects to a fully musical treatment. The flying Dutchman, condemned to wander the seas, was already Ulysses, and this same Ulysses, when he freed himself from the arms of Calypso and fled the allurements of Circe, prefigured Tannhäuser; similarly the myth of Zeus and Semele lived again in that of Lohengrin.[43] In 1847, when Wagner had finished the composition of *Lohengrin*, reading Aeschylus sent him into "complete delight." "The intoxicating effect of the production of an Athenian tragedy" passed before his eyes "so that I could see the *Oresteia* with my mind's eye." His "ideas about the whole significance of the drama and of the theatre were, without a doubt, moulded by these impressions," he said.[44] These ideas were expressed in the series of theoretical works he wrote at the end of the 1840s and the beginning of the 1850s, before undertaking his tetralogy.

Greek tragedy, which "Art and Revolution" celebrates as "the ideal expression of art," was born under the auspices of Apollo, "the head and national deity of the Hellenic race." To "those involved in passionate action," the conqueror of Python, the dragon of chaos, presented "the peaceful, undisturbed mirror of their innermost, unchangeable Grecian nature." Thus also "inspired by Dionysus, the tragic poet saw this glorious god," when "to all the rich elements of spontaneous art, the harvest of the fairest and most human life, he joined the bond of speech, and concentrating them all in one focus, brought forth the conceivable form of art—the *Drama*." And the people would come "seat themselves before it, in order to understand its action, in order to identify themselves completely with its essence, its collective soul, its god, and in this way return to the most noble and deep calm, what had a few moments earlier been the most tireless agitation and the most outrageous individualization."[45]

If Wagner only mentions Dionysus again after meeting Nietzsche, in his 1871 essay "The Destiny of Opera" he does however assign music no less a decisive role in the genesis of ancient tragedy.[46] "Birth from [aus] music: Aeschylus. *Décadence*—Euripides," we read in a note from 1849 that will be developed two years later in *Opera and Drama*.[47] It was from the "maternal womb" of music that tragedy was born: "conditioned by melody," that spontaneous expression of the "primitive emotional faculty of man," thanks to the natural rhythm of the Greek language, it would reach "a fitting union of word and gesture" in the chorus singing and dancing on the "orchestra."[48]

Yet the action drew tragedy toward "intellectual reflection," and bit by bit the songs of the chorus were replaced by "the exclusively iambic discourse of the actor." The lyrical-musical element remained, but the poet henceforth made use of it in a didactic and "fully self-conscious" manner— "less honestly, therefore, and less directly" than when he used spoken language; and "the Folk soon noticed that [tragedy] did not want instinctively to move their Feeling, but arbitrarily to rule their Understanding. Euripides had to shed blood beneath the lash of Aristophaneian ridicule, for this open blurting of the lie."[49]

An inevitable decadence: the chorus having both to contribute to the action and to comment on it, the dialog impeded the free development of the lyrical-musical element. Therefore the chorus disappeared from theater, splitting up into independent characters—whence the superiority of Shakespeare over the Greek tragedians, as regards dramatic technique. And, its original function would be fulfilled only in the orchestra of modern musical drama, which alone "will keep the melody in the requisite unceasing flow, and thus convincingly impress the motives on the Feeling."[50]

Any reader at all familiar with *The Birth of Tragedy* will easily recognize most of its principal themes. Beginning with the place of choice reserved for myth, which "gives music the highest freedom,"[51] and through his inversion of the traditional hierarchy established for the Greek tragedies. Nietzsche, following Wagner, rated Aeschylus above Sophocles and Euripides, conventionally classified as archaic, and favored by the "Weimar standard bearers"— Goethe and Schiller. Similarly, the ironical reference Wagner makes to "the transparent gaiety" of the Greeks in his essay "About Conducting"[52] (which Nietzsche had read in manuscript in 1869), can be found again in *The Birth of Tragedy*, where the same "'Greek cheerfulness'" only signifies a "senile, unproductive love of existence."[53] This was a debt that Nietzsche recognized, something rather rare for him to do toward those still living. This acknowledgement, moreover, came with a certain reticence in 1871 in his speech "Greek Musical Drama," which he dedicated to Wagner:

> From you, my revered friend, and you alone, I know that with me you distinguish between a true and a false concept of "Greek serenity," and that you encounter the latter—the false one—all over the place in a state of assured contentment; from you as well, I know that you hold it to be impossible starting from this false concept to gain insight into the essence of tragedy. . . .
>
> As for those whose praise stops at the transparency, the clarity, the definiteness and harmony of Greek art in the belief that protected by this model they can come to terms with the horrors of existence—a species that you have already, my revered friend, brought to light with incomparably sharp features in your memorable text "On Conducting"—they need to be convinced that it is in part their own fault if the foundation of Greek art seems so thin, and also in part due to the innermost essence of that Greek serenity. . . . For Greek art has taught us that there is no truly beautiful surface apart from some terrifying depths.[54]

It was as a connoisseur that Nietzsche later distinguished "two types of genius: one which above all begets and wants to beget, and another which prefers being fertilized and giving birth."[55] "In it one sees a gifted man imbued with R.'s ideas in his own way," Cosima recorded after Nietzsche had read to her some passages from *The Birth of Tragedy*.[56] In the "strange collaboration" with Wagner from which was born Nietzsche's first book, Nietzsche can be credited with the duality of Dionysus and Apollo—an idea which, if not having conceived, he set in sharp relief. Moreover, Nietzsche cast the god of music in the primary role; this went against German aesthetics, according to which the image of Hellenic civilization, since Winckelmann, had been characterized by the supremacy of the plastic arts and, since Lessing, by the opposition between these arts and poetry.[57] "I was the first to take seriously that wonderful phenomenon which bears the name Dionysus as a means to understanding the older Hellenic instinct, an instinct still exuberant and even overflowing," Nietzsche rightly said in *Twilight of the Idols*.[58] Wagner, then, understood as an "oracle" Genelli's picture which presided over their conversations: "A remarkable, and even marvelous coherence, I should like to say, of my whole life with itself, which starting from that image I see represented for me in your thought," he wrote to Nietzsche in November 1871.[59]

Without Wagner's example, however, and without the hold his music had over him, Nietzsche would surely have not attributed primacy to Dionysus. In October 1869, he wrote to Erwin Rhode:

> Wagner was naturally the greatest help to me, above all, as an exemplar ungraspable by past aesthetics. It is above all a matter of getting beyond Lessing's *Laocoö*: which one can hardly dare say without inner anxiety and shame.[60]

Nietzsche was also original in that when he borrowed Wagner's ideas, he showed himself to be more Wagnerian than Wagner. Unconcerned about history—"all of us suffer from a debilitating historical fever"[61]—the disciple did not recoil before the flagrant anachronisms that his model had carefully avoided.

Indeed, it is the modern symphonic orchestra as whole that Nietzsche projects into the ancient chorus—"the chorus as orchestra," "the dithyramb as symphony," we read in his notes from the spring and summer of 1871[62]—whereas Wagner had only seen in the chorus its distant and necessarily incomplete prefiguration. As an expression of the popular soul, melody had given birth to tragedy, but for Wagner, faithful in this to classical aesthetics, music only played in it a supporting role, which was subordinated to the ideal of plastic beauty that impregnated a whole culture devoted "to the purely exterior forms of man." The Greeks cultivated music only "sufficiently to serve as a prop for Gesture, whose tale was already expressed melodiously by Speech itself."[63] In addition, he posited that it existed only in association with dance. The laws of rhythm so "strictly governed verse and melody, that Greek music (a term which almost always included Poetry) may be regarded merely as Dance expressing itself in tones and words."[64] One could also say, in Schopenhauerian terms, that it went with the world of appearances. Once this paradise of appearance that was the Hellenic world had been lost forever, it was through "the spirit of Christianity" that music "rewoke to life." And it then acquired progressively that power that we experience "in the opening chords of a symphony by Beethoven," which has the effect of abolishing all the lies of our civilization "as the light of day, the lamp light."[65]

Nietzsche takes up this formulation in *The Birth of Tragedy*, but to apply it to what he imagines must have been authentic, "Dionysian" Greek music—the light of Apollo scattered by the frantic chromaticism of *Tristan*. This formulation follows a reference made in passing to what Wagner rightly had taken to be the only music known to the Greeks: "a wave-like rhythm with an image-making power which they developed to represent [Darstellung] Apollonian states." "The music of Apollo was Doric architectonics in tones, but in tones that were merely suggestive, such as those of the *cithara*." This could not be really qualified as music, since consequently it lacked "the uniform flow of melody, and the utterly incomparable world of harmony."[66] More than the birth of tragedy, it was the triumph of Wagnerian drama, *Tristan* as it turns out, that Nietzsche celebrated in Greek décor. But if Wagner sometimes took himself to be a new Aeschylus, at least unlike his excessive disciple he never depicted Aeschylus as an earlier incarnation of himself.

What is more, if Wagner thought that there existed a particular affinity between the Greek and the German spirit that predisposed his compatriots to find inspiration in Hellenic art, he never lost sight of what separated ancient Greece from nineteenth-century Germany. Ancient drama was "so distinctly a native product of the Hellenic spirit, its religion, ay, its State itself, that to assume the possibility of a modern imitation must necessarily lead to the gravest errors," he had written in March 1871,[67] fully aware of the theses that were going to be presented in *The Birth of Tragedy*, which its author had already revealed, a year earlier, in "Greek Musical Drama":

> Constrained yet graceful, multiplicity and yet unity, many arts at the
> peak of activity, and yet *one* work of art—this was ancient music-drama.
> But anyone for whom this vision recalls the ideal of the current reformer
> of the arts must immediately say that the work of art of the future is not a
> brilliant yet deceptive mirage: what we are hoping for from the future
> has already been a reality—in a past more than two thousand
> years old.[68]

Nietzsche, caught up in his Greco-Wagnerian passion, imagined a "German rebirth of Hellenic antiquity" for which Bayreuth would be the seat—"for it is in it, and in it alone that lies every hope we have of a renewal and a purification of the German Spirit by the magical play of music." Wagner, for his part, since 1849 had already relinquished such chimerical aspirations, which were so contrary to his vision of history. In "Art and Revolution," he wrote:

> No, we do not wish to revert to Greekdom; for what the Greeks knew
> not, and, knowing not, came by their downfall, that know *we*. It is their

very fall, whose cause we now perceive after years of misery and deepest universal suffering, that shows us clearly what we should become; it shows us that we must love all men before we can rightly love ourselves, before we can regain the true joy in our own personality.

The Slave, by sheer reason of the assumed necessity of his slavery, has exposed the null and fleeting nature of all the strength and beauty of exclusive Grecian manhood, and has shown to all time that that *Beauty and Strength as attributes of public life, can then alone prove lasting blessings, when they are the common gifts of all mankind.*[69]

In 1869, it was not time for the restoration of a fallen civilization but for revolution, as the necessary prelude to the free development of art. Thus, after having expressed his rejection of modern society and his faith in the ideal by means of Christian symbols, Wagner set aside Christianity in *The Flying Dutchman, Tannhäuser,* and *Lohengrin* equally, believing the regeneration of humanity was then possible and even close. Taking the world as the kingdom of evil, it was the "direct antithesis of art," which presupposes "pleasure in itself, in existence, in community."[70] What is more, the religion of renouncement that Wagner had admired in Christianity had, through the treason of the churches, made itself an accomplice of "the slavery of money," set up by "a far worse mistress—Commerce."

Inspired by Feuerbach, this double condemnation—which Wagner would soon judge incorrect and inexact, as the very example of music "regenerated by Christianity" demonstrated—did not prevent Wagner, however, from making his own the egalitarian and universal message Christianity contained, a message that he would never deny; any more than the pro-slavery attitude of the Greeks weakened in his eyes the ideal of beauty that they had made into a religion. In complementing each other, both of these should work for the building of a free society in which the artistic nature of man would flourish.[71] Whence the invocation of the "two sublimest teachers of mankind" that concludes *Art and Revolution:* Jesus, who has "shown us that we all alike are men and brothers," and Apollo, who will stamp "this mighty bond of brotherhood with strength and beauty."[72]

With no apparent awareness of the paradox he was presenting, Nietzsche in *The Birth of Tragedy* only denounces the existence of a "slave class" in the modern world.[73] However, this was a short-lived and superficial indignation, since it was not its very existence that troubled him, but the contradiction with "the optimistic vision of existence" sustaining modern Alexandrian existence that it revealed. His working notes from this period leave no doubt about his deep conviction:

The "dignity of labor" is a modern fantasy of the worst sort. It is the dream of slaves. . . . Slavery belongs to the essence of any culture.

Art is the surplus force of a people that has not been squandered in the struggle for existence. Here the *cruel* actuality of a *culture* shows itself—to the degree that it builds its triumphal gates on servitude and annihilation.[74]

Here lay the seed of the misunderstanding that would break out over *Parsifal*, when Nietzsche reproached Wagner for the Christianity to which Wagner had been "converted," its "slave morality" and its negation of art.

"A New Year's Eve"

Whatever their differences, however tacit, may have been, Wagner must have felt responsible in good part for his young friend's daring innovations. Thus, when *The Birth of Tragedy* had suffered the harsh criticism of a number of eminent philologists, he did not hesitate to defend it vigorously in an open letter—something that Nietzsche would never forget. So in 1888 he could write:

Has anyone ever understood to the slightest extent what I am—understood *me?* One did, and one alone: Richard Wagner, a reason for me to doubt that he was truly German. . . . Who, among my German "friends" (and in my life, the word "friend" is always to be written in quotation marks) could even have approached the *depth* of insight with which *sixteen years ago* Wagner made himself my prophet . . . ?[75]

As for Wagner, at the moment when, after long years of tribulations, land seemed in sight, his encounter with Nietzsche must have felt like an act of grace. From the university, for which he felt little respect, had come to him a young, brilliant mind who was thrilled to meet him and who would, perhaps, help him carry out his mission. "Let yourself be seen as you are. I have not yet had many delightful experiences with Germans compatriots," Wagner declared in his first letter in June 1869. "Save my faith, which is not totally unshakable, in what I call—with Goethe and a few others—German freedom."[76] Three years later, he would add: "Strictly speaking, you are, after my wife, the one good thing that life has brought me."[77] And the following year: "I take you to be the one person who knows what I want." Nietzsche and his friends seemed to him "a new and admirable species of men" that until then he had not thought possible. In October 1872, Wagner wrote to Erwin Rhode, "With and through Nietzsche, I mingle with an excellent society. You cannot know what it means to have passed so many years of one's life in a poor or at least stupid society."[78] Nietzsche was hardly exaggerating when some years later he wrote that *The Birth of Tragedy* had been "for Wagner the happiness that had the greatest resonance in his life; he was ecstatic, and in *Götterdämmerung* there are magnificent things that he brought forth in his condition of an unexpected, extreme hope."[79] In 1870, thanking Nietzsche for having sent the text of his lecture "Socrates and Tragedy," Cosima referred to the happy effects that this had had on the composition of the third act of the opera:

> Your present and the attention it garnered has marked a turning point in the atmosphere at Tribschen. We were so morose that we no longer even read in the evening, the pilgrimage we took thanks to your intermediary to the heart of the most beautiful ages of humanity had such a positive effect on us that the next morning the master had his *Siegfried* played, accompanying its joyous theme of the Rhine with strong and petulant acrobatics on the violin; hearing this, the Rhine maidens, filled with hope, made your motif sound forth.[80]

In 1872, after having received *The Birth of Tragedy*, Wagner himself was enthusiastic and will write to Nietzsche how much his book stimulated him:

> I still always use it to put myself into the right mood between breakfast and work; for since reading it I have returned to the composition of my last act. Alone or together [with Cosima], exclamations constantly accompany our reading. For my part, I do not understand how it was granted me to experience something like this.[81]

Yet life at Tribschen, that "isle of the blessed," did not always take place at such a high altitude. The young professor participated in family gatherings. He was present on 25 December 1870 when, for her thirty-eighth birthday, Wagner presented Cosima with the first performance of his *Siegfried Idyll*. And the following year, when *The Birth of Tragedy* appeared, as though Nietzsche wanted to say, "I, too, am a composer," he dedicated to Cosima his *Nachklang einer Sylvester Nacht*, whose first version of piano and violin went back to 1863.

This was a piece filled with meaning and emotion for Nietzsche. With the nostalgia for the Christmases of his childhood it provoked in him, each year's end for him was a propitious moment for meditation: one of those all too rare hours when, dominating time, "the soul stands still and can survey a period of its own development."[82] Moreover, he found the dedicatrice charming: Cosima, "the only woman of high style it has been given me to know, at bottom the only woman I have venerated," he will later write. And in his notes for *Ecce Homo:* "as for myself, I have always considered her marriage to Wagner as a simple act of adultery . . . the case of Tristan."[83] Cosima-Isolde—the Ariadne of Wagner-Theseus, to whom, in January 1889, just as he was falling into madness, he will address this card: "Ariadne, I love you. Signed, Dionysus."[84]

However, except for an obstinate rhythmic figure, the god of intoxication and ecstatic dance can hardly be heard in this composition, which once again underscores the occasional character of Nietzsche's inspiration, the difficulty he had in giving form to his ideas, in developing and fusing them into a unified whole. What he lacked—as his books also indicate—is that sense of transition that Wagner took to be the secret of his art.[85] That he felt no embarrassment in submitting it to the composer of *Tristan* indicates that he also lacked the clairvoyance and tact proper to the "first psychologist of Europe," as he one day will flatter himself to be. We can understand that Wagner must have smiled at the clumsy mistakes of a short-winded improviser whom, the preceding year, he had advised to confine himself to philology while allowing himself to be "directed by music."[86] The humble and grateful disciple had responded to this: "If it is true, as you once wrote, to my pride, that music is my conductor, then you are at all events the conductor of this music of mine; and you have said yourself that even something middling, if *well* conducted, can make a satisfactory impression."[87]

"LONG LIVE THE NOBLE TRAITORS!"

*N*ietzsche followed Wagner's advice so well that he became a philosopher, in this way freeing up the true music to be found in him: that of language—but, for all that, without renouncing composing and thus cultivating what Goethe called a "false tendency." In April 1872, four months after the appearance of *The Birth of Tragedy*, he finished his *Manfred-Meditation* duet for piano, in which we catch more than just an echo of the Dionysian music praised in his book. Although it suffers from the same clumsiness of almost all his other compositions, this score is better constructed, more elaborated than his previous one, *Nachklang einer Sylvester Nacht*, from which—and this was a characteristic feature of the musician from the start, one shared by the writer—it borrows a few themes, but they are dealt with this time in a more somber and tormented mode. Louis Kelterborn, who had played it several times with Nietzsche while a student at Basel, will write many years later: "Nothing expresses the very soul of Nietzsche as I knew it and venerated it than this 'Manfred-Meditation' . . . so singular and abrupt in form, but so great in soul and thought, so deep in feeling." And, he adds, "I have not the slightest doubt that at the bottom of his heart [Nietzsche] had a certain weakness for this volcanic effusion from his musician's soul, even though he wrote me that it was a musical monster that had awakened an excessive sympathy in me."[1]

Cruelty, Pleasure, and Vengeance

As a sign of gratitude for the performances of *Tristan* that had so over-whelmed him, Nietzsche dedicated "Manfred-Meditation" to Hans von Bülow, who, moreover, was an enthusiastic reader of his book and who de-voted himself to making it widely known. "Go ahead, make fun of me, I merit it," Nietzsche wrote, sensing that the conductor's admiration un-doubtedly would not extend to the author of such a "dubious piece of music."[2] Well-known for his ferocious wit and his aggressive outbursts, Bülow lived up to his reputation—unless it was a "joke," "a parody of the alleged music of the future," this meditation was the height of fantastic ex-travagance, nothing less, "in the musical sphere," than "the equivalent of a crime in the moral realm."

> I could not discover in it the least trace of Apollonian elements, and, as for the Dionysian, to tell you frankly, it made me think of the morning after a bacchanalian orgy rather than of an orgy itself. If you really have a passionate need to express yourself in musical language, it is urgent that you assimilate the basic elements of this language. A fantasy still intoxi-cated with Wagnerian resonances is not a good starting point for crea-tion. In Wagner, unprecedented strokes of audacity, not to add that they spring from a dramatic texture that is justified by the words . . . are al-ways grammatically correct even in the smallest details of the notation.
>
> Once again—don't take this badly—you yourself say your music is "detestable"—it is, actually, more detestable than you believe, not in a way detrimental to the common interest, but worse than that: detrimen-tal to you, who cannot more hideously waste your excess of leisure than in this kind of rape of Euterpe.[3]

This was certainly a harsh verdict. But if Nietzsche, challenged by his philological colleagues, thought to take revenge as a composer, this "telling correction" would not leave any room for hope. What is more, three months passed before he could even reply to von Bülow. In the draft that preceded this letter, an almost obsequious Nietzsche seeks to gain absolution, as we have seen, by attributing his "detestable music" to a purgative fit of "barbaric frenzy." However, he is forced to acknowledge, not without some pretense of remorse, that it also was due to another, perhaps less excusable impulse:

> It is now unfortunately clear to me that the whole, with its mélange of pathos and malice, corresponded precisely to an actual mood and that in

writing this music down I experienced a pleasure as never before. There is something very sad here about my music and even more so about my feelings. What does one call a condition where pleasure, contempt, exuberance, and sublimity are all mixed together?[4]

While not answering the question, Nietzsche did define the dominant tonalities of his future philosophical work almost as though music was its clumsy prelude. In this sense, it was in his composing that the future author of *The Genealogy of Morals* will have first expressed, if not felt, cruelty, which he will say "belongs to the sources of art."[5] We read in one of his notes from the autumn of 1885: "Somber or turbulent, a spirit that in all that it imagines takes vengeance for something it has done (or for *not* having done something)—who does not understand happiness without cruelty."[6] Upon what is the *Manfred-Meditation* wreaking vengeance? The beginning of an answer appears in the letter that Nietzsche did send to von Bülow. Referring to the joy that his music had always brought him, Nietzsche comments:

I have always asked myself, where did this joy come from? There was something irrational. . . . Precisely this Manfred-music gave me a feeling of such fierce, even scornful pathos that I enjoyed it as though it were a devilish irony! . . . The very title was ironic—for I can barely think of Byron's *Manfred*, which fascinated me as a boy and was almost my favorite poem, except as an absurdly shapeless and monotonous monster.

But I will keep silent regarding all that . . .[7]

Sixteen years later, when "read backwards," "this long phase of his life" will seem to hand over all its meaning, the author of *Ecce Homo* will be more explicit:

The Germans are *incapable* of any notion of greatness; proof: Schumann. Simply from fury against this sugary Saxon, I composed a counter-overture for *Manfred* of which Hans von Bülow said that he had never seen anything like it on paper, and he called it rape of Euterpe.[8]

These lines from 1888 are from the same Nietzsche who, in October 1864, paid homage at Schumann's tomb in Bonn before delighting himself with the piano redaction of *Manfred*. Two years later, the mordant psychologist of culture who flares up in *Beyond Good and Evil* had not spared the composer of *Manfred*, that work which he then regarded as "an error and misunderstanding to the point of an injustice":

> Schumann with his taste which was basically a *small* taste (namely, a
> dangerous propensity, doubly dangerous among Germans, for quiet lyri-
> cism and sottishness of feeling) . . . this Schumann was already a merely
> *German* event in music, no longer a European one, as Beethoven was
> and, to a still greater extent, Mozart. With him German music was
> threatened by its greatest danger: losing *the voice of the soul of Europe* and
> descending to mere fatherlandishness.[9]

Already in 1879 in "The Wanderer and His Shadow," Nietzsche
treacherously praised Schumann for having been the one Romantic who
had succeeded in depicting the "eternal youth." It was true, he added, that
"there are moments when his music recalls the *eternal 'old maid.'*"[10] The musician had preceded the writer: In 1872, the Wagnerian Nietzsche, who saw
in "the artwork of the future the annunciation of and incitement to a new society," took his vengeance on the Schumannian Nietzsche who, withdrawn
within his nostalgic inwardness, "indifferent to the destiny of humanity,"
had become lost "in a debauchery of personal, petit-bourgeois, treacly feelings."[11] Filled with chromatic runs, appoggiaturas, and modulations that
break up Schumann's music and subvert it with suggestions of *Tristan*, the
Manfred-Meditation expresses one of those "twists" by which Nietzsche, rejecting and burning what he had at first admired or adored, attacks himself
from the rear "as an adversary and mortal enemy of his own thought"—
always on campaign against himself. "I only attack things I have known
thoroughly—that I have myself experienced, that, to a point, I have *been*."[12]

Whoever Loves, Punishes Himself as Well

Indeed, there was not one of his inclinations that Nietzsche did not deny, not
one that he did not struggle to overcome, not one among those whom he admired that did not slander or betray. "Long live the noble traitors!"[13] he exclaimed during the fateful summer of 1876, announcing in this way the
praise of Brutus found in *The Gay Science*: "Independence of the soul!—that
is at stake here. No sacrifice can be too great for that: one must be capable of
sacrificing one's dearest friend for it, even if he should also be the most glorious human being, an ornament of the world, a genius without peer."[14] Behind Caesar's mask, it is easy to recognize Wagner.

Following Schumann and along with Schopenhauer (already half
"surmounted" in *The Birth of Tragedy*) Wagner was the object of the most
spectacular of Nietzsche's reversals. And this took place the day after Wagner's triumph in Bayreuth in 1876, that consecration of the musician that

Nietzsche's fourth essay in *Unfashionable Observations* celebrated as the "call to arms before the battle" for "the liberation of art." Twelve years later, Bayreuth will be equated with the hydrotherapy resort where it is located; and Wagner, with Cagliostro.

This was the central episode in Nietzsche's life, judging from the space it occupies in his books and even more so in the posthumous fragments. His Wagnerian adventure was the detonator of a tremendous chain reaction that, over ten years, step by step, from *Human, All Too Human* to the *Twilight of the Idols* in 1888 (and not without other "twists") ends in a radical critique of values and modern ideas. For "one has almost completed an account of the value of what is modern once one has gained clarity about what is good and evil in Wagner"[15]—from progress to socialism, passing through labor, revolution, and democracy, those heirs of Christianity—and leaving out neither nationalism nor anti-Semitism (Nietzsche, sharing the prejudices of his milieu and faced with the example of Schopenhauer and Wagner, showed some symptoms of anti-Semitism in his youth before becoming, in the words of Erich Heller, "the most radical anti-anti-Semite in German literature since Lessing").[16]

"Whoever attacks his own age," we must not forget, "can only be attacking *himself*; who can he have in sight if not himself? Even in others one is glorifying oneself. Self-annihilation, self-deification, self-distrust—these are for us what it means to condemn, love, hate."[17] "Connoisseur-executioner of himself" is how Zarathustra will name himself. By way of Wagner, as by way of Socrates, Christ, or Germany—to cite only the principal protagonists of his inner drama, his most intimate enemies—Nietzsche continued to struggle with and against himself. His struggle was sharper with Wagner, since for him Wagner and his art were "the great passionate love of his life." "I loved and venerated Richard Wagner more than anyone," we read in his preparatory notes for *The Case of Wagner.* "I loved him and no one other than him. He was a man after my own heart."[18]

"Wounded by an unfulfilled, nostalgic, and solitary youth," Nietzsche will say that he "could not have endured it without Wagner's music."[19] At an age where, ordinarily, enthusiasms, desires, torments get fixed on other objects or find other outlets, it was in and through this music—with its unequaled power to express "all the deepest-hidden secrets of the human heart" and immediately to impregnate it with its tonalities—that Nietzsche's, for the first time, really became known to him by becoming identified so to speak with visceral sonorous figures, with vital sounds, as immediately recognizable as a familiar voice, and which never would allow themselves to be forgotten.[20] This was an experience both of liberation and of possession that his friendship with the composer and his wife could only make even more intense and dangerous. Hence the role that personal elements and the psychological background of their relations played in Nietzsche's taking leave of them: clashes between two equally strong characters, blunders that turned into wounds: the (classic) jealousy of the bashful young man toward Cosima's husband; the "metaphysical jealousy" of an emerging genius towards an already recognized one, of a disciple himself impatient to dominate, to fulfill his mission, which included much pride—Valéry called it "the pride of being right, Protestant, and of not thinking as others do"—along with a good dose of *ressentiment*, for which Nietzsche gave such a lucid analysis.[21]

The personal element infuses many pages of *Human, All Too Human*, where we sense that the author, to speak as he does, often "attacks problems" in order to "be right against persons" and even to get the better of them. "I could say something about every one of the sentences I read, and I know that that represents a victory of evil," was Cosima's reaction.[22] Nor was she spared: "One always loses by too familiar association with friends and women; and sometimes what one loses is the pearl of one's life."[23] She was especially hurt by the aphorism entitled "Voluntary sacrifice." Living only for Wagner and his work, she could not without pain recognize herself in the "women of consequence" who "alleviate the life of their men . . . by becoming, as it were, the receptacle of the general disfavour and occasional ill-humour of the rest of mankind" or that "then the man can feel very contented—assuming, that is, that he is enough of an egotist to endure the proximity of such a voluntary lightning-, storm- and rain-conductor."[24]

As for the "great man" in question, that "genius (as we say)," the veneration, the cult of which he is the object really stems from superstition. They depend on the credulity and the vanity of human beings, "for only if we think of him as being very remote from us, as a *miraculum*, does he not aggrieve us."[25] Even worse is the fact that he himself comes to experience the "religious awe" that he inspires.

> It is in any event a dangerous sign when a man is assailed by awe of himself . . . when the sacrificial incense which is properly rendered only to a god penetrates the brain of the genius, so that his head begins to swim and he comes to regard himself as something supra-human. The consequences that slowly result are: the feeling of irresponsibility, of exceptional rights, the belief that he confers a favour by his mere presence, insane rage when anyone attempts even to compare him with others. Let alone to rate him beneath them, or to draw attention to lapses in his

work. . . . In rare individual cases this portion of madness may, indeed, actually have been the means by which such a nature, excessive in all directions, was held firmly together: in the life of individuals, too, illusions that are in themselves poisons often play the role of healers; yet, in the end, in the case of every "genius" who believes in his own divinity, the poison shows itself to the same degree as his "genius" grows old.[26]

Wagner died too soon to have been able to note that Nietzsche had thus foretold his own fate. But neither he nor Cosima was completely surprised by their young friend's evolution, except perhaps for the violence with which he tore himself away from them. Already in 1871, Cosima sensed within him "an addiction to treachery, as it were—as if he were seeking to avenge himself for some great impression."[27] And on 3 August of the same year, she again writes in her diary: "It is as if he were trying to resist the overwhelming effect of Wagner's personality."[28] Despite the bitterness he felt, the composer, who in many ways was a more perceptive psychologist than his disciple, understood that Nietzsche was moved by irresistible forces, that the flowering of his personality would undoubtedly demand a hardening of their relations and perhaps even a complete break. A letter that he will write in October 1879 to Franz Overbeck, Nietzsche's most faithful friend, bears witness to this:

> Even if I always felt that Nietzsche, in his association with me, was subject to the laws of an essential life crisis, and even if I always found it surprising that this crisis could engender in him an outburst of such vivid, shining, heated thoughts, as it did, to everyone's surprise; even if I recognized with horror in the decisive turn in his evolution the intolerable weight that this crisis must have been for him, I had to realize that one cannot relate such a violent psychic phenomenon to moral norms, so that the only possible attitude is a deeply felt silence. But I am afflicted to feel myself so totally excluded from Nietzsche's life and sufferings.[29]

If his Tribschen idyll had not been interrupted by the Wagners moving to Bayreuth, Nietzsche would have probably in some way or another arranged for it to end. No doubt, the "independence of his soul" was at stake, but a soul that only felt fully alive when in opposition. Any agreement was only the provisional, deceptive resolution of those dissonances that came forth beneath his fingers when "the demon of music" took hold of him with a "barbarous frenzy." There is no mutual agreement that does not rest—and rest dangerously!—on some misunderstanding. In all of Nietzsche's disavowals, in all his declarations of war, there resounds an unmistakable hint of relief, of satisfaction, sometimes jubilant in its aggressiveness. It is almost as if he had been long waiting for the right occasion to break off a harmonious relationship that his basically bellicose nature was unable to prolong except at the price of a fatal relaxation. "At the very deepest level, I am convinced that I owe more to those of my feelings aroused by hostility than to my friendly ones," he notes in 1884.[30] Only hostility was creative. Whence the necessity of being an "enemy," wherein Nietzsche saw a condition "inherent in every strong nature," while denouncing the reactive character of the "decadent" that he also was and only managed to become himself at the cost of what he admired.[31] Here again we see the "deep kinship" he gladly acknowledged with Wagner for whom, by his own admission, anger was as necessary as "bile was for blood." In this they were both typically *modern:* noisily clamoring to be understood and secretly fearing that they would be, they conformed to Schiller's figure of the "sentimental" artist, who comes to life only when irritated by reality, caught between nostalgia and invective.[32]

In the case of Wagner, at least, Nietzsche did not commence hostilities with a light heart: "What is all of Hamlet's melancholy compared to that of Brutus?"[33] The pain and bad conscience he must have felt contributed to the insistence with which he returned again and again to the necessity of being unfaithful as the "condition of mastery":

> Because we have sworn to be faithful, perhaps even to a purely fictitious being such as a god, because we have surrendered our heart to a prince, to a party, to a woman, to a priestly order, to an artist, to a thinker, in a state of deluded infatuation that made that being seem worthy of every kind of sacrifice and reverence—are we now ineluctably committed? Were we not indeed at that time deceiving ourselves? Was it not a hypothetical promise, made under the admittedly silent condition that the beings to which we consecrated ourselves were in reality what they appeared to us to be? Are we obliged to be faithful to our errors, even when we realize that through this faithfulness we are injuring our higher self?—No, there exists no law, no obligation, of this kind; we *have* to become traitors, be unfaithful, again and again abandon our ideals. We cannot advance from one period of our life into the next without passing through these pains of betrayal and then continuing to suffer them.[34]

And besides, in spite of the suffering that it provokes, "open contradiction" often has calming and even conciliating effects:

When someone publicly declares that he differs from a celebrated party leader or teacher in a matter of dogma all the world believes that at that moment he must harbour a dislike of him. But sometimes it is at precisely that moment that he ceases to dislike him: he ventures to set himself up beside him and is free of the torment of unspoken jealousy.[35]

That all relations between the two men should have ceased following the appearance of *Human, All Too Human* therefore does not imply, for all that, that Nietzsche "broke" with Wagner—any more than he "broke" with Socrates, Christ, or Germany, to all of whom he was attached by the same love-hate that he had for himself. He denied it anyway, when speaking of *Human, All Too Human* in *Ecce Homo*, he writes: "What reached a decision in me at that time was not a break with Wagner: I noted a total aberration of my instincts. . . . I was overcome by *impatience* with myself."[36] As Thomas Mann, who was both Wagnerian and Nietzschean, has emphasized, "We may say that Nietzsche's relationship to the preferred objects of his criticism was simply one of passion—a passion without specific sign, for it was constantly shifting between the negative and the positive."[37] Even at its paroxysm, in his last pamphlets, his polemic against Wagner presupposes a prior adhesion: "There is nothing to do about it, one has to begin by being a Wagnerian . . ." In the same way, such polemics refuse any merely external adhesion. If Nietzsche, with his passion for distance, found it difficult to admit that his esteem for or condemnation of a person gave another the right to esteem or condemn in turn[38]—which amounts to acknowledging his fellow man as an equal—in the case of Wagner, he resented this claim to equality as an intrusion into his privacy.

It goes without saying that I do not grant lightly anyone the right to appropriate for himself my estimation [of Wagner], and none of the disrespectful rabble who teem like lice on the body of contemporary society is authorized even to have on their lips, whether in praise or opposition, a name as great as that of Richard Wagner's.[39]

In any case, it was "only too easy to be right against Wagner":[40]

It is difficult to attack him on some point of detail and not be correct; his art, life, character, his opinions, his inclinations, and aversions all have their weak points. But as a whole, his appearance is above every attack.[41]

Nietzsche's critique of Wagner was not as useless as one might suppose, however. As Thomas Mann writes, at least "by means of it we can learn more about Wagner, and draw from it a more lucid enthusiasm for him than from all the simple-minded panegyrics." Lucid, we will savor all the more this "inexhaustible source of delights and despair" for having the antidotes so as not (overly) to succumb to it.[42] And for that, Nietzsche might have added: Wagnerians all know, and ought to thank me.

THE DISAPPOINTMENT OF BAYREUTH

*O*fficially, it was at Bayreuth, in 1876, during the first festival—"the greatest victory an artist has ever achieved"[1]—that things began to go badly. As Montherlant put it, "we betray lost causes out of cowardice, and victorious ones out of delicacy." Nietzsche only went after victorious causes, which also had the advantage of enhancing the traitor and, in his eyes, of ennobling him.

"For us, Bayreuth signifies the morning consecration on the day of battle," proclaims Nietzsche's fourth "unfashionable observation," which appeared a few weeks before the festival's opening.[2] A battle for the regeneration of culture, which, itself, would lead to the birth of a "new society." For, Nietzsche emphasizes, "One could do us no greater injustice than to assume that for us it is a matter of art alone, as if it were to function as a medicine and narcotic with which we could cure ourselves of all other miserable conditions. In the image of the tragic work of art at Bayreuth, we witness precisely the struggle of these individuals against everything that confronts them as a seemingly invincible necessity: against power, rule of law, tradition, convention, and the whole order of things."[3]

Against this prevailing order, against the "cultural state" denounced in the third essay in *Unfashionable Observations*, Bayreuth will represent a kind of counterpower. But there was nothing political, properly speaking, in the authority that Wagner might exercise. For at about the same time, Nietzsche, who would one day name himself "the last apolitical German," poses the question: "How could a political innovation possibly be sufficient to make human beings once and for all into contented dwellers on this earth?"[4]

Admittedly, three years earlier, shortly after the German victory over France, Nietzsche had "linked his hopes for a *German* renaissance of the Hellenic world" to "the bloody glory that the name German [then] bore." "The only productive *political* power in Germany [i.e., Bismarck's Prussia] has triumphed in the most prodigious way and henceforth shall rule what is German right down to its atoms," he wrote in 1871, in his dedication to Wagner in his lecture "Socrates and Tragedy."

> This fact is of inestimable value, for this power will make something
> perish that we hate as the true adversary of all deeper philosophy and
> aesthetics, that sickly state from which the German has suffered since the
> great French Revolution, whose cramping effects keep returning to para-
> lyze even the best-constituted German natures, to say nothing of the
> masses, whose name for this illness ignominiously profanes what is
> meant by the word "liberalism." This liberalism built entirely on a
> dreamed up dignity of man, and of the generic concept of humankind,
> will together with its crude brothers, bleed to death at the hands of that
> inflexible power.[5]

Yet, he adds, "And what purpose will this inflexible power serve, which over the centuries has always been born in violence, conquest, and carnage, if not to prepare the way for the genius?" And quickly, Nietzsche—who had been plunged into a sense of horror and despair at the erroneous report that the Communards had burned down the Louvre—interpreted the victory by arms as a defeat of culture for the benefit of the State ("the coldest of cold monsters," Zarathustra will say), before seeing in this, "under the pompous pretense of founding a *Reich*," the irrevocable and definitive abdication of the German spirit to "a leveling mediocrity, democracy, and 'modern ideas'!"[6]

Suffering and tragedy—this was the real lesson of war, which reinforced Nietzsche's deepest convictions. "A happy life" was a contradiction in terms, "an impossibility," and "to desire happiness" was to reveal that "he has not elevated his gaze above the horizon of the animal."[7] Only a "heroic life" was worth living, and it was up to philosophy to prepare men for it, as shown by Schopenhauer, whom Nietzsche designates in 1874 as "the one teacher and only initiator that he [could] glorify." The task that fell to his disciples was to make his works, and even more, his exemplary life known to the "free spirits," then to rally them away from the state in order to initiate "a movement" that could, if not defeat, at least keep at bay selling our soul "to moneymaking, to social life, or to scholarship."[8]

Two years later, Nietzsche will add music to philosophy. Exalted by Wagner, more than ever before "the soul of music wishes to form a body for itself . . . it seeks its path to visibility in motion, action, institution, and morality!"[9] Awakened by it to the transformative power of art, men in ever greater numbers are beginning to understand "as though for the first time what it means to found a state on music—something that the ancient Greeks not only understood but also demanded of themselves. And these same understanding people will condemn the state just as unconditionally as most people already condemn the church."[10] To "those who can hear," Wagner asks them to help him discover the culture that his music proclaims because it is the rediscovered language of the *"correct feeling"* and because this has always been perceptible in the music of the German masters, which is "the enemy of all convention, of all artificial alienation and unintelligibility between human beings."[11] Hence the audience at the festival at Bayreuth will be themselves "worthy of interest," and like all the participants, will "seem untimely: their fatherland is elsewhere than in the present moment." There is little risk there of encountering the habitués of "our theatrical institutions," which are so vulgar "when we simply compare them to what Greek theater had been"—those "cultivated people" and "lovers of art" "for whom the very word Bayreuth signifies one of their profoundest defeats." No, what one will find there are men "prepared for and initiated into tragic contemplation, at the heights of their happiness, and who sense in it all their being coming together in order to strengthen them with an even broader and higher will."

German Revels

Such spectators, in an exalted mood, were no doubt present at the first performances of *The Ring of the Nibelungen:* musicians (Tchaikovsky, Bruckner, Saint-Saëns), painters, and writers were numerous. But these were eclipsed by high-flying guests: two emperors—including Wilhelm I, who in 1849 would no doubt have willingly seen the revolutionary Wagner before a firing squad; two kings, and in their train a swarm of richly dressed and bejeweled representatives of the new empire. Far too many *Reichsdeutschen* for Nietzsche's taste: "Poor Wagner!" He, whose art, if it were to be understood, demanded "refined artists," a "cosmopolitanism of the mind," and taste, "where had he landed!—If he had at least entered into swine! But to descend among Germans!"[12]

Gathered together were all the leisured riffraff of Europe and the first prince who arrived walked in on Wagner as into his own home, if it were nothing more than one more amusement. And, at bottom, it was nothing else. Besides the familiar pretexts, they had found a new, artistic one, a grand opera *with obstacles:* they found in Wagner's music, which was so insinuating owing to its hidden sexuality, a "cement" for a society wherein everyone pursued his *pleasures.*[13]

Aggravated by a suffocating heat, the atmosphere was that both of a spa and a jolly party. In the crammed inns, instead of the contemplation into which tragic catastrophe is supposed to plunge the "artist-spectator," gripped "by the voice arising from the deepest depths of things," there were only lively, laugh-filled conversations amid the smoke of sausages and cigars and great streams of "*German* beer." The first souvenirs were already on sale: medallions of the Nibelungen and Wagnerian neckties, announcing those Grails in red glass and Parsifal pants that were so to amuse Willy and Colette.[14]

Shy, distant, a little stiff, the son of a provincial pastor whom the university had hardly made sociable, the young professor from Basel was less inclined than ever to laugh—with that strident laugh he would attribute to the *Übermensch.*[15] In vain he tried to revive his lyrical erudite's dream. "Wherever was I? There was nothing I recognized; I scarcely recognized Wagner."[16] The Aeschylus of Tribschen, who lived as though on a "distant isle, cut off from the world," had been transformed into a showman, at once conductor, stage director, actor—directing, singing, mimicking, leaping about (he was sixty-three years old) like a Nibelung, sometimes at the risk of breaking his neck, in order to breath his soul into all the characters into whom he had projected himself—gods, giants, dwarfs, heroes, and Valkyries, not to mention the orchestra or the stagehands; sometimes like an animal trainer, sometimes charming, alternating between anger, caresses, and easy jokes, without ever for a moment deviating from his goal: the realization of an artistic miracle no one believed possible.

In the presence of this demiurge who enjoyed, sometimes naively, the legitimate triumph of having given life to the world he created, Nietzsche was "upset, almost always silent," notes Edouard Schuré, who came to know him at this time. Could his "pride suffer that inferiority"?

In his initial intimacy with Wagner, Nietzsche had set himself on an equal footing with his master. He had dedicated his first book to him as "to my sublime predecessor" [meinem erhabenen Vorkämpfer]. Perhaps he was thinking of the reform of Germany as a school of philosophy, aesthetics, and morality, for which Schopenhauer would be the venerated ancestor, Wagner the artist and producer, and he, Nietzsche, the prophet and supreme legislator. It is certain the hurly-burly Valhalla of Bayreuth, with its imperious and sovereign Wotan, hardly resembled the dream of this Schopenhauerian professor. The author of *The Birth of Tragedy* disappeared along with everyone else in the apotheosis of the master, and this latter, taunting him a bit but seriously outraged and upset to see his disciple so morose, and not really understanding anything, seemed to cry out to him, like Loki, the fire demon, from the top of the rainbow that led to the palace of the Immortals: "Why these complaints? Rejoice in the sunshine of the gods!"[17]

Rather than this theatrical sun, which hurt his weak eyes, Nietzsche preferred the memory of the rainy but "incomparable" days when the foundation stone had been laid in May 1872, when to the accents of the "Hymn to Joy" (one of his most stirring emotions) in the "thrill of a return to health," "tragic men celebrated their dedicatory festival as the sign of the beginning of a new culture." "Our wonderment at Pentecost," he wrote in his notebooks. "This was not a musical festival. It seemed like a dream."[18] The "small group" of the faithful brought together for the ceremony "had belonged, had celebrated, and did not need first to acquire fingers for delicate matters."[19] It was nothing like the court of devotees who would henceforth surround Wagner: "A band abandoned by the gods and the spirit, with a strong stomach, devouring in good faith everything that the 'Master'" let fall, who did not have sufficient pride to distrust their flattery. The Wagnerians won the day over Wagner—those "blind disciples" who, through the weight of stupidity they bring to a cause, do so much to topple it into success.[20]

No, there was definitely "not the shadow of a resemblance" between the sad, vulgar today and those olden days, suddenly just as distant as the Greeks among whom Nietzsche had found "a perfect conception of life," which Bayreuth was supposed to resurrect. But what would Nietzsche have written about those Greeks, engulfed by the pathos of distance and near whom he took refuge in thought, if after having conversed with Aeschylus and Sophocles on the nature of tragedy, myth, and religion, he had for the first time attended the famous festival at Athens? No doubt, it would have been with the same refined disgusted face as Plato, Alciphron, or Theophrastus that he would have mixed with and depicted the gaudy and smelly crowd of spectators: philistines taking pleasure in their contentment at being there, a claque paid to cover up the disapproval of the connoisseurs, elegant youth applauding at the wrong moments in order to draw attention to themselves, ordinary citizens, finally, munching on olives and sausages while the noble hero was crushed by the gods. If, subsequently invited to visit the playwright, who, surrounded by his admirers, would have addressed only a few distracted words to him, perhaps our young philosopher would have quit Athens for Delphi or some other place on the spot, there to fill his tablets with pointed reflections on this master of illusion, on the actors, on Greeks and humanity in general. In *Ecce Homo*, he will write:

> Enough; in the midst of it I left for a couple of weeks, very suddenly. . . .
> In Klingenbrunn, a small town concealed in the wood of the *Böhmerwald*,
> I dragged around my melancholy and contempt for Germans.[21]

However, what Nietzsche omits mentioning is that more than melancholy it was illness that took him from Bayreuth: violent headaches, accompanied by troubles with his eyes and vomiting, from which he had been already periodically suffering for over a year, made the long rehearsals difficult to bear. The previous summer he had already had to abstain from attending them. Yet, after a week, the pain having gone down, he returned to Bayreuth for the first cycle of *The Ring*. "When we left together," reports Schuré, "no word of criticism or disapprobation escaped his lips, but he had the resigned sadness of someone who had been beaten."[22]

Physiological Objections

Beaten, all of Nietzsche had been by the testing spectacle of "the full work of art" whose realization he had expected from Wagner.[23]

That it was necessary to "present the arts in isolation" had seemed to Nietzsche, five years earlier, "a modern travesty,"[24] the sign of a dislocated world, as represented by the dismembered body of Dionysus, who longed for rebirth in his original unity, amid the "enchanting" accents of "ecstatic music." In 1870, he could write in "Greek Musical Drama" of the recent and much to be regretted principle

> that the connecting of two or more arts cannot generate a heightening of
> aesthetic pleasure, but is rather a barbarous aberration of taste. But this
> principle demonstrates, above all, the wretched modern habituation to
> being no longer able to enjoy as whole human beings: the absolute arts
> tear us to pieces, as it were, and we also enjoy only by bits, now as ear-
> people, now as eye-people, etc.[25]

Nietzsche had read the composer's theoretical works—*The Art-Work of the Future, Opera and Drama,* and *On the Application of Music to the Drama,* in particular—wherein Wagner deplored the state of alienation from which, according to him, the arts in the modern world suffered because they were cultivated separately to pursue some "egotistical" end, whereas, like men, they could only truly accomplish their mission through obedience to the law of love.

> Artistic man can only fully content himself by uniting every branch of art into the *common* artwork [Gesamtkunstwerk]: in every *segregation* of his artistic faculties he is *unfree,* not fully that which he has the power to be; whereas in the *common* artwork, he is *free,* and fully that which he has the power to be. . . . The purpose of each separate branch of art can only be fully attained by the reciprocal agreement and co-operation of all the branches in their common message.[26]

Opera gave an exemplary illustration of the decadence provoked by such separation: behind the appearance of mutual support, poetry, music, and dance each tried to shape its part so that it preserved its independent existence. This chaotic aggregate yielded only a caricature of Greek tragedy where these three arts spoke to the whole man thanks to a fruitful union that allowed each of them to produce its maximum effect. However, after the long age of dissociation that had followed the death of tragedy, a new synthesis now appeared possible: in musical drama where, under the impulse and authority of the "poet-musician," the arts would once again be united, not simply mixed together, as some wrongly believed, but by conserving their specific role in "the Perfected Drama."[27]

Stretching the composer's ideas somewhat, Nietzsche, in 1874, believed it "seriously possible that Wagner will spoil for the Germans their preoccupation with the arts taken in isolation. Perhaps," he added, "his influence will even produce the image of a unified culture [Bildung] that cannot be achieved simply by the accumulation of skills and information."[28] Imbued with this hope, *Richard Wagner in Bayreuth* hails in Wagner "the genuinely free artist, who cannot help but think simultaneously in all arts, who mediates and conciliates between apparently separate spheres, who restores to the artistic faculty a unity and totality that cannot be divined or inferred, but only demonstrated through actions."[29] This is what Wagner had done in giving "every dramatic event in a threefold rendering, through words, gestures and music":

And the music transmits the fundamental internal emotions of the drama's characters immediately to the souls of the audience, who then perceive the first visible signs of those inner events in the gestures of the same character, and recognize in this character's verbal expression a second, paler manifestation of these, translated into a more conscious form of willing. All these effects occur simultaneously and without disrupting one another, and they compel those to whom such a drama is presented to adopt a new mode of understanding and experience, just as if suddenly their senses had become more spiritual and their spirit more sensual . . .[30]

This is how the spectator overcome by *Die Meistersinger* and *Tristan* expressed himself. But, shortly after this praise had appeared, on the eve of the inauguration of the Bayreuth theater, Nietzsche, following the festival, retracted his judgment and soon after was quick in his notes to denounce the composer's "tyranny" and his "pretentiousness":

Anyone who, *one at a time,* has assimilated first poetry (language!), then transformed this by eye into action, then has discerned and lived himself into musical symbolism, and has even fallen in love with all three at once—will enjoy exceptional pleasure. But how demanding! It is impossible, except for brief moments—because too exhausting, this tenfold total attention on the part of eye, ear, understanding, and feeling, that receptive activity pushed to the maximum without *any* productive reaction whatsoever!—Rare are those who can do this: whence then the effect on *so many?* Because one's attention is *intermittent,* dulled for long periods, and one attends now to the music, now to the drama, now to the scenery *in isolation*—and this *divides* the work up.—But this is then to condemn the *genre:* the result is not drama, but an instant or an *arbitrary* selection. The creator of a *new genre* will need to pay attention here! Not a matter of *the arts always alongside each other*—but rather the *moderation* of the ancients, which conforms to human nature.[31]

"It is to be feared that confronted with a work of this kind, one will break it into pieces in order better to assimilate it," he wrote in 1870 with regard to Greek musical drama.[32] And he did not ascribe this failure to the genre per se but to the lack of preparation on the part of the modern spectator, that is, to the infirmity this latter suffered from, because his overly specialized senses and intellect had lost their original harmony.

A bit later in his notes from 1878, however, Nietzsche gives a more favorable interpretation of how he had adapted to the spectacle of Wagner's tetralogy:

> Wagner's music is *always* interesting in some way: now feeling, now understanding can take a rest. It is for this total relaxation and excitement of our being that we are grateful to it.[33]

"To direct our attention sometimes to the music, sometimes to the drama, sometimes to the scenery," appealing successively to understanding and feeling, this is what therefore would conform to the "moderation of the ancients." Yet it is precisely here that, nine years earlier, Nietzsche had seen "the Achilles' heel of ancient drama," the source of its "disintegration."[34]

As a development of the primitive dithyramb, of "the originary one," expressed in the simultaneity of word, music, and gesture, "Greek musical drama"—because "one could not sing everything that had been written"—had to string together musical and spoken moments. "The condition in which the human being *sings* provided the standard."[35] Yet "one held two worlds side by side, which more or less alternated with each other, with the result that the world of the eye disappeared when that of the ear began, and vice versa." There was not so much mediation between these two worlds as there was "confrontation." Between "the *torrents* of pathos," when "the kingdom of the heart" kept silent, "understanding" was able to "assert its rights." Yet "here is where the unfortunate consequence happens," Nietzsche noted in 1869: "If we make an unnatural separation between heart and mind, music and action, intellect and will, each separated part wastes away." Thus tragedy "committed suicide."

Believing themselves to have discovered "the secret of ancient music," the Florentine circles in which opera was born at the end of the sixteenth century, in reality, reproduced this fatal separation in the *stile rappresentativo* that, "sung/spoken," "quickly shifted the accent sometimes to the comprehension of the audience, sometimes to its musical sense." As he puts it in *The Birth of Tragedy*, "something so utterly unnatural and likewise so intrinsically contradictory both to the Apollonian and the Dionysian artistic impulses, that one has to infer an origin of the recitative lying outside all artistic instincts."[36] Stage designers and machinists would soon add their costly artifices to this "heterogeneous conglomeration," thereby completing the ruin of what little power music still preserved. But happily "the Dionysian spirit" was about to take revenge in Germany.

Therefore, it looks as though after having celebrated Wagner in 1874 as the restorer of ancient drama through the union of the arts under the aegis of music, Nietzsche reproached him four years later for having done so too successfully. In large measure, this is, as we have seen, because the spectator at the first festival in Bayreuth in 1876 was no longer the high-spirited prophet who, exalted by *Tristan* and *Die Meistersinger,* had announced "in the somber desert of a worn out civilization" the formidable reawakening of tragic myth and the German spirit. Confronted with the experience of the four dramas of *The Ring,* compelled to the sustained, multifaceted attention they demanded, Nietzsche now suffering pain in his eyes and violent migraines, retracted his earlier statements. The eulogist of Dionysus no longer possessed the physical means for his ecstasies: "the springlike instinct," the "fresh, dawnlike sense, ready for the festival" that made the Athenian capable of enjoying tragedy as a "complete man."[37] As illness aggravated "the tyrannical disharmony of his nature," Nietzsche was and would become less and less this complete man. "My objections to the music of Wagner are physiological objections," he will write in *The Gay Science,* "why should I trouble to dress them up in aesthetic formulas? My 'fact' is that I no longer breathe easily once this music begins to affect me; that my foot soon resents it and rebels. . . . But does not my stomach protest too? my heart? my circulation? my intestines?" These are symptoms that leave out those more serious ones from which Nietzsche had been suffering ever since 1874 and which he had not apparently felt before this date, neither at the performances of *Die Meistersinger* and *Tristan,* nor when he enthusiastically played the piano redactions of these works. It is left to the "enlightened Wagnerian" whom Nietzsche addresses in this aphorism to quite rightly reply: "'Then you really are merely not healthy enough for our music?'"[38] We ought not to be surprised, therefore, that in the same book Nietzsche comes almost to rehabilitate opera as he had previously condemned it, that offshoot of "theoretical man," by praising recitative: "this kind of half-music is only supposed . . . to give the musical ear a little rest (rest from the *melody* as the most sublime but therefore also most strenuous enjoyment of this art)."[39]

Before Nietzsche, Rousseau too had complained that it was "very fatiguing for him to follow overloaded scores." Having begun by stating his great admiration for Rameau, from whose *Treatise on Harmony* as an autodidact he learned the principles of composition, Rousseau, the author of the destitute *Devin du village,* turned against his idol, who was guilty in his eyes for having misunderstood him, and condemned his operas for being useless and tedious complications (without even bringing the visual element into his judgment): "The effect of these beautiful songs vanishes as soon as they are heard all at the same time . . . because it is impossible for the ear to lend itself to several melodies at the same time, and because—since one effaces the impression of the other—the result of all this is mostly confusion and noise."[40] This comparison of Nietzsche with Rousseau is all the more enlightening, because in many aspects—the fusion of recitative and aria in an instrumental arioso, the approximation of a "continuous melody," and the omnipresence and richness of the orchestra—Rameau's lyrical tragedy prefigures Wagner's musical drama.[41] And both composers would not have more virulent adversaries than their two former disciples with musical pretensions, who both turned an infirmity of their body or mind into an aesthetic principle.

6

TRAGEDY'S DECADENCE

$\mathcal{A}$s for Wagner, he, too, was not satisfied with the festival. He told Cosima, "I should not like to go through all that again! It was all wrong!"[1] The visual presentation had particularly disappointed him, as it did most of the critics who found the scenic effects mediocre or worse. However, this was not Nietzsche's reaction. In his notebooks, he wrote, "Least of all do I agree with those who were displeased with the decorations, scenery, stage machinery at Bayreuth."[2] The disappointment he had felt on the aesthetic level was deeper and concerned the "naturalism of the mime, of the singing, in comparison with the orchestra." The spectacle of *The Ring of the Nibelungen* was not accidentally, but necessarily flawed, owing to its very nature. Intended to protect the spectator against "the Dionysiac violence of the myth," the "Apollonian illusion" woven of words, gestures, and images here took on too much solidity compared to music whose full unfolding it prevented, thereby reducing its effect. Like ancient tragedy of which it was supposed to be a rebirth, Wagnerian drama in turn perished through "the excessive preponderance of the Apollonian element."[3]

If since the writing of *The Birth of Tragedy* Nietzsche had in part "gotten beyond" Schopenhauer in exalting the "avidity of the will" and the "pleasure of existing," he had however remained faithful to his conception of music. Expressing the "quintessence of life," the "innermost essence of the phenomenon," the "will itself," it could not be subordinated to the anecdote of an opera libretto, with which it maintained only an "analogical relation," except at the risk of becoming "a mere means of expression," "an alienated slave of the phenomenon" by losing its "exclusive property." This "generality" is tied to a "strict precision," which "gives it such a high value and makes it the remedy for all our ills."[4]

Music: End or Means?

In reaction against the opera of his day, the reforming Wagner of the 1850s, who did not yet know Schopenhauer, had said the opposite. "The *error* in the Operatic art-genre consisted in 'that a means of expression (Music) had been made the end while the End of expression (the Drama) had been made a means,'" he wrote in *Opera and Drama*.[5] Triumphing through Rossini's "artificial flowers" and "intoxicating narcotic melodies" and Meyerbeer's "effects without causes," this "radically defective" genre was dominated by the musician, who bent the poet to his demands along with the singers and the dancers, too often to the harm of the dramatic logic.

> To rescue her supremacy, Tone contracts with Dance for so many quarters-of-an hour which shall belong to the latter *alone:* during this period the chalk upon the sole-shoes shall rule the stage, and music shall be made according to the system of the *leg-*, and not the *tone-*, vibrations; item, that the singers shall be expressly forbidden to indulge in any sort of graceful bodily motion,—this is to be the exclusive property of the dancer, whereas the singer is to be pledged to complete abstention from any fancy mimetic gestures, a restriction which will have the additional advantage of conserving his voice. With Poetry Tone settles, to the former's highest satisfaction, that she will not employ her in the slightest on stage; may, will as far as possible not even articulate her words and verse, and will relegate her instead to the printed text-book, necessarily to be read *after* the performance, in Literature's decorous garb of black and white. Thus, then, is the noble bond concluded, each art again itself; and between the dancing legs and written book, Music once more floats gaily on through all the length and breadth of her desire.[6]

Such degeneracy could be wiped away only through the restoration of drama where opera's unrealized ideal would be reached through "an equal and reciprocal penetration of music and poetry," to which would be joined the other arts. Only the poet-musician could succeed where the poet or the musician had to fail. This inevitable failure was a result, we know, of the dissociation of the arts brought about by the decline of ancient tragedy. Having continued to draw apart from each other ever since, they had claimed to be self-sufficient, each becoming its own object, whereas, cut off from their popular sources, each only obeyed more and more abstract laws that condemned them to an ever increasing isolation and, hence, to sterility.[7] Separated from poetry and dance, music had become autonomous: "absolute."

Wagner was undoubtedly the first to make use of this qualification in this way—in the program prepared for the performance of Beethoven's Ninth Symphony that he conducted at Dresden in 1846.[8] He was, in fact, taking up again an idea that had appeared in German aesthetics at the end of the eighteenth century, at a moment when instrumental, and especially symphonic music was in full swing, but by now giving it a negative sense. Far from being only a deficient form of vocal or dramatic music, such music, owing precisely to its lack of an object or any precise destination, incarnated the very essence of music and, as a result, became a revelation of the infinite. That it was listened to for its own sake simultaneously conferred upon it aesthetic autonomy and metaphysical dignity. This idea, found in Wackenroder and Ludwig Tieck, was strikingly formulated by E. T. A. Hoffmann, in 1810, in his well-known analysis of Beethoven's Fifth Symphony.

> When one speaks of music as an independent art, does not the term properly apply only to instrumental music, which scorns all aid, all admixture of other arts (poetry), and gives pure expression to its own peculiar artistic nature? . . . Beethoven's music sets in motion the machinery of awe, of fear, of terror, of pain, and awakens that infinite yearning which is the essence of romanticism. He is there a purely romantic composer. Might this not explain why his vocal music is less successful, since it does not permit a mood of vague yearning but can only depict from the realm of the infinite those feelings capable of being described in words? Beethoven's mighty genius intimidates the musical rabble; they try in vain to resist it.[9]

This preeminence conferred on instrumental music, which flowed from the Romantics' distrust of language and rationality, ran counter to the dominant Western tradition both in practice as well as in theory. From Plato, who defined music as the covenant between rhythmic harmony and the Logos, to Rousseau, for whom, the original identity of music and language being unquestionable, genuine music was that which was sung.[10] On the other hand, the fact that music freed itself from language and from its traditional social functions (in the theater, church, and court) did not necessarily imply that it lost any definite object. On the contrary, thanks to the increasing differentiation of its language and means, as seen largely in the development of the orchestra, like all the other arts, it was able to convey a poetic, dramatic, or philosophical content, to be meaningful, otherwise, as Hegel said (to whom Wagner will be close on this point), it would risk losing itself in equally sterile virtuosity or abstractness. This aspiration, which became manifest in the eighteenth century with the aesthetics of feeling (*Gefühlasthetik*)[11] blossomed with Romanticism, which tended wholly toward expressiveness.

However, even if during most of the nineteenth century, opera and its derivatives, comic-opera and operetta, along with chamber music, remained the dominant genres, not to mention religious music (oratorio, which was so popular in England), the notion of absolute music gradually came to prevail in German aesthetics before impregnating the whole of European musical culture. At the turn of the century, the "lovely forehead" of Madame Verdurin "swells forth" on hearing Beethoven's last quartets, which real connoisseurs hold to be above everything else, and her grand-nephews, taking the sense of purity even further, will hear in Bach's suites for solo cello or his *Art of the Fugue* surprising sonorous premonitions of nonfigurative painting. "The beauty of music is a specifically musical kind of beauty. By this we understand beauty that is self-contained and in no need of content from outside itself, that consists simply and solely of tones and their artistic combination," wrote Edward Hanslick in his influential essay "On Beauty in Music" (1854), where the ideal defined by Hoffmann lost its metaphysical content and was reduced to a formalist conception of music.[12]

Besides the fact that the public, overall, did not share this view—audiences, said Schindler, listened to Beethoven's symphonies as "operas in disguise"—this change did not occur without running into resistance, most spectacularly that of Wagner, whom Hanslick specifically opposed. Before launching himself on the composition of *The Ring*, concerned to assure the legitimacy of his undertaking, the composer built, with *The Art-Work of the Future* and *Opera and Drama,* an ambitious historico-mythological construct (the equivalent for his work of Hugo's preface to *Cromwell* for his play) meant to demonstrate that musical drama was the necessary goal of the movement of history. Within this perspective, Beethoven's development of absolute music counts as the antithesis of a dialectical process. The "infinite nostalgia," the "objectless desire" that is apparent to the highest degree in Beethoven's symphonies indicates an intermediary state where instrumental music, forgetting its origins, has not yet attained its destination: "satisfaction in an *object*." It does so in the Ninth Symphony, when, with the "Ode to Joy," the irresistible "redemption of sound by words" comes about. Like

Christopher Columbus, who in discovering America was persuaded that he had reached India, Beethoven, in developing in an incomparable way the possibilities of instrumental music, thought he was forging a purely musical language, whereas this language really depended on drama, through which it was aspiring toward its full expressive power and in which his audacious innovations would find their full justification. But in experiencing the necessity, *as a musician,* to throw himself into the arms of the poet, Beethoven wrote "the Last Symphony" and opened the way to "the realm of universal art."[13]

Twenty years later, Wagner's theoretical positions seem to have completely reversed themselves. An example of this is again, on Beethoven, in an essay written on the occasion of the hundredth anniversary of his birth:

> Seeing that Music does not portray the Ideas inherent in the world's phenomena, but is itself an Idea of the World, and a comprehensive one, it naturally includes the Drama in itself; as Drama, again, expresses the only world's-Idea proportionate (*adäquat*) to Music. . . . As a drama does not depict human characters, but lets them display their immediate selves, so a piece of music gives us in its motives the character of all the world's appearances according to their inmost essence (*An-Sich*). Not only are the movement, interchange and evolution of these motives analogous to nothing but the Drama, but a drama representing the [world's] Idea can be understood with perfect clearness through nothing but those moving, evolving and alternative motives of Music's. We consequently should not go far astray, if we defined Music as man's qualification *a priori* for fashioning the Drama.[14]

"I would gladly have called my dramas deeds of Music brought to sight," Wagner will add two years later.[15] In the meantime, he had read Schopenhauer (whose words are easily recognizable); and if it was especially his pessimism and his theory of the will that attracted Wagner, the positive philosophical interpretation that Schopenhauer gave of music could not fail to affect him as well. Always taking for granted the moral weakness or bad faith of his adversaries, which a bit of genealogy would suffice to reveal, Nietzsche will explain Wagner's change of heart solely in terms of opportunism:

> He grasped all at once that with the Schopenhauerian theory and innovation *more* could be done *in majorem musicae gloriam* [for the greater glory of music]—namely, with the theory of the *sovereignty* of music as

Schopenhauer conceived it: music set apart from all the other arts, the independent art as such, *not* offering images of phenomenality, as the other arts did, but speaking rather the language of the will itself, directly out of the "abyss" as its most authentic, elemental, nonderivative revelation. With this extraordinary rise in the value of music that appeared to follow from Schopenhauerian philosophy, the value of *the musician* himself all at once went up in an unheard-of manner, too: from now on he became an oracle, a priest, indeed more than a priest, a kind of mouthpiece of the "in itself" of things, a telephone from the beyond.[16]

That Wagner may have felt flattered by this elevation of the musician is likely—and only incidental. In reality, his reading of the philosopher, whose musical aesthetic stemmed from Romanticism, had reawakened for him the ambivalence and contradictions of his early theoretical writings, which despite their having been written in the style of a manifesto and, hence, deliberately in a simplifying way, had made apparent. Music, enriched by the poet, was nevertheless the "maternal womb of drama," "the beginning and the end of language just as mythology [was] the beginning and end of history," as we can read in *Opera and Drama*. And whereas absolute music represented an intermediary step in the full accomplishment of drama in the Hegelian philosophy of history that Wagner had adopted, the Romanticist metaphysics from which Wagner also drew opened "the marvelous realm of the infinite" and was intermingled with the essence of things.[17]

Wagner reconciled these two sides of his aesthetic by superimposing them: on the metaphysical level, music reigned supreme, unconditioned, as the origin of drama; on that of empirical reality, not being able to become manifest without some external intervention, it was conditioned by drama.[18] This conclusion can be seen in his "open letter" of 1857, "On Franz Liszt's Symphonic Poems," in which the change in his ideas is apparent in the uneasy formulation, even if not openly admitted:

> Hear my creed: music can never and in no possible alliance cease to be the highest, the redeeming art. . . . But it is equally manifest, equally sure that Music will let herself be seen in forms first borrowed from an aspect or utterance of Life, which originally strangers to Music obtain through her revelation of the music latent in them. Nothing is less absolute (as to its appearance in Life, of course) than Music, and the champions of an Absolute Music evidently don't know what they're talking about; to utterly confound them, one would only have to bid them shew us a music

without the form which it has borrowed from either bodily motion or spoken verse (as regards the causal connexion). . . . [19] On this point, then, we are at one, and admit that in this human world it was necessary to afford divine Music a point of attachment, nay—as we have seen—a "conditioning moment," before ever she could come to appearance.[20]

In clearer terms: that music in order to exist needs a motif external to itself does not prevent it from being absolute in its essence, or the listener from receiving it as such. If Wagner no longer uses the expression "absolute music" to not appear to contradict himself, he continued to hold to the validity of this notion, which his polemics against Rossini and Meyerbeer had initially led him to deny. There are other signs that show that his siding with it was not merely theoretical but based on a deep-seated affinity. One example is his increasing admiration for Bach's instrumental works, whose study he had returned to while composing *Tristan*. Whereas "the others, Mozart, Beethoven, were closer to being poets," he confided to Cosima one day, "Bach was a true musician."[21] Another time, he laughingly said, "I like Bach better than myself. . . . It is like the voice of the thing-in-self; in comparison, the sensitive and the sentimental seem trivial."[22]

For all that, even though Schopenhauer had, from a philosophical point of view, condemned opera—which in daily life he much appreciated[23]—the Wagner of the years 1860–70 did not disown drama. And, by drama, contrary to what a number of his commentators have said, he did not mean first and foremost the text for which the music, as in Gluck, should have been merely the servant,[24] all the more so since he had discovered, to his surprise, the effect his works could produce on a public that did not know German.[25] In his "Beethoven" he writes, "For we know that it is not the verses of a text-writer, and were he a Goethe or Schiller, that can determine Music. Drama alone can do that," that is, "the drama that moves before our very eyes," or, more profoundly, that reveals itself to us in that "state analogous to somnambulistic clairvoyance" provoked by the music's expressive intensity to reduce the power of our sight: in belonging then directly to the world dreamt by the musician, we understand it without having to see it.[26]

A pure or absolute musician, therefore, is not what Wagner laid claim to be. If, at the end of his life, tired of theater ("after having invented the invisible orchestra, would that I had also invented the invisible theater," he will say in 1878),[27] he dreamed of writing symphonies with the "ideas" and themes that had not been included in *Parsifal*, we can clearly suspect, in light of the instrumental pages that punctuate his dramas and other works like his *Faust* overture or *Siegfried Idyll*, that they would not have obeyed a purely musical logic given how much the "drama" was the motor of invention for him.[28] "He says he sometimes wishes he were just a musician and did not have other thoughts," notes Cosima.[29] But "the musician who only writes music from morning to night, completely ignoring the world of ideas, must be inhuman," Wagner added, "for he lacks much more than those who, knowing nothing about music, observe the world." And again: "If only I were not a musician! This wretched note-writing—into what category of uneducated people has it pitched me?"[30] The pure musician was a product of the dissociation of the arts and the division of labor that fragmented the modern world into pieces; Wagner's activity made sense only if he aspired to rediscover, by new pathways, the plenitude enjoyed by the ancient Greeks, to realize that "total man" also dreamed of by the young Marx and Nietzsche.

Even while judging himself inferior to composers of instrumental music such as Beethoven and Bach, Wagner was no less aware of his manifest and perhaps unsurpassable originality: "The main thing is that one should be out of the ordinary. In me the accent lies on the conjunction of poet and musician, as a pure musician I would not be of much significance."[31] From this union—or better: from this interpenetration so extolled in *Opera and Drama*, which he himself was never able really to explain to himself clearly—was born a unique language, one where poetry only exists through music, while this latter, through its evocative power and symbolic richness, becomes a higher and spellbinding form of poetry. Even when absent, the word, through the interplay of instruments, timbres, and motifs, "imbues the sound, parasite like, from the interior" while simultaneously being its prefiguration.[32] Having reread Wagner's librettos when he was writing his own for *Die Frau ohne Schatten*, Hofmannsthal found himself "really knocked out" by "the inaccessible quality," "the inimitable perfection with which the musical realization is there brought about through anticipation— just as rivers shape a landscape, so here, the poetic landscape is shaped by the streams and rivers of the melody, already known to the poet."[33] In these librettos, notably in those of the tetralology, the irregular versification, the rhythmic freedom in the declamation, the particularities of the syntax, as well as the numerous assonances and alliterations, constitute a sort of "verbal instrumentation," a premusic waiting to be realized as used to be said of the figured bass in ancient and baroque music.[34] This explains why Wagner made minor changes to his text when he turned to composition, and then only rarely, because it stood in the way of the music. Even though, not without some repugnance and remorse, he published them before the composition was completed, his librettos had been conceived in music's "maternal womb."

> It would be totally impossible for me to set another's text to music for the following reason:—It is not my practice to choose a subject at random, to versify it and then think of suitable music to write for it;—if I were to proceed in that way I should be exposed to the difficulty of having to work myself up to a pitch of enthusiasm on two separate occasions, something which is impossible. No, my method of production is different from that:—in the first place I am attracted only by those subjects which reveal themselves to me not only as poetically but, at the same time, as musically significant. And so, even before I set about writing a single line of the text or drafting a scene, I am already thoroughly immersed in the musical aura of my new creation, I have the whole sound and all the characteristic motives in my head so that when the poem is finished and the scenes are arranged in their proper order the actual opera is already completed, and its detailed musical treatment is more a question of calm and reflective revision, the moment of actual creativity having already passed. But for this to be so, I must choose only subjects which are capable of an exclusively musical treatment.[35]

Nine years later, having completed the poem for *The Ring*, he announced to Liszt:

> As to the form of it, it is quite ready in my mind. . . . All I want is sufficient *charm* of *life* to get into the indispensable cheerful mood from which motives spring forth gladly and spontaneously.[36]

No doubt these declarations include some illusion designed to facilitate his task—the composition of *The Ring* would take almost a quarter century. But when it was interrupted in 1857, this was for musical reasons connected to a change of Wagner's inner disposition. While working on *Siegfried*, melodies and motifs welled up that were alien to that work, which drew him toward "the realm of melancholy," he wrote to Otto von Wesendonck on 22 December 1856.[37] Three days earlier he had said: "*Tristan*, for the time being, music without a text," had "got in my way with a melodic thread that kept spinning up whenever I wanted to leave it."[38] "It is true I sometimes felt inclined in my disgust to throw everything into the gutter," he will later say, "and in fact I eventually did so, unwilling as I was to do any more work."[39] "At that time I felt an uncontrollable urge to luxuriate in music."[40] And, as "in the *Nibelungen* the requirements of the drama frequently forced him to restrict the musical expression" but driven by his passion for Mathilde Wesendonck, Wagner "had felt the urge to express himself symphonically for once, and that led to *Tristan*."[41] Wagner evidently meant the word *symphonic* in the loose sense of a network of thematic relations and transformations using every possible asset of the symphonic tradition, as regards development and instrumental technique, but not bound by restrictive conventions—harmonic logic and symmetrical design—all of which he thought to be inherent in the symphonic form, from which drama allowed him to free himself. For it is the drama that gives meaning and much of the coherence to the score of *Tristan*. Yet the action being so simple, "he had had to make use of the richest resources of musical expression."[42] And whereas "in his other works the musical motifs serve the action; in this, one might say the action arises out of the motive."[43] "No one but a musician was in a position to explore such a subject to its very depths and remain at the same time attractive."[44]

More than his reading of Schopenhauer, it was this experience in which the musician let himself go with incomparable independence and sureness that led Wagner to modify his conception of drama, by allowing him to say clearly that it was music that gave it birth. "For every theory was clean forgotten by me," he will write a few years later. "But since here I moved with fullest freedom and the most utter disregard of every theoretic scruple, to such an extent that during the working-out I myself was aware how far I had outstripped my system."[45]

From *Tristan* to Ballet

As it happens, *Tristan* is the only work that Nietzsche cites in *The Birth of Tragedy* as an example of the resurrection of Greek musical drama, even though unlike *Die Meistersinger* he had not yet seen it performed and only knew it through its piano redaction and a few extracts heard in concert. "It is a drama with the severest austerity of form, overwhelming in its simple grandeur,"[46] reduced to a diagram, the words in it only form a "musical mist," and the singers are submerged by that "greatest possible symphony" to which Wagner seemed "unconsciously to aspire."[47] In contrast to "the impractical realism of *The Ring*," the stage designer Adolphe Appia will write, "the *exclusively interior* action of *Tristan* remains alien to the representative form that we would have liked it to shape."[48] Whence the satisfaction Nietzsche felt when he attended two performances of the work in Munich in June

1872, six months after the appearance of his book. "A profound difference" struck him, as compared to the usual spectacles of opera and the theater:

> There was a spontaneous striving [on the part of the actors] to maintain even in the most passionate moments a *calm greatness:* essentially, one saw noble sculptural groups moving moderately, and for the most part almost immobile. . . . I told myself that the music and the singing must have been the reason why nothing moved as quickly as it does in ordinary life or in spoken tragedy . . . Thus I had a premonition of an extremely fruitful future for our sculptural tasks, which are to invent sublime positionings and groupings to correspond to such sublime music. Here again music appeared to me as the redeemer of our time.[49]

Coming after the revelation of *Tristan*, the tetralogy that Nietzsche discovered at Bayreuth in 1876 could only have been a disappointment. Its often demonstrative theatricality, aggravated by the epic character of many episodes, could only intermittently retain the Dionysiac impulse arising from "the echo of innumerable shouts of pleasure and woe in the 'wide space of the world night.'"[50] Like Euripides and his "dramatized epic" in relation to Aeschylus and, above all, to original dithyramb, *The Ring* in fact marked a decadent step in relation to *Tristan*, that reincarnation of ancient tragedy, where the role of the chorus was taken by the orchestra, the source of the Dionysian vision, of which the stage setting, like a mirage, was but an emanation.

Indeed, at the origin, at the primitive stage, Nietzsche emphasizes, when "the natural bond between the language of words and of tones" had not yet been broken,[51] tragedy amounted to the chorus and only the chorus. Issuing from popular songs, the choral song, sustained by instruments, was characterized by a simple harmony and by "the richness of its means of rhythmic expression." Simultaneously, "the structure of musical and rhythmic passages, which closely parallel the text, were accompanied . . . by the movement of the dance, the orchestric. The chorus movements that unfolded before the spectators' eyes like arabesques on the large surface of the *orchestra* were experienced like a music that had somehow become visible."[52]

"Musical facts become visible"—this is how Wagner would define his works after *Tristan*. But to renew the ideal of primitive "Greek musical drama," which had degenerated into spoken drama and, later, into opera, Nietzsche, when he was working on *The Birth of Tragedy*, once again showed himself to be more Wagernian that Wagner. In some of his notes starting from *Tristan* we can see Nietzsche radicalizing its formula. Since in that work the voices often are assimilated to instruments to the point of merging with the orchestra, particularly in the second and third acts his first move is to "get rid of the singer," to "completely erase" that "nonsense" that, moreover, imposes a "repulsive spectacle." Yet as "one cannot really get rid [of him] for he has the most soulful sonority," and because "the orchestra is not sufficient," the singer must "be placed in the orchestra" where he will act "like a *chorus*, that is, as the full sonority of the human voice taken into the orchestra." "The *unnaturalness* of the singer's singing in the orchestra, while the mime moves on the stage, is in no way contrary to art." The result of this is the "restoration of the chorus," which, associated with the orchestra, "*has a vision and describes enthusiastically what it sees*," while, above, is "the world of the image, the mime," in the "ancient purity of the scene."[53] Then, from that scene freed from "the central principle" of theater, music alone "bursts forth and regenerates all vitality," to quote Mallarmé. "Then the audience will feel that if the orchestra suddenly stopped pouring forth its influence, the actor would immediately become a statue."[54]

Citing Mallarmé alongside Nietzsche is no accident. The "reverie of a French poet" and that of the young philologist have the same origin: their shared dissatisfaction with the compromise that Wagner had made with a theatrical convention encumbered by and struck by "an impending obsolescence" instead of "simplifying the attribution of his art to the point of that initial insight," which they both described in similar terms. Still, Wagner had come close to it, and Nietzsche was not wrong to remark that "one could almost draw a conception like [his own] from *Tristan*." Yet the work of art of the future that Nietzsche thereby announces, in his notes from 1871, is not Wagnerian drama but, beyond *Tristan*, the dramatic ballet accompanied by voice that will flourish at the beginning of the twentieth century: Ravel's *Daphnis et Chloé*, Stravinsky's *Pulcinella* and *Renard*, and especially his *Noces*, that strange "ballet cantata," wherein, shortly after its creation in 1923, André Schaeffner will see "a new metamorphosis of the ancient chorus" and "the fulfillment of a prediction coming from Nietzsche's fantasies and probably forgotten among the pile of his unused notes."[55] Actually, Nietzsche had not completely forgotten it, as shown by a note from the summer of 1878 in which, referring to "the ways that remain—or rather, still *remained* open, apart from Wagner's influence," he indicates that "it is necessary *to surpass* Wagner: *dramatic choral music.*—Dithyramb. An effect of unison."[56] This is the very spirit of the primitive dithyramb that Stravinsky, who was little influenced by Wagner, rediscovered in assigning the prime role to the chorus associated with the orchestra, the singers being placed in the pit, while their doubles move on a stage freed from every naturalistic inclination. The dramatic action, too, recalls the original stage of tragedy since it is a succession of ritual ceremonies of popular origin culminating in a vast orgiastic dance, and the unfolding of the whole obeys the unbending pulse of an "elementary" ensemble of percussion instruments.

Beyond rediscovering the rhythmic richness of a Dionysiac music, as evoked in *The Birth of Tragedy*, Nietzsche would have loved the chorus "singing without interruption, like an orchestra . . . or rather delirious, possessed by the admirably calculated rhythm; thereby returning, behind the false appearance of a weak melodic invention, to what must be, in its very essence, *the* melody: a *voice*, a raucous, primordial cry, torn from a human being, like at the beginning of the first tableau of this work, that *e* piercing through the notes thrown up by the pianos and xylophones."[57]

> No doubt the philosopher of the Eternal Return [would he not have equally] loved the vivifying pessimism that emerges from the work as a whole, where a feeling of despondency is mixed with an ardent sense of life; something weighty but which rebounds, like the material percussive noise that resolves into exultant sonorities; as in the *Sacre*, a pungent sadness, a drowsiness as at the beginning of the world, a heavy resignation charged with a new *heroism*. Would Nietzsche have recognized in all this "the metaphysical comfort—with which . . . every true tragedy leaves us—that life is at the bottom of things, despite all the changes of appearances, indestructibly powerful and pleasurable"?[58]

Yes, undoubtedly. And this is all the more so in that the rebirth of ballet at the beginning of the twentieth century can be seen as responding to the expectation of Wagner's former disciple, who had become an enthusiast for "a god who dances."[59] "The Wagnerian incapacity to *walk* (much less yet to *dance*—and without dance there is for me neither relaxation nor happiness) has always plunged me into distress," he notes in his notebooks in 1886.[60] The sworn enemy of the spirit of heaviness, the *"free spirit* par excellence"* will dance "even near abysses," "to the light sounds of everything possible." "Thinking has to be learned in the way dancing has to be learned, *as* a form of dancing"; "for *dancing* in any form cannot be divorced from a *noble education*, being able to dance with the feet, with concepts, with words."[61]

That Nietzsche refers so often to dancing at the end of his "positivistic" period, and in particular in his last books, fits with the preference he then gives to physiological interpretations, anchored in the body, and with his renewed fervor for Dionysus, "nature's genius" who, to express himself, demands "the entire symbolism of the body . . . not the mere symbolism of the lips, face, and speech but the whole pantomime of dancing, forcing every member into rhythmic movement."[62] But modern music, Nietzsche complains, is nothing more than "a mere residuum of Dionysian histrionics." For music to constitute itself as an independent art it was necessary to reduce the part taken by the other senses besides hearing, at the beginning, in musical enjoyment—that especially of muscular enjoyment, "so that man no longer straightway imitates and represents bodily everything he feels. Nonetheless, *that* is the true Dionysian normal condition."[63]

Nietzsche was not alone in feeling such nostalgia. Around 1900, tied to the rediscovery of the body that is also apparent from the growing vogue for sports (in 1896 the first modern Olympic games were held in Athens), a return of the Dionysian transformed the art of dance, and its first artisans openly drew on Nietzsche. These included Rudolf Laban, the principal force behind the principal home of this counterculture, which until just after the First World War was to be found in the Swiss village of Ascona, where we find such notables the psychoanalyst Otto Gross, D. H. Lawrence, C. G. Jung, and Hermann Hesse; Mary Wigman, his associate and the founder of the German school of modern dance; and, finally, also a regular at Ascona, Isadora Duncan, the well-known American dancer and choreographer.[64]

"Nietzsche was the first dancing philosopher," proclaimed Duncan,[65] and she placed him among her teachers—a setting that would have horrified him—alongside the Rousseau of *Emile* and Walt Whitman. "It is only with Nietzsche that you will arrive at the complete revelation of the expression in dance you are looking for," one of her German friends, the writer Karl Federn, who had introduced her to Nietzsche's writings in 1902, had told her.[66] The ground had been well prepared. Shortly before this, desiring to revive ancient tragedy—it was the era of the flourishing of neo-Hellenism—Duncan had made a pilgrimage to Greece during which, one evening in the amphitheater of Dionysus in Athens, she had imagined, thinking of Aeschylus's *Suppliants*, a spectacle that until Stravinsky's *Noces* one might well have taken as illustrating Nietzsche's intuitions. In this ballet accompanied by voices, which was afterward performed in Vienna and Berlin, Duncan danced in a tunic with bare feet, while a dozen young Greeks, also clothed in loose, multicolored tunics, sang choruses from Aeschylus to music inspired by ancient Greece, for which she had found the scales and motifs in scholarly works in the library in Athens. Her preferred movement was to throw her head back—the very movement of trance in Dionysian rites, as shown on vase paintings representing the cultural processions of this god of ecstasy and transgression. Breaking with the stereotyped, expressive, and stylistic figures of academicism, Duncan's "other dance" announced the innovations of Fokine and especially of Nijinksy that Diaghilev would bring to triumph in Paris starting in 1909.[67]

"Who will invent tragic ballet with music for us?" Nietzsche asked himself in 1881.[68] And four years later, referring to Slavic music, he wrote: "The historical-cultural ballet:—has surpassed opera."[69] If he could have seen the Ballets Russes, Nietzsche would have seen there the fulfillment of the "new task" that the development of the "Greek musical drama" assigned to the "poet-musician": "that of being an imaginative master of ballet."[70]

From Drama to Absolute Music

It is not certain, however, that after having sketched out the theory of the new dithyramb and expressed his desire for "tragic ballet," Nietzsche would not have turned against their scenic realization with the same repugnance that he had felt at the time of the creation of *The Ring of the Nibelungen.* "The theater corrupts everything, even a Stravinsky," Cocteau will say, who had read Nietzsche and read him well.[71]

The Birth of Tragedy is supposed to be a book in praise of theater. No less than two divinities, Dionysus and Apollo, preside over the gestation of Attic drama and its heir, Wagnerian musical drama. But, for Nietzsche, one cannot be too cautious; theater does not signify action. At the origin, the chorus was "older, more original and important than the 'action' proper."[72] A note in *The Case of Wagner* makes this clear: "It has been a real misfortune for aesthetics that the word *drama* has always been translated "action" [*Handlung*] . . . Ancient drama aimed at scenes of great *pathos*—it precluded action (moving it *before* the beginning or *behind* the scene)."[73] Without saying so expressly, Nietzsche basically substitutes for Aristotle's *praxis* the German *Stimmung*—atmosphere, mood, impression—that music is particularly apt to create and sustain. The more music, the less action there is: the music slows down the action, even immobilizes it, which *Tristan* had been celebrated in 1872 for doing.

However, we read in *The Birth of Tragedy* that this work would not be bearable unless the myth, the image, and the word, the Apollonian elements, protected us against its Dionysian unfurling. We would be crushed by the music without the intervention of the god of "good appearance," who in ancient Greece, transformed into an aesthetic phenomena the "deadly sorcerer's poison" of Dionysianism, "made up of voluptuousness and cruelty." Indeed, can we "imagine a human being who would be able to perceive the third act of *Tristan and Isolde,* without any aid of word and image, purely as a tremendous symphonic movement, without expiring in a spasmodic unharnessing of all the wings of the soul?" asks Nietzsche in a key passage of this work that deserves fuller citation.[74] "But if such a work could nevertheless be perceived as a whole, without denial of individual existence; if such a creation could be created without smashing its creator— whence do we take the solution of such a contradiction?"[75]

> Here the tragic myth and the tragic hero intervene between our highest musical emotion and this music—at bottom only as symbols of the most universal facts, of which music can speak so directly. But if our feelings were those of entirely Dionysian beings, myth as a symbol would remain totally ineffective and unnoticed, and would never for a moment keep us from listening to the re-echo of the *universalia ante rem*. Yet here the *Apollinian* power erupts to restore the almost shattered individual with the healing balm of blissful illusion: suddenly we imagine we see only Tristan, motionless, asking himself dully: "The old tune, why does it wake me?" . . . The glorious Apollinian illusion makes it appear as if even the tone world confronted us as a sculpted world. . . . It presents images of life to us, and incites us to comprehend in thought the core of life they contain. With the immense impact of the image, the concept, . . . the Apollinian tears man from his orgiastic self-annihilation and blinds him to the universality of the Dionysian process, deluding him into the belief that he is seeing a single image of the world (*Tristan and Isolde*, for instance), and that, *through music*, he is merely supposed to *see* it better and more profoundly. . . . By means of the pre-established harmony between perfect drama and its music, drama attains a superlative vividness unattainable in mere spoken drama. . . . While music thus compels us to see more and more profoundly than usual, and we see the action on stage as a delicate web, the world of the stage is expanded infinitely and illuminated for our spiritualized eye.[76]

"Here we understand *why* the music demands images," remarks Nietzsche in one of the preparatory notes for this sibylline passage, inspired by Schopenhauer and Wagner's "Beethoven." "It calls for Apollo the healer. Such is the relationship of the drama to the music."[77] But this is a less necessary relation than it may appear. Reading too quickly, we may be tempted to conclude that (Dionysian) music can be listened to only when accompanied by some spectacle. Was not the reference to the composer the first to succumb without the mediation of Apollo? Music "demands images" but these emanate from an inner vision—as indicated by the phrases "we believe," "it seems"—analogous to a dream, which, in the case of drama, can eventually coincide with the spectacle itself in increasing its visibility (the passage from the one to the other is hardly discernible in Nietzsche's text).

The irruption of the Apollonian force therefore takes place apart from any scene, as in the primitive dithyramb where, according to Nietzsche, "this is simply experienced as a vision of the chorus" shared by the public, whereas in tragedy properly speaking the symbolization of the music will take on an increasing materiality and density with the appearance of the actor. But the fact that the "charitable Apollonian illusion" comes about within the music—otherwise, remaining a "purely Dionysian being," the composer would not be able to write it down—does imply that music, which is Dionysian by nature, must also be Apollonian. However, Nietzsche seems to exclude this. If he does mention the existence in Greece of an Apollonian music—"Doric architectonics in sounds"[78]—it is only in passing, and in order to deny it the quality of really being music owing to its overly plastic, too-phenomenal character. For the same reason, he ridicules "the arithmetic abacus of the fugue and the dialectic of counterpoint," incapable of giving voice to the Dionysian, and yet at the same time he salutes Johann Sebastian Bach for being the first to have reawakened it in Germany—almost as though Bach had expressed himself other than through musical language.[79]

Yet, if we assume that, following Schopenhauer, music could "continue to exist even though the universe did not exist," it could only do so by taking on a phenomenal appearance. In his essay on Beethoven, Wagner had made reference to Schopenhauer's theory of dreams in order to describe this creative process. In "the lighter, allegoric dream which immediately precedes our awakening," he writes, the composer who floats in the flood of harmony, "the most inalienable element of Music," imposes a rhythmic order on it without which music would be imperceptible. "So the musician makes contact with the plastic world through the rhythmic ordering of his tones, and that in virtue of a resemblance to the laws whereby the motion of visible bodies is brought to our intelligence."[80] Yet, when he draws upon this reference in his book, Nietzsche leaps, so to speak, over this purely musical step to bring immediately into play myth, word, and image ("the Apollonian makes living images appear before our eyes"). Prior to this, however, the first "analogous substitute" that music borrows in order to exist is simply the form (what Wagner in his text calls the "rhythmic order").[81] If the composer and his listeners are not to be bowled over by its unfolding it is because the composer has known how to impose upon it that form Nietzsche the musician had so much difficulty mastering.

Nietzsche's suggestion that music could be purely Dionysian betrays his own inexperience as a composer, which, we have seen, rarely got beyond the stage of transcribed improvisations. After having devoted some time to composing fugues and counterpoint to discipline his talent a bit, he abandoned himself to "a kind of frenzy," to free sonorous outpourings to the point of sometimes getting caught up in, if not chaos, at least "the perilous domain of the lunatic" where "exuberance, pathos, and cruelty" intermixed—especially when he yielded to the charms of Wagner's music, that is, to *Tristan,* where the composer seemed to have rejected the forms and conventions through which Nietzsche had sometimes been able to make his demon speak. But, as Hans Sachs in *Die Meistersinger* recalls to Walther, there is no music without form or convention.

"The Tristan-sensation. Unbearable—when art is lacking," he notes.[82] The purely Apollonian, the form in itself, without the aid of images or words, must therefore be inherent to music. The conclusion of his book suggests this: "Where the Dionysian powers rise up as impetuously as we experience them now, Apollo, too, must already have descended among us."[83] Moreover, that an "immense gap . . . separates the *Dionysian Greek* from the Dionysian barbarian," as he emphasizes in his opening pages, indicates not that there are two versions of the god of drunkenness but, rather, that the Dionysianism of the Greeks, even before the birth of tragedy, was impregnated with the Apollonian, that the Apollonian music that they then practiced was enlivened by feverish harmonies and orgiastic rhythms coming from Asia.[84] "The purely Dionysian is impossible," he writes in another of his notebooks, but he then adds, returning to the thesis he had defended in his book, "tragedy is the natural remedy" for the Dionysian.[85] This is the ambiguity, not to say contradiction, that *The Birth of Tragedy* contains. Nietzsche cannot make up his mind whether to say clearly that as soon as a combination of sounds merits the name *music* it is both Dionysian and Apollonian.

Beside the fact that Nietzsche's own music practice hardly inclined him in this direction, this median position did not fit with the antinomic vision that he spontaneously adopted toward everything. And however little he will say he was "enlightened by the magic of extremes," Nietzsche usually did not take a notion to be valid except by taking it in its most radical sense. Finally, and above all, it was difficult for him explicitly to call into doubt the alliance between music and theater without which his book, undertaken to celebrate Wagnerian drama, would lose its raison d'être. Doubts persist however and, we have seen, this alliance turns out to be less imperative that it might seem. At least two long fragments from this period in his notes confirm this in announcing his subsequent attacks against Wagner and his "theateromanie."

Using Wagner's late writings as a starting point and his essay on Beethoven, in particular, Nietzsche refutes the theoretician of *Opera and Drama* and *The Art-Work of the Future*. But he goes even further:

> To the extent that it is certain that music can never become a means in service of the text but in each case surpasses it, to the same extent it surely becomes bad music if the composer breaks every Dionysian force that arises in it with an anxious glance at the words and gestures of his marionettes. If the librettist has only offered him something like ordinary schematized figures, with their Egyptian regularity, then the value of the opera will be all the greater the more the music unfolds in a free, unconditioned, more Dionysian fashion, and the more it disregards all so-called dramatic requirements. Opera in this sense is then, in the best case, good music and music alone—whereas the buffoonery it presents is as it were no more than a fantastic disguise for the orchestra and above all for its most important instruments, the singers, a disguise from which the insightful spectator will turn away from in laughter.[86]

If the music is submitted to the requirements of the drama, Nietzsche continues, it is reduced to a *"purely conventional symbol"* made up of "mnemonic signs" and to "a stimulant for dulled or tired nerves." But if it frees itself and becomes "absolute music, acting for itself," then "at each instant where its Dionysian violence penetrates the listener, the glance that sees the action and that gets lost in the individuals before him clouds over: the listener now *forgets* the drama and only reawakens to it when the Dionysian charm quits him."

As much as his personal experiences, Nietzsche here is recalling Wagner's essay on Beethoven where the composer comments that, in its most intense moments, vision loses its force and sharpness under the effect of the music, which, saturated with the composer's poetico-dramatic vision, makes us comprehend the action without our being aware of what we are seeing.[87] For his part, Nietzsche questions whether music, if it is really Dionysian, can obey images or any poetic intention, or even proceed from them. "Music can engender images from itself that are then only schemata, examples, as it were, of its true universal content," he writes as a good disciple of Schopenhauer. "But how could image, representation engender music?" "In Wagner, there is first of all hallucination: not in sounds but in gestures," he will say in *The Case of Wagner* to show that the composer was not a "musician by instinct" but only a man of the theater who *"made himself a musician"* to serve "his talent for exhibition."[88]

The Wagner of the years 1860–70 distinguished in terms of a dialectical relation the metaphysical plane where music reigned, sovereign, unconditioned, and absolute, and the empirical reality where it could not be born without external intervention. Nietzsche for his part affirms that it is equally in the practice of composition that music must be absolute.

> What an enterprise unnatural and even impossible this must be, to want to illustrate a poem through music and thereby to procure a conceptual language for music: an enterprise that seems to me similar to that of a son's wanting to engender his father.[89]

> When a musician composes a lyrical song what excites him as a musician is neither the images nor the feeling-language of the text: rather a musical incitement coming from wholly different sphere *chooses* this song-text as an analogical expression of itself.[90]

The ideal would be, as at the birth of tragedy, that music, images, and words all spring up simultaneously. Lacking this, the music must precede and be *unconditioned* in every way. In this way the philosopher, always in quest of "the originary one," theorizes the failures of the composer. For him, we know, music and language were profoundly dissociated. Besides the fact that Nietzsche was rarely his own poet, the music preceded the words that he had then to adapt to it, and not easily. Yet deprived of this "rudder," Nietzsche did not tarry in losing himself on "the ocean of sounds" once he ventured beyond short, traditional forms. He was neither truly an absolute musician, then—except perhaps in the small outburst of an improvisation—nor, even less, a poet-musician. To conclude from this, the blessed day of Hellas having passed, that the poet-musician was an impossibility or something feigned required just one more step, one that Nietzsche will take against Wagner, by not acknowledging the extent to which musician and poet were intimately combined in him. Wagner was all the more reprehensible in that he had gotten so close to rediscovering the lost unity (the closer one gets to an ideal, the more the remaining gap is insupportable). Wagner "forced language back into a primal state in which it conceives almost nothing with the help of concepts, a state in which it itself is still poetry, image, and feeling."[91] But other than in *Tristan*, for which the libretto was simply "musical froth" and where "the highest symphony," his unconscious objective, succeeded (above all in the third act) in "surmounting the original problem of the opera," Wagner's essentially theatrical nature enslaved him to the words and gestures of his singing "marionettes."[92]

Corrupting music at its source, words equally harm its reception. Just as musician and poet were irremediably dissociated since the decline of Attic drama, modern spectators according to Nietzsche were "hardly in a position any more to enjoy text and music at the same time."[93] In the most worked-out preparatory fragments for *The Birth of Tragedy* the "hardly" disappears, and Nietzsche even affirms that the text must not be understood. This is the lesson that he draws from the "extraordinary last movement of Beethoven's Ninth Symphony."

> That Schiller's poem "Ode to Joy" should be absolutely incongruous with the dithyrambic world-redeeming jubilation of this music, and that it should even be submerged like pale moonlight by this sea of flames, who can deprive me of this totally certain feeling? And who would dispute my affirmation that this feeling finds its cry of expression, when hearing this music, only because the music has deprived us of every capacity for images and words, and because *we hear almost nothing of Schiller's poem?*[94]

To affirm that in this movement "Beethoven solemnly confesses the limits of absolute music and even opens the door to a new art in which music would be able to portray image and concept, . . . was a monstrous aesthetic superstition," concludes Nietzsche, with a scornful allusion to *Opera and Drama*. "Only for the one who also sings" are the words comprehensible, and "therefore there is a vocal music: the listener confronts this as if it were absolute music."[95] If sometimes Nietzsche happens to believe "possible, in song, a truly organic connection between music and words,"[96] their disunion, which as a composer he had so much difficulty in surmounting, also appeared obvious to him as a listener when illness diminished his attentive capacity. To juxtapose the poet and the musician is a challenge, he will note in 1880, for the first "lets the drive to know *play*" whereas the second "lets it *rest*" (as though music, unlike language, always produced an immediate effect, without ever having to pass through the intellect).[97] Hence, "as soon as one no longer comprehends the words, everything returns to order: and this happily is the rule."[98]

Distancing himself from the theory he himself put forth in *Opera and Drama*, Wagner in his essay on Beethoven (1870) emphasized that in hearing the "Ode to Joy" it was not "the meaning of the Word" nor the "thought expressed in Schiller's verses" that grip us, but rather "the human character "of the voice: and "the choral chant."[99] And as we have seen, Wagner had become skeptical about the text of his own works, but this skepticism was counterbalanced by the growing confidence he had in the evocative power of music, thanks in particular to his mastery of the leitmotif technique, which allowed him to bring about a veritable semantization of sound.[100] "In my works the action is everything," he commented in 1871. "To a certain extent it is a matter of indifference to me whether people understand my verses, since the will certainly understand my dramatic action."[101] One could say as well that the music, even apart from the words but contaminated by them, was reduced to the state of being a "means of expression, of underscoring gestures, of suggestion." It was no longer music "but language, instrument, *ancilla dramaturgica*," Nietzsche indignantly complains, forgetting his own Wagnerian *musical* emotions, for whom, more than ever, action was a synonym of bad theater (supposing there had ever been good).[102]

We are far from the Nietzsche who in 1869 in agreement with *Opera and Drama* described music as "a means of expression in view of some end . . . Upholding the poem, reinforcing the expression of feelings and our interest in situations, without interrupting the action or disturbing it with unhelpful ornaments."[103] This was the Nietzsche who went on to deplore "the separation of heart and understanding, of music and action," for ancient drama broke down by giving birth "to *absolute music* and *everyday drama*."[104] Presented in *The Birth of Tragedy* as remedies for the elemental, devouring power of music, image, word, and myth were in reality only inconvenient analogical substitutes that music dissipates with its free and sovereign unfolding:

> In the supreme revelations of music, we feel even involuntarily the *grossness* of every figuration in images and of every affect introduced by analogy: it is in this way, for example, that the last quartets by Beethoven put to shame any kind of graphicness and in general the entire realm of empirical reality. In the face of the supreme God in his actual revelation, the symbol no longer has any meaning: it appears instead as an insulting exteriority.[105]

As his working notes and a few ambiguous pages from *The Birth of Tragedy* demonstrate, in less than three years Nietzsche had undergone the same evolution as did Wagner between 1850 and 1870, but Nietzsche had radicalized it. Initially drawn to positions that the composer had partly abandoned when he knew him, Nietzsche, more Wagnerian than Wagner, projected modern musical drama—as it turned out, only *Tristan*—back on ancient tragedy. Later this extreme yet partial adhesion to Wagner's aesthetic led him, via Schopenhauer, to rebuff the compromise that Wagner had come to make with his own theory and the philosopher's principles. In 1874 Nietzsche summed up the change that had occurred in the composer's ideas: "Means and end—music and drama—earlier teaching. *Generality* and *example*—music and drama—more recent teaching." And he concludes: "If the second is true, generality has no right whatsoever to be dependent on the example, in other words, if absolute music has its right, the music of drama too must be absolute music."[106]

"Wagner broke off the course of things disastrously, with no possibility of regaining the right course," Nietzsche will comment four years later.[107] "I had in mind a *symphony coinciding* with drama. . . . But the opera, the effect, what is not German led Wagner in another direction." Among the ways that, however, "still remained open," Nietzsche indicates, as we have seen, besides a return to the dithyramb "by overbidding Wagner": "absolute music rediscovering the laws of organic composition and only making use of Wagner as a preparation."[108]

Therefore, if we read *The Birth of Tragedy* with an eye on Nietzsche's working notes and recall that for him chorus and dithyramb were the ancient equivalents of the modern orchestra and symphony, it is clear that in his book he offers a refusal of drama and a barely disguised plea for absolute music. Moreover, before citing *Tristan* in that work, he cannot repress the confession that

> in giving this example, I must not appeal to those who use the images of what happens on the stage, the words and emotions of the acting persons, in order to approach with their help the musical feeling; for these people do not speak music as their mother tongue and, in spite of this help, never get beyond the entrance halls of musical perception, without ever being able to as much as touch the inner sanctum.[109]

PORTRAIT OF THE ARTIST AS AN ACTOR

The appearance of Richard Wagner was "like a volcanic eruption of nature's entire, undivided artistic ability. For this reason, one can vacillate when considering what to call him, whether he should be called—taking each designation in its broadest possible meaning—a poet, or a sculptor, or a composer, or whether a new designation must not in fact be created for him."[1] Yet Nietzsche's hopes in the total work of art, that resurrection of Greek tragedy, did not survive the experience of the Bayreuth Festival. Aided by his illness, it fueled the philosophical and musical objections and doubts that Nietzsche nourished and which until then he had confided only to his notebooks. They come to light in *Human, All Too Human:* "The mixed genres in art bear witness to the mistrust their originators felt towards their own powers; they sought assistants, advocates, hiding places—for example, the poet who calls on philosophy for aid, the composer who calls on the drama, the thinker who calls on rhetoric."[2] Abandoning any prudent and allusive pretense, seven years later—Wagner was dead—Nietzsche will diagnose a symptom of decadence in such "mixers of the arts," typical of "late French romanticism," notably Delacroix, with whom he associates Wagner: "as a musician" the latter "belongs among painters; as a poet, among musicians; as an artist in general, among actors."[3]

"Was Wagner a Musician?"

Nietzsche's criticism extends even to denying Wagner the very name of musician. If, in fact, Wagner makes use of other arts it is because "he has no real confidence in music,"[4] because he needs the theater and literature to "persuade the world to take his music seriously," thus betraying not the mediating power of the sovereign artist endowed with a "polyphonic being" like what was celebrated in *Richard Wagner in Bayreuth*, but rather a poverty of invention and the lack of discipline of a dilettante for which the lack of concentration of his youth, marked by a "feverish haste to try everything," was a presentiment. "Was Wagner a musician at all?" asks the truly dilettante composer of a certain *Night of Saint Sylvester*, that maladroit reply to *Siefried Idyll* (and like it dedicated to Cosima), which had made the composer of *Tristan* smile.

But the Wagner whose mastery of his art Nietzsche ends up denying was the same man he had initially admired as a musician before turning against him as a theoretician. (In this, he differed from most of his contemporaries, who were so obsessed with the dramatist that the latter concealed from them the composer, on whom indeed not much has been written.) It was because Wagner had made "fidelity to the spirit of music" his "religion," Nietzsche wrote in 1875, that "almost *all* other music sounds to our ears like a superficial, conventional, servile language."[5]

> In all other music there are only brief moments that make us suddenly hear the language that we *ceaselessly* hear in Wagner's music: rare moments of forgetfulness that seem to take hold of it, where it speaks to itself of itself and raises our eyes to the sky like Raphael's Saint Cecilia, far unlike those listeners who expect it to divert them, to give them pleasure or lessons. I do not know by what other way than Wagner's music I should have been able to take part in *so pure* a happiness, illumined by such a sun: and all this even though it is far from always speaking of happiness; rather, it speaks of terrible, disquieting, subterranean forces, of human tumult, of the suffering there is in all happiness and of the finitude of our happiness; therefore it has to be in its way of speaking that the happiness it dispenses is to be found.

And this musician, who *"has increased music's capacity for language to the point of making it immeasurable,"*[6] was, moreover, endowed with an unequalled capacity for composition, for organization. Taking up the "language of passion" created by Beethoven, he alone knew how to realize the "grand form" that Beethoven *"hinted* at" through the organic contrast of the movements of his symphonies, whereas his immediate successors—Schubert, Schumann, Mendelssohn—lacking the passion to understand this and make it their own, were content to juxtapose movements in a purely formal way that were never justified by the whole, but merely in their details.[7] Whence those "extended scenes," those acts and even whole dramas governed by "a sense of monumental rhythm" and a "sovereign symphonic intelligence."

> Wagner is never more Wagner than in those moments when the difficulties multiply tenfold and he can govern great relationships with the joy of the lawmaker. Subduing turbulent, resisting masses into simple rhythms, asserting one will throughout a confusing multitude of demands and desires—these are the tasks for which he feels himself born, in which he feels his freedom. Never does he lose his breath; never does he arrive panting at his goal.[8]

> His greatest force is to feel the unity in diversity. . . . He embraces many relationships in a single glance and is not a prisoner of the details. He orders everything on the grand scale; one will always make a false judgment concerning him if one judges him in terms of some one detail, as much in his music as in his drama.[9]

Wagner's success was so overwhelming that Nietzsche, who knew something about these matters, thought that all the musicians subjugated by Wagner and who were nonetheless eager to compose should "limit themselves to *the smallest form* . . . the musical epigram, for which perhaps wit [Witz] would suffice along with a talent for arrangement; and these can be honest, and even give rise to something magnificent, as with the Greeks, who went for the smallest form when the great ones had preempted."[10]

A dozen years later, a complete reversal has occurred: Wagner, not knowing how "to create a totality made in one piece,"[11] the grand form in him is only "a patchwork," a "lie," which his ancient thurifer, now "the first psychologist of Europe," has no difficulty penetrating (without ever informing us how he could have allowed himself to be deceived for such a long time). To his "wicked ear," Wagner's "large-scale audacious frescos," so admired by the naïve (encouraged perhaps by having read the fourth essay in *Unfashionable Observations*), betray the anarchy of their constitutive elements—which, by the way, are often "real treasures" but whose composite character and juxtaposition are characteristic of the "style of *decadence.*"

If one would admire him, one should watch him at work at this point: how he separates, how he gains small units, how he animates these, severs them, and makes them visible. But this exhausts his strength: the rest is no good. How wretched, how embarrassed, how amateurish is his manner of "development," his attempt to at least interlard what has not grown out of each other. His manners recall those of the *frères* de Goncourt, who are quite generally pertinent to Wagner's style: one feels a kind of compassion for so much distress.

. . . Once more: Wagner is admirable and gracious only in the invention of what is smallest, in spinning out the details. Here one is entirely justified in proclaiming him a master of the first rank, as our greatest *miniaturist* in music who crowds into the smallest space an infinity of sense and sweetness.[12]

"One need not hesitate to put down my name . . . where the text has the word 'Wagner,'" Nietzsche will write of *Richard Wagner in Bayreuth*.[13] But this advice holds as much if not more for *The Case of Wagner*, where the projection is even more obvious and enlightening. When Nietzsche, against all evidence, claims that Wagner has "disguised" as a "dramatic style" "his incapacity for giving organic form," which is characteristic of Wagner's "bold habit" of stating "a principle where he lacks a capacity," it is himself that he is describing.[14] When Nietzsche refers to Pascal's *Pensées* (which are not aphoristic by design but owing to the author's death) to affirm that "the most profound and most inexhaustible books always have something aphoristic and unexpected about them," what is Nietzsche doing if not stating a principle of writing precisely where he himself lacks a capacity: that of development and organization. Except for several short pieces, the music he wrote before his books exhibited this weakness, which worsened with his decline in health. "I had to omit about twenty *longish* thought sequences, unfortunately essential ones, because I could not find the time to extract them from my frightful pencil scribbling; the same was already true last summer," he writes, for example, to Peter Gast in October 1879 regarding "The Wanderer and His Shadow." "In the interim the connections between the thoughts escaped my memory; I have to steal the minutes and quarter-hours of "brain energy," as you call it, steal them away from a suffering brain."[15] And a month later, he adds: "Grounds for misunderstanding are so often close by in this work: the brevity, the accursed telegraphic style to which my head and eyes constrain me, is the cause."[16]

By disguising his own impotence through a literary parti pris, Nietzsche tried to respond to criticisms made by others as well as himself that he was merely an improviser, capable only of brief efforts, despite his ambition to write a classic book, a monument, not just collections of aphorisms and essays. But his "philosophy of the future"—as a riposte to "the work of art of the future," itself accomplished—will only subsist as a "prelude," *Beyond Good and Evil,* still in a fragmented form. The object of several successive plans, with changing titles ("The Will to Power," "The Reevaluation of All Values"), this great, longed-for work will remain enmeshed in an accumulation of notes. "The literary problem in general is to tie things together," Valéry has said, himself confronted with a large number of fragments meant to serve as the basis for a work that their accumulation made impossible.[17] To tie things together—this was Nietzsche's constant difficulty, since he no doubt lacked sufficiently strong "artistic gifts" to counterbalance the vigor of his critical faculties. Reproaching Wagner for having barely "pieced together" "elements that were not from the same mold," Nietzsche drew on almost the exact same terms his friend Rohde had used with regard to *The Birth of Tragedy* (which had cost him a lot of pain to complete). "Certain pieces," Rohde had written to Nietzsche, give the impression of having been *"first written for themselves,* and then, without being completely recast in the flow of metal, having been incorporated into the whole."[18] Nietzsche will comment in 1881 that

> *The great form of a work of art* will come to light when the artist has the great form in his *being!* To require a great form in itself is only twaddle that spoils art, and comes down to seducing the artist into hypocrisy. . . . An artist who does not have such a force in his *character* is *honest* in not seeking to have it in his works:—if he absolutely repudiates it and denigrates it, that is comprehensible and at least excusable: he *cannot* surpass himself here. Thus Wagner . . .[19]

What must be kept in mind regarding Nietzsche's attitude toward Wagner's "structuring force," which was capable of producing variations and transitions on a grand scale that weave together "the endless melody" into which "miniatures" and closed forms are blended—these were what Nietzsche himself was able to master as a composer, and even more so as a writer. This was a mastery by default, and one that he recognized as such. From book to book, none of which from *Human, All Too Human* on were really finished; his aphorisms become merely disjointed fragments, provisional inklings of a thought process that was always underway. In this, it was as German and as unappeasable as the flow of Wagner's music, but without its formal continuity, as though it could only express itself intermittently, like bits of melody emerging, fleetingly, from an incessant harmonic rumination.[20]

Whence the ambivalence toward this "endless melody" first manifested by Nietzsche, after 1876, which in *Human, All Too Human* he praises and criticizes in almost the same terms within the space of a few pages.[21] It is this "artistic style"—where "the fixed form is constantly being broken up, displaced, transposed back into indefiniteness, so that it signifies one thing and at the same time another"—that makes Lawrence Sterne, who Nietzsche uses to depict an ideal version of himself, "the most liberated spirit of all time." Digressive, ironic, both profound and a buffoon, this "great master of *ambiguity* . . . produces in the right reader a feeling of uncertainty as to whether one is walking, standing or lying: a feeling, that is, closely related to floating." This is why, of all the great writers, Sterne (which is to say, Nietzsche) is the one who "ought least to be imitated": "he raises himself above that which all artists in writing demand of themselves: discipline, compactness, simplicity, restraint in motion and deportment."[22]

Wagner, too—because he "fears . . . petrifaction, crystallization, the change of music into the architectonic"—seeks to "break" and even to "mock" all "mathematical symmetry of tempo and force." Whereas ancient music constrained one to "dance" and in "needful preservation of orderly measure compelled the soul of the listener to a continual *self-possession*," this kind of art desires a different movement of the soul related to "floating": as though "gradually relinquishing a firm tread on the bottom and finally surrendering unconditionally to the watery element: one is supposed to *swim*." A too facile and uncontrolled imitation of Wagner's principal innovation risks "the brutalization and decay of rhythm itself" through adherence to "the *all too feminine* nature of music."[23]

Therefore, where Sterne's—or Nietzsche's—reader takes flight, Wagner's listener, as an effect of the same causes, risks sinking. Nietzsche will soon deplore in Wagner the absence of what, under the cover of Sterne, he flattered himself for magisterially ignoring: discipline, completeness, constancy of intentions—as when in *Die Meistersinger* the marker Sixtus Beckmesser finds no cadence or conclusion or, in fact, "any trace of melody" in Walther's song, that abbreviated specimen of infinite melody.[24] Henceforth stigmatized as "the exact contrary of melody," the "infinite melody" will be a "counterfeit," "a veritable polyp in music" charged with artificially bringing into harmony "the motifs, gestures, and formulas" from which works are confectioned that, behind an appearance of continuity, reveal themselves to be fundamentally fragmentary.[25]—Like those of Nietzsche.

"It would be easy to produce the impression of a completed whole through the art of illusion, but I want to remain honest," he wrote in 1875, while working on the fourth of his *Unfashionable Observations*.[26] A facile honesty for one who had been denied such facility. From here, to claim that there is no "completed whole" without some illusion or imposture is something Nietzsche will not fail to do in the case of Wagner, even though in the prefaces he added to his earlier books in 1886, and even more insistently in *Ecce Homo*, he tries to present his own works as the organized and coherent product of a unique, continuous will—yet, not completely a fool, crafty in his way, and not without pretending to confuse a unified work with a system, which he proclaims himself proud not to have built. For every system betrays "a lack of probity"—like those large-scale deceitful frescoes painted by Wagner, who was "too vain" to "admit" or even "know" that above all else "yes, he is the master of the very minute."[27] It is "concealed," even concealed from himself, "in the corners of his frescoes," that, in a Nietzschean way despite himself, "he paints his real masterpieces all of which are very short, often only a single measure in length."[28] Ergo: the miniature is the truth of Wagner's art since it is Nietzsche's, who, in unmasking his old god, simultaneously appears as his real double and faithful disciple. At the same time, "the unsettling discordance" that the composer-writer experienced between his taste (for Wagner) and his creative force finally finds its resolution: long humiliated, the latter takes vengeance on the former by denouncing in it an error, a "misunderstanding."

But how are we not to recognize in this "master of suspicion," well accustomed to "sound[ing] out idols," the man of *ressentiment* that he would not have so strongly condemned if he had not been one himself: the ancestor of a swarming posterity of failed creators who, incapable of works, denounces every completed work as an illusion or imposture, who glories in cleansing or deconstructing it in order to reveal its truth in the fragmentation of its elements, the tentativeness of its sketches, or the disorder of its first drafts?

Music Guilty and Innocent

Alongside *ressentiment* we need also to make room for Nietzsche's passion for contradiction. Anticipating the snobbish criticism of the duchess of Guermantes who will only retain "a few horn notes" of *Tristan*, his praise of Wagner's real "masterpieces"—"all of them short things of five to fifteen measures, all of it music *nobody knows*"[29]—will allow the "untimely" one to distinguish himself "from the laymen and imbeciles who immerse themselves in art and want to impose their taste," above all from the crowd, enthused by those "impudent frescoes" uniquely conceived to seduce it (even while he asks himself, albeit in his notebooks, "What is it the laymen find in Wagner?" for it is necessary to be a musician, and even to possess "a higher musical culture" to appreciate him).[30] In this way is reestablished the *distance* so dear to Nietzsche, which theater in its very nature abolishes. For "the theater is a form of demolatry in matters of taste . . . a plebiscite *against* good taste."[31]

> In the theater one is honest only in the mass; as an individual one lies, one lies to oneself. One leaves oneself at home when one goes to the theater, one renounces the right to one's own tongue and choice, to one's taste, even to one's courage as one has it and exercises it between one's own four walls against both God and man. No one brings along the finest senses of his art to the theater, nor does the artist who works for the theater. There one is common people, audience, herd, female, pharisee, voting cattle, democrat, neighbor, fellow man; there even the most personal conscience is vanquished by the leveling magic of the great number; there stupidity has the effect of lasciviousness and contagion; the neighbor reigns, one becomes a mere neighbor.[32]

But if even the spectator blessed with the most personal self-awareness succumbs to this leveling magic it is because the artist has first given into it. With the simultaneous development of dramatic music and democracy, the "herd" has got into his mind and dictated its taste to him. Rather than the servant of princes and the Church he had formerly been, the artist has become the servant of the people.[33] This is a change of masters that has only aggravated his dependence, for "never yet has the integrity of musicians, their 'authenticity,' been put to the test so dangerously."[34] "Mass success" presupposes expressive demagogy, a consummate sense of the effect of staging, display.[35] Hugo, Michelet, and George Sand, those "flatterers of the plebians" in literature correspond in music to "those three marvelous and dangerous men, Paganini, Liszt, and Wagner . . . whose instinct divined everything that could be found and dispensed with an eye to exposing, expressing, influencing, enchanting, and seducing."[36]

The most "dangerous" (and "marvelous") of these "demonic intermediaries" is, of course, Wagner, "the Victor Hugo of music"[37] whose hold is particularly strong, and frightening, on women, and even more so on young people. "Trembling, they hear how the *great symbols* approach from foggy distances to resound in his art with muted thunder."[38] But, when in *Thus Spoke Zarathustra*—whose "*finale*," as a sign of fate, "was finished exactly in that sacred hour in which Richard Wagner died in Venice"[39]—Nietzsche wanted to set himself up as a rival to him, steal these subjugated youth away from the Minotaur, it was also by making such "great symbols" thunder, while "great winds" sweep the peaks. Clothed in a heavy panoply of evangelical emblems, his prophet, appearing from the forest, delivers his oracles to incredulous crowds in a language stuffed with etymological and alliterative games that recall in many ways those of the heroes of *The Ring* cycle. Nietzsche compared his book to a "symphony" (the only one, by the way, that he succeeded in orchestrating from end to end). But to a reader endowed with a "wicked ear" it sounds rather like a pastiche of Wagner that has withstood the passage of time less well than the original, no doubt owing to the lack of music. Having received a copy of *Zarathustra*, Jacob Burckhardt (a good judge) merely asked Nietzsche whether "he planned to try his hand at a play one day."[40]

This is the paradox that catches Nietzsche: contemptuous of the masses and of theater, he has to make recourse to rhetoric and the artifices of the theater to proclaim his disgust for them—like Rousseau, who became an author in order to denounce the lie of literature by proclaiming "that virtue lies in silent wisdom."[41] Hence, when the preaching failed to be heard, his invocation to the future elect, those as yet unborn "aristocrats of the spirit" that Nietzsche will designate as the real audience for his books, and the proud apology of the solitary walker who meets his best thoughts while walking "six thousand feet above human things," far from the "big city" peopled by "the scribble- and scream-throats, the overheated ambitious and conceited,"[42] where he did not find ears ready to listen to him. What is more, the very ambition to be heard would corrupt at its source the thoughts and music that sprang from his singular soul: The "herd" would again get on the inside and impose its bad taste on them. Above all, "there is something insulting about being understood. Being understood? Do you know what that means?—*Comprendre, c'est égaler* [To understand is to be equal]."[43] Wagner wanted to be understood by the greatest possible number. And if Nietzsche praises Wagner because "he gave a language to everything in nature that until now had not wanted to speak,"[44] his praise is ambivalent. To say that music is a language implies that it lowers itself to communicate; but one only communicates what is, and makes "common."[45]

Rather than "art conceived in the presence of witnesses," rigged, invalidated by a concern to please, the true artist, therefore, will prefer "monologue": an art "based *on forgetting*" the world, which is "the music of forgetting."[46] As for the public, it needs to learn how to listen with "the finest part of [its] honesty," for when it applauds and acclaims, it has "the artists' conscience in [its] hands—and woe betide if they notice you are incapable of distinguishing between innocent music and guilty music!" It is not a question of "good" and "bad" music, "both species include both good and bad music." No, "what I mean by *innocent music* is music which thinks wholly and solely of itself, believes in itself and has forgotten the world in contemplation of itself—the self-resounding of the profoundest solitude, which speaks to itself of itself and no longer knows that outside there are hearers and listeners, effects, misunderstandings and failures."[47] The essence of Dionysian art entails that the artist pay no attention to the listener, Nietzsche had already noted in 1871: "the dithyrambic servant of Dionysus . . . is understood only by his own kind."[48] In fact, listeners are unnecessary, apart from those who too can forget the world, who are rare, among the chosen, solitary preferably. For, "in the century of the herd," music and public have become antinomies. *"Good* music never has a 'public,'" he notes in 1885. "It never is, and never can be 'public,' it belongs to the most select, it must always only be "chamber" *music*."[49] There, locked away in his irreducible difference, "the intoxicated man" himself becomes "a work of art without a public."[50]

There we find again "the eternal young man" (if not the *eternal old maid*) pouring himself out, dreaming, tormented, nostalgic, at his piano: Schumann, the musician "of solitary intimacy, of the amorous and imprisoned soul that *speaks to itself*," Roland Barthes will say, whose works for piano were written "only for one person, the one who plays it."[51] Even though in 1886 Nietzsche will again lambaste his first model and inspiration in *Beyond Good and Evil*, in his preparatory notes Nietzsche remarked that Schumann possessed a *"purer* nature" than Wagner, which was an obstacle when the latter "went to meet" the Reich Germans.[52] But was it not exactly in order to get out of his "room" and to transcend that "muggy" inwardness where he lazed in the company of this "sugary Saxon" that this same Nietzsche had embraced the cause of Wagner fifteen years earlier, animated by the hope that the realization of the "total work of art" in the Bayreuth theater would bring about "a renewal and purification of the German spirit" and even of German society? "The bond between human beings," he then wrote, is "renewed by the magic of the Dionysian":

> Transform Beethoven's "Hymn to Joy" into a painting; let your imagination conceive the multitudes bowing to the dust, awestruck—then you will approach the Dionysian. Now the slave is a free man; now all the rigid, hostile barriers that necessity, caprice, or "impudent convention" have fixed between man and man are broken. Now, with the gospel of

universal harmony, each one feels himself not only united, reconciled, and fused with his neighbor, but as one with him, as if the veil of *māyā* had been torn aside, and were now merely fluttering in tatters before the mysterious primordial unity.[53]

"The isolated man of our age seeks artistic pleasure in communication with his equals," Wagner had said. And he found it in drama, "the fullest expression of Community."[54] Nietzsche enthusiastically sought to contribute to the realization of this "supreme work of art in common." "Wagner's art speaks a *theatrical* language," he noted in 1874, "it has no place in the drawing room, in the chamber. It is a popular discourse, and this is inconceivable unless even what is most noble in it be made coarse. It has to work at a distance and cement together the chaos that is the people."[55]

For Nietzsche, therefore, the desire for communion won out at least once over his sharp sense of distance. Next came the time of solitude that, he said, his "task" required of him, and that his work exalted: "O solitude! O my *home*, solitude!" exclaims Zarathustra. "Too long have I lived wildly in wild strange places not to return home to you in tears." This "whole subterranean, concealed, mute, undiscovered solitude that among us is called life" is "a virtue for us, as a sublime bent and urge for cleanliness which guesses how all contact between man and man—'in society'—involves inevitable uncleanliness."[56]

Yet these strong words, and others as haughty or lyrical, ought not to be overinterpreted. There is something about them that resembles the insistence of one who preaches in order first to convince himself. The itinerant hermit was "avid for men, like a pirate." It was not so much from the multitude that Nietzsche suffered as it was from solitude, he for whom almost every one of his musical compositions was offered to or dedicated to someone, many of them even having this gesture as their unique raison d'être.[57] "O solitude of those who give," Zarathustra also complains. "Alas, ice surrounds me, my hand meets icy contacts." "Solitude is at times crushing," Nietzsche will write to Overbeck. "I am not made for it, and at the current hour, when I do not know how to get out of it, I feel overwhelmed, almost every week, by such a sharp distaste for existence that I am sickened by it." "The longer it lasts, the more dangerous it is," for "in solitude the beast everyone carries within himself grows."[58]

As an ardent heir of Romanticism who fought against it with an equal ardor, Nietzsche illustrates in his hyperbolic manner the modern tension between the individual and society on which the former nourished himself, as much in music as in literature. A melancholy or haughty withdrawal into oneself, a trust in the "happy few" was counterbalanced by the desire for an art for all that would give expression to a free and united people. If Beethoven in his best-known works combines an affirmed subjectivity and a personal language with the ambition to conquer a public that extends to the whole of mankind, Schumann experienced this double aspiration as a torment, which his composition of popular or patriotic choruses did not suffice to ease. "My prayer from morning to night," he said, "is called German opera." This prayer would be answered—by Wagner, a no less subjective artist than the author of the *Nachtstücke* but one endowed at the same time with an ability to project himself superior even to that of Beethoven. Cursing the world, which the Flying Dutchman and Lohengrin flee, did not prevent the composer of *Tristan* from allowing it to be the witness of his most intimate confessions, or even less from wanting to convert it, to make it submit to his art, and this on the a priori least likely terrain—opera—by creating a community of faithful followers and proselytes from a public whose frivolity he castigated.[59] He was in the process of doing just this when Nietzsche first knew him.[60] How could such an example not have been contagious? Before treating Wagner as a rival that he intended to supplant among Germans, Nietzsche could well imagine that Wagner might also be the intermediary through which the new thoughts he felt growing in him and which, he believed, extended those of the composer while clarifying them, might reach a wide audience and transform German culture.

Therefore neither the presence of too *Reichsdeutsch* a public at the first Bayreuth festival nor his illness suffice to explain the disillusion he felt at the time. As can be seen from the accumulating reservations in his notes against Wagnerian drama, this had first of all to do with the very nature of theater, which Nietzsche, contrary to his natural inclinations and due to his fascination for Wagner, had taken for a time to be an instrument of regeneration.

Birth of the Actor

The edifice, the laying of whose foundation stone on the hill at Bayreuth he had watched with emotion in 1872, was not at that time to his mind a theater like others. "What equivocal objections one must combat, if only to prevent anyone from confusing the Bayreuth event of May 1872 with the foundation of a new theater, or to explain on the other hand why no existing theater could satisfy the spirit of such an undertaking," he wrote in 1873 in his "Appeal to Germans," written to stimulate the collection of the necessary funds to complete its construction.[61] Consistent with his neo-Hellenic dream, Nietzsche imagined it on the model of Athenian theater as he had conceived of it; as the good son of a German pastor, he never could think without a shudder that his dear Greeks might in all good conscience go to the theater for amusement. If, in reality, he experienced more attraction for the *birth* of tragedy than for tragedy itself, beyond his passion for the "originary," this was for the same reasons when, as an adolescent, he preferred oratorio to opera. At its "primitive stage," almost in a state of nature, tragedy did not yet exist as a spectacle but rather was a sacred festival, an ecstatic moment of "profound communion" where the spectators metamorphosed into participants.[62]

"In the great age of Attic drama" when there still "subsisted in the soul of the spectator something of the Dionysian life of nature,"[63] "a public of spectators as we know it was unknown to the Greeks: in their theaters the terraced structure of concentric arcs made it possible for everybody to actually *overlook* the whole world of culture around him and to imagine, in absorbed contemplation, that he himself was a chorist."[64]

The vision of the sufferings and victory of Dionysus, irradiated by the chorus, was so intense that it rendered "the spectator's gaze insensitive and unresponsive to the impression of 'reality' and to the cultured people occupying the rows of seats around" one. One was unaware of being a "neighbor." The distance between beings was at once incommensurable and abolished since each one of them found himself projected beyond himself into the ideal community of the singing, dancing chorus.

Similarly, the dithyrambic chorus was a kind of "group in fusion" constituted by "a chorus of transformed characters whose civic past and social status have been completely forgotten: they have become timeless servants of their god . . . a community of unconscious actors who consider themselves and one another transformed."[65] "It is not that drama begins with someone's disguising himself in the desire to deceive other people but, rather, with the human being's being outside himself and believing himself magically transformed."[66] The conclusion is that "such magic transformation is the presupposition of all dramatic art."[67] At this stage, therefore, there was no representation properly speaking since "only the chorus in the *orchestra* [was] real, whereas the world of the stage, the characters and the events that appeared there, were only visible as living images, shining apparitions from the Apollonian fantasy-projection from the chorus,"[68] aroused by the musical incantations and dances, which were themselves extremely elementary. Apollo, certainly, was already present, but so to speak in degree zero. Nietzsche's primitive stage is an empty one—where the vision of the dismembered, then reunited body of Dionysus trembles among the unifying "commotion" of the chorus and instruments.

However, Dionysian intoxication, which prompts man to see "every-where only the horror or absurdity of existence," with "its annihilation of the ordinary bounds and limits of existence" and the "danger of longing for a Buddhistic negation of the will," called for a corrective, that is, for "no-tions with which man can live."[69] This was the salvific work of Apollo, who populated the stage with images that were visual and no longer just vir-tual. For intoxication was substituted "playing with intoxication"[70]: art that imitates it by imposing a limit on it and that as a result "strives not after truth, but after *plausibility*."[71] This "intermediary world between truth and beauty," "floating between the two" thanks to the covenant concluded be-tween Dionysus and Apollo—this was Greek tragedy.

With Apollo, therefore, the actor comes on stage, but at least initially in his most transparent figure. Without falling completely into intoxication, he is yet impregnated to the point that he "sees the role he is supposed to play quite palpably before his eyes," the suffering god or hero he represents, and for whom he is the mask.[72] He plays at intoxication, but does so re-maining near to the "instinctive poet, singer, dancer"[73] (which must have still been the case when Sophocles and Aeschylus themselves played their leading roles).[74] If he speaks, it is to the accompaniment of instruments that keep his words under "the dominant influence of the music."[75] Finally, he is not "isolated," since he is barely distinguishable from the chorus, which al-ways predominates, into which the members of the public continue to pro-ject themselves, no longer as participants, but as "artist-spectators" prey to a beneficial "illusion."

This was tragedy at its birth: a moment of extreme tension, a unique and necessarily ephemeral conjunction, since the covenant that made it pos-sible is also the principle of its disintegration. Indeed, under the irresistible force of the Apollonian element the action continues to develop to the detri-ment of the vision, bit by bit pushing the music and the chorus into a sup-porting role. Hence the stage quickly came to dominate the orchestra like the "colony does the metropolis."[76] And then we see the triumph of the ac-tor on this invasive stage, the actor who, in the prosaic plays of Euripides, often evokes everyday life, making himself the fully aware and docile inter-preter of the plebe, for whom Socrates is both ventriloquist and spokesman. If we add critics and journalists to the picture, the disaster will be complete.

In this, tragedy ended up like Faust. The culminating moment of its existence (*der höchsten Augenblick*) was also that of its death. And since this began with its birth, once it had hatched from the dithyramb, tragedy was condemned. The advent of the actor "who plays" signaled the progressive and irremediable degradation of the festival into a "spectacle."[77]

Concerned especially with opposing music to Socrates—held to be "the one turning point and vortex of so-called world history"[78]—in a spectacular duel that simultaneously glorified Wagner and also elevated himself, Nietzsche, in 1871, slides over this precocious symptom of the decline of tragedy. That this was a crucial point, though, is shown by the disenchantment he experienced five years later at Bayreuth, when he brings to the fore his denunciation of the actor with all the virulence of a return of the repressed.

To Represent Is to Profane

"What is the drama to me? What, the convulsions of its moral ecstasies which give the common people satisfaction? What, the whole gesture hocus-pocus of the actor? You will guess that I am essentially anti-theatrical," Nietzsche will exclaim in 1882 in *The Gay Science*.[79] Cut off from his sacred roots plunging into a mythic past, the actor is nothing more than a ham who destroys the "beneficial illusion" with which tragedy was supposed to envelop the "artist-spectator." "Supposing *one* actor creates it, another immediately destroys it, or *in any case* the theater and the people who surround us do. How dull and unconvincing is Mozart's *Don Juan* compared to that of Mérimée's *Don Juan!*"[80] In 1878, having read the libretto for *Parsifal*, Nietzsche was unable to restrain his admiration—despite the Christian character of this work—for "the situations and their sequence," which, he writes to a friend, stem from "the highest poetry." But, he adds, "much that is tolerable to the inner eye will be almost insupportable in performance—imagine our actors praying, trembling, with ecstatic throats."[81] And it was not (just) because *Parsifal* included scenes of religious inspiration that Nietzsche got his back up. Nine years later, shortly before praising *Carmen* in *The Case of Wagner* as the supreme antidote to *Parsifal*, Nietzsche forcefully forbids himself from attending any new performances of the work, for the music is "corrupted" by the drama and "the antinaturalness" of the actors.[82]

So, it is not the object of representation that is at issue, but rather the very fact of representing anything. And this was not a late reaction on Nietzsche's part, provoked by the disappointment of Bayreuth. At the very moment when his supposed extolling of tragedy was about to appear, we find growing in his notes, in reference to Shakespeare, that insurmountable distaste that any "scenic realization" inspired in him:

> One feels a kind of *desecration*, and one tries to explain away this impression of shortcomings of the staging, a misunderstanding of Shakespeare

on the part of the actors, and so forth. None of this will work: for even in the mouth of an actor capable of conveying the deepest conviction a profound thought, a metaphor, basically each and every word sounds weakened, withered, desacralized; we do not believe in this language, we do not believe in these people, and what touched us as the most profound revelation about the world now appears to us as a repulsive masquerade.[83]

Ought we not to compare this instinctive, Puritan-like repulsion for the theater with the remoteness Nietzsche felt during the same period toward painting: landscapes alone pleased him, whereas "the representation of the human body remained always alien" to him,[84] for he "lacked any feeling for the plastic arts." This lack, combined with Protestant iconoclasm, betrays, in the future apologist of the body, a fundamental difficulty in representing or accepting incarnation.

If therefore, during his most Apollonian phases, Nietzsche would have applauded Sophocles, Aeschylus, and the revival of the dithyramb in Stravinsky's *Les Noces*—just as he had applauded *Die Meistersinger, Tristan,* and *Carmen*—once past this "limit point," this "culminating instant," the irrepressible movement of his nature would have led him to leave them and to disparage the spectacle in favor of music, which "leads more and more to interiority"[85] and to "honesty"[86] and in which always resounds more or less the echo of a sacred festival or of a moment of solitary intoxication celebrating the reconciliation of the individual with himself. Therefore, it is not in *Richard Wagner in Bayreuth* that Nietzsche overdid his taste and thinking in the service of Wagner, as has often been suggested, but already with *The Birth of Tragedy*, where, turning away from his deepest instinct, he had been led to glorify theater due to the passionate admiration that he felt for the composer of *Tristan*. This was something for which Wagner was to pay dearly.

In the fourth *Meditation* itself, the actor stands out beneath the "dithyrambic dramatist," though ennobled by a comparison with the great man of German culture: like Goethe, for whom "whom "literature was a kind of compensation for his thwarted desire to be a painter," Wagner had "a natural theatrical gift that had to renounce the most traditional, most trivial means of attaining satisfaction, and that discovered its compensation and salvation in the merging of all the arts to form a great theatrical revelation."[87] And if "his life had a theatrical aspect, and even of a singularly grotesque kind," it was "as seen close up and without any affection."[88] However, Nietzsche's preparatory notes testify to more ambivalent feelings:

His relationship to music is that of an actor: this is why he can in a way speak through various musical souls and place side by side very diverse worlds (*Tristan, Meistersinger*).[89]

As an actor, he wanted to imitate the human being only insofar as he is most effective and most real: with the highest affect. [But] affect is suspect because it lends itself easily to effect.[90]

Comic situation: Wagner is unable to persuade the Germans to take theater seriously. They remain cold and comfortable—he gets worked up as though German salvation depended on this.[91]

Whoever in our day applauds at the theater is ashamed of it the next day, for we have our home altar, Beethoven, Bach—there the memory pales.[92]

Two years later, the inauguration of Bayreuth will lift the obstacles that restrained Nietzsche from openly expressing his hostility. This theater was just a theater like all others, and its very resemblance to the Greek model (set in a field and with concentric bleachers) only made more apparent the gulf between dream and reality. The mythic festival had degraded into a festival consecrating *"the emergence of the actor in music,"*[93] "the most enthusiastic mimomaniac of all time."[94] His response is as one would expect: "A democratic age praises the actor to the skies, in Athens just as today."[95] Behind the features of the "venerated master" stood a clever maestro, a stage director consumed by his work and himself:

Stop it, you actor! You counterfeiter! You liar from the bottom! I recognize you well! . . . You peacock of peacocks, you sea of vanity, *what* were you playing before me, you wicked magician? In *whom* was I to believe then . . . ?[96]

A fatal discovery, as dramatic as that of the lie of appearance by the young Jean-Jacques Rousseau, whose shock wave would continue to sound in Nietzsche's works. Disillusioned, one becomes a moralist, and to get vengeance, a psychologist:

My portrait of Wagner went beyond its model, I depicted an *ideal monster.* . . . The real Wagner, the real Bayreuth, were for me like a bad version of an etching, the very last one on poor paper. My need to see real people and their motives was extraordinarily stimulated by that humiliating experience.[97]

"Everything Becomes Histrionics"

Enlightened and prodded by his reading of French moralists, Nietzsche was about to cultivate the very classic suspicion that all men wear masks and necessarily conceal within themselves barely honorable motivations. "Everyone puts their being in appearing," said Rousseau. But unlike Rousseau, who was caught up in a persecution mania, the author of *Human, All Too Human,* through one of those heroic and voluptuously cruel reversals against himself of which he was a virtuoso, would soon take up the defense of appearances and give an apology for masks against suspicion, which itself would be in turn suspected of being merely a barely disguised form of *ressentiment.* For "whatever is profound loves masks,"[98] and "anyone who does not *want* to see what is lofty in a man looks that much more keenly for what is low in him and mere foreground—and thus betrays himself."[99] Nietzsche was masked in his day-to-day life—or at least he wished to appear so. Lou Salomé reported that

> Nietzsche's behavior gave a similar impression of reclusivity and secretness. Usually he displayed great courtesy, almost feminine mildness, and an even-tempered geniality. He took pleasure in stylish conventions and thought highly of them. Moreover there was an enjoyment in his costuming, as mantle and mask covered a rarely exposed interior. I remember that when I first spoke with Nietzsche during a day in the Spring of 1882 in St. Peter's in Rome; his studied, elegant posture surprised and deceived me. But not for long was one deceived by this recluse who wore his mask so awkwardly, like someone who has come out of the wilderness and mountains and who is dressed conventionally. Very soon a question surfaces, which he formulated in these words: "Whenever a person permits something to become visible, one can ask: 'What does it hide? From what does it wish to divert someone's gaze? What conception should it arouse?'" And further: "To what extreme does the subtlety of this disguise go? And does he misperceive himself in all that?"[100]

Nietzsche practiced this art of disguise more successfully in his books. A paradoxical rehabilitation of the theater—but of an imaginary theater, where like "the Dionysian chorus, which ever anew discharges itself in an

Apollinian world of images,"[101] Nietzsche, increasingly alone, projects himself with more veracity and shamelessness when in *Ecce Homo* he will finally decide to say who he really is. For example, his melancholic analysis in *Human, All Too Human* of "Goethe's two errors"—having taken himself first for a painter, then for a scientist—it is not difficult to recognize Nietzsche's own in the painful oscillation of his nature between art (music) and knowledge. Or even more so in his loaded portrait of Socrates in *Twilight of the Idols:* "Everything about him is exaggerated, *buffo,* caricature, everything is at the same time, hidden, reserved, subterranean. . . . Socrates was the buffoon who *got himself taken seriously.*"[102] "I do not want to be a holy man; sooner even a buffoon," he will add a few years later[103]—a buffoon "condemned to entertain the next eternity with bad jokes," he adds in a letter he addressed to Jacob Burckhardt, 6 January 1889, when he had already fallen into madness.[104]

A buffoon—which is to say, the parodic, derisory version of the supreme actor—Wagner—into which, to the end, Nietzsche continued to project himself, but without ever allowing Wagner himself to wear a mask or to lie, a sign that the "old enchanter" was too close for Nietzsche to be able to manage to save the appearances. As the author of *Ecce Homo* leads us clearly to believe, it was not just in *Richard Wagner in Bayreuth* but throughout his whole work that every time the name Wagner appears, we should not hesitate to substitute his. As early as *The Birth of Tragedy,* when some newspapers treated him as the composer's "literary lackey,"[105] *Wagner* in reality was his pseudonym. As proof: "It was only from that moment on that Wagner's name elicited high hopes."[106] (Thus the unknown disciple had given birth to the already crowned master, in whom, at the time, he had saluted a new father.) At this point, their names became so interchangeable, Nietzsche goes on to say, that if "I had published my *Zarathustra* under another name—for example, that of Richard Wagner—the acuteness of two thousand years would not have been sufficient for anyone to guess that the author of *Human, All-Too-Human* is the visionary of *Zarathustra.*"[107]

To Wagner, *Ecce Homo,* then his last letters, in an accelerating tempo, add other frontmen beneath which he concealed himself in his works, or whom the Eternal Return, undoubtedly, made him borrow in earlier lives: Schopenhauer, Dionysus (who is also the true spouse of Ariadne-Cosima), and the Crucified, to whom we may add the Buddha, Alexander, Caesar, "Lord Bacon, the poet of Shakespeare," Voltaire, and Napoleon.[108] "At bottom, every name in history is me," he triumphantly announces to Burckhardt.

"There are people who want to be seen in no other way than shining through others. And there is a great deal of prudence in that," we read in *Daybreak*.[109] But the delirious succession of masks that Nietzsche presents during his last weeks of conscious life denounces the truth of this feigned prudence: an uncertain, discontinuous, even contingent identity—I am only "a fragment, riddle, lugubrious chance," confesses Zarathustra—vacillating at the edge of chaos, whose attraction at the end will prove to be irresistible. "Ah, give me madness, you heavenly powers! Madness, that I may at last believe in myself," implored the "solitary and agitated minds," "the most fruitful men of all times" in *Daybreak*.[110] "Give deliriums and convulsions, sudden lights and darkness, terrify me with frost and fire such as no mortal has ever felt, with deafening din and prowling figures, make me howl and whine and crawl like a beast: so that I may only come to believe in myself!"

"Nietzsche never believed in himself," commented his friend Franz Overbeck, who knew his taste for masks so well that, as the first witness of his "mental darkening," he could not help thinking of the "horrible idea that it was simulated."[111] But, after having displayed in *Ecce Homo* the euphoric and most successful version of the self-falsification that drives his works— "Why I am so wise," "so clever," "so free of *ressentiment*," I who "was never a Christian a single hour of my life," and so on—Nietzsche, finally, no longer concealed himself. And along with the actor equally vanished the artist, these two terms being synonymous for him.

> The problem of the actor has troubled me for the longest time. I felt unsure (and sometimes still do) whether it is not only from this angle that one can get at the dangerous concept of the "artist"—a concept that has so far been treated with unpardonable generosity. Falseness with a good conscience; the delight in simulation exploding as a power that pushes aside one's so-called "character," flooding it and at times extinguishing it; the inner craving for a role and mask, for *appearance;* an excess of the capacity for all kinds of adaptations that can no longer be satisfied in the service of the most immediate and narrowest utility—all of this is perhaps not *only* peculiar to the actor?[112]

This uncertainty was more rhetorical than real—simulated, for a few more years, out of concern not to take on Wagner head-on. As his notebooks demonstrate, even before the Bayreuth Festival, Nietzsche was convinced that "in what he called the 'artist,' the force *proper to the player* was the principal element." To become aware of this "exceptional problem," which returns under his pen as an insistent leitmotiv, to "discover and recognize the actor at bottom of every artist," it was necessary that he should have first known Wagner.[113] "Wagner never calculates as a musician, from some sort of musician's conscience: what he wants is effect, nothing but effect," Nietzsche writes in 1888. "One is an actor by virtue of being ahead of the rest of mankind in one insight: what is meant to have the effect of truth must not be true."[114] In other words, as everyone knows, the actor simulates what he does not experience (or no longer experiences) in order to better produce the effect. Too "sentimental" in Schiller's sense, too self-aware—which for Hegel indicated the end of art—and too much aware of his public, the accomplished dramatic musician that was Wagner substituted reflection, calculation, professionalism for instinct; his music was therefore doubly "guilty."

When he saw in Wagner the new "dithyrambic dramatist," it was to Euripides that Nietzsche addressed such criticism. Euripides had precipitated the "death agony of tragedy" because he obeyed his public and was "the first to follow a conscious aesthetic," whereas Aeschylus, on the contrary, owed "the best of his work to unconscious creation."[115] Less than ten years later, however, impatient to exorcise the fascination for genius he had undergone, Nietzsche will take an almost diametrically opposite stand to this Romantic-Schopenhauerian vision of the creator in *Human, All too Human*. Without denying any role to inspiration, he now put the accent on work, patience, cunning. A perfect work is no less the result of work—as learning numerous musical scores, and, *a contrario*, his less happy experiments as a composer had taught him. In short, it was a more balanced conception, but one as precarious as that of tragedy balanced between Dionysus and Apollo, for it proceeded above all from a reactive aspiration (against Wagner and the idea that shallow people had of him) and not from serene, disinterested affirmation. We can sense this in the insistence and polemical tone with which Nietzsche expresses himself: as though he wanted first to convince himself of something every lucid creator takes for granted.[116] If this was not the case for Nietzsche, it was because his sought-after Apollonianism in fact remained much more dependent on the original source of inspiration than his picture of the artistic process as a kind of determined tinkering suggests. Doomed to the aphorism, which henceforth would be his trademark, the writer found again in it that state of innocent, "forced" creation the musician had known, especially in his youth when "the demon of music" took hold of him and which he turned loose at the piano, like thunder, "this pure willing that the intellect does not disturb," in Dionysian improvisations where Apollo seemed to play no part.[117] When ideas "took hold" of him with as imperious a force as did sounds, the aphorism allowed him to experience an almost ideal coincidence between intuition and form and to communicate his thoughts with their immediate vibration. The actor waited in the wings and only intervened once the essential action had been carried out, to finish things up, a finishing touch that did not betray the truth of the first sketches, as delicate as this must sometimes have been. We can understand why, being short-winded, Nietzsche held that "what can be done well today, what can be masterly, is only what is small. Here alone integrity is still possible."[118]

It is hardly surprising that at the end of his "positivist" period, Nietzsche, taken again with music that he had for a time abandoned, returned to his initial conception. "What is 'mind' to me? What does knowledge matter?" he then writes to Lou Andreas-Salomé. "I treasure nothing except *impulses*."[119] Zarathustra tells his disciples to become children, for "the child is innocence and forgetting . . . a self-propelled wheel, a first movement, a sacred 'Yes.'"[120] And a few years later the author of *The Antichrist* will designate "a complete automatism of instinct," such as he had admired in Siegfried, as "the precondition for any kind of mastery, any kind of perfection in the art of living," to the point of denying "that anything can be made perfect so long as it is still made consciously."[121]

In his impassioned study of the early Greeks Nietzsche had had a vision of a beautiful existence and a perfect art, because they were governed by sureness of instinct (his vision of the natural state). "We ought to include among the number of [their] beautiful qualities the fact that they could not transform the best of what they had into reflection," he told his students in 1871.[122] At the primitive stage of tragedy, even before Aeschylus and Sophocles, when it still did not have an author but, like an image of the universe, engendered itself from music "where the power of instinct dominates,"[123] everything was in everything else: not indistinct, but undivided in a flawless cohesion, where everything fit together without any *play*.[124] Compact, vibrant with intoxication and terror, this original unity was fissured, dismembered, like the body of Dionysus, with the appearance of the author-actor, that figure of otherness, the initial source of our alienation. In this way the duality from which free will proceeds was made manifest, which the artist pushes to its best—by sacrificing his ego to a "higher," more noble, stylized self out of a creative ambition[125]—and at the same time at its worst, since this imaginary self, born from self-consciousness, is a *played-at* self, the creator of illusions. This split implies duplicity: "But the poets lie too much."[126]

Ever since that initial fissure, the decadence—of which Socrates was already a late symptom—has not ceased. And Wagner, far from "taking up again the thread broken several thousand years ago," as Nietzsche for a moment believed, was the latest sign of this; this "Cagliostro of modernity" incarnated it with as much force as did Nietzsche himself, his alter ego. "We have reached the opposite of perfection in life and creation, and we even *wanted* to reach it—the most extreme awareness, where the human being and history see through themselves . . ."[127] "Everything" as a result "becomes play-acting."[128]

Irremediable decadence, unless—a modern paradox—to claim to recreate voluntarily (like Wotan) what was only worthwhile owing to its very spontaneity. Whence, for the late Nietzsche, the temptation of eugenics and training, which alternates with that of a cosmic dissolution into Dionysian intoxication. But one "cannot leap over his shadow" as Zarathustra demands; one throws oneself into "sparkling irreflection" only at the price of damnation and madness, Thomas Mann will say in *Doktor Faustus*, whose hero, Adrian Leverkühn, is inspired specifically by Nietzsche. And it was an unconscious buffoon, a pitiable creature possessed by Dionysus that his friend Overbeck was to discover in Turin in January 1889. Nietzsche sang, danced, pounded on the piano, "incarnating in a frightening way the orgiastic conception of sacred furor that is at the base of Greek tragedy."[129]

The other great reproach, bound to the preceding one, that Nietzsche makes to the actor, and therefore to the artist, is the actor's faculty of metamorphosing himself (as though there were no difference whatsoever between the author who draws works and characters from his multiple personality and the actor who interprets them). Wagner's crime was being able to make works in succession with such different contents and tone as *Tristan* and *Die Meistersinger*. Without being able to conceal his admiration initially—for he cherished these two works above all others—Nietzsche yet was quick to see in this protean character of the artist precisely a character flaw, one that explains his "dishonesty," or let us say, his indifference, if not distrust, for truth. But to surrender himself "to changing psychological moods of each period in his life, representing them in works that contradict each other intellectually, but that are all beautiful and worth preservation"—this is the prerogative of the artist, his very definition, according to Thomas Mann, and precisely with regard to Wagner.

> To the artist, new experiences of "truth" mean new stimuli to play, new expressive possibilities—nothing more. He believes in them—takes them seriously—only to the degree that is necessary in order to bring them to the highest pitch of expression and make the deepest possible impression with them. Consequently, he is very much in earnest about them, earnest to the point of tears—but then again, not totally, and there-

fore not *at all*. His artistic earnest is "playful earnest," and absolute by
nature. But his intellectual earnest is not absolute, for it serves as a
means to the end of play.[130]

"Leave off! . . . I did all this only as a game. Such things belong to my
art," admits the old enchanter, which is a transparent portrait of Wagner,
when Zarathustra hits him with his stick for having counterfeited Dionysian
inspiration.[131] Nietzsche doesn't play. If he too did so metamorphose himself—to the point where his commentators often find it difficult to find any
unity other than a thematic one in his works—it was in order better to track
down truth, but without renouncing art, that "beneficial" lie," and in order
to put an end to their divorce, which plunged him into a "sacred indignation."[132] Nietzsche was condemned therefore to live, in permanent tension,
in that "intermediary world between truth and beauty" where he had seen
shine, fleetingly, Greek tragedy. The "player" whom he bragged about having "found and recognized at the bottom of every artist" was only the gri-
macing figure of the artist he would have liked to discover in himself. If
Wagner had elevated the art of the actor to the level of genius, as Nietzsche
said, it is also with genius that Nietzsche played the comedy of art.

Siegfried contra Parsifal

$\mathcal{T}$here is one instance in which it seems that Nietzsche would have preferred for Wagner to be more playful. This concerns the treatment of Christianity in *Parsifal*. This had been Nietzsche's tone in *Zarathustra*, parodying the Bible and the Gospels in a frankly farcical manner. In 1888 he will write:

> I should really wish that the Wagnerian *Parsifal* were intended as a prank—as the epilogue and satyr play,[1] as it were, with which the tragedian Wagner wanted to say farewell in a fitting manner worthy of himself—to us, to himself, and above all to *tragedy*, with an excessive, sublimely wanton parody on the tragic itself, on all the former horrid earthly seriousness and earthly misery, on the *most stupid* form, of the anti-nature of the ascetic ideal. After all, Parsifal is operetta material par excellence. Is Wagner's *Parsifal* his secretly superior laughter at himself, the triumph of his ultimate artistic freedom, his artistic *non plus ultra*—Wagner able to *laugh* at himself? Clearly, one should wish that.[2]

Several times previously Nietzsche had been tempted to try to convince himself that Wagner's last work could not be born "from any serious intention." Perhaps it was simply out of a concern for respectability that Wagner had made use of Christianity, just as he had sought the favor of princes?[3] Did he think it possible to "play a bit at being a Christian, a new convert, in order to facilitate his recent reintegration into German society"?[4]

More likely, lacking any great ideas and drawing on anything and every-thing, he came to borrow as well from "Christian feelings—not really Chris-tian thoughts."[5]

It is true that the former revolutionary of 1848, prohibited from enter-ing Germany for twelve years, had been married in the Protestant church in Lucerne in 1870. He had had his son Siegfried baptized, overseen the reli-gious education of his children, and even went to church. Yet, when in 1876, most likely, just before beginning to work on *Parsifal*, he spoke to Nietzsche about "the joy he felt in receiving (Protestant) Christian communion," Nietzsche's initial response was to see in this a kind of hypocrisy, which also was revealing about what the "great actor" Wagner was at bottom: "But without restraint and inwardly prey to anything that strongly intoxicates."[6] Since Nietzsche often associated intoxication with creation, we might say that Wagner did not compose *Parsifal* because he had become a convert but rather because, in working on this project, which he had long planned to write, he developed within himself the necessary emotional and intellectual disposition. Thus at this time he both plunged into reading historians of Christianity and, unconsciously replaying the scenario of the composition of *Tristan* initiated by Mathilde Wesendonck, was smitten by Judith Gautier, who lends her charms to Kundry, whose presents of perfumes, satin, and silk stimulated his creative activity. For an artist everything is grist for his mill, especially when, persuaded he has a spiritual mission to fulfill, which is the case beginning with Romanticism, he seeks to be a prophet and the re-deemer of humanity—twenty years earlier, the "Magus" Victor Hugo forti-fied his oracular powers by consulting a Ouija board.

Before deciding that Wagner was "beaten," Nietzsche had for a time considered such an interpretation. "The actor has spirit but little conscience of spirit," says Zarathustra. "Always he has faith in that with which he in-spires the most faith—faith in himself."[7] In 1874, when *Parsifal* only existed in a rough draft, Nietzsche even seemed not to doubt that the new "dithyra-mbic dramatist" held the same attitude toward religion as did his long dis-tant predecessors:

> If Wagner sometimes takes up the Germanic Christian myth, sometimes
> marine legends, sometimes pagan German ones, sometimes the Protes-
> tant bourgeoisie, it is clear that he feels *free* as regards the *religious* mean-
> ing of this myth, and that he requires the same freedom of his listeners,
> just as the Greek dramatists and already Homer did. . . . A poet is never
> *pious*. . . . Wagner found himself at a formidable point in time: *where all*

religion of all previous ages wavers in the dogmatic effects of its idols and
fetishes: he is the tragic poet of the end of all religion, of the "twilight
of the gods."[8]

Wagner, indeed, did not believe in God, at least not in the God of
the Old Testament, whom he regarded as the basis for a narrow-minded,
repressive, and violent religion. Wagner "could not imagine God," he said
to Cosima, "only the divine." By which he meant, as a good disciple of
Feuerbach and Schopenhauer, as a "religious atheist," not a "light that illu-
mines the world from the outside, but the light that we project on the world
from inside ourselves, that is, knowledge through pity."[9] And this knowledge was manifest in its most complete, most "redemptive" form in Buddhism—which inspired a dramatic project in him, "The Conquerors," the
essence of which was absorbed into *Parsifal*—and above all, in the words of
Jesus, for he addressed himself to all men without distinction of caste or
race.[10] If Wagner did "play," it was not in the heavy-handed manner Nietzsche appreciated (*Parsifal* as a farce, or an operetta—what a witty Saxon
joke!) or with the ironic distance that Thomas Mann will attribute to him to
prevent his annexation by the Nazis.[11] He was sufficiently "serious" to merit
the reproach that Zarathustra directs against the old magician. After all,
he had no less ambition or pretension in the philosophical domain than did
Nietzsche in the artistic one. His abundant theoretical writings attest to it,
from *Art and Revolution* in 1849 up to the essay "The Feminine in the Human," which he had just drafted when death overtook him. ("Men most
willingly undertake what they least know how to do: Wagner the *writer*;
Nietzsche the *composer*," remarks aptly Martin Gregor-Dellin).[12]

From legends and myths, Wagner was determined to express the
"eternally and purely human" content by projecting into them the duality
of his nature, caught between "an indomitable desire to live" and an anar-
chistic pessimism to which his reading of Schopenhauer provided a basis
and a philosophical formulation. "Tragic poet of the end of religions," according to him, the role of art was to save "the spirit" of moribund religion,
"recognizing the figurative value of the mythic . . . and religious allegories,"
which it took to be an ideal presentment of the allegoric figure, which led
"to apprehension of its inner kernel, the truth ineffably divine" through an
ideal, freely invented representation.[13] In this way, he defended himself from
the charge of having "the Redeemer" in mind in imagining the character of
Parsifal.[14] Indeed, this latter, half-savage, half-good soul with a dash of heroism resembles less the Christ of the Gospels than his Romantic substitutes,
to which Wagner himself had failed to add his own quite human version, in

1849, with a "Jesus of Nazareth" that did not get beyond the stage of an initial project. Borrowing some of the features of Ernest Renan's "incomparable young man," whom Wagner had read about in Renan's *Origines du christianisme* as a means of getting started, this Jesus was close to Dostoevsky's *Idiot,* as Nietzsche would point out, for whom Christ was "a fascinating combination of the sublime, the sick and the childish."[15] But Parsifal also recalls Heracles freeing Prometheus and Achilles healing King Telephus with the same lance with which he had struck him, for according to the oracle, "let the one who has wounded him cure him." If the communion of the knights in the Temple of Monsalvat has all the appearances of the Roman Catholic Eucharist, there is one major exception, which is often overlooked today: freely interpreted by Wagner, the mystery of the Grail inverts the miracle of the Last Supper since for him the blood turns into wine, which "permits us to turn our gaze refreshed back to earth, whereas the conversion of wine into blood draws us away from the earth."[16] Heaven is no less present in the form of the dove of the Holy Spirit and, except for the second act, which unfolds in the realm of the sorcerer Klingsor, the whole work is suffused with an undeniable religious poetic and sonorous climate. Whence the subtitle of *Parsifal:* a scenic sacred festival (*ein Bühnenweihfestspiel*). But the fact that Wagner considered it to be "the most sacred of his works"[17] indicates that to his eyes there was just a difference of degree, not one of nature between it and those that preceded—the very pagan *Ring, Tristan,* where the word God is never pronounced. Combining, thanks to music's sovereign ambiguity, very disparate philosophical and legendary elements, what he took to be the "essence of religion" was founded on an art that had itself become a religion, Wagner saw in it an instrument of salvation, as did many other artists and writers of the nineteenth century.

This is the significance of the sibylline words—*Erlösung dem Erlöser* (redemption of the redeemer)—that the chorus sings at the work's end, after Parsifal has taken the Grail from its reliquary while asking that "it never again be locked away." In Wagner's opinion, Christ's message, prisoner of a religion that had betrayed it and become sclerotic in its dogmas and rites, was once again addressed to the whole human species. And the agent of this "redemption," which Parsifal represents on-stage, is no other, in reality, than the artist himself, "the Tone-poet seer," whose priesthood, inherited from a worn-out spiritual power, reveals in turn that "this insistent World of Will, is also but a state that vanishes before the One." "Wafted beyond the temple walls, the holy strains of Music" teach "redemption-starved mankind a second speech in which the Infinite can voice itself with clearest definition."[18] The high priest of art, Wagner liked to say, is the only one who has never lied.

With *Parsifal*—in embryonic form already in 1845, the year of *Tann-häuser* (so "Christian" in its finale), which takes up again the theme of the Grail outlined in *Lohengrin*—his work seemed to him to circle back on itself. If *The Ring* pleased him because there was not "in it the least spark of Christianity," nevertheless, Wagner did think, without seeing any contradiction in this, that "Siegfried ought to have turned into Parsifal and redeemed Wotan" from the curse of power, just as he could have "redeemed" Tristan from the spells of love.[19] At the end of his life, looking back at his finished works as a harmonious whole, Wagner was not yielding to a retrospective illusion. The seeds for all the parts of this whole were present during the first ten years of his creative activity, and they give the impression of having been developed in succession with the rigor of a genetic program, each one reflecting, in the color proper to it, one of the facets of the poet-composer—to the point where inquiry into their chronology can seem superfluous.

During the course of their genesis, though, certain inflections or changes had occurred. Perhaps Parsifal would not have succeeded Siegfried if this latter, born from the revolutionary hope of 1848 (with Bakunin as his godfather), had not perished under the blows of a firmly restored order, leaving no other exit to his creator than exile and resignation.

"Whoever Awakens Me Wounds Me"

Siegfried represented the "male-embodied spirit of the perennial and sole creative Instinct (*Unwillkür*) . . . of *Manhood* in the utmost fulness of its inborn strength and proved loveworthiness."[20] Nietzsche recognized the vague aspirations that tormented him in this "free and fearless man, the fruit of a union against all ethics"[21]—whom for a time Wagner cherished more than any of his heroes and as "the most beautiful of my life-dreams."[22] This identification was all the easier for Nietzsche since it was under the sign of Siegfried that his first visits to Tribschen took place. Wagner was then completing, with Dionysian accents, the composition of the work that retraces his heroic deeds. Three years later, Nietzsche will write to Wagner:

> Have I already told you that I rediscovered the passage you were composing the first time I came to see you in Tribschen?
>
> It was the Saturday evening of Pentecost, stifling, heavy, luxuriant; around us, all was growing, everything fragrant. For a long time I did not dare to enter the house; I waited awhile, hidden among the trees, just in front of the window from which came, with the greatest insistence, the

echo of a series of repeated chords. I swear that it was the passage "Whoever awakens me wounds me."

As if in bronze, those sounds have remained engraved in my memory, and I played and sang them to myself a long time before having [the score] in hand. They seemed to me to say so much.[23]

To be sure. Without being revolutionary, Nietzsche will soon see in Siegfried the incarnation of a vital force capable of sweeping away "our old exhausted Socratic-Alexandrine-civilization." And in its music he will believe himself to hear "the earthquake through which some primeval force that has been dammed up for ages finally liberates itself—indifferent whether everything else that one calls culture might begin to tremble."[24] A passage from *Richard Wagner in Bayreuth*, generally overlooked by commentators (even though it is one of the key texts on his approaching disenchantment), bears witness to the enthusiasm the slightly gauche yet respectful philologist then felt for this sylvan enemy of laws. Its "optimistic" tone echoes Heine's solemn prophecy concerning the reawakening of the German gods of nature:

No golden age, no cloudless sky is allotted to these coming generations toward which Wagner's instinct directs him. . . . Nor will suprahuman goodness and justice stretch like an immobile rainbow over the fields of this future. Perhaps this generation will seem on the whole even more evil than the present one—for it will be *more open,* in evil as in good; indeed, it is possible that if its soul were ever to speak out in a full, free voice, it would shake up and terrify our soul in much the same way as if had heard the voice of some previously hidden evil spirit of nature.[25]

Ten years later, in *Beyond Good and Evil,* after having shown that Wagner, having drawn upon the late French Romanticism of the 1840s, was not as "German" as his friends claimed, Nietzsche nonetheless concludes with praise for Siegfried, that purely German hero:

Perhaps it will be found after a subtler comparison that, to the honor of Richard Wagner's German nature, his doings were in every respect stronger, more audacious, harder, and higher than anything a Frenchman of the nineteenth century could manage—thanks to the fact that we Germans are still closer to barbarism than the French. Perhaps Wagner's strangest creation is inaccessible, inimitable, and beyond the feelings of the whole, so mature, Latin race, not only today but forever: the figure of Siegfreid, that *very free* man who may indeed be much too free, too hard, too cheerful, too healthy, too *anti-Catholic* for the taste of ancient and mellow cultured peoples.[26]

And too much to the taste of his creator, Nietzsche clearly implies, since he renounced him in *Parsifal:* the rebellious scherzo of the "son of the woods" had precipitated a liberating cataclysm, yet above the ruins of the ancient world arose anew the *lamento* of hunted-down, accursed, wounded heroes in quest of nothingness or redemption that will be brought about by a "pure fool" (*reine Tor*), a "country simpleton" filled with pity. "By new ways toward ancient Hellenism," notes Nietzsche in 1884, "I thought I could redeem the *German in you*—Your Parsifal, caricature of your Siegfried."[27] If *Parsifal* was "meant seriously," then was it, like the Gospel, an "apostasy," a work of rancor and vengeance, "and ultimately a self-negation, a self-cancellation on the part of an artist who had hitherto aimed with all the power of his will at the reverse, at the *highest spiritualization and sensualization* of his art? And not of his art only, of his life, too."[28]

Against Wagner-Wotan, the old, worn-out, incurably Schopenhauerian god, who "casts a longing glance" at the cross, Nietzsche will want to be the heir of Siegfried in order "to accomplish the task whose accomplishment had been refused to the god."[29] The "hammer" of the philosopher who smashes idols, who "breaks history into two," is no longer that of the piano tuner attentive to his "hollow sounds," the hammer with which the "utterly free" hero has succeeded in forging his sword, instinctually, disregarding knowledge intoned by the dwarf Mime. And when Nietzsche will dream of a new elite, destined to fight against the "shrinking and leveling down of European man," how can we fail to see in Siegfried the first sketch of those "tall blond Germans," primitive yet carefully chosen, who will give men again the taste for adventure and unbelief, after having pronounced an inexorable condemnation "against everything that had been believed, demanded, hallowed so far"?[30]

"You can now free me from much, even from half of my mission. And maybe in so doing you will fully be serving your own," Wagner had written to Nietzsche in February 1870, before appointing him his "prophet" in 1872 in the "open letter" in which he defended *The Birth of Tragedy* against the attacks philologists had directed against it. There he said,

What we expect of you can only be the task of a lifetime, of the lifetime of a man for whom we have the most urgent need, such as you proclaim yourself to be to all those who call upon the purest sources of the German spirit, with the great seriousness that he brings to everything to which he devotes himself, insight into and indications of what German culture must be, in order to assist the reborn nation to attain its noblest goals.

"Wagner was finally right," Nietzsche will note in 1888. "*Now* he is right. I am the only *major force* strong enough to save the Germans, and in the end, not just the Germans. . . . Perhaps he forgot that if I was destined to show the way to culture, I had also perhaps to show it to Richard Wagner. Culture and *Parsifal*—they don't go together."[31] Wagner, in his eyes, had stopped along the way, held back by the sirens of the ancient world—something for which Nietzsche would not forgive him, as can be seen from the constant way in which he broods over his deception in his books and even more so in his notes:

> 1878: "I imagined . . . I had discovered in Wagner's art the way to a German paganism, at least a bridge toward a specifically un-Christian view of the world and human beings."[32]

> 1884: "I only loved the Wagner that I knew, that is, an upright atheist and immoralist, who had invented the character Siegfried."[33]

> 1886: "Old Romantics collapse and find themselves, who knows how, prostrated before the cross: this is also what happened to Richard Wagner. To have to view the degeneration of such a man is one of the most painful experiences I have lived through."[34]

> 1887: "What I appreciated in Wagner was the good bit of Antichristian represented in his art and his manner (oh, so clever!). I am the most disappointed of all Wagnerians; for at the moment when more than ever it was respectable to be pagan, he turned Christian."[35]

A Belated Courage

If we are to believe Nietzsche, and many docile commentators who followed, the separation must have had the quickness and sharpness of a duel. "By a miraculously meaningful coincidence," he will write in *Ecce Homo*, at the very moment when two copies of *Human, All Too Human* were on their way to Bayreuth, "I received . . . a beautiful copy of the text of *Parsifal*, with

Wagner's inscription for me, 'for his dear friend, Friedrich Nietzsche, Richard Wagner, Church Councilor.'—This crossing of the two books—I felt as if I heard an ominous sound—as if two swords had crossed."[36]

Seeking to stylize his existence retroactively, Nietzsche was hardly going to let the facts get in the way. The libretto of *Parsifal* had come to him on 3 January 1878, four months before the publication of *Human, All Too Human*. And Wagner's actual dedication said: "To his dear friend Friedrich Nietzsche, Richard Wagner (member of the church council—to be communicated in a friendly way to Professor Overbeck)." Since Franz Overbeck, of all Nietzsche's friends the one Wagner liked most, had published a pamphlet recommending a critical theology wholly free toward Christianity, Wagner's dedication had an ironic sense, the opposite of the one Nietzsche attributes to it (and which, taking him at his word, all his commentators subsequently attribute to it). As for the libretto, its contents could hardly have surprised him. Nietzsche had read an early prose draft on 25 December 1869 at Tribschen, in the company of Cosima.[37] "May the marvelous promise of *Parsifal* console us in all those situations where one needs consolation," he wrote to her on 10 October 1877. Therefore, if, as he will note ten years later, it was starting in 1876 that he had understood "with terror what Wagner wanted to get to," his "compromised will" nonetheless remained silent.[38]

"One only belatedly has the courage for what one really *knows*," he will note a number of times in his notebooks from 1886 to 1888.[39] Without a clear, imperative consciousness of one's strength and one's goal, which protects against too precocious an adaptation to a situation or a task, by setting aside "the dangers of modesty," the best one can do is to dissimulate: "To defend oneself against [other people's] love with an involuntary distrust, to learn to maintain silence by concealing it by speaking, to create for oneself inner recesses and undivinable solitudes for moments of relief, tears, sublime consolation—until one is finally strong enough to say: 'What do I have to do with *you?*' and go off on one's *own* way."[40] Reports about Nietzsche during his youth and his years of teaching describe him as calm, timid, modest, measured in his speaking to the point of affectation; it was not easy to see in him, given the thoughts he concealed, any touchiness or the "explosive violence" to which he was sometimes subject.[41] "Dissimulating, devious, subterranean," like Socrates in *Twilight of the Idols*, what most preoccupied him "more than anyone else, he could lock away within himself, keeping it hermetically sealed with an extraordinary energy," Overbeck will write (just as he was the one who said that his friend had never believed in himself):

I had this experience many times, but the impression I have kept of him was never so vivid as in 1874–75 when he confided in me what he thought about Wagner and his *Lohengrin*. These confidences already anticipated *The Case of Wagner*. They passed in front of my stupefied eyes and disappeared with the rapidity of a bolt of lightening, not to return again for many years. Indeed, over the course of our relationship and for a long time, Nietzsche did not again allow such things to escape him, and, in 1876, he wrote *Richard Wagner in Bayreuth* for the public.[42]

In 1876, however disappointed he might have been by Bayreuth or whatever reservations he might have had about *Parsifal,* as he would confide in his notes, Nietzsche was too "solidly bound to Wagner, by all the bonds of a profound unity of needs, by gratitude, by his irreplaceability and absolute readiness to sacrifice" that he saw before him, to abruptly break free and go his own way.[43] Even when he risked doing so, in *Human, All Too Human*, it was not with that "prodigious assurance" trumpeted by *Ecce Homo*, since at first he wanted to publish it under a pseudonym. But as it was impossible to leave Wagner uninformed, Nietzsche planned to write him (the rough draft was found among his notes):

In sending you the enclosed books, I place my secret trustingly into your hands and the hands of your noble spouse, and I assume that from now on it will be your secret too. This book is by me: in it, I have brought to light my innermost feelings about people and things and, for the first time, encircled the periphery of my own thinking. In times that were full of paroxysms and torments, this book was a means of solace which never failed when all other means failed. Perhaps I am alive today because I was capable of writing it.—A pseudonym had to be chosen, first of all because I did not want to interfere with the effect of my earlier writings; and then, because the public and private defilement of my personal dignity was thereby to be prevented (my health no longer can endure such things); finally and especially, because I wished to make an *objective* discussion possible, one in which also my so intelligent friends of all kinds could participate without any delicacy of feelings getting in the way as earlier.[44]

But his publisher refused to go along with this stratagem. He wanted Nietzsche's signature and welcomed a bit of scandal. So Nietzsche wrote a dedication to Wagner, meant to be bantering to suggest that one was not to take the book too seriously. Comparing his "new child" to a "recently born kid" impatient to "romp in the mountains," the "free Spirit" that had brought it to light asked for "the Master's benediction, and the wise graces of the mistress."[45] Previously, though, the name Wagner had everywhere been removed and replaced by the word "artist." However, the sometimes hurtful allusions that targeted the composer and Cosima could not be missed by them or any alert reader. If *Parsifal* is not named, it is indicated by an unmistakable innuendo: against the torments provoked by knowledge, frivolity or melancholy is always better than "a romantic return and desertion, an approach to Christianity in any form: for, given the current state of knowledge, one can no longer have any association with it without incurably dirtying one's intellectual conscience and prostituting it before oneself and others."[46] Yet in 1882 a sign from Wagner would probably have sufficed so that Nietzsche would have attended the premiere of *Parsifal* at Bayreuth, where he would have run into Lou Salomé with whom he was much taken at that time.[47] "This time, I will shine by my absence from Bayreuth," he wrote in January to Ida Overbeck, "at least if Wagner does not give me a personal invitation (which would fit perfectly with my conception of a 'higher propriety')."[48] That Wagner did not take propriety to the point of forgetting *Human, All Too Human*, "The Wanderer and His Shadow," and *Daybreak* left this "extra-lucid psychologist" bitterly deceived and vexed.[49] "Two years ago," he writes to Heinrich von Stein on 22 May 1884, "I spoke with a kind of anger of the fact that an event like *Parsifal* had to unfold far away from me, precisely from *me*; and now again, when I have a second reason for going to Bayreuth—namely, *you*, my dear Doctor, who are part of my great 'hopes'—now again I doubt whether I *may* go there. For the following reason: the law that stands over me, my *task*, leaves me no time."[50]

From now on Nietzsche feels completely free to accomplish his *task* without having to disguise himself or to take precautions: Wagner had died the preceding year. Stirred up by the rancor that he had felt since the success of *Parsifal* at seeing himself deprived of "all those, in Germany, whom it would make sense to affect," he can allow his hostility to express itself publicly.[51] The blows from his rod that Zarathustra, the anti-Wotan and anti-Parsifal, inflicts on the "old magician" in the last part of the book of the same name, written between 1883 and 1885, are a prelude to the "third essay" of *On the Genealogy of Morals* and the last pamphlets. Nietzsche fights against Wagner's influence, however, with less restraint once he has persuaded himself that in so doing he is remaining faithful to the ideal that his old mentor had betrayed: "One must liberate Richard Wagner's great cause from his personal defects, defects that became principles; in this sense I mean to lay a hand, gladly, on *his* works and to prove, retrospectively, that we did not come together merely 'by accident,'" he writes to Overbeck in 1884. Two years later, he again writes: "It's marvelous how all Wagner's partisans still like me; they ought to know that I believe today as much as in the past in the ideal that Wagner believed in—it doesn't matter that I stumble over the many human, all too human things with which Wagner himself blocked his way."[52]

An Insurmountable Kinship

Precipitating the hesitations and doubts that had built up within him, Wagner's "conversion" was experienced by Nietzsche as a "mortal offense," a betrayal (every traitor to a cause begins by claiming that it is the cause, through its degeneration, that has betrayed him) for it occurred at a time when, sustained by his Greco-Wagnerian vision, Nietzsche had the feeling of having freed himself of the Christian religion and he could believe that the work of the "new dithyrambic dramatist" would purge the German soul of it as well.[53] "I hoped that art might make the Germans sick of *stale Christianity*— seeing German mythology weakening, accustoming them to polytheism, etc. What horror when I see the *restorative* currents!"[54]

In the antiliberal climate the followed the failure of Bismarck's *Kulturkampf* against the Roman Catholic church, which deepened the sense of moral and cultural uneasiness provoked by the rapid industrialization of the Reich, the success of *Parsifal* had an air of something like a religious "revival," of a challenge to the forces of modernity. This is what the "horned Wagnerians" by means of the *Bayreuther Blätter* hastened to accredit, by making the testament of the master's work the gospel of a Germano-Christian religion marked by strong nationalist and racist overtones. Nietzsche, who at bottom would never deny his allegiance to the Enlightenment as contracted in *Human, All Too Human,* could only lambaste the "frightful obscurantism of Bayreuth."[55] "Never has there been such a mortal *hate* of knowledge," he will say about *Parsifal* in *The Case of Wagner* after having accused its author, in large part for tactical reasons—although Wagner detested Catholicism—of preaching "the road to Rome," thereby confusing him with Liszt.[56] And since he proclaimed himself the heir of the "true Wagner," he had to present the "apostasy" of *Parsifal* as an "unexpected event"[57] caused by accidents of circumstance: opportunism, the effects of age—"it was the old Wagner against whom I had to defend myself"[58]—and, above all, the role of Cosima: "Liszt's daughter with her Catholic instincts" through whom the composer, who "did not merit her" (read: who a Nietzsche did merit!), is supposed to have "succumbed, out of respect for her," we read in his notes.[59] This, at least, is the allusive version suggested in *The Case of Wagner,* but those in the know could not fail to get the point:

> The danger for artists, for geniuses . . . is woman: adoring women confront them with corruption. Hardly any of them have character enough not to be corrupted—or "redeemed"—when they find themselves treated like gods: soon they condescend to the level of the women.— Man is a coward, confronted with the Eternal-Feminine—and the females know it.—In many cases of feminine love, perhaps including the most famous ones above all, love is merely a more refined form of parasitism, a form of nestling down in another soul, sometimes even in the flesh of another—alas, always decidedly at the expense of "the host"![60]

This is how, according to the official version of his old propagandist, Wagner became "Wagnerian"—instead of becoming Nietzschean.

Yet this betrayal, as Nietzsche had to acknowledge more or less implicitly in his books, could not have taken place without the blind eye he had turned toward Wagner and toward himself. Was not the fact that the composer of *Siegfried* could easily transform himself into that of *Parsifal* the result of some profound logic? Beyond the fact that this new metamorphosis served to unmask the actor in Wagner, it revealed that his music, and with it all Romantic music of which it is the quintessence, once freed of external constraints was in fact rooted in "the desolation of the ancient world" and its misleading idealism.

But what Nietzsche himself—whose first musical impressions were closely tied up with religious emotions—had first loved about Wagner, according to his own admission, was "as in Schopenhauer . . . the ethical air, the Faustian odor, Cross, Death and Grave, and so on."[61] Following which, strengthened in his desire to forge for himself the soul of a Hellenic Siegfried, he concealed from himself the true nature of the pleasure this music so often gave him, and not just this music. Later, in his notebooks, he will admit, not without a touch of the casuist's duplicity, "disguised pacification of the *religiosi*," music allows one to assuage those impulses that want "*to be, in any case, satisfied.*"[62]

> That music itself ignores words, concepts, images, oh, how well it knows how to draw its advantage from this, the cunning feminine "eternal feminine"! . . . Even the most honest conscience need feel no shame—it remains outside. It is healthy, and clever, and insofar as it expresses shame

in the face of the paltriness of all religious judgment, it is even a good sign . . .

If, on the other hand, one opposes to this, as Wagner did . . . religious symbolism as in *Parsifal* . . . such music gives rise to indignation.[63]

If these misdemeanors had a bit of hypocrisy about them, one was nonetheless permitted to assuage his religious instinct on the condition that it was on the sly, almost unknown to oneself, and seasoned with regret. With his incorrigible taste for theater, the Wagner of *Parsifal*, in effect, had compromised this illicit pleasure: the intellectual conscience being plainly involved, it was impossible to allow oneself the least indulgence. Yet a year earlier Nietzsche could ask Peter Gast, "Has Wagner ever done *better?*" having heard the prelude to the work for the first time at Monte Carlo. Always the casuist, this was a "purely aesthetic" judgment, he hastened to add, in order to allow to himself as musician what he forbade himself as philosopher.

> The finest psychological intelligence and definition of what must be said here, expressed, *communicated*, the briefest and most direct form for it, every nuance of feeling pared down to an epigram; a clarity in the music as descriptive art, bringing to mind a feeling, experience, happening of the soul at the basis of the music, which does Wagner the highest credit, a synthesis of states that will seem incompatible to many people, even "loftier" people, with a severity that judges, an "altitude" in the terrifying sense of the word, with an intimate cognizance and perspicuity that cuts through the soul like a knife—and with a compassion for what is being *watched* and *judged*. Something of that sort occurs in *Dante*— nowhere else. Has any painter ever painted such a melancholy gaze of love as Wagner did with the last accents of his prelude?[64]

This letter rivals the analysis of the prelude to *Die Meistersinger* that appears in *Beyond Good and Evil*. But in his working notes prior to this letter, Nietzsche, before putting on the mask of the Antichrist, offers a more sincere version of what he really felt:

> Prelude to *Parsifal*, the greatest satisfaction granted me in a very long time. . . . I know of nothing that grasps Christianity at such a depth and that so sharply leads to compassion.
>
> As though after many years someone finally spoke to me about the problems that disturb me, not naturally to give them the answers that I

hold ready, but Christian answers—though mine has ultimately been the answer of stronger souls than our last two centuries have produced. Indeed, on hearing this music one sets aside Protestantism as a misunderstanding: just as Wagner's music at Monte Carlo led me, I don't want to deny it, also to set aside as a misunderstanding of music the *very good music* heard in other places (Haydn, Berlioz, Brahms, Reyer's *Sigurd* overture). Strange! As a child I gave myself the mission of bringing the mystery onstage . . .[65]

Five years earlier, while he was helping his sister to hear *Parsifal*, Nietzsche had had the troubling impression that it was "precisely the kind of music" he practiced in his youth when he composed his oratorio. "The *identity* of *mood* and *expression* was fabulous! Yes, a few parts . . . seemed to us more moving than anything we had played from *Parsifal*, and yet they were wholly Parsifalesque!" (Having preceded Wagner before "surpassing" him, Nietzsche, to be sure, could only have done better). And it is with a "real fright" that he had seen "*how* closely [he was] *akin* to Wagner."[66] In 1887, on hearing the prelude, the sense of that kinship will exasperate him: once again, and with no possible "Tartufferie" this time, in "drinking the forbidden cup," Nietzsche discovered that the genial actor was telling him the profound, indisputable truth of his nature. Whence the attacks and sarcasms of *The Case of Wagner*, which include this admission: "I admire this work; I wish I had written it myself; failing that, *I understand it*."[67]

From Flower Maidens to the Maidens of the Desert

Experienced in "looking in every nook and cranny" of the soul—at least of his own, if not that of others—Nietzsche must have indeed felt closer to the characters in this "antinature" drama than to Siegfried, the solar hero driven to conquer the woman because of the fear she made him feel for the first time. If Nietzsche stigmatizes Wagner for having apparently rejected a sensuality whose healthy and liberating character he had praised in his youth, following Feuerbach, it is with the same indignation that this bard of the body condemns him for having made it the demoralizing impulse of his music ("sensuousness which in turn makes the spirit weary and worn-out").[68] This includes *Parsifal*, in which "the nebulous ideal" of Catholicism "allows the 'spell' to act on one unknowingly, innocently, *Christianly*."[69] Far then from rejoicing that the music insidiously contradicts what it is supposed to make one believe, in his notebooks and letters during 1888 Nietzsche denounces it for its "repugnant sexuality," "that incredibly sick sexuality" said to have been "the curse of Wagner's life,"[70] in this way yielding to the pressure of something repressed that over the last years of his conscious life will bit by bit overcome his defenses (his declaration of love to Ariadne-Cosima will be another flagrant example of this).

"Do I need to add that Wagner also owes his *success* to his sensuality? That his music wins over the lowest of instincts? . . . —Who has dared to name, *really* to name the ardors of the music of *Tristan?* I put on gloves when I read the score of *Tristan*," he exclaims, shifting from the invective of a Lenten preacher to the tight-lipped tone of a Wilhelmian bourgeois,[71] typical of that "moraline-sour, old-maidish Germany" he makes fun of in *The Case of Wagner* for having "crossed themselves against Goethe, against the 'unclean spirit' in Goethe."[72]

"It is simply not possible that a human being should *not* have the qualities and preferences of his parents and ancestors in his body, whatever appearances may suggest to the contrary."[73] As the descendant of a long line of pastors, Nietzsche could not escape his heredity. And far from deviating from them, in his case appearances—the grandiloquent poses of Zarathustra, the vengeful aphorisms against women drawn from two or three comic misadventures—only confirm this. Even during his first visits to Tribschen, the irregular character of the liaison between Wagner and Cosima, still at the time a von Bülow, bothered him a lot. And when their marriage made things legal, no one was happier or more relieved.[74] Wagner was often irritated by Nietzsche's chastity, "and he would suddenly break forth in the coarsest and most objectionable expressions concerning himself and Frau Cosima," reports Elisabeth Förster-Nietzsche, who we can trust on this point, given that she was so concerned to defend her brother's virtue.[75] "I am, for example, by no means a bogey, or a moralistic monster—I am actually the very opposite of the type of man who so far has been revered as virtuous. Between ourselves, it seems to me that precisely this is part of my pride. I am a disciple of the philosopher Dionysus: I should prefer to be even a satyr to being a saint," he boasts in *Ecce Homo,* he whom his neighbors in Genoa called *"il piccolo santo."*[76] "A Puritan turned boaster," Paul Valéry will say.[77]

The Puritan shows himself twice over in the partial, mutilated conception he offers of Christianity, following in the wake of Schopenhauer, and that he pins on *Parsifal:* all belief in God, in transcendence weakens humanity and depreciates life. "Open your ears: everything that ever grew on the soil of *impoverished* life, all of the counterfeiting of transcendence and beyond, has found its most sublime advocate in Wagner's art," he warns in *The Case of Wagner.*[78] And shortly thereafter, in *Twilight of the Idols,* he writes, "a Christian who is at the same time an artist *does not exist.* . . . Let no one be childish and cite Raphael as an objection . . . Raphael said Yes, Raphael *did* Yes, consequently Raphael was not a Christian . . ."[79]

Besides the fact that these two statements, subsidiarily, seem to deny Wagner the status of being an artist, they violently ignore the central tenet of Christianity that distinguishes it from other religions: the Incarnation— "the Word was made flesh and dwelt among us." By assuming human nature to bring about the salvation of human beings, Christ raised creation to God and conferred on each individual human, body and soul, a singular, unique value. Moreover, it is significant that Nietzsche set Christ in opposition not with the figure of Apollo, that "apotheosis of the *principium individuationis,*"[80] but with his martyr, Dionysus, whose body was dismembered by the Titans and divided into an infinity of suffering individuals who only aspire to regain their original unity. As the distance he took regarding paintings of the human body and his hostility to theater already predicted, Nietzsche, whose illnesses never allowed him to forget the infirmities of the flesh, resented incarnation as a painful fatality.

Assuredly, Raphael could be both Christian and artist at the same time, as were those other artists who celebrated the mystery of God made man, which constitutes the background of the Grail legend that Wagner used in *Parsifal.* Wagner illustrated this in his own way in the scene called "The Enchantment of Holy Friday"—the highest point of the work for many—where in union with transfigured nature every creature gains its "day of innocence" by participating in the transcendent. Nietzsche says not a word about it—and could not say anything after having suggested that Wagner was not an artist, other than, given this passage of great musical beauty, that he, Wagner, was clearly not Christian.

Furthermore, in accusing religion of being fundamentally antiartistic, Nietzsche was turning back against the composer a theme that he himself had briefly defended in 1849 in *Art and Revolution* before recognizing that "the soul of music" had been "redeemed" by Christianity.[81] This is an ironic reversal of which Nietzsche seems not to have been aware, for if he had recalled this work, he would certainly not have failed to cite it as supplementary proof of Wagner's recantation. But neither was this thesis always his own, contrary to what Nietzsche claims in his last writings where he strives to show that opposition to Christianity—"Dionysus contra the Crucified"— formed a permanent, if not dominant, theme in his work from the beginning. In *Human, All Too Human,* where it is said that "music was the *Counterrenaissance* in the domain of art," he nevertheless does acknowledge, following Wagner, "how profoundly indebted we are to the religious life," for without it, modern music filled with "feeling" would not have seen the light of day.[82] *The Birth of Tragedy* had already hinted at this. The true target of this hymn to art, he affirms in the 1886 preface, could easily be deduced from "the careful and hostile silence with which Christianity is treated throughout the whole work. . . . Christian teaching, which is, and wants to be, *only* moral and which relegates art, *every* art, to the realm of *lies . . .* judges, and damns art."[83] But there is no need for "an ear behind the ear" such as Nietzsche asks from his readers to perceive that far from being hostile, this silence—which perhaps is more embarrassed than prudent—allows a favorable evaluation on the aesthetic level to leak out. Indeed, if Nietzsche does not go so far as to openly associate the Dionysian with religion, he does present them almost as fellow travelers, even as accomplices in the long traversal across the desert that followed the downfall of ancient tragedy.

Expelled from Hellenic soil by Socrates, he writes, Dionysus "sought refuge in the depths of the sea, namely the mystical flood of a secret cult which gradually covered the earth"[84] (it is easy to recognize a reference to Christianity, as several working notes from this period confirm).[85] "In its strangest metamorphoses and debasements, [it] does not cease to attract serious natures,"[86] and the Dionysian spirit ends up returning to the light of day in the German Reformation, thanks to the chorale created by Luther— "this calamity of a monk," *Ecce Homo* will say, who restored "Christianity, at the very moment *when it was vanquished.*"[87]

> It is from this abyss that the German Reformation came forth; and in its chorales the future tune of German music resounded for the first time. So deep, courageous, and spiritual, so exuberantly good and tender did this chorale of Luther sound—as the first Dionysian luring call breaking forth from dense thickets at the approach of spring. And in competing echoes the solemnly exuberant procession of Dionysian revelers responded, to whom we are indebted for German music.[88]

This, *The Birth of Tragedy* concludes, culminates in Wagner, rejected six years afterward for his "conversion" to Christianity, that religion which "denies and damns all art." From *On the Genealogy of Morals* to *Nietzsche contra Wagner,* Nietzsche will concentrate his fire regarding *Parsifal* on two notions linked to this theme, without being specifically Christian: chastity and pity; the former in particular, which he turns into Wagner's ultimate credo by confusing it with continence, with renunciation. It is true that the magician Klingsor's self-mutilation has made him continent, even while continuing to desire, because he only saw in love the domination of the body. But Wagner did not take love—the union of bodies and souls—to be a curse, as *Siegfried* and *Tristan* demonstrate. Amfortas is the son of Titurel and Parsifal, we know, the father of *Lohengrin*. "How did Wagner fall for that?" sniggers Nietzsche. But what would his sarcasm have been if Wagner (like some "feminist" directors today) had concluded with the union of his "country simpleton" and Kundry, that "hysterical woman," that "old, corrupt woman" only just escaped from a place of ill repute?[89] "The preaching of chastity remains an incitement to anti-nature," he repeats. "I despise everyone who does not experience *Parsifal* as an attempted assassination of basic ethics."[90] His insistence on this is revealing if we compare these texts with his notes from the same period, in which Nietzsche (before Freud) maintains that art draws its "affirmative" character from being the fruit of a sublimated sexuality, or, to use his own term, "idealized." As it is "one and the same force that one spends in the conceiving of art and the sexual act," he writes, "one's dominant instinct *wants* the artist to be chaste," for "if he wastes himself in the sexual act he betrays himself. . . . This can be a sign of decadence and, in any case, reduces the value of his art in an incalculable way."[91] And again: "Making music is also in a way to make children: chastity is simply the economy of the artist."[92]

However disputable it might be—think, among others, of Bach with his twenty-eight children and more than three hundred cantatas, to say nothing of the rest of his production—this simply physiological, mechanistic conception of artistic creation, like a zero sum game with an economic, shameful sexuality, at least provides an unmistakable autobiographical accent.

"The most virulent utterances against the senses have *not* come from the impotent, *nor* from ascetics, but from those who found it impossible to be ascetics, from those who stood in need of being ascetics . . ."[93] By his own admission, possessing only an "impoverished" vitality ("my father's *wicked* heritage"), Nietzsche no doubt reproached himself for not having resisted the advances of the "flower-maidens" as calmly as Parsifal: this is what that poem in *Thus Spoke Zarathustra* suggests, that poem addressed to the "daughters of the wilderness"—those "felines, Doudou and Souleika"—that "orientalized poem" in whose "grotesquely jesting tone" Thomas Mann discerned "the pangs of mortified sensuality."[94]

A Super-Ascetic

There wasn't always a piano available to allow Nietzsche to turn away from the apparitions "of spangles and gauze," of "flashing skirts promising many things." And his health, as is well known, suffered cruelly as a result. It was Amfortas more than Parsifal that he resembled: the wounded, sinful king, victim of Klingsor's spells, whom adoration of the Grail, the source of life for knights, condemns to torture—until a simpleton, made clairvoyant by pity, can bring him a cure.

Yet Nietzsche, who day after day had to conquer each thought, each page through suffering, could only rear back before such a Schopenhauerian celebration of pity, to which Wagner's music lends powerful seduction. This is all the more so since, unlike Amfortas, who renounced fulfilling the sacred office in order to put an end, through death, to his sufferings, Nietzsche, for his part, saw in his own sufferings, those of the body confirming those of the spirit, a justification of his *task*. It was out of his experience of pain and by taking sides against himself that the author of *Human, All Too Human* understood that he had rediscovered his own path and found the truth again.[95] "Only great pain is the ultimate liberator of the spirit."[96] And "it almost determines the order of rank *how* profoundly human beings can suffer."[97] Starting in 1876, whenever he speaks of *his* philosophy, he always refers to it as that "which mistreats him to the very root of his being."[98]

> Spirit is the life that itself cuts into life: with its own agony it increases its
> own knowledge. Did you know that? [demands Zarathustra]. . . . You
> know only the spark of the spirit, but you do not see the anvil it is, nor
> the cruelty of its hammer.[99]

That Nietzsche sought suffering "consciously and passionately," like a privilege, a sign of election—what he also called the "decadent" side of his nature—was something Lou Salomé realized soon after meeting him. The poem "To Pain" that she sent him shortly thereafter could not have been better chosen:

> Life without you—certainly it would be beautiful
> But you as well, pain, you are worth experiencing.[100]

Nietzsche could not read these verses without weeping. It sounded "like the resonance of a voice" that he had been "waiting and waiting for since childhood."[101] A short time later, in August 1882, when *Parsifal* was triumphing at Bayreuth, he took up an old composition and set to it another of Lou Salomé's poems with a similar tone: "Prayer to Life," which would become the "Hymn to Life," and he wished that this "lied" could somehow be performed publicly—"in order to seduce people to [his] philosophy."[102]

As the friend loves the friend,
O Mysterious Life, thus I love you!
Whether I rejoiced in you or I wept
Whether you gave me joy or pain,
I love you with all your good and bad!
And when you have to crush me,
I will tear myself from you with pain,
like a friend from the arms of a friend!
With all my strength, I embrace you!
Let your flame set my spirit ablaze!
In the fire of struggle let me discover
The solution to the riddle of your being!
To think and live for millennia
Throw me that with which your hands are filled
If you have no more happiness to give,
You can give me your pain![103]

On receiving this work, Gast was astonished by its "very somber" character. The music "sounds Christian," he wrote to Nietzsche. "If you had sent it to me without the text I would have taken it for a 'Crusaders' March'—Christianity ready for battle [Christisch-Kriegerisch]. The sharp dissonances which you multiply give me the impression of shields clashing. In its sonorous translation there is a vindictive and warlike emotion."[104] And when Nietzsche replied that he considered this piece "as a commentary on *The Gay Science*, a sort of accompanying bass," the "faithful Kurvenal" set aside his customary deference: "Contrary to what you say, I affirm that my idea of music for *The Gay Science* does not correspond to what you have composed—otherwise you are not very far from the philosophy of the knights of the Grail" (an allusion to the martial choruses from the first act of *Parsifal*). "It's true church music! [É la vera musica ecclesiastica!]," exclaimed two Venetian musicians for whom he played the hymn a few years later. Protesting the label "church music," Gast translated the text for them, and one of the two commented that then it was not what he had imagined, for in hearing the work he had in mind the night of Calvary with its stations of the Cross.[105]

Nietzsche did not reply to these judgments, a sign that they must not have displeased him, all the more so since Gast, his judgment clouded by "the idyllic heroism" of *The Gay Science*, could not understand the significance they had for his "Venerated Professor."[106] Thanks to the counterpoint of music and text, Nietzsche probably believed that he had composed a work that was "Parsifalesque" (as, in his opinion, was the oratorio he had composed in his youth) yet more genuinely religious than *Parsifal* and that proclaimed a contrary message, by radicalizing the basic theme of Wagner's drama through the lyrical acceptance of suffering. This conviction would confirm itself in that, after having heard the prelude to *Parsifal*, Nietzsche asked Gast, in 1887, to adapt his hymn for orchestra and mixed choir, then tried to get it performed, albeit unsuccessfully.

Twice stated, the first time *fortissimo*, the second *pianissimo*, between heavy silences, the final verse—"You can give me your pain! [Wohlan! Noch hast du deine Pein . . .]"—was meant to sound like "the ultimate of *hubris* in the Greek sense, in its blasphemous challenging of destiny by an excess of spirit and exuberance." "I still feel a slight shudder when I see (and hear) the phrase," he will say to Gast, adding (a reflection that Gast evidently was incapable of grasping), "this small link with music and almost with composers, to which this hymn *does* testify, is something of inestimable value with respect to the psychological problem that I am."[107] In *Ecce Homo*, he associates this work with Zarathustra, all the while desiring that one day it will be sung in his memory:

> Whoever can find any meaning at all in the last words of this poem will guess why I preferred and admired it: they attain greatness. Pain is *not* considered an objection to life. . . . Perhaps my music, too, attains greatness at this point.[108]

Without a doubt, Nietzsche saw in it the fulfilled expression of that *amor fati* he had taken as his motto. "Not merely bear what is necessary, still less conceal it . . . but *love* it."[109] Beneath a stoic exterior, the hermit of Sils-Maria had, in reality, moved from religion, which gives meaning to suffering, to a religion of suffering, since this latter, the privileged instrument for knowledge and criterion of truth, alone gave meaning to life. No god any longer presided over the sacrifice nor received the offering—but rather man himself, at once disgusted and intoxicated with himself.

Far from testifying against life, suffering for Nietzsche was the highest proof of it, which he administered to himself with a cruel pleasure. "Self-annihilation, self-deification."[110] An expert at self-mortification, as so many pages filled with a disturbing acuteness show, perhaps he became that ascetic demiurge imagined in *Daybreak*, whose passion to distinguish himself, his passion to dominate, pushes him to "hurt others in order thereby to hurt *oneself*, in order then to triumph over oneself and one's pity and to revel in an extremity of power."[111] Like King Vishvamitra of Hindu legend, "who through millennia of self-torture acquired such a feeling of power and self-confidence that he endeavored to build a *new heaven* . . . [and] whoever has at some time built a 'new heaven' has found the power to do so only in his *own hell*."[112] Will to power, will to suffering—and vice versa. In a Nietzschean version of *Parsifal*, Amfortas, having become one with the Grail, would be consumed in a dreadful ecstasy.

To give in to pity or to provoke it, apart from the fact that his strict sense of distance forbad such a thing to Nietzsche, would be to indulge in a vain, whining suffering, and to add to the contagion—a characteristic symptom of an age of weakness, of decadence.

> I reproach those who are full of pity for easily losing a sense of shame, of respect, of sensitivity for distances; before you know it, pity begins to smell of the mob and becomes scarcely distinguishable from bad manners—and sometimes pitying hands can interfere in a downright destructive manner in a great destiny, in the growing solitude of one wounded, in a privileged right to heavy guilt. The overcoming of pity I count among the *noble* virtues.[113]

Just as the artist "wastes" himself in sexuality, "one loses strength when one pities" (always that idea of a fixed quantum of energy that has to be managed parsimoniously!). More serious: "Pity on the whole thwarts the law of evolution, which is the law of *selection*. It preserves what is ripe for destruction; it defends life's disinherited and condemned; through the abundance of the ill-constituted of all kinds which it *retains* in life it gives life itself a gloomy and questionable aspect."[114] Whence the anathema Nietzsche pronounces against altruism, for "man is finished when he becomes altruistic";[115] his exhortations to hardness—and first of all against oneself; finally, his call for the unpitying selection that the lords of the future, intoxicated by "great health," must exercise. "The weak and ill-constituted shall perish: first principle of *our* philanthropy. And one shall help them to do so."[116]

And yet, after having written in his notebooks that "the *instincts of decline* have become master over the *instincts of rising life*, the *will to nothingness* over the *will to life*," he asks himself, "is this TRUE?" "Is there not perhaps a greater guarantee for life, for the species, in this victory of the weak and mediocre? . . . And would we really want a world where the influence of the weak, their subtlety, their considerateness, spirituality, *flexibility* would be lacking?"[117] "I know nothing that grasps Christianity at such a depth and leads so bitterly to compassion," he had said about the prelude to *Parsifal* in January 1887, at a moment when Dostoevsky's *House of the Dead* made him "shed hot tears."[118] Two years later, at Turin, like Parisfal, the "pure fool" who is overcome with pity over the agony of the swan that he has just killed, the Antichrist, so contemptuous of pity, will throw himself weeping at the neck of a carriage horse being maltreated by his driver, before identifying himself in his last letters as both Dionysus and the Crucified.

"In me, Christianity triumphs over itself by surpassing itself," Nietzsche wrote three months before this in *Ecce Homo*. But if Christianity so upset him in *Parsifal*, it was because Nietzsche took it more seriously than did Wagner; because, for Nietzsche, who announced the death of God, it was still alive. Was it not to this "immortal stain on humanity" that he owed "the best piece of ideal life" he had known?[119] Besides, hardly had he said that he regretted the fact that Wagner did not quit the scene with a joke than he reproaches him for having dragged "the sublime symbols and practices" of Christianity onto a theatrical stage "where they do not belong."

> To say it once more, the Christians of today are too modest for my taste.—If Wagner was a Christian then Liszt was perhaps a church father!—the need for *redemption*, the quintessence of all Christian needs, has nothing to do with such buffoons.[120]

Wagner, it will have been understood, turns out to have been doubly guilty: for having become Christian, and for not having done so sufficiently; for having succumbed to the influence of ascetic ideals but without daring to draw the ultimate consequences, to "overcome" them by means of themselves so as to attain a kind of asceticism of asceticism: the Christian Passion justified by the sufferings of Dionysus—a "hyper-Christianity."[121] For, contrary to what a quick reading may suggest, the author of *Beyond Good and Evil* never breaks with an ideal or a value unless it be *also*, even above all, in the very name of that ideal or that value, in going one step further than them. "Overcoming" for him always signifies overtrumping. If he condemns Christianity, it is both as a doctrine, because it is harmful, and as an adulterated doctrine, because the churches and their faithful, while professing Christian ideals, do not practice them, or at least not sufficiently enough. In *Daybreak*, the work that inaugurates his "campaign against morality," he comments that "it does in fact exhibit a contradiction and is not afraid of it: in this book faith in morality is withdrawn—but why? *Out of morality!*"[122]

Contradictory as Nietzsche is, we shall not be able to get hold of him unless we think of him as a general commanding two enemy armies, which he throws one against the other for the gain of a third, mysterious, hypothetical one.[123] From this third, sometimes called the *"Übermensch,"* Nietzsche expected a victory over himself that he never achieved, that it would triumph over the "warring factions" whose "buzzing and roaring" he heard within himself ever since his youth.[124] In a letter from 1876, after having depicted himself ideally as "a man who desires nothing more each day than to lose some belief, that is, one more comfort, and who seeks, and finds his happiness in this liberation that is each day more total," he lucidly concluded: "Perhaps even I *want* to be a freer spirit than I *can* be?"[125]

9

"Cave Musicam!"

$\mathcal{Y}$et, if we were to believe his books, particularly the last ones, Nietzsche was a free spirit, a disciple of Dionysus who from his youth, in fact, always (since "one becomes only what one is") had said yes to the tragic fullness of existence. In *The Gay Science* he writes:

> It may perhaps be recalled, at least among my friends, that initially I approached the modern world with a few crude errors and overestimations and, in any case, hopefully. . . . I understood the philosophical pessimism of the nineteenth century as if it were a symptom of a superior force of thought, of more audacious courage, and of more triumphant *fullness* of life than had characterized the eighteenth century. . . . In the same way, I reinterpreted German music for myself as if it signified a Dionysian power of the German soul: I believed that I heard in it the earthquake through which some primeval force that had been dammed up for ages finally liberated itself—indifferent whether everything else that one calls culture might begin to tremble. You see, what I failed to recognize at that time both in philosophical pessimism and in German music was what is really their distinctive character—their *romanticism*.[1]

Romanticism, that is, the pessimism of weakness, in opposition to the Dionysian pessimism of strength. The product of a weakening of the vital instinct, which entails a complaisance toward suffering, and a longing for peace, for nothingness—it found its "most expressive form in the Schopenhauerian philosophy of the will and in Wagnerian music," the latter being only the translation in tones of the former. Returning to this aphorism six years later in *Nietzsche contra Wagner*, Nietzsche will add, "It is plain what I misunderstood in, equally plain what I read into, Wagner and Schopenhauer—myself." That is, everything began as a "misunderstanding."[2]

Pessimism, Vegetarianism, Socialism

It is true that, starting from the implacable Schopenhauerian concept of the will, in *The Birth of Tragedy* Nietzsche turns it against itself in order to end with a justification of life, "even what is most terrible, most equivocal, and most deceitful in it." In effect, tragedy reveals the horror of existence: "the terrible destructiveness of so-called world history as well as the cruelty of nature."[3] This revelation may lead to a "Buddhistic negation of the will" (as recommended by Schopenhauer) unless art transforms it into "representations that make life possible." The dithyrambic chorus, the instrument of this "act of salvation," was reincarnated in German music, particularly "in its vast solar orbit from Bach to Beethoven, from Beethoven to Wagner."[4]

This is where the misunderstanding took place. "What I heard as a young man listening to Wagnerian music had really nothing to do with Wagner," Nietzsche will write in *Ecce Homo*. "When I described Dionysian music I described what *I* had heard—that instinctively I had to transpose and transfigure everything into the new spirit that I carried in me."[5] That is, just the contrary of what in reality the composer had expressed, for during the course of composing *The Ring*, Wagner had succumbed to the grip of Schopenhauer at the very moment when Nietzsche was preparing to "overcome" him. His "disavowal" of *Parsifal* was, in fact, inevitable, even though during the same period, in his second pamphlet against Wagner, Nietzsche still presents it as an "unexpected catastrophe" If one looked closely, *The Ring* already had "a nihilistic conclusion (avid for rest and an end)."[6]

"Half his life, Wagner believed in the Revolution as much as ever a Frenchman believed in it," says Nietzsche in *The Case of Wagner*. "He believed that in Siegfried that he had found the typical revolutionary" who "overthrows everything traditional, all reverence, all *fear*." His union with Brunhilde is "the sacrament of free love; the rise of the golden age; the twilight of the gods for the old morality—*all ill has been abolished*."

> For a long time, Wagner's ship followed *this* course gaily. No doubt, this was where Wagner sought his highest goal.—What happened? A misfortune. The ship struck a reef; Wagner was stuck. The reef was Schopen-

hauer's philosophy; Wagner was stranded on a *contrary* world view. What had he transposed into music? Optimism. Wagner was ashamed. Even an optimism for which Schopenhauer had coined an evil epithet— *infamous* optimism. He was ashamed a second time. He reflected for a long while, his situation seemed desperate.—Finally, a way out dawned on him: the reef on which he was shipwrecked—what if he interpreted it as the *goal,* as the secret intent, as the true significance of his voyage? To be shipwrecked *here*—that was a goal, too. . . .

So he translated *The Ring* into Schopenhauer's terms. Everything goes wrong, everything perishes, the new world is as bad as the old: the *nothing,* the Indian Circe beckons.

Brunhilde was initially supposed to take her farewell with a song in honor of free love, putting off the world with the hope for a socialist utopia in which "all turns out well"—but now gets something else to do. She has to study Schopenhauer first; she has to transpose the fourth book of *The World as Will and Representation* into verse. *Wagner was redeemed.*

In all seriousness, this *was* a redemption. The benefit Schopenhauer conferred on Wagner is immeasurable. Only the *philosopher of decadence* gave to the artist of decadence—*himself.*[7]

For having been cited or referred to ad nauseum by his disciples and many of his commentators, this petulant summary of nonetheless is incorrect. The original poem was completed in December 1852—and published the following February in an edition of fifty copies—two years before Wagner had read a line of Schopenhauer. And if afterward he hesitated over the conclusion he ought to give to his work, it remains that, after having struck out a few "Feuerbachean" verses from Brunhilde's peroration, which were too "sententious" for his taste (but which he did set to music for King Ludwig II), Wagner also set aside the version written in 1856 that was inspired by Schopenhauer. "Siegfried, see, your wife hails you in ecstasy!"—these are Brunhilde's final words, and the work ends with the so-called "redemption through love" theme with which Sieglinde, in the third act of *Die Walküre,* had greeted the announcement that she carried "in her womb the most noble of heroes." The twilight of the gods leads not to the end of the world, but of *a* world, as is attested to by the presence among the ruins of survivors, who, the libretto says, "grasped by a violent emotion, contemplate the flames that reach to the sky" while the deeps of the Rhine engulf the accursed ring. Nor are we purely and simply brought back to the beginning (as with Nietzsche's eternal return of the same), since, meanwhile, the domination of gold and of Wotan's defective law have been abolished. Whatever Nietzsche may have said—and whatever some "creative" directors today may claim—Wagner's first conception was also, twenty-two years later, his final one.[8]

At the beginning of the 1850s, while revising the poem of *The Ring*, Wagner had undergone a serious crisis of pessimism following the events of 1848–1849, which had sent him into exile and brought with them the failure of his marriage. His discovery of Schopenhauer in 1854 only made clear to him "the truth about human affairs" he had already "unconsciously admitted" to himself. (This was already manifest in his *Lohengrin*, his most pessimistic work, which was composed before the revolution.) Schopenhauer's "chief idea, the final negation of the desire of life, is terribly serious, but it shows the only salvation possible," he wrote to Liszt. "To me of course that thought was not news, and it can indeed be conceived by no one in whom it did not preexist."[9] Applying this yardstick drawn from his reading to the work in progress, Wagner recognized in Wotan the Schopenhauerian will driven to self-renunciation.[10] But since his vital instinct was not slow in counterbalancing this desire to flee the world—"this terrible will, desire of life, which again and again dims my vision and throws me into a chaos of contradictions," as he will write to Liszt a year later[11]—Wagner quickly became aware that the philosopher's absolute pessimism did not agree with what he himself thought and felt.

Where Schopenhauer denounced history as an immense illusion having no goal, Wagner, who was attached to the idea of evolution, of "becoming," did not despair that man would succeed in ennobling himself, perhaps through art and, in particular, through his own works. "We recognize the cause of the fall of Historic Man, and the necessity of his regeneration; we believe in the possibility of such Regeneration, and we devote ourselves to its carrying-through in every sense," he will write in 1881 just as he was completing *Parsifal*.[12] Yes, he no longer believed in revolution, but neither did he renounce all the aspirations of his youth or the sympathy that he showed for socialist movements. "As then, he is still expecting socialism to take over," Cosima records on 2 June 1879, "the only difference being that he does not foresee its happening at any particular time."[13] The legislation Bismarck had passed against socialism upset him, and he approved of the Russian nihilists. "I am always on the side of the rebels!" he exclaimed one evening in 1881 to an alarmed Cosima.[14] A year earlier he had concluded *Religion and Art*, his aesthetic and philosophical testament, with his wish for "a sincere and intimate union among modern socialism, the so-called vegetarian societies, the societies for the protection of animals, and all the temperance societies." In it he also denounced the arms race of the European states, which strongly risked one day blowing up "through some incalculable accident."[15] Similarly, the author of "A Capitulation"—that "insult" to the vanquished France of 1871 that Nietzsche will reproach him for as "real badness"[16]— soon repented for having placed his hopes in Bismarck's Reich built on "blood and iron." "I am ashamed that so many people have proved me wrong" who knew "what would become of the German Reich under Prussian leadership," and that "a Pomeranian *Junker* would never understand German culture," he confessed in 1878.[17] At another time he offered this lament, which Nietzsche surely would have appreciated: "But how difficult it is to find good things to say of the Germans!"[18]

A positive pessimist like Hans Sachs, Wagner therefore could have replied to his old disciple that in fact pessimism was not *"necessarily* a sign of decline, decay, degeneration, weary and weak instincts."[19] But to Nietzsche's eyes, the panaceas that Wagner recommended in his operas for stemming decadence—love and compassion—were the surest way of accelerating it. His apology for temperance would not have displeased him, though, for ever since his youthful participation in a few student drinking parties, Nietzsche had never stopped deploring his compatriots "tendency to drunkenness." On the other hand, Wagner's plea in favor of vegetarianism totally exasperated him, and rightly so. In fact, when they had first met in 1869, Nietzsche was practicing this kind of diet and Wagner, having tried it and decided that "he would not live very long if he went on with it," was irritated by Nietzsche's naivety. "You are an ass!" he exclaimed when Nietzsche refused to eat meat.[20] Crestfallen, the young philologist allowed himself to be convinced by the "venerated Master" about the "absurdities of that theory and such practice." "The most important thing for me," Nietzsche wrote at the time to Gersdorff, who had introduced him to this diet, is that "here is another tangible case of that optimism which keeps cropping up, in the strangest forms—now as socialism, now as cremation instead of burial, now as vegetarian doctrine—and in countless forms; just as if the removal of a sinfully natural phenomenon could mean the establishment of happiness and harmony. Whereas our sublime philosophy teaches that wherever we reach out our hands we grasp total ruin, the pure will to life, and here all palliatives are useless." To abstain from meat for a time for dietetic reasons could be useful. "But," he concludes, "why, to quote Goethe, make a 'religion' of it? But then that is inevitably entailed in all such eccentricities, and anyone who is ripe for vegetarianism is generally also ripe for socialist 'stew.'"[21] That a dozen years later the composer returned to his original convictions and, like all good social reformers, without himself taking up the practice—because, he said, of his delicate condition—was something that Nietzsche could not pass up. Wagnerian music, he will write in *The Case of Wagner,* has the same effect as a vegetarian diet: it increases weakness and, for that reason, like vegetables "weaken the vegetarian," it attracts "the weak and exhausted."[22]

As for socialism, which inspired an early antipathy in Nietzsche, he took it to be "the fanciful younger brother of the almost expired despotism whose heir it wants to be."[23] Its will to "negate life" made it akin to Christianity. If it could play any "useful or healthy role," it was as a "subversive mole in a society addicted to idiocy," where it would retard "the advent of peace on earth and the debonair character of the democratic herd," thereby provisionally protecting "Europe from the threatening *marasmus femininus*," that avatar of the "Eternal Feminine" Wagner had made one of the leading themes of his work.[24]

No, certainly the author of *The Gay Science* would have to rebut the "old Romantic" soothsayer, against whom he invokes "the honest, atheist immoralist" he had known. And in his notebooks we see Nietzsche venting his anger and scorn on that organ of Wagnerian "obscurantism," the *Bayreuther Blätter,* which had been Nietzsche's idea and of which Nietzsche had hoped to be the editor:

> What a quagmire! The muddiest mishmash of arrogance, Germanic nonsense, and confusion of concepts, an unbearable sugar of the "sweetest" compassion, and along with that, the aforementioned taste for green vegetables and that premeditated unction and sentimentality towards animals,[25] *right beside* a sincere, genuine, and deep hatred for science. . . . —Overall, the impudence of a pontiff saturated with incense who dispenses his obscure impressions like revelations regarding every imaginable realm of thought which precisely escapes him and is forbidden to him: all this in a German that is a veritable swamp of obscurity and exaggeration, such as even the disciples of Hegel, the greatest enemies of the German language, have not managed to attain![26]

From Tragic Sun to Romantic Night

Their vision of history was not the only point on which Wagner found himself in disagreement with Schopenhauer. If to the end of his life Wagner professed admiration for the philosophy of the "sage of Frankfurt," he did so by insisting on its ethical aspect and only after having given it a no less decisive twist than did Nietzsche in *The Birth of Tragedy.* When, after 1854, Wagner speaks of a negation of the will it is the individual, egoistic, sterile will he refers to, not the universal will that Schopenhauer refused to believe could ever be good.[27] What is more, Wagner places love on a par with pity among the means human beings have at their disposal for overcoming their wills, an idea completely foreign to Schopenhauer, who easily lost his temper on hearing the word "love" and who saw in it merely a ruse that the will uses to ensure the perpetuation of the species.

Wagner was plainly aware of this divergence in beliefs when he ended *Tristan*, so much so that, on rereading the philosopher's masterwork, he even thought about correcting it in order clearly to demonstrate that "the pathway to complete pacification of the Will [passes] through love, and that no abstract love of mankind, but the love which actually blossoms from the soil of sexual love."[28] It is not by renouncing the longing that makes the will objective that Tristan and Isolde know absolute peace, but by intensifying it to the point where they cease to be separated individuals and meet in the universal will. This is the meaning of Isolde's "love death," or rather "transfiguration," at the work's end. She attains this revelation in "supreme voluptuousness," whereas King Mark, the ascetic saint according to Schopenhauer, pardons her with a despairing tenderness without having understood.

As Nietzsche rightly comments in one of his notebooks in 1875, "*Love in Tristan* must not be understood in a Schopenhauerian manner, but rather as Empodoclean . . . it is the sign and guarantee of an eternal unity."[29] And in *The Birth of Tragedy,* it is "the impulses of the universal will," the "desire to exist" that the Dionysian spectator, at the risk of "shattering," hears rising from "the immensity of the night of worlds": "'Longing! Longing! In death still longing! for every longing not dying!'"[30] This longing, however, cut off from any end in existence, is only fulfilled in death. It is because they think they have drunk a death potion that, at the end of the first act, Tristan and Isolde confess their love to each other. Yet while correcting Schopenhauer, Thomas Mann will say that *Tristan*—"Wagner's most extreme work"—is also the one in which he shows himself closest to Schopenhauer. Wagner had written to Liszt, after having announced his providential discovery of the philosopher:

> If I think of the storm of my heart, the terrible tenacity with which,
> against my desire, it used to cling to the hope of life, and even if now I
> feel this hurricane within me, I have at least found a quietus which in
> wakeful nights helps me to sleep. This is the genuine, ardent longing of
> death, for absolute unconsciousness, total non-existence; freedom from
> all dreams is our only final salvation.[31]

He goes on to say, "I have worked out in my head *Tristan and Isolde*. The simplest but most full-blooded musical conception; I shall cover myself to die with the 'black flag' that floats at the end of it." This letter, along with some of the most gripping pages of the work that it announces, also at times seems like a paraphrase of Schopenhauer: "Dying is the moment of that liberation from the one-sidedness of an individuality which does not constitute the innermost kernel of our true being, but is rather to be thought of as a kind of aberration thereof. The true original freedom again enters at this moment which in the sense stated can be regarded as a *restitutio in integrum*."[32]

Night—prelude to death. And this, which the lovers celebrate in ecstasy, is not just a refuge, propitious to the effusions that the world condemns, but rather the apotheosis of German Romanticism, a metaphysical night where the sufferings of individuation disappear along with all sensible appearances:

Ich war	I was
wo Ich von je gewesen,	where I had been before I was,
wohin auf je Ich geh:	where I am to go:
im weisten reich	the immense realm
der Weltennacht,	of universal night.
Nur ein Wissen	A single knowledge
dort uns eigen:	there belongs to us:
göttlich ew' ges	immemorial forgetfulness,
Ur-vergessen!	divine, eternal![33]

No doubt this exaltation of longing (which later Nietzsche will denounce as the symptom of a "repugnant sexuality") was damped for him, as for many other spectators, by the dark side of the Dionysian that the music evokes with an unequaled power and seductiveness.

In *Richard Wagner in Bayreuth*, Nietzsche writes: "*Tristan and Isolde*, the true *opus metaphysicum* of all art, a work on which lies the shattered gaze of a dying man with his insatiable, sweetest of all longings for the mysteries of night and death, far removed from life, which, as what is evil, deceptive, and divisive, shines in the piercing light of a horrible, ghostly dawn. It is a drama with the severest austerity of form, overwhelming in its simple grandeur and precisely suited to the mystery of which it speaks, the mystery of death in life, of unity in duality."[34]

If following the performances of July 1872 Nietzsche sang the praises of the "beneficial force of *Tristan*" and spoke of it as "the healthiest of beverages," he knew these were words dictated by the modesty of someone (he would later confess) for whom the "total upheaval" he had just undergone had at first taken away all language and turned him in on himself. The beverage, in truth, had more to do with the potion absorbed by the two lovers "consecrated to night" than with some restorative drink, as can be seen from the impressions he conveyed to Erwin Rohde a few months later after having heard at Mannheim, under the very direction of Wagner himself, the prelude and finale of the work:

> Everything else, that which cannot be grasped in terms of musical relations, engenders in me disgust and horror. And when I returned from the Mannheim concert, I actually had an oddly intensified, weary dread of daily reality, because it seemed no longer real to me but ghostly.[35]

"As soon as this everyday reality re-enters consciousness," we read in *The Birth of Tragedy*, "it is experienced as such, with nausea: an ascetic, will-negating mood is the fruit of these [Dionysian] states."[36] That art (myth, word, and image) should not have sufficed to protect someone with a delicate sensibility like Nietzsche should not surprise us when we recall the state of shock, not to say trance, into which *Tristan* plunged a number of his contemporaries (and others as well since), which Wagner moreover had anticipated with a mixture of apprehension and pride: "Child! This *Tristan* is becoming something *terrible*. This last act!! . . . I fear the opera will be forbidden—unless the whole is turned into a parody by reduction," he wrote to Mathilde Wesendonck in April 1859 while he was composing the third act. "Nothing but indifferent performances can save me! Completely good ones are bound to send folks crazy—I can see nothing else for it."[37]

In fact, *Tristan* began its ravaging effects on its first performers before any audience heard it. The victim of a chill but also of his exalted effort, the tenor Ludwig Schnorr died a short time thereafter and in a kind of Wagnerian delirium. His wife, Malvina, as his Isolde, was then struck by hallucinations and never really recovered from this double ordeal. As for Hans von Bülow, who had begun rehearsals of the work on the very day that his wife Cosima was giving birth to Wagner's first child, it was the "coup de grâce." If he was subsequently to concede that "one has to pardon everything from a man who could compose this," the first performances were a descent into hell, and he barely avoided committing suicide.

If less extreme, the reactions of the spectators nonetheless confirmed the composer's suspicions. In 1889, for example, at Bayreuth, William Lekeu, a young disciple of César Franck, fainted during the prelude and had to be carried from the hall. A few years previously in Munich, on hearing the first notes of the same prelude, Chabrier, the author of the *Joyeuse marche*, broke out in sobs, confiding to his neighbor and friend, Vincent d'Indy: "Oh, it's awful, I can't stop myself, for ten years I have been waiting to hear *that* from the cellos!" Even Ravel, "apparently so cold and cynical," on hearing the same section at a concert "trembled convulsively and cried like a baby."[38]

As if reality were not enough, fiction rapidly took over. Giorgio, the hero of d'Annunzio's *Trionfo della morte*, a sadistic aesthete whom *Tristan* has led to madness, ends up committing suicide and taking with him Ippolita, his Isolde, albeit unwillingly. It is also to suicide, but a long and voluptuous one, that Frau Klötherjahn abandons herself in Thomas Mann's novella *Tristan*, savoring at length the chromatic philtre, whereas on each hearing the councilor Spatz is threatened with dyspepsia and stomach cramps, which may also recall the "facial neuralgia" that the same music provokes in Mme Verdurin, the "goddess of Wagnerianism and migraines." "They did not all die, but all were shaken." So we can understand that sixteen years after the first revelation at Munich, the author of *Ecce Homo* should have preserved intact this feverish memory:

> But to this day I am still looking for a work that equals the dangerous fascination and the gruesome and sweet infinity of *Tristan*—and look in all the arts in vain. All the strangenesses of Leonardo da Vinci emerge from their spell at the first note of *Tristan*. This work is emphatically Wagner's *non plus ultra*. . . . I take it for a good fortune of the first order that I lived at the right time and among Germans, of all peoples, so that I was *ripe* for this work: that is how far the psychologist's inquisitiveness extends in my case. The world is poor for anyone who has never been sick enough for this "voluptuousness of hell."[39]

The Orpheus of All Secret Misery

Still, before proudly proclaiming that one had to be sick to appreciate *Tristan* and then acknowledging that he himself suffered from such a "weakened vitality," Nietzsche, looking inductively back over Wagner's works to their author, had begun by bringing this diagnosis to bear on Wagner. For Wagner, it is an "impoverishment of life," not a "fullness of life," that became creative, he says in *The Gay Science*.[40] And six years later, the composer dead, Nietzsche comments bluntly: "Wagner increases exhaustion: that is why he attracts the weak and exhausted. . . . Wagner represents a great corruption of music. . . . And with that he has made music sick."[41]

Yet in *Tristan* Wagner, divided like Nietzsche himself between what Baudelaire, in this respect their psychological counterpart, called "the ecstasy and horror of life," had exorcised his nostalgia for death. Cosima one day, like Isolde, had sighed to him, "I should like to die," and he unperturbedly replied, "and I to live."[42] What is more, immediately after *Tristan* he wrote an opera opposite in color to it: *Die Meistersinger,* in which under the authority of Hans Sachs, art, love, and society reach in C major a reasonable and democratic compromise.[43] While Nietzsche much appreciated this work for its music, he says nothing about its content. And for good reason: democracy was not his forte—nor was comedy. What does Zarathustra do with laughter? He "sanctifies" it. In the same way, Nietzsche could not simply accept life. He had to "divinize" it, provided, to be sure, that it was "problematic, heroic, terrible." What could be more fundamentally, more pathologically Romantic?

If Wagner was "sick," it was in a "healthy way," Thomas Mann will say, and as a creator.[44] As for Nietzsche, he aspired to health in an unhealthy way, not possessing artistic gifts sufficient to be, except in *Zarathustra,* more than critical and reactive. Sick in body as well after 1874, his receptivity to music was heightened, especially to the music of Wagner, which did not require this to move him. In 1885 he notes, "Here was the other side of the coin, the indisputably *detrimental* and destructive action this venerated music exercised on me."[45] What was once qualified as Dionysian, German Romantic music was merely a "nervous crisis of the first order." To those who suffer, everything is suffering; to those who are ill, everything is sickness.

In his first book, where the antinomies that later will split into contradictory aphorisms are still linked, Nietzsche had undoubtedly intellectually moved beyond Schopenhauer—while still projecting himself into Siegfried, he invoked for the service of life Wagner's most Schopenhauerian work, the one to which he was most closely attached. This is why he does not attack it in *The Case of Wagner,* where the accusation of pessimism is wrongly directed against *The Ring* before reaffirming his allegiance to it in *Ecce Homo,* on the threshold of madness, with a homage no less frank and sincere than his reactions to the prelude to *Parsifal* the previous year. Nietzsche had understood this hymn to the night in which the malediction of alterity vanishes, not poorly, but rather too well. He noted in his notebooks in 1878, "As a student, I said: 'Wagner is Romanticism. Not the art of the golden mean and plentitude, but of the last quarter hour: soon it will be night.' This view made me a Wagnerian, I could *do* no other, but I *knew* it better."[46]

Assuredly, to present *Tristan* as he would later do, as the crowning of the "vast solar orbit" of German music, is at least paradoxical, all the more so in that Dionysian music was not supposed to play on the feelings and emotions. As Nietzsche had remarked in 1871, "to all those who can only reach music through their emotions, it must be said that they will always remain in the narthex and never have access to its sanctuary."[47] And *The Birth of Tragedy* castigates the decadent music of Euripides' plays, which aimed at "*the dramatized epos*—but in this Apollinian domain of art the *tragic* effect is certainly unattainable."[48] But it was also himself that Nietzsche castigated in this way, the unfulfilled, solitary young man who, better than in Schumann, found in Wagner's art a remedy for his torments, a potent means of calming the bitterness caused by the unfocused character of his faculties, and that at the same time assuaged the bad conscience he felt over having chosen to be a teacher, thereby betraying a vocation he felt to be more in conformity with his personality and his expectations. Nietzsche will admit almost all of this in his notebooks, a short time after his "break" with Wagner. He writes in 1878:

> Wagner's art is made for those who are aware of an essential *fault* in the conduct of their life: either they have stifled a noble nature in some vile activity, or squandered it through laziness or conventional marriages. Here to flee the world means TO FLEE ONESELF.[49]

A few pages later we find this admission:

> To suffer from life neither so extremely, nor so weakly and emotionlessly, that Wagner's art is *necessary* to us as a remedy. This is the capital reason for OPPOSITION not impure motives.[50]

Even when he will subsequently refer to "impure motives," he will rarely do so without associating them with this "capital reason," which will sometimes be admiring, sometimes hostile, since his opposition to Wagner's music was born from the attraction he felt to it. Thus when in *The Gay Science* he reproaches Wagner for wanting, out of vanity, to overlook that he is "the master of small things," this theme, destined for a good future, is introduced by revealing praise of the incomparable art with which the composer knows how to discover "the tones out of the realm of suffering, depressed, tormented souls" and to give "speech even to dumb animals":

> Nobody equals him in the colors of late fall, the indescribably moving happiness of the last, very last, very briefest enjoyment; he finds sounds for those secret and uncanny midnights of the soul in which cause and

effect appear to be unhinged and any moment something can come into being "out of nothing." More happily than anyone else, he draws from the very bottom of human happiness—as it were, from its drained cup, where the bitterest and most repulsive drops have merged in the end, for better or for worse, with the sweetest. He knows how souls drag themselves along when they can no longer leap and fly, nor even walk; his is the shy glance of concealed pain, of understanding without comfort, of farewells without confessions. As the Orpheus of all secret misery he is greater than anyone.[51]

Seven years later, Nietzsche will accuse Wagner of having made music "sick" because he set out to seduce the "weak and the feeble"—he was speaking whereof he knew, both in terms of cause and effect. His music was merely a short-term remedy, made double harmful by the excess of emotion it produced. And, once again, what is expressed through these now difficult to endure emotions was perhaps not so much the desire to rediscover some lost unity, proclaimed by the musician god of the Greeks, as it was the nostalgia for a "world" that Nietzsche found it difficult to accept no longer believing in. "The translation of music into metaphysics" that he had turned to "was an act of veneration and gratitude; basically all religious people so far have had this kind of experience."[52]

We can understand, therefore, why in the autobiographical preface he will add to *Human, All Too Human* in 1886, Nietzsche, after having accused Wagner, "a decaying, despairing romantic," of suddenly sinking down "helpless and shattered before the Christian cross," immediately takes off after Romantic music:

> I began by *forbidding* myself, totally and on principle, all romantic music, that ambiguous, inflated, oppressive art that deprives the spirit of its severity and cheerfulness and lets rampant every kind of vague longing and greedy, spongy desire. *'Cave Musicam'* [Beware music] is to this day my advice to all who are man enough to insist on cleanliness in things of the spirit; such music unnerves, softens, feminizes, its 'eternal womanly' draws *us*—downwards![53]

From the Dark Night of Romanticism to Enlightenment

In truth, as his schoolboy and university letters attest, Nietzsche did not need to wait until this time to be prudent regarding music or even to impose periods of abstinence on himself, either because he was caught up in his studies or because his violent headaches prevented him from indulging any emotion. But it was not just because of circumstances, as Cosima's answer to one of his letters (which one of her daughters will destroy at the beginning of our century) demonstrates: "I understand all the better the hatred for music that I myself have experienced and why I flee music as the enemy of all rational existence," she wrote to him in August 1872, probably alluding to the period of her unhappy marriage to von Bülow.[54] This confidence and what it allows us to guess about what Nietzsche had said testifies to the ambivalent reactions awakened by the power music had acquired since the birth of Romanticism, so much so that Eduard Hanslick did not hesitate, before Nietzsche came along, to denounce the "pathological" effects of Wagner's music. "In the hierarchy of the arts, music on the grand scale as created by modern masters provides a real parallel with the powerful, the almost superabundant, resources other moderns have been able to create in the realm of material enterprise," Paul Valéry will say.

> Music plays upon us, saddening, enlivening, intoxicating, rending us thoughtful, at its own will making us more passionate or profound, tenderer or stronger than man ever was before. Just as our machines can perform our labors for us, giving us the benefit of speeds which far exceed our natural capacity, so music—with its ecstasies and rages always in wait to seize on us, its limitless imaginings, its almost total powers of possession—offers and inspires us with states of feeling that are half unreal yet more powerful than most of our real ones. Not one of the other arts can claim such sovereignty.[55]

But at the same time, this had to raise suspicion. "My 'unfairness' toward music," Valéry will also say, "may perhaps be due to a feeling that something as powerful as that is capable of animating us to the point of absurdity."[56] Nietzsche's illness made him more aware than ever of this danger by provoking in him "a sudden resistance," an "instinctive reaction."[57] The disappointment of Bayreuth and Wagner's "conversion" did the rest. "Henceforth alone," starting in 1877, Nietzsche will take sides against himself, and up to *The Gay Science* it will be against music that he philosophizes, by challenging or refuting in the name of knowledge or even of science almost everything that he had affirmed until then. He began with the very ground of the metaphysics of the artist that had underlain *The Birth of Tragedy* and his Wagnerian commitment: the idea of the "sovereignty of music" that he had borrowed from Schopenhauer. Because dramatic music had conquered for the tonal art "an enormous domain of symbolic means," it had usurped an unjustified preeminence:

> In itself, no music is profound or significant, it does not speak of the 'will' or of the 'thing in itself'; . . . It was the intellect itself which first *introduced* this significance into sounds: just as, in the case of architecture, it likewise introduced a significance into the relations between lines and masses which is in itself quite unknown to the laws of mechanics.[58]

In this phenomenon of projection, which had allowed Schopenhauer to confer a metaphysical status on the tonal art, it is not difficult to discern the cunning of the old religious instinct: to claim that music spoke of the will and the thing in itself was merely a barely disguised way of transforming it into "a kind of mouthpiece of the 'in itself' of things, a telephone from the beyond."[59] The religious origin of modern music predisposed it to play this role.[60] And when religion declined, the sentiment the Enlightenment philosophers had expelled from it threw itself into art. It thereby grew "more profound and soulful" but also took on a "higher, gloomier colouring" in which we recognize that human beings remain impregnated with "that dread of spirits, the odour of incense and the shadows of churches."[61]

As the twin of religious neediness, metaphysical neediness also finds a refuge in art:

> Even when the free spirit [let us read: Nietzsche] has divested himself of everything metaphysical the highest effects of art can easily set the metaphysical strings, which have long been silent or indeed snapped apart, vibrating in sympathy; so it can happen, for example, that a passage in Beethoven's Ninth Symphony will make him feel he is hovering above the earth in a dome of stars with the dream of *immortality* in his heart. . . . If he becomes aware of being in this condition he feels a profound stab in the heart and sighs for the man who will lead him back to his lost love, whether she be called religion or metaphysics. It is in such moments that his intellectual probity is put to the test.[62]

Signs were not lacking that in the Europe of the day music was transforming itself into disguised metaphysics or "contraband religion." The success of Bayreuth, it has been noted, was contemporary with that of Lourdes. Even the country of Voltaire—Nietzsche's new master, to whose memory *Human, All Too Human* is dedicated—was struck by this plague. In 1882, in an amusing "paradox about music," Paul Bourget (from whom Nietzsche would borrow the word "nihilism") presented a kind of Rameau's nephew that lashed out against this new idolatry accompanied with appropriate ceremonies: "Idolatry and ceremony increase every day. On Sunday, the people no longer go to mass, they go to a concert!"[63] Mallarmé said that he went to them as to vespers—and this was not just a quip, as can be seen from his chronicle from 1893, "Plaisir sacré," where referring to concerts he says, "it is not a question of aesthetics, but of religiosity. . . . It being understood that, apart from official celebrations, Music presents itself as the last and most sufficient human worship."[64] One of his close friends, Camille Mauclair, in a book with the significant title *La Religion de la musique*, held that "music is the last prayer."[65] In more and more, and ever larger concert halls were released "the latent energies of metaphysics that did not want to die and that, no longer dependent on coarse language, had turned into sound in order to recommence the conquest of souls."[66]

Nietzsche probably would not have been surprised, he who had designated Paris, because of its refinement, as the "real soil" for Wagner.[67] But he would most likely have added that French culture possessed enough psychological and intellectual antidotes to resist it, whereas music flattered the "obscure, undecided, ominous, elemental, intuitive" taste that particularly characterized the "German nature."[68] And, if Germans had such bad writing, it was because they gave themselves over too much to music,[69] which lacks "accents for enrapturing the mind,"[70] only addressing itself to feelings and the senses. Whereas in 1875 he had seen in the flowering of music in the nineteenth century both a response to and a remedy for worn-out language,[71] Nietzsche now made of the art of prose an artistic and even political ideal, "for better writing means better thinking," and in the long run "this will prepare for that distant state of things when the good Europeans would acknowledge and take in hand their task: to direct and oversee world culture in its entirety."

In fact, music exercised an all the more disastrous effect on the Germans since it had further added to the "two great European narcotics," "nowhere else . . . so viciously abused"—Christianity and alcohol. ("How much *beer* there is in the German intellect!")[72] Christianity reduced to "pure folly" (*Parsifal*) and the increasing consumption of "music and spirituous drinks" was not limited to them. Along with the "despiritualization and dumbing down of taste," they characterized a sick civilization of work that had abolished slavery by generalizing it, and where as a result art, in particular music, as in the time of Euripides, had no other function than to "stim-

ulate exhausted nerves" or to relax them.[73] "The wearied worker," "this typical figure . . . encountered in all classes of society," expects "drunkenness,
commotion, tearful crises" from it, and the relaxation and rest that tourism
was also beginning to provide. The "man of the evening, with the 'wild instincts lulled to sleep' of which Faust speaks, requires the health resort, the
seaside, the glaciers, Bayreuth. . . . In ages like this, art has a right to *pure
folly*—as a kind of holiday for the spirit, the wits and the heart. Wagner understood that. *Pure folly* is restorative . . ."[74] (Imagine what Nietzsche would
have written today, confronted with the flourishing of a phenomenon whose
beginnings he had observed with concern: a governing class that, for the
first time in history, prides itself on working more than do its subordinates
and that numbed by work, nonetheless claims to dispense and oversee culture . . .)

Music, "that art of the night and shadows," fueled and amplified
"German hostility to the Enlightenment," whose herald Nietzsche would
now appoint himself while rehabilitating French classical aesthetics. Indeed, just as music "produces a *magical* effect only when we hear the language of our own *past* speaking out of it," so, too, "as the late fruit of every
civilization," it "resounds into a new and astonished world like the language of an age that has vanished," taking "extinguished, faded ideas and
restoring to them a little colour.[75] Whence its importance in the Romantic
period for Germans, who were set "against the Enlightenment and against
the revolution in society which was crudely misunderstood as its consequence: piety towards everything that exists sought to translate itself into
piety towards everything that ever had existed, to the end that heart and
spirit might once more become *full* and no room be left for future and novel
goals. The cult of feeling was erected in place of the cult of reason, and the
German composers, as artists of the invisible, emotional, fabulous, unsatisfied, built a new temple more successfully than any of the artists of words or
of ideas."[76]

Such was the case with Wagner, whose art expressed with "the greatest intensity" the ideas and sentiments of that "age of reaction and restoration" that followed the French Revolution. "In Wagner there are elements
that seem *reactionary*," Nietzsche noted in 1875, "the Christianity of the
Middle Ages, princes, Buddhism, the fabulous . . . the German national element. Because this is how he could gain a large number of followers. These
are his *means of expression*, language that is still understood but that has received a *new content*. For the future he seeks analogies with what has been:
for the artist, these things are to be taken in an artistic fashion and not dog-

matically."[77] Two years later, rejecting the future that Wagner's works were meant to announce, Nietzsche had abandoned the artistic point of view and condemning it as well:

> Wagner's appropriation of the old Germanic sagas, his ennobling dispos-
> ing of the strange gods and heroes contained in them—who are actually
> sovereign beasts of prey with occasional impulses to thoughtfulness,
> magnanimity and world-weariness—the reanimation of these figures, to
> whom he added the Christian-medieval thirst for ecstatic sensuality and
> asceticism, this entire Wagnerian giving and taking in regard to subject-
> matter, souls, forms and words, would also be clearly expressed in the
> *spirit of his music* if, in common with all music, it were able to speak of it-
> self with complete lack of ambiguity: this spirit wages the *ultimate* war of
> reaction against the spirit of the Enlightenment wafted across from the
> preceding century into this, likewise against the supra-national ideas of
> French revolutionary enthusiasm and English-American sobriety in the
> reconstruction of state and society.[78]

In 1888 Nietzsche will again denounce in his notes the "anti-intellectualism" of German Romantic music, "its hatred for the 'Enlighten-ment and reason'":

> The decay of melody is the same thing as the decay of the "idea," of di-
> alectic, of freedom of intellectual movement—how much struggling
> against *Voltaire* there is in German music![79]

Barely six years after having greeted in its "vast solar orbit" a rebirth of the Dionysian spirit, Nietzsche fears that the Germans, as they had already done with the Reformation, will once again deprive the European spirit of the fruits of its latest blooming. For those who "would like to make the world intoxicated on music and think this will mean the advent of cul-ture" simply forget that "until now drunkenness has been always followed by something other than culture."[80] But who other than Nietzsche himself had forgotten that in *The Birth of Tragedy* he had announced the eruption of a new culture engendered by music and that he had condemned Socrates, whose "negative, dissolving, and optimistic" dialectic had precipitated the downfall of ancient drama? "Music achieves great power only among people who cannot or are not allowed to discourse. . . . The Greeks, as a vol-uble and disputatious people, could therefore endure music only as a *sea-soning* for those arts that could actually be talked about and disputed over:

whereas it is hardly possible even to *think* clearly about music," is what he now says.[81]

Along with these anti-Dionysian Greeks, it is dialectic and its inventor, Socrates, that Nietzsche rehabilitates—"this simplest and most imperishable of intercessors," the one most likely, along with Montaigne and Voltaire, his faithful heirs, to serve as a "guide to morals and reason."[82] "This Enlightenment we must now carry further forward: let us not worry about the 'great revolution' and the 'great reaction' against it which have take place—they are no more than sporting of waves in comparison with the truly great flood which bears *us* along."[83]

From *Human, All Too Human* through *The Gay Science* it is with great jubilation that Nietzsche evokes the work of elucidation that needs to be accomplished in every domain. Humans think they know, while they are victims of illusions, lies that conceal reality from them, victims of appearances harassed by the "free spirit" in search of the "depth of things" with the same extreme passion that the author of *The Birth of Tragedy* had brought to their celebration in art. And certainly "we have Christianity, the philosophers, poets, musicians to thank for an abundance of profound sensations," but "if these are not to stifle us we must conjure up the spirit of science, which on the whole makes one somewhat colder and more skeptical and in especial cools down the fiery stream of belief in ultimate definitive truths."[84] In fact, metaphysics "leads to a contempt for what is *actual:* it is finally in this sense *hostile to culture*." As for musical culture, it "refuses science."[85] "Why were scholars absent from Bayreuth?" notes Nietzsche during the summer of 1878. "They had no *need* of that. I would previously have held it against them. But now . . ."[86] Like Hegel in his *Aesthetics*, Nietzsche now announces that the scientist has to succeed the artist. It will be up to him henceforth to teach us how to "take pleasure in life" as art has taught us, but which "now reemerges as an almighty requirement of knowledge."[87] Believing himself cured of the spell of Wagnerian music, Nietzsche bids farewell to art, like Wotan bids farewell to Brunhilde, in the red glow of twilight:

> Perhaps art has never before been comprehended so profoundly or with
> so much feeling as it is now, when the magic of death seems to play
> around it. Recall that Greek city in south Italy which on *one* day of the
> year continued to celebrate their Greek festival and did so with tears and
> sadness at the fact that foreign barbarism was triumphing more and
> more over the customs they had brought with them; it is to be doubted
> whether the Hellenic has ever been so greatly savoured, or its golden
> nectar imbibed with so much relish, as it was among these declining

Hellenes. The artist will soon be regarded as a glorious relic, and we
shall bestow upon him, as a marvelous stranger upon whose strength
and beauty the happiness of former ages depended, honours such as we
do not grant to others of our own kind. The best in us has perhaps been
inherited from the sensibilities of earlier ages to which we hardly any
longer have access by direct paths; the sun has already set, but the sky of
our life still glows with its light, even though we no longer see it.[88]

And since in Germany there is no sobering up or return to equilibrium
after a metaphysical-lyrical swerve without a few bows to Goethe, Nietzsche, is now pleased that the sage of Weimar, whom Nietzsche at one time
had judged very inferior to Beethoven,[89] should have adopted "a prudent attitude toward music." "It was advantageous," he notes in 1880, "that the
German tendency toward lack of clarity did not find a supplementary artistic backing."[90]

A half-century after the reversal of *Human, All Too Human,* Harry
Haller, the rather Nietzschean hero of Hermann Hesse's *Steppenwolf,* will see
in the "rather dire but touching bond" he has with music "the fate of every
German intellectual":

> In the German spirit the matriarchal link to nature rules in the form of
> the hegemony of music to an extent unknown in any other people. We
> intellectuals, instead of fighting against this tendency like men and ren-
> dering obedience to the spirit, the Logos, the Word, and gaining hearing
> for it, are all dreaming of a speech without words that utters the inex-
> pressible and gives form to the formless. Instead of playing his part as
> truly and honestly as he could, the German intellectual has constantly
> rebelled against the word and reason, and courted music. And so the
> German spirit, carousing in music, in wonderful creations of sound, and
> wonderful beauties of feeling and more that were never pressed home to
> reality, has left the greater part of its practical gifts to decay. None of us
> intellectuals is at home in reality. We are strange to it and hostile. This is
> why the part played by intellect even in our German reality, in our his-
> tory and politics and public opinion, has been so lamentable a one.[91]

Thomas Mann will offer a similar disenchanted judgment at the end
of a spiritual adventure similar to that of Nietzsche.[92] In his *Reflections of a
Nonpolitical Man,* written during the First World War against "self-righteous
democratic and anti-German propaganda," the author of "Tristan" opposes
music, the symbol of Germanness, of his apolitical idealism, of "culture," to

the literary "civilization" of the Allied powers who want to make Germany "progress" from "music to democracy," from "music to politics." Yet this book had hardly been published when, anxious about the effects the war and defeat were having in Germany and about reactionary abuses of irrationalism, whose threat be believed was increasing, Mann quickly turned in favor of the republic and against Romantic music, that of Wagner in particular, to which however he owed the revelation of himself and unforgettable "hours of deep and solitary happiness." And Nietzsche—who had overcome Romanticism—then seemed a model to him, and even something like "a guide toward a new human future."[93]

Behind the "nostalgic, cunning art" of the old magician, it was music itself that Mann had in his sights: "the unformulated, equivocal, irresponsible" something that had already inspired in one of the characters in his *Magic Mountain*, Settembrini, "an antipathy of a political order." "Despite all the logical and moral rigor it sometimes affects, it seems to me rather to stem from a spiritual world whose irreproachability I cannot guarantee, when considered from the perspective of reason and human dignity," Serenus Zeitblom will say in *Doktor Faustus*, which retraces the tragic destiny of a musician whose work reaches its conclusion as Germany is about to fall into barbarism.

"Music has always been suspect, especially for those who love it most intensely, like Nietzsche," Mann wrote a short time later in his diary.[94] And, almost like echoing the old Wagnerian who, in order better to overcome himself, drew near to Goethe, he will add, having read a collection of Beethoven's letters:

> Once again I share Goethe's retractile feeling before "that unbridled
> man." Once again I ponder the relations of music and spirit, of music
> and the world, of music and humanity. Does musical genius, moreover,
> have anything in common with a sense of humanity and of an "im-
> proved society"? Doesn't music run head on against the latter?[95]

"DA CAPO" AND FINALE

To be sure, the regimen with no music that Nietzsche had adopted following the conception of *Human, All Too Human* did not last. However good he might claim to be at "the art of dividing [himself] and forgetting for years one of [his] halves,"[1] "impulses" of a religious or sentimental origin did "want, all the same, to be satisfied." This led, initially, to the somewhat purgative denials following from the well-understood moral hygiene his conscience adapted with just a touch of casuistry:

> Well, we let music make us sad and we sigh like weeping willows in the wind—but then with a joyous laugh we shake off all that and exclaim: music could do all that, grief and tears *with no ground!* To live in feeling without missing the causes of hearing! And then, forward into the real world, our soul is freer and has overcome its sickness![2]

However, the real world soon lost the colors of daybreak that Nietzsche had rediscovered in escaping the nocturnal spells Wagner's music had lavished on him, when a "light-hearted taste for knowledge" had carried him to the "summits" where he triumphed over all "martyrdom and despair."[3] For his "positivist" reaction to Romanticism was so radical, so extreme, that it bore within itself an inevitable disenchantment. Science was not as "gay" as Nietzsche believed or pretended to believe. "Knowledge turns back on itself and ends up biting its tail," he had already written in 1870, "and modern man begins to suspect the limits of the Socratic pleasure in knowing."[4] This suspicion was also to dawn on Nietzsche himself, if he had ever in fact lost sight of it. Truth is perhaps sad, thought Renan, and, in every way, insufficient—worse, it is a lure, since, God being dead, the idea of the perfection of Being on which it had been grounded had also gone under. Deprived of this horizon, science could only turn into nihilism: an accumulation of bits of knowledge against the backdrop of ultimate ignorance. *The Gay Science* in reality is a "knowledge of nonsense, of the insignificance, the meaningless character of everything that exists."[5] And everything that exists, with no goal, is bound to repeat itself in an "eternal *da capo*"[6] that human beings must therefore transform into an ever repeated affirmation of life for its own sake.

That Nietzsche should make use of a musical metaphor to characterize what he calls his "high noon Thought" is neither accidental nor gratuitous. When he had an intuition of the eternal return and of Zarathustra, it was during one of those moments of lyrical exaltation where all contradictions seemed to have resolved themselves, and shortly before this, he had begun to compose again or at least to work again on some of his old scores. "We want to experience a work of art again and again," he noted during the same period. "One shall fashion one's life in such a way that one has the same wish with respect to each of its parts! The capital thought."[7] Since a work of art for Nietzsche always meant music, it is not surprising that a return to music and the eternal return should be so closely connected; all the more so since Nietzsche would henceforth conceive of music as the best symbol of a world without meaning and, at the same time, as a kind of mirage that in transfiguring this world would help humans to affirm themselves in it:

> And do you know what "the world" is for me? Shall I show it to you in my mirror? This world: a monstrosity of forces, with neither beginning nor end; a fixed sum of forces, hard like bronze, that neither increases nor diminishes, that never consumes itself but only transforms itself, whose totality is of invariable size . . . surrounded by "nothingness" as by its limit, without anything spilling out, without waste . . . a sea of stormy forces, in perpetual flux . . . an ebb and flow of forms, from the most simple to the most complex, from the calmest, most rigid, coldest to the most ardent, wildest, most self-contradictory, returning from fullness to simplicity, from a play of contrasts to the pleasure of harmony, always affirming its being in the sameness of its courses and years, blessing itself as that which must eternally recur, as a becoming that knows neither satiety, nor surfeit, nor weariness: this is my *Dionysian* world of eternal self-creation, of eternal self-destruction, a mysterious world of

doubly voluptuous pleasures, my beyond good and evil, with no goal,
unless in the happiness of the circle there is a goal, without will, unless
a ring has goodwill toward itself—do you want a *name* for this world?
A *solution* for all its riddles? . . . —*This world is will to power—and nothing
besides!*[8]

Blind, contradictory, irresistible, the same forces are at work in the
ego—the "pseudo-ego," that fortuitous assemblage, that obscure mixture of
instincts, aspiring only to "experience in a cosmic manner" before dissolving, ecstatically, into the totality without any purpose. Converted into an
aesthetics of rupture, this Dionysian vision, which presupposes an experience of the absurd, was to make Nietzsche one of the patron saints of the
twentieth-century's spontaneously expressive avant-gardes—especially in
Germany, where the final collapse of his mind and reason would add to the
prestige that ever since Hölderlin and Schumann was allotted to madness,
to which was attributed great liberating virtues.

The Return of Apollo

However, we must not reduce the thought of the late Nietzsche to this "moment" (or this temptation), for simultaneously he made it the premise—like
"intoxication" in the process of creation—of an overcoming from which
would be born the authentic individual, master of his "inner explosives"
and proudly solitary in his difference. If Dionysus returns in force in Nietzsche's work, beginning with *The Gay Science*, as a symbol of the most affirmative will to life and not just of music or the creative instinct, it will be to
Romanticism and Christianity that Nietzsche will oppose him from now on,
not any longer to Apollo with whom the god of trance seems to be so intimately connected (above all, in dance) that he, we might say, incorporated
him into himself. We can see this in *Twilight of the Idols* where Goethe is
depicted as the ideal incarnation of the Dionysian spirit (even if his idea
of what was "Greek" was "incompatible with that element out of which
Dionysian art evolved—the orgy").[9] The accomplishment that Nietzsche
most admired in Goethe—that he said yes to life, that he had *created* himself
like a work of art, in overcoming "sentimentality, idealism, irrealism," and
surrounded himself "with limited horizons on all sides"—is the most successful modern version of what he now most appreciates about the Greeks:

Oh, those Greeks! They knew how to live. What is required for that is to
stop courageously at the surface, the fold, the skin, to adore appearance,

to believe in forms, tones, words, in the whole Olympus of appearance. Those Greeks were superficial—*out of profundity.*[10]

Even though Apollo is not named, the worship of appearance unequivocally points to him. However, Nietzsche has broken less than it might appear with something hinted at in *The Birth of Tragedy,* where more than a few indications seem to point to an underlying inclination for his rival, Dionysus. When he writes, for example, that "we, as it were, pass through the chief epochs of the Hellenic genius, analogically in *reverse* order,"[11] we can deduce, without forcing the argument, that the new tragic age that Wagner was supposed to initiate would be followed by a new Apollonian age analogous to that of the Olympian Greeks, that "striking society" in which everything, good or bad, was deified.[12] The book's conclusion also seems to confirm this, since—after having pointed out that "where the Dionysian powers rise up as impetuously as we experience them now, Apollo, too, must already have descended among us"—Nietzsche adds, "and the next generation will probably behold his most ample beautiful effects."[13]

What is hinted at here in counterpoint was to take on fuller amplitude in his later work, beginning with *Daybreak,* even if once again the name Apollo is absent. "How much life shines with beautiful appearances!" he writes in his notebook for 1885.[14] But there is no beautiful appearance without some constraining form. "The greatness of an artist is not to be evaluated by the 'beautiful feelings' that he gives rise to. . . . But by the extent to which he is capable of a grand style. . . . To master the chaos that one is: to constrain one's chaos to take on form; to become necessity in this form; to become logical, simple, unequivocal, mathematics; to become *law*—that is the great ambition."[15] By "grand style" (which apes Wagner), one could guess that Nietzsche means classical style: "To be classical, one must have *all* strong apparently contradictory gifts and desires; but in such a way that they go together under a common yoke" and submit to convention; for "convention is the condition of great art, *not* something that prevents it."[16]

> What music lacks for us is an aesthetic that would impose rules on musicians and create a conscience; what is also lacking is a consequence of this, a genuine struggle for "principles." . . . In fact, this creates a great difficulty: we no longer know how to *justify* the notions of "model," "mastery," "perfection"—we grope blindly in the realm of values, with the instinct of an ancient love and admiration, we almost believe that "anything that pleases *us* is good . . ." What awakens distrust on my part is to see Beethoven on all sides innocently baptized "classical": I am pre-

pared to uphold resolutely that in the other arts what one means by classical is something opposite to Beethoven.[17] Yet when one goes so far as to teach and venerate as a "model," as "mastery," as "progress," the perfect, blinding disintegration of Wagner's style, his so-called "dramatic style," my impatience knows no bounds. Dramatic style in music as Wagner understands it is the renunciation of all style whatsoever, with the presupposition that something else is a hundred times most important than music: namely, drama . . .

What's the use of the expansion of the means of expression if what expresses itself here, art itself, has lost the law that determines it? The painterly splendor and the power of sound, the symbolism of the tonality, rhythm, tone-colors of harmony and dissonance, the suggestive significance of the music with respect to other arts, the whole *sensuality* of music so dominant in Wagner—all this Wagner acknowledged in music, drew out, and developed. Victor Hugo did something similar for language: but now, already, the question is asked in France, in the case of Victor Hugo, if not to the detriment of language . . . if, in intensifying the sensuality in language, one has not suppressed reason, intellect, deep conformity to laws.[18]

From this comes Nietzsche's praise for the "great century" and court society brought to perfection by Louis XIV: this was another way of responding to Wagner, who, in *German Art and German Politics* (1867) dated the decadence of France to Louis XIV and imputed the "superficiality" of French civilization to its aristocratic character.[19] In fact, it was because they addressed themselves to an aristocratic society, well-skilled in the art of the masque, that Corneille and Racine, following the example of the "great Greeks," imposed "the law of a refined, clear intellectuality on the brutish claims of colors, sounds, and forms." As for Wagner, he had no such demands imposed upon him. "It was *not* the public of Corneille of whom Wagner had to be considerate," but just a lowbrow nineteenth century, and even worse, "mere Germans."[20] Similarly, it was because he knew how "to subdue through Greek moderation a soul many-formed and equal to mightiest thunderstorms of tragedy" that Voltaire was not only the last of the great dramatic poets, but also "the last great writer to possess a Greek ear, Greek artistic conscientiousness, Greek charm and simplicity in the treatment of prose speech."[21]

"The stern constraint the French dramatists imposed upon themselves in regard to unity of action, of place and of time, to style, to construction of verse and sentence, to choice of words and ideas, was as vital a schooling as that of counterpoint and fugue in the development of modern music."[22] (Here are rehabilitated the "mathematical rigidity of the counterpoint and the dialectic of the fugue" that Nietzsche had mocked in *The Birth of Tragedy*.) On the contrary, the "restlessness" of the modern Romantic spirit, its "hatred for bounds and moderation" combined with the idea of "inspiration for its own sake"—three characteristics combined to the highest degree by Wagner—far from augmenting the creative force of artists, fatally condemns them once the evolutionary thread has been broken to "become experimenting imitators and foolhardy copiers, however great their powers may have been at first."[23] "If we look at our artists," he notes in 1885, "are not almost all of them perishing from a lack of discipline? They are losing their ability to tyrannize, and so they no longer know how to tyrannize themselves."[24] "Dancing in chains," such is the ideal of the Greek poets and writers, who were not content "to allow a multiplicity of constraints" to be imposed upon them but instead devised "an additional new constraint" and imposed it upon themselves so as to "conquer it with charm and grace: so that both the constraint and its conquest are noticed and admired."[25]

Strict constraints, hardness, order imposed by fierce struggle, tyranny, bridle, yoke, chains—Nietzsche enjoys hyperbole. But perhaps it was because discipline was unnatural to him, and chaos, always near, that he makes use of this vocabulary of the animal trainer, not to say the torturer, when he speaks of attaining any self-control and mastery of style. It is difficult, indeed, to become what one is not, to stop being German and Romantic. A classical education, by all accounts, will not suffice; one has to impose *hyperclassical* coercion (wherein we also rediscover the proof of excellence gained through suffering).[26]

This is all the more so since Romanticism is not just the adversary of moderation and measure: as the aesthetics of feeling, it set up emotion as the criterion of taste. No doubt, in our day, sentimentality forms the principal pleasurable ingredient music provides, particularly when it speaks "the language of our own past" to us. But it is also "always the expression of a *depressed* nervous activity," and if thought gives way to laziness, it will lead us "in the direction of Wagnerian mists."[27] "Feeling and passion as surrogates, once one no longer knows how to reach a high spirituality and the *happiness* of it (for example, that of Voltaire)." Moreover, "from a technical point of view, 'feeling' and 'passion' are *easier*—they presuppose the poorer artists."[28] In short: subjectivity is the enemy!

"As they increase in intensity Dionysian emotions lead to the forgetfulness of self," we already read in *The Birth of Tragedy*, in which Nietzsche separated music from the domain of affects and feelings exploited by Euripides, the gravedigger of ancient drama. Nietzsche's preparatory notes for this book provide the philosophical rationalization for this separation. As Schopenhauer was finally linked to the aesthetics of feeling in making the will the origin of music and of this separation that reflects it, "the universal and imageless language of the heart," Nietzsche does not hesitate in radicalizing his conception of the will and, as an indirect consequence, the metaphysics of music that followed from it.[29] Music does not emanate from the will but from "something that remains undecipherable to us" and situated "beyond all individuation." The will, which music takes for its object, is a "manifestation" (*Erscheinung*) of this undecipherable something, which "reveals itself to us as sensations of pleasure and displeasure." As for feeling, "already penetrated by conscious or unconscious representations that saturate it," this is only a symbol or metaphor for music, not "its direct object." "In the realm of creation, feeling is absolutely not artistic in itself, and only its complete exclusion permits the artist to lose himself without reservation in disinterested contemplation." Nietzsche does not specify how the relation between the undecipherable, situated beyond all individuation, and the artist's disinterested contemplation—in other words, between Dionysus and Apollo—establishes itself. But it is clear from his notes that for him, who so much had to guard himself against his own emotions, emotions can be neither the condition nor the content of music. To be sure, this strict prescription also applies to its listeners. In those "who sense an effect on their affects . . . the distant, furtive power of music appeals to an *intermediary order* that gives them a sort of foretaste, a symbolic preconception of music properly speaking." But to rest there or to be unable to surpass this stage (as when one needs theater to draw near music, to experience it) condemns one to remain in the peristyle of the sanctuary. Genuine, that is, absolute music can make sense and yet not be, for all that, the "language of the heart." Already in 1862, we recall, when the "impetuous waves" of *Tristan* were beginning to wash over him, Nietzsche had commented that these waves and a classic counterfugue must "have something in common, which is the essence of music," and he had concluded: "Feeling absolutely does not constitute a criterion for music." This point of view was developed two years later in reply to a correspondent who had reported the effects, especially the physical effects, that music had upon him:

> Very different musical works produce a similar impression. Don't forget
> that [the excitation of the nerves] is simply physical effect; this is pre-
> ceded by a spiritual intuition, which in its singularity, its greatness, and
> all that it portends, acts on the human being like a sudden miracle. Don't

believe that the ground of this intuition lies in feeling, in sensation; no, it
lies precisely in the most elevated and refined part of the knowing spirit.
Is it not for you as though a vast, unsuspected space opens up; don't you
have the impression of looking beyond into another universe that is ordinarily concealed from human being?

Thanks to this spiritual intuition the listener comes as close as possible to the composer. Indeed, in art there is no higher effect than this; it
is itself a creative force. Do you now find the expression inappropriate
that I myself adopted two years ago when I wrote a number of pages on
this subject to my friends? I referred to the effect as "daemonic." If there
are portents of higher worlds, this is where they lie concealed.[30]

Nietzsche was later to suspect that these intimations of higher worlds,
which earlier he had assimilated with the divine, were nothing more than a
ruse of the religious instinct and its double, the metaphysical instinct, but
without ever really denying the spiritual intuition from which they proceeded. And his reservations concerning feelings will turn into open hostility once he has experienced their debilitating effects, as multiplied by Wagner. In this, Nietzsche turns out to be quite close to Hanslick, who, in *On the
Musically Beautiful*, speaks out strongly against the sentimental conception
of music and, in the first place, against "the sung and fiddled opium-trance
for whose cult, if you please, a temple all its own, has been dedicated in
Bayreuth."[31] No doubt the Viennese critic was thinking of Wagner's public
when he described "the continually crepuscular or exalted state" of "sentimental listeners":

> Slouched dozing in their chairs, these enthusiasts allow themselves to
> brood and sway in response to the vibrations of tones, instead of con-
> templating tones attentively. How the music swells louder and louder
> and dies away, how it jubilates or trembles, they transform into a nonde-
> script state of awareness which they naively consider to be purely intel-
> lectual. These people make up the most "appreciative" audience and the
> one most likely to bring music into disrepute. The aesthetical criterion of
> intellectual pleasure is lost to them. . . . Some sit there mindless at ease,
> others in extravagant rapture, but for all the principle is one and the
> same: pleasure in the elemental in music.[32]

These are lines that Nietzsche will recall in his anti-Wagnerian dia-
tribes, along with others that denounce the infinite melody as "the absence
of melody turned into a principle." For Hanslick, the value of a work of

music is not determined by the effect it produces on the feelings, but by a factor of an intellectual order. To the excitation of the emotions he opposes "pure contemplation" and the comprehension of the beautiful revealed by the form, which is "the true content, the true *ground* of music," for in this "sound is its own end for itself."[33] Nietzsche, however, could not bring himself to rally to this formalist conception of music. The purely formal apprehension of a musical work was only possible in his eyes at a "primitive" stage of music and its reception. For modern music, even when labeled as absolute, is a "symbolism of form speaking to the understanding without poetry after both arts had been united over a long course of evolution and the musical form had finally become entirely enmeshed in threads of feeling and concepts."[34] To refer to a work only in terms of its formal beauty, therefore, is either to overlook the symbolic capacity of musical language through a lack of learning or, like Hanslick, to deny its existence by coldly taking refuge behind the façade of Apollonianism.

"What a spectacle, when our latter-day aestheticians, with a net of 'beauty' peculiar to themselves, pursue and clutch at the genius of music whirling before display activities which are not to be judged by the standard of eternal beauty any more than by the standard of the sublime," he writes in *The Birth of Tragedy,* threatening these "patrons of music at close range . . . indefatigably crying: 'Beauty! Beauty!'" who "must some day appear before the unerring judge, Dionysus."[35] In fact, their defense of beauty comes down to "a struggle against the *moralizing* tendency in art," he will say in *Twilight of the Idols.* "But this very hostility betrays that moral prejudice is still dominant. When one has excluded from art the purpose of moral preaching and human improvement, it by no means follows that art is completely purposeless, goalless, meaningless, in short, *l'art pour l'art*—a snake biting its own tail."[36] Similarly, in his notebooks from the same period, we read: "*L'art pour l'art:* the virtuosic croaking of frogs, chilled to the bone, who despair in their ponds."[37]

A barely disguised adept of absolute music, Nietzsche, at bottom, remained impregnated by the Romantic metaphysics that underlay the definition Tieck and Hoffmann had given to it. In its very absence of an object or a precise destination it revealed the infinite, what at first Nietzsche called the divine, then higher worlds. In his last writings, what gets substituted for these pitfalls of idealism, evaded by "the free spirit," is "life," life that itself tends to become a synonym for truth and that, in taking on a central place in his thought, was rapidly to win him a large following. Except for the euphoria of his last weeks in Turin, "life" is exalted with as much vehemence as Nietzsche, "crushed" by solitude and the almost continual presence of pain, struggles against a distaste for existence and other human beings. Art must be in the service of life—*The Birth of Tragedy* had already announced this. But following his first book, Nietzsche had perceived that the pessimism of the nineteenth century, upon which he had founded such great hopes, could have two opposing origins. Either it was the reflection of a "superabundance of life" giving rise to a tragic vision of existence and a Dionysian art or, on the contrary, it betrayed an "impoverishment of this life" and art, in this case, was called on to give "rest, silence, a glassy sea, self-forgetfulness, and at the opposite pole, intoxication, frenzy, dizziness, and madness." In this ambivalence of pessimism or nihilism we rediscover, transposed, the determining ambivalence of Nietzsche's musical experience.

His polemical intent led Nietzsche to generally infer from the effects of a phenomenon that their cause has to be of the same nature: sick music exists whose most complete model, whose archetype is the Wagnerian love potion. "That the dear old Germans know how to indulge in primal feelings of Teutonic efficiency and strength, belongs to the most farcical signs of German psychological culture—for us Wagner's music means a visit to the hospital. . . . For him, such morbidity is not willed, not a matter of chance—it is the essence of his art, its instinct, its 'unconscious,' it is its *innocence* . . ."[38] "He is a master of hypnotic tricks, he manages to throw down the strongest like bulls. . . . this decadent corrupts our health."[39] Here again, when he writes these lines, the author of *The Case of Wagner* knows what he is talking about. As Julien Gracq will put it, "he takes revenge for years of sensual servitude to his old master."[40] For, let us not forget, in the anathemas and sarcasm that Nietzsche throws at his old idol, the insurmountable reflexes of a Puritan are always mixed in along with the protest over threats to the vital instinct. In this, the author of *Beyond Good and Evil*, sometimes wrongly taken to be a kind of immoral anarchist, shows himself to be the faithful heir of one of his closest enemies: Plato, who out of concern to "purify the city" would banish from it all rhythms and harmonies suspected of leading to intoxication and indolence and permitting only those that "expressed a rule-governed and courageous life."[41]

Indeed, some music does stimulate life, provoking or increasing that joy, that full, complete adhesion to existence, without remorse or second thoughts that lies on the horizon of Nietzsche's last writings. For example, in the spring of 1887 he writes:

> I am not happy enough, not in good enough health for all this Romantic
> music (Beethoven included). What I require is a music where one forgets

one's suffering; where animal life feels divinized and triumphant; to which one wants to dance; with which perhaps—a cynical question—comes good digestion? Life lightened by *light*, bold rhythms, sure of themselves, exuberant, life gilded by *golden*, tender, kind-hearted harmonies—this is what I extract from all music . . . But these are physiological, not aesthetic judgments: simply—I no longer have any aesthetic![42]

But at the same time that he celebrates instinct, Nietzsche also tends to consider the body as "the ground of things," the originary ground he never stopped looking for: "the ultimate fact to which we can descend" for which ideas, feelings, emotions are just its "ciphered language." "The ultimate irreducible element I find within myself is sensation," he already had written a decade earlier.[43] There is no false sensation he might have added. But the body itself, he was soon to suspect, was itself only a second-order phenomenon, the interpreter of the will to power, that score open to an infinity of interpretations.[44] Music begins with the body, but it does not exhaust its meaning. The "spiritual intuition" it provokes is not determined by feeling or sensations but proceeds from "the most elevated and most refined portion of the knowing spirit," he wrote in 1862. It is through the body to the spirit that music must speak:

> Our music, which can transform itself into everything and has to transform itself because, like the demon of the sea, it has in itself no character: in the past this music followed the *Christian scholar* and was able to translate his ideal into sounds; why should it not in the end discover that brighter, more joyful and universal sound which corresponds to the *ideal thinker?*—a music which knows how to *be at home* only floating up and down among the broad soaring vaulted arches of *his soul?*—Our music has hitherto been so great, so good: nothing has been impossible to it! So let it then show that it is possible to feel these three things at the same time: sublimity, deep and warm illumination, and the joy of perfect consistency.[45]

From One Modernity to Another

Anti-Romanticism, classicism, Enlightenment, intellectual delight: the aesthetic outlined in Nietzsche's works starting with *Human, All Too Human* stood in complete opposition to Wagnerianism and to almost all of its Austro-German posterity. That he should have sometimes been connected with this latter or was thought of in terms of it in most cases reveals a misinterpretation caused by misunderstanding or by simply overlooking certain essential aspects of his thought.

In the case of Mahler, this misunderstanding only lasted a short while. "What he has to say comes from Nietzsche," the critic William Ritter will write after hearing Mahler's Fourth Symphony. "From Nietzsche he acquired a passionate and sarcastic vehemence that encourages him to risk all in order to assert his passions, his enthusiasms, his monumental, side-splitting humour, and no doubt his utter contempt for humanity."[46] But if he was initially "enchanted" by the philosopher's work—he set the midnight dancing song from *Zarathustra* to music in his Third Symphony in 1895[47]—Mahler soon turned away from it, shocked by its anti-Christianity and "the anti-ethics of the Overman." The discovery that his future wife, Anna Schindler, had Nietzsche's books plunged him into indignation, and he unsuccessfully requested that she burn them. This episode would surely have pleased the author of *The Gay Science*. What else could be expected of a former disciple who had converted to Catholicism, even if he did so in large part to advance his career? And what sarcasm Nietzsche would have directed against Mahler's "theatrical symphonies," with their false naïveté, their whining, and the compulsive need for redemption that sounds so loudly in them!

Richard Strauss would, probably, not have found favor in Nietzsche's eyes, at least up to his *Ariadne auf Naxos*. That he should have made Zarathustra dance a Viennese waltz, and a quite banal one to boot, would have seemed to Nietzsche an act of profanity, as would have that other waltz, more frenetic than Dionysian, that ends *Elektra*, even though in this work Strauss wanted to "contrast this possessed, exalted Greece of the sixth century with Winckelmann's Roman copies and Goethe's humanism."[48] Yet, under the deliberately prosaic exterior of a Barvarian *Bürger*, Strauss concealed a cultivated mind and more than a slight affinity with Nietzsche, whom, by the way, he discovered at the same time he came to know Greece. Under the blow of this double initiation, in 1892, he modified the ending of his first opera, *Guntram*. Instead of submitting to authority and leaving the stage with an act of renouncement, the hero, a kind of Parsifal touched by love, delivers a profession of faith in individualism, Nietzschean individualism: "My life is dictated by the one law of my spirit: it is to me alone that my god speaks and he speaks only to me." Still, this is a highly discreet god. Little interested in metaphysics, Strauss was even less concerned about religion. If in *Salomé* Jokanaan preaches repentance to the daughter of Babylon, Strauss, who had no "sympathy for this kind of man," thought him to be "an imbecile and at first wanted him to be slightly grotesque."[49] "I don't see from what I need to be saved," he liked to say. This is a saying that Nietz-sche would certainly have claimed as his own. The composer of *Daphné* was a pagan but naturally and tranquilly so, with no need to "overcome him-self." What is more, Nietzsche would undoubtedly quickly have perceived that this was a Wagnerian in form rather than in content. Having inherited the language forged by *Tristan* and *The Ring*, Strauss made use of it, except in his first operas and then again later in *Die Frau ohne Schatten,* for wholly other ends than the exploitation of Romantic pathos and the pangs of sub-jectivity that, after Wagner, already felt overdone. ("Wagner *is* terribly cloy-ing," says Julien Gracq.) So we can understand that Debussy and Ravel might have appreciated Strauss, while they did not conceal their hostility toward Mahler. In 1903, "Monsieur Croche" will say:

> His eyes and gestures are those of a *Superman,* to quote Nietzsche, from
> whose teaching he must have imbibed his energy. From Nietzsche too he
> must have learned his lofty scorn of feeble sentimentalities and his
> desire that music not go on forever providing a more or less satisfactory
> illumination for our nights, that it should shine like the sun. I can assure
> you that there is sunshine in the music of Strauss.[50]

After *Salomé* and *Elektra,* those bloody nocturnal dramas, the sun shone in his work, albeit filtered through Mozart, the discovery of whom re-vealed to Strauss his own profound nature. "I don't want to force myself any more," he confided to Romain Rolland, following a visit to the Louvre where he had much admired paintings by Watteau. "I need to make sweet, happy music. No more heroic things."[51] In 1941, while war was raging, this return to Mozart would produce its most successful effort: *Capriccio.* In a chateau near Paris, in a lively dispute between admirers of Gluck and admirers of Puccini, six characters discuss, with a love subplot thrown in, the relations between words and music, of which Nietzsche, like Strauss, could have said that they "had always been the problem of [his] life." Strauss would add: "*Capriccio* solves with a question mark."[52] But the music by itself concludes this mixture of irony, pastiche, and parody expressing in a light-hearted mode what Thomas Mann calls "the historical exhaustion of the means available to art "at the same time that it obstinately refuses the horrors sur-rounding it.

Strauss, who felt a "vocation to become the Offenbach of the twentieth century,"[53] had abandoned without regret or remorse the exaltation of anxi-ety and suffering, against the background of Austrian decadence and Ger-man apocalypse, to the audacities and modernist experiments of the Viennese avant-garde. Perhaps Nietzsche would have approved of the return to order and formal conciseness introduced by Schoenburg in reaction to the post-Wagnerian dissolution of chromaticism. But as the strict serialism of his heirs confirmed, the dodecaphonic system tends irresistibly to eliminate all physical and physiological references of musical perception—consonance, hierarchy of notes, rhythmic pulse—to the profit of purely abstract combinations. The author of *Human, All Too Human* had foreseen this "intellectualization of art" and condemned it as an impasse:

> By virtue of the extraordinary exercise the intellect has undergone
> through the artistic evolution of modern music, our ears have grown
> more and more intellectual. We can now endure a much greater volume,
> much more 'noise,' than our forefathers could because we are much
> more practised in listening for the *reason in it* than they were. Because
> they at once inquire after the reason, the 'meaning,' and are no longer
> content to know that a thing 'is,' all our senses have in fact become some-
> what blunted. . . . In this matter our ears have become coarser. Then, the
> ugly side of the world, the side originally hostile to the senses, has now
> been conquered for music . . . our music now brings to utterance things
> which formerly had no tongue. In a similar way, some of our painters
> have made our eyes more intellectual and have gone far beyond that
> which was formerly called pleasure in form and colour. Here too the side
> of the world that originally counted as ugly has been conquered by artis-
> tic reason.—What will be the consequence of all this? The more capable
> of thought the eye and ear become, the closer they approach the point at
> which they become unsensual: pleasure is transferred to the brain, the
> sense-organs themselves grow blunt and feeble, the symbolic increas-
> ingly replaces the simple being—and along this path we thus attain to
> barbarism as certainly as along any other.[54]

The intellectualization of art, and its consequent impoverishment, went hand in hand with other, no less pernicious evils that Nietzsche again and again deplores: "the counterfeiting in the imitation of big forms for which nobody today is strong, proud, self-assured, *healthy* enough; excessive liveliness in the smallest parts; excitement at any price; cunning as the expression of *impoverished* life; more and more nerves in the place of flesh."[55] Decadence was irremediable. Wagner had only "speeded up the tempo" (for other reasons, to be sure, Wagner thought the same thing: "the history of music will have been short," he said toward the end of his life).

However, particularly outside Germany, another musical "modernity" was getting ready to blossom—colorful, dancing, hedonist, then ludic and neoclassical, for which Paris would be the principal center. Its representatives—French (Debussy, Ravel, Roussel, then the group of six), Russian (Stravinsky, Prokofiev), Spanish (Albeniz, Granados, Falla), Hungarian (Bartók)—were careful to preserve a national originality in the face of the Wagnerian hegemony and its sequel. But often, they followed the same aesthetic motifs as did Nietzsche. Nor was it unknown that they, like Debussy and Bartók, had read him to their own profit.[56] ("Let us read again Nietzsche's *The Case of Wagner*," Cocteau will later say. "Never have shallower or profounder things been said."[57]) For the most part, what these composers had in common was a refusal of the "sentimental blackmail" that had become music's specialty. And more than any other work *Le Sacre du printemps* symbolizes this reaction, which, for Stravinsky—revolted by the spectacle of *Parsifal*, that "aping of a religious rite"—was aimed also at "this unseemly and sacrilegious conception of art as religion and the theater as its temple."[58] Perhaps Nietzsche, before Cocteau, might have judged that Stravinsky, too, in spite of everything, was contaminated by the "theater bug." What is certain is that, unlike Adorno, far from seeing in *Le Sacre* a sign of historical regression, he would have greeted it as a deliverance.

Nietzsche died too soon to see this renaissance, which he hoped for without really believing in. But the early warning signs did not escape him. His books and correspondence starting with *The Gay Science* bear witness to this.

The Case of Brahms

However, since his taste never fit perfectly with his creative force—all the more so in that after a certain point he contradicted a good portion of himself, if not his deepest nature—the adaptation he made at this time of Lou Salomé's "Hymn to Life" stops well short of his ideal. "Great artists have a dual character," Baudelaire had noted, "which drives them as critics to praise and analyze more lovingly the qualities they themselves most need as creators, and which serve as a foil to those they possess in superabundance."[59] Just as the piano piece of 1874, which Nietzsche drew on, predicted, the Wagner-like torments of his *Manfred-Meditation* were forgotten in favor of an affirmation of classicism. But the "pure" style of the chorale, cultivated during his youth, which the composer now employs, does not reflect, as we know, the "heroic idyll" to which he aspires as philosopher.[60] Here Nietzsche is thinking above his musical and emotional means. As Peter Gast puts it, in listening to this "Protestant music which mounts to the sky with a heavy step," one thinks of Brahms, to whom, by the way, Nietzsche sent a copy of the score at the same time he had his publisher send a copy of *On the Genealogy of Morals*.[61]

The resemblance was no accident. Nietzsche had experienced more than sympathy for Brahms's music. This increased when, at the beginning of the summer of 1874, he heard Brahms's *Triumphlied* both in Basel and in Zurich under the composer's direction. Following the first concert, Nietzsche writes to Erwin Rohde, "One of the most difficult tests of aesthetic conscience for me has been this confrontation with Brahms. I am beginning to form some sort of opinion about him, but still a very timid one."[62] Oddly, Nietzsche does not allude to the highly nationalistic character of this work, which celebrates the German victory of 1871, even though this, we have seen, quickly inspired morose reflections on his part and even though he would reproach Wagner brusquely (*corruptio optimi pessima*) for his strongly anti-French attitude during the time of his favorable attitude toward the *Reich*.[63] But this "small idea" he was beginning to have of Brahms—certainly an unfavorable one—did not prevent him from bringing the score to Bayreuth a few weeks later. There was something provocative about this gesture, for Nietzsche was not unaware of how little Wagner thought of his young confrere and, in particular, of the highly critical lines he had devoted to him in his essay on conducting.[64] This was not unfounded. In 1860, seven years earlier, the one whom Schumann had greeted as the messiah of German music had, along with four other musicians including Joseph Joachim, signed a manifesto directed against "the so-called music of the future," that is, against Liszt and Wagner. Such a profession of faith, along with the conservatism of his works, destined him for the admiration of Hanslick, Wagner's great adversary, who made himself the champion of Brahms in his crusade against "musical pathology." Were he to show himself at all magnanimous, Wagner would have had to have demonstrated much more tolerance than genius usually does toward its contemporary equals or even lesser talents.

When Nietzsche played the *Triumphlied* for Wagner, he laughed "loudly at the idea of setting such a word as *Gerechtigkeit* [justice] to music."[65] But things worsened two days later when, after another performance of the piece, Nietzsche did not hesitate to praise it, contrary to Wagner's opinion, and Wagner exclaimed, quite irritatedly, "Handel, Mendelssohn, and Schumann wrapped in leather."[66] After having "caused R. many difficult hours,"—having maintained among other things that "the German language gives him no pleasure, and he would rather talk Latin"[67]—Nietzsche left Bayreuth, to which he would not return until 1876. He noted angrily in his notebook: "The tyrant cannot tolerate any individuality but his own and those close to him. The danger is great for Wagner if he won't tolerate Brahms, etc., or the Jews."[68] Yet the fourth essay in *Unfashionable Observations*, on which the future emulator of Brutus was just then beginning to work, was to echo favorably the tyrant's anger. It is not difficult to recognize Brahms in it among those musicians ("a purely convenient plural," comments Schaeffner) who "banish themselves with anxious eagerness to the circle of the old masters, and prefer to base their 'independence' on Schubert or Handel rather than on Wagner. To no avail! By fighting against their own better conscience they become smaller and pettier as artists; they ruin their character by having to put up with bad allies and friends; and after making all these sacrifices, it still happens, perhaps in a dream, that they have ears only for Wagner."[69] Two years later, following his farewell to Bayreuth, we find a new turn or, rather, semi-turn—but this time in his notebook:

> The most salutary appearance is that of Brahms, in whose music flows more German blood than in Wagner's—by which I mean to say something good but by no means *only* something good.[70]

More German blood—we can take this to mean that Brahms was not corrupted by the theater, which was often contrary to his inclination since, like Mendelssohn and Schumann, he was very attracted to opera. Nietzsche was not unaware of this,[71] and no doubt he would have credited the composer for his ineptitude in this domain. "Brahms is *no* actor," we read in the second postscript to *The Case of Wagner*[72]—a high compliment. But an earlier portion of this text proves clearly that Nietzsche did not mean just to say something good about Brahms.

> His good fortune was a German misunderstanding: he was taken for Wagner's antagonist—an antagonist was *needed*.—That does not make for *necessary* music, that makes, above all, for too much music. . . . His is the melancholy of incapacity; he does *not* create out of an abundance, he *languishes* for abundance. If we discount what he imitates, what he borrows from great old or exotic-modern styles—he is a master of imitation—what remains as specifically his is *yearning*.—This is felt by all who are full of yearning and dissatisfaction of any kind. . . . In particular, he is the musician for a certain type of dissatisfied women. Fifty steps more, and you have got the female Wagnerian—just as fifty steps beyond Brahms you encounter Wagner—the female Wagnerian, a type that is more incisive, more interesting, and above all *more charming*.[73]

It was not by returning to older forms that one could successfully battle Wagner, however. As a nostalgic rebel for tradition, Nietzsche had tried it, following Brahms, with his "Hymn to Life," whose first version for piano had anticipated his turning away from Wagner. This probably accounts for his sending a copy to Brahms as an indication of a return of sympathy for his music. "The best instruction, the most conscientious training, intimacy on principle, even isolation in the company of the old masters—all this remains merely palliative—to speak more precisely, illusory—for one no longer has the presupposition in one's body."[74] The reaction against the evolution since Beethoven of instrumental music toward drama had been "unable to fill the Classic form with Life" without "distorting it" and "the reactionary party" has merely exposed ineptitudes, Wagner had written in 1879 in a transparent allusion to Brahms and his "symphonic revival," which surely did not escape Nietzsche.[75] As Nietzsche will say to the "ear of the Conservatives" in *Twilight of the Idols*, "what was formerly not known, what is known today or could be known—a *reversion*, a turning back in any sense and to any degree, is quite impossible. . . . There is nothing for it: one *has* to go forward, which is to say *step by step further into décadence* (—this is *my* definition of modern 'progress' . . .). One can *retard* this development and, through retardation, dam and gather up degeneration itself and make it more vehement and *sudden:* more one cannot do."[76]

The impotence for which he stigmatizes Brahms is also his own as a composer formed from the classic mold. Nietzsche is just as incapable of rejuvenating it as he is of successfully freeing himself from it. If, therefore, for lack of anything better, while awaiting the still worse from which the dreams of new may perhaps spring, one was to imitate the old masters, Nietzsche desires it without being able to achieve it, and he does so with a smile, "the smile of a spoiled man, lately arrived at refinement, who, at the same time, never ceases to *make whole-hearted fun* of the good old days and its music, so good, so old, so worn out—but a smile filled with love, even with emotion . . ."

> What, is this not the best attitude that we *can* adopt today toward the
> past in general?—to look back to it with gratitude, to acknowledge it,
> and even to imitate "the ancients," with much joy and love for all that an-
> cestral worthiness and unworthiness from which we stem, but also with
> that sublime speck of contempt without which all love prematurely gets
> corrupted, rots, and becomes "stupid" . . .[77]

Nietzsche believed he found this loving, yet ironic form in his "faith-ful Kurwenal," Gast, whom he did not hesitate to proclaim a "new Mozart" and the "last classical musician." With the pale talent of an epigone, Gast had in fact composed a *Lion of Venice* to the libretto of Cimarosa's *Secret Mariage*, which was performed a single time—in Danzig in 1891—only thanks to Nietzsche's madness and his sudden fame, before falling into almost complete oblivion.[78] Too bad that Nietzsche never heard *Ariadne auf Naxos, Pulcinella, Apollon Musagète*, or *Capriccio!*

Echoes of the "Good Old Days"

If it was necessary to advance step by step into decadence, it is surprising that what Nietzsche condemns in Brahms he praises in Mendelssohn: "good taste applied to all that had previously been good."

> It always points back behind itself. How could it have much "before it," much future!—But then did he *want* a future? He possessed a virtue rare among artists, that of gratitude without mental reservations: and this virtue too always points back behind itself.[79]

Maybe Mendelssohn was no genius. But as a victim of the cult that it engenders, genius often loses all sense of measure, believing itself to enjoy "exceptional rights."[80]

> It is precisely the original heads among the artists, those who draw on resources that are their own, who can sometimes produce the empty and the hollow, while the more dependent natures, the so-called talents, full of recollections of everything imaginable are able even when they are at their weakest to produce something tolerable. If the originals are deserted by themselves recollection renders them no aid: they become empty.[81]

This is a return to a childhood admiration. As a student at Pforta, Nietzsche had sung in the choruses of *Oedipus at Colonus* and the *Lorelei* (an unfinished opera) by Mendelssohn, who at the time he held to be one of the "six pillars" of German music. At that time he will say, "it was Mendelssohn's high culture that set the tone; and we owe to it our great caution as regards vulgarity and presumption *in rebus musicis et musicantibus*."[82] Under Wagner's influence, Nietzsche had subsequently rejected this admiration. Invited by the composer's son, Karl, who was a professor at the University of Freiburg im Breisgau and a reader of *The Birth of Tragedy*, to accompany him on a trip to Greece that would have brought them to Athens, Naxos, and then to Crete, Nietzsche said no.[83] "After my book," he wrote to a friend, "it has become impossible for me to reconcile what we call *our* Hellas with my memories of Mendelssohn's *Antigone*."[84] In Wagner's eyes, the music Mendelssohn had composed for Sophocles' tragedies passed for the leading example of the misunderstanding Greek antiquity suffered from in educated, high German circles.[85] What is more, the composer of *Elijah,* along with Meyerbeer, was the principal target of his pamphlet, "Jews in Music," which he had just reissued in May 1869 when Nietzsche was beginning his visits to Tribschen. Mendelssohn, whom he renamed "Handelssohn" was the very incarnation of the "cultured Jew," who, thanks to "his learned and paid-for culture," turned toward music, "that art which is just the very easiest to learn" and that "affords such plenteous possibility of talking in it without saying any real thing." But having become a musician, his lack of roots in the "people" condemned him to babble, repeating what had already been said like a parrot.[86]

To praise Mendelssohn, therefore, was a way for Nietzsche to attack Wagner, whose prejudices against the Jews he had shared for a time, on one sensitive point, and clearly to set himself apart from the "anti-Semitic villain." When on the edge of madness Nietzsche will dream of "sending [Wagner] to the firing squad."[87]

> Mendelssohn, in whom they [i.e., the Wagnerians] deplore the absence
> of any force of elementary emotion (let it be said in passing: the talent of
> the *Jews* of the Old Testament), without finding any compensation in
> what he does have: freedom under the law, and noble affects within the
> bounds of beauty.[88]

> With a little bit of Goethe that's not to be found anywhere else.[89]

This "halcyon master" had been "the beautiful *intermezzo* of German Music," whereas Schumann "was already a merely *German* event in music."[90]

It was no accident, then, that Chopin ranks near Mendelssohn on Nietzsche's list at the end of his Wagnerian period. Chopin had "freed music of its German influences, of its propensity for the ugly, the gloomy, the petit-bourgeois, for heaviness and pedantry." When Nietzsche discovered him, Beethoven seemed alongside him "a semibarbaric nature whose great soul had been badly educated so that it had never learned to distinguish clearly between the sublime and the adventurous, between the simple and what was mediocre and in bad taste."[91] Like the Greek poets, Chopin knows how to play and dance "in fetters" (i.e., with the traditional forms of melody and rhythm), "like the freest and most graceful of spirits—and does so, more-over, without turning them to ridicule."[92] A genius at composing the musi-cal aphorism, he knew so well how to make moments of happiness sing that in listening to his barcarole "the gods themselves could on hearing it desire to spend long summer evenings lying in a boat."[93] Nietzsche often asked Gast to play this piece for him, which he had heard in Basel played by Hans von Bülow, as well as many others, even if this were to be to the detriment of his health, as Gast recounts in his memoirs:

> End of March 1880.—Nietzsche came to see me Tuesday and I played Chopin's Barcarole for him, in my best manner, several times over. We cannot get enough of these charming sounds, of the fantastic richness of all that is implied in them, of its perfection of form. Nietzsche then played for me a number of times a typical piece of his from when he was fifteen. Then I had to play more Chopin again. Here, curtly, is a list: the Impromptu, op. 29 (which we call "The Dancing Muse"); the Prelude, op. 28, no. 15 in D-flat; the Berceuse, op. 57; the Largo from the Sonata, op. 58; the principal theme of the Rondo in E-flat, op. 16; the Variation, op. 12; the addition to the Allegro of the concerto, op. 46, including the brilliant modulations in thirty-second notes; and finally the grand Fan-tasy in F-minor, op. 49. In this way, we passed two hours of joyous exalta-tion. Nietzsche said to me in parting: "I am going to pay for all that." And, indeed, the day after I found him laid low by awful suffering.[94]

Nietzsche did not turn these migraines into "physiological objec-tions" against Chopin's art, as he did with Wagner, but they may neverthe-less have been the source of one reservation that he confided to his notebook

> Unfortunately . . . Chopin comes too close to a dangerous current of the French spirit, and it is not all that rare that his music comes across as pale, lacking sunlight, oppressed, even though elegantly and richly clothed—the strong Slav did not know how to defend himself against the narcotics of an overly refined culture.[95]

But there was nothing like this to fear with Mozart. "I have the im-pression of having recovered from an illness," he writes during the summer of 1879. "I am thinking with unspeakable sweetness of Mozart's *Requiem*. I have regained my taste for simple foods."[96] Ten years later, however, Jo-melli's *Requiem* will seem to him to come from "another world than that of

Mozart's *Requiem*." And he adds, "The older Italians, with their depth of sweet melancholy feeling, [were] the *aristocratic* musicians *par excellence;* the most sublime voice was found in their tones."[97] From this observation, we can guess that Nietzsche would have welcomed the rediscovery of Baroque and Renaissance music that was beginning at that time—just as Wagner, eight years earlier in Naples, had been strongly touched by Leonardo Leo's *Miserere.* (Leo was one of Jomelli's teachers). "That is true music," he had told Cosima, "which makes everything else look like child's play. . . . Art of the noblest, most impersonal kind."[98]

In Jomelli and Leo both Wagner and Nietzsche appreciated the music of a world that, when measured against Romanticism, seemed not to know the Romantic expression of subjectivity and the conventions of drama, what Nietzsche might have called the denaturing of music. Nietzsche hints at this in "The Wanderer and His Shadow" in discussing "musical performance," which Mozart himself may have participated in, if not actually inaugurated. Protesting against the dramatization of music (imputable to Wagner, even if he is not named), which consists in giving every piece "as much *high relief* as possible," Nietzsche, addressing himself to the performers of his own day, asks: "do you think that all Mozartian music should be equated with 'the music of the stone guest'? And not only Mozartian music but all music?"[99] In other words, one starts by being taken with the Commandatore scene in *Don Giovanni,* and then, sooner or later, one finds oneself in the grasp of Wagner, who, as above all else a man of the theater, seeks only "a genuine *actio* with an *haut-relief* of gestures, a scene that *throws* people."[100]

That Mozart may have been, with this "terribly serious" scene," at the origin of the change in aesthetic values that will triumph in the nineteenth century, does not therefore authorize interpreting all his works in such a dramatic fashion. That would be "simply a sin against the spirit, against the cheerful, sunny, tender, frivolous spirit of Mozart."[101] But the change had been so great that Nietzsche doubted whether the modern soul had a refined enough ear to hear it:

> The "good old time" is gone, in Mozart we hear its swan song. How fortunate *we* are that his rococo still speaks to us, that his "good company," his tender enthusiasms, his childlike delight in curlicues and Chinese touches, his courtesy of the heart, his longing for the graceful, those in love, those dancing, those easily moved to tears, his faith in the south, may still appeal to some *residue* in us. Alas, some day all this will be gone.[102]

"Off to Crete"

Nietzsche was excessively pessimistic. In fact, hardly had the Wagnerian mists invaded the theaters, from which Mozart had almost completely disappeared, than in 1880–90 a reaction set in. In Munich—"where live my antipodes," said Nietzsche—the home of a triumphant Wagnerism whose festivals were beginning to compete with Bayreuth, a Mozart Festival was held in 1895, with "model" performances of *The Marriage of Figaro*. The orchestra was reduced, the recitatives accompanied by a harpsichord; and the conductor was Hermann Levi, who had directed the premier of *Parsifal* at Bayreuth thirteen years earlier. The following summer, the *Marriage* was succeed by *Don Giovanni*, presented exactly according the Prague score under the baton of Richard Strauss. The recitatives that he improvised on the spinet piano were one of the attractions of these performances. Among the audience in the hall—which was perfectly suited to this work, a small theater of the palace where Mozart himself had presented *Idomea*—there were numerous foreign music lovers who would spread the good news. Among them were Edward J. Dent, whose book on Mozart's operas, published in 1913, would quickly become considered a classic; Théodore de Wyzewa, one-time codirector of *Le Revue wagnérienne* who with Georges de Saint-Foix was to undertake a big musical biography of Mozart whose first two volumes in 1912 would mark an important step in Mozart studies and in musicology in general; and Alfred Boschot, who in 1901 along with Saint-Foix would found a Mozart Society destined to make known his overlooked and little known works, which is to say, most of them.

This same year, 1896, *Don Giovanni* was also the order of the day in Paris. Carvalho, the director of the Opera-Comique, "reconstructed" it, once again on the basis of the Prague manuscript. And although the final scene was not restored, he nonetheless emphasized how its spectacle was in conformity with the spirit of the work. In *Le Fiagro* Carvalho declared, "What must not be forgotten is that *Don Juan* was called an *opera giocoso*, that is, a light opera, by its composer." A reduced orchestra, to which "new"—that is, very old—instruments were introduced to make this clear, and immediately Debussy recognized that "in returning to Mozart's orchestra one arrives at emotional effects as considerable and above all more sincere" than with the large-scale orchestra and "odd instruments" of the modern school.[103] Also in 1896, this time in Vienna, Emperor Franz-Josef and his court attended with much pomp the inauguration of a monument erected to the glory of Mozart. It was the first time, it was said, that a ruler of Austria had taken part in such a thing. This belated redress was to culminate ten years later with a "Mozart Festival" conducted by Gustav Mahler in honor of the one hundred fiftieth anniversary of Mozart's birth. This movement even carried over into England thanks to Thomas Beecham, who would later say, "Nothing so noteworthy has happened in the course of my life as the reevaluation of which Mozart has been the object throughout the whole world."

Having begun with his operas—not just *Don Giovanni* and *The Marriage of Figaro*, but also with *Così fan tutte*, forgotten by then or badly disfigured—this reevaluation went on to include Mozart's instrumental works. By the end of the century, his concertos and symphonies were reappearing on concert programs, as was his chamber music. There was a thirst for simplicity, for transparency, and Mozart was not the only figure to be rediscovered: Bach, Handel, Rameau, Palestrina, and even Monteverdi were back— all masters of music prior to Romanticism, to music that had become drama and highly expressive. For "it was only starting with Beethoven that music had in general taken on an aspect of the *translation* of the psychological into the musical order," said Paul Dukas at that time, in an article that surely would have pleased Nietzsche.

> We can even say that the major part of the pleasure today's listener takes in music is provided to him by the impression of the *struggle* the composer must engage in in order to express musically ever more complicated inner phenomena. Whence those leaps—those sudden explosions, those heartbreaking moments, and all those strange beauties that one delights in considering as characteristic of art at present. Looked at from the point of view of absolute music, they can only be seen as clear signs of degeneracy. From Beethoven to Richard Strauss *translation* music has made great progress. This is due without a doubt to the fact that it addresses itself to and continually must address ever growing masses who are incapable of taking pleasure in a uniquely musical emotion.

On the other hand, "everything Mozart touches naturally transforms itself into music without one ever having, in listening to it, the impression that he had been seeking, for whatever feeling, a *translation* for whose expression he had to make his music undergo some deformation, however small." If "shaken by the oftentimes cruel blows of modern art . . . and that earthquakelike atmosphere it brings with it," we seek to get back to a "*musical* music," then "we can take refuge in his music like some forgotten Eden."[104]

Coincidentally, thirty years earlier, when Bayreuth was in the planning stages, this nostalgia for an almost lost world already gripped, if not

CHAPTER TEN

Wagner himself, at least the guardian of the Grail: Cosima-Ariadne. After having heard Wagner and Hans Richter play the andante from the *Jupiter* symphony for four hands, it was with accents worthy of the future apostate—to whom, perhaps, she confided—that she poured out her feelings to her diary:

> Listening to the Andante, I found myself thinking of Beethoven, and I felt as if one might say to him, "Alas, alas, you have destroyed it, this beautiful world." . . . The gods have ceased their sweet and blessed playing, and instead of Paradise we have life, with all its terrible agony and the salvation which flows from it.[105]

Salvation, redemption: Wagner's "opera is the opera of redemption. Somebody or other always wants to be redeemed in his work," Nietzsche will ironize in *The Case of Wagner*.[106]

> *Sursoum!* Boumboum! Virtue is always right, even against counterpoint. . . . We will never tolerate that music should "serve for relaxation," that it should "please" us, give us pleasure. *Never do we give in to pleasure!* We are lost if we start to think of art as hedonists. . . . Drink, O my friends. Drink the philters of this old magician! This Klingsor of all Klingsors! How he speaks to all the cowardice of the modern soul, with his siren's accent!
>
> Ah, this old robber. He robs our youths, he even robs our women and drags them into his den.—Ah, this old Minotaur! The price we have had to pay for him! Every year trains of the most beautiful maidens and youths are led into his labyrinth, so that he may devour them—every year all of Europe intones the words, "off to Crete! off to Crete!"

That the boisterous finale of the first act of *La belle Hélène* (preceded by an allusion to General Bouboum of *La Grande-Duchesse de Gerolstein*) should break into Klingsor's poisonous garden is not just a brilliant polemist's gesture. For some time Nietzsche had been distracting himself in the company of the organizer of the *"fête imperiale"* whom Rossini (not without some toadying) nicknamed "the Mozart of the Champs-Elysées."

> Offenbach, French music, with a Voltairean spirit, free, exuberant, with a touch of sardonic humor, yet clear, witty to the point of banality (no *make up* whatsoever)—and without any affectation of a morbid or blonde Viennese sensibility.[107]

And again:

The Jews attained genius in the sphere of art with H. Heine and Offenbach, the most witty, most exuberant of satyrs, who as a musician holds
to the great tradition and . . . represents a true redemption from the sentimental and basically *degenerate* musicians of German Romanticism.[108]

Coming after Wagner, this light-hearted music had the same restorative effect on Nietzsche as did reading of Petronius's *Satyricon* after the New
Testament: "Serenity is said to be a sign of a lack of depth: but that it can be
serenity after an overly rigorous tension, who knows that?"[109] And far from
being offended by this parody of Greek mythology—which the critic Jules
Janin had labeled a "sacrilege of Holy Antiquity"—the author of *The Birth of
Tragedy* would surely have felt some complicity with Hélène when she sings:

Il faut lutter contre les hommes
 Il faut lutter contre les dieux.

In this operetta, as in *La Périchole, La Grande-Duchesse de Gerolstein,* and
La fille du tambour-major, which he hears in 1888 in Nice (where, by the way,
he is living on Rossini Street), Nietzsche appreciates not only "the most
exuberant buffoonery" that the composer succeeded a number of times in
achieving but also that there was "a classic taste, an absolute logic" to it. It is
"a paradox that is paradoxical only today: that the stricter principles and the
more serene music go hand in hand," he writes to Gast, whom he wants to
encourage to move in this direction.[110]

What is more, Offenbach is "so marvelously Parisian"! This is about
the highest praise Nietzsche can offer as he moves away both physically and
intellectually from Germany. When he was twenty-four and dreaming of
going to Paris to study "and see the cancan," he spoke of Paris as "the highest school of existence."[111] It was in the French capital in 1882, at his instiga-
tion, that the "trinity" he formed for a time with Lou Salomé and Paul Rée
planned to spend the winter. "As an *artist,*" he writes in *Ecce Homo,* "one has
no home in Europe, except Paris.[112] If he had spent time there, perhaps he
would have said, as did the very Viennese Stefan Zweig in 1913, "I am happy
and light-hearted, thank-you, Paris!"[113] "Without a doubt, it is France that
today represents the oldest and most refined culture in Europe: the spirit of
Paris is its quintessence!" he wrote in 1880. And where is this spirit expressed with the most grace and nimbleness if not in operetta? In Nice, and
then in Turin, in the four years that precede his "collapse," Nietzsche ab-

sorbs a lot of this genre, then triumphant on the Paris stage and far beyond. "Today what is the dominant melody in Europe, *l'idée fixe musicale?* An operetta melody (except, naturally, for the deaf and for Wagner)," he had already written in 1876 shortly after the Bayreuth Festival.[114] One work in particular especially moves him, Audran's *La Mascotte,* which he hears several times in Turin while enjoying ice cream. He writes to Gast, on 27 September 1888, about it:

> This music, which never falls into vulgarity, with so many pretty, little melodies, belongs totally to the idyllic kind of existence that is so necessary to me these evenings. (As *contrepartie:* "The Gypsy Baron" by Strauss: I left *quickly* in, disgust—the two aspects of German vulgarity: animality and sentimentality, combined with quite horrible attempts to pose as a *refined* musician here and there. Heavens! How much the French surpass us in matters of taste.)[115]

We find the same expression of admiration and pleasure two months later in another letter to Gast:

> Three hours and not *a single* measure of *Viennoiserie* (that is, of trash). . . . They are at present in France, in this domain, real geniuses for witty exuberance, wicked kindness, archaism, exoticism, things wholly *naïve* . . . . There is a true science of finesse in taste and effects. I swear to you, *Vienna is a pigsty.* . . . For *our* bodies and our souls, dear friend, a little poisoning *à la parisienne* is a wonderful "redemption"—we become *ourselves,* we stop being horned Germans.[116]

Were he to have witnessed the present Parisian craze for fin-de-siècle Vienna (and, in particular, for Mahler), Nietzsche no doubt would have concluded that "poor sick France" had become incurably ill. But his will to light-heartedness, joined to an increasing sensitivity to external impressions, was at the time so strong that he did not hesitate in finding Offenbach (and even Audran) "more inspired" than Wagner.[117] One thinks of Proust's narrator who, having replaced the score of Vinteuil's sonata with that of *Tristan* on his piano's music stand, amusingly comments, "In admiring the Bayreuth master, I had none of the scruples of those who, like Nietzsche, are bidden by a sense of duty to shun in art as in life the beauty that tempts them, and who, tearing themselves from *Tristan* as they renounce *Parsifal,* and, in their spiritual asceticism, progressing from one mortification to another, succeed, by following the most bloody stations of the cross, in exalting themselves to the pure cognition and perfect adoration of *Le Postillon de Longjumeau*."[118]

Gluck's Fault

If Offenbach and Audran can make one forget Vienna, they themselves, however, are pushed aside by something more "roguish," more "mischievous": *La Gran Via*, a "Spanish operetta" (actually a *zarzuela*) by Joachim Valverde and Frederico Chueca, which Nietzsche hears in Turin three weeks before collapsing.[119] *La belle Hélène*, which followed, "was a sorry falling off." Even *Il Barbiere di Siviglia*, his favorite opera by Rossini, seemed "too kind-hearted" in comparison.

And yet, as he had recently written in *Ecce Homo*, Nietzsche cannot "get along without Rossini."[120] This was a belated discovery in his life; it was at Genoa in 1881–82, on the advice of Gast, that he really began to listen to Rossini's works, which had been pretty well abandoned in favor of Verdi's dramas, which Nietzsche had many reasons to avoid or dislike.[121] In Rossini, he senses an "overflowing animal vitality" and, like Schopenhauer, an "ultimate lack of regard for words. With just a little more impertinence, Rossini would have had everybody sing nothing but la-la-la-la."[122] In any case, *Il Barbiere di Siviglia* displeases him. The Seville he imagines is quite different (more Spanish, undoubtedly, even African . . .). "To please me," he writes to his mentor, "music must be very passionate or very sensual. This is neither the one nor the other: the extreme virtuosity is as tiresome to me as a clown's."[123] What is more, "without three or four tears it is difficult to take gaiety for a long time," he will add after having "breathed the air of Bellini at Messina,"[124] whom he also discovered at Genoa where he heard his *Romeo and Juliet* and *La Somnambula* several times. "We old smitten Wagnerians are the most grateful listeners of Rossini and Bellini," he writes in his notebook.

> The best music doesn't mean much unless the voice and art of a male or
> female singer plunges us into a mild intoxication—in *this* case *mediocre*
> music finds itself unspeakably elevated.[125]

Similarly, at Bayreuth, one evening three years earlier, Wagner had confided to Cosima, after having played some themes from *Norma* and *I Capuleti e i Montecchi* on the piano:

> For all the poverty of invention, there is real passion and feeling there,
> and the right singer has only to get up and sing it for it to win hearts. I

have learned things from them which Messrs. Brahms & Co. have never learned, and they can be seen in my melodies.[126]

"Sing, sing, sing it again and again, forever, you Germans!" This is how he exhorted his fellow countrymen in an article about Bellini in December 1837, before conducting *Norma* in Riga where his reputation in the Italian and French repertoire had brought him.[127] Having discovered the "earnest life" that runs through Bellini's music, Wagner complained, in tones worthy of Stendhal, about "the painstaking pedantry with which we Germans, as a rule, brought naught but laborious make-believe to market."[128] To be sure, Nietzsche might have added, but Wagner had pirated, Germanized his model. The infinite melody—complex, shapeless, so German in its incompleteness—is "the exact contrary" of melody, as the Italians had invented it and brought it to perfection: that pure, *absolute* melody that Wagner condemned in *Opera and Drama*. They are opposed like being and becoming; Nietzsche, now under the luminous spell of Apollo, feels an increasing nostalgia for the former. "To impose an aspect of being on becoming, that is the highest Will to Power": to fasten to the *Ur*-melody of the eternal return the destiny of human beings otherwise condemned to the eternally transitory. So he, for whom as composer, melody rarely stems from harmony, henceforth requires a "purely melodic" music.[129] In March 1882, he writes to his friend Gustav Krug:

> Modern music is just the progressive withering of the melodic sense. Melody, as the ultimate and most sublime art of art, obeys logical principles that our anarchists would like to decry as slavery. But all that is certain to me is that they are unable to reach high enough for these sweetest and ripest fruits, the most sweet and richest of all. To all composers, therefore, I recommend the most delightful of asceticisms: consider that harmony had not yet been invented, and engage collection of pure melodies from Beethoven and Chopin.

"Truly, everything good in music should be able to be whistled," he had said two years before this to Gast, "but Germans have never known how to sing and lug their piano along with them everywhere; whence their insatiable desire for harmony."[130] In this, Nietzsche links up again with Stendhal—his last discovery—whose *Life of Rossini* he had recently read. To the ears of this lover of Italian music in the manner of the eighteenth century, only vocal melody found favor, and as for everything else, like Rousseau, he disdainfully baptized it "harmony": in particular all "insolent" symphonic accompaniments—that "instrumental din" born in the depths of Germany—which "overstepped the limits of polite conversation concerning singing." "At the piano, what is essential is to let the song *sing* and the accompaniment *accompany*," notes Nietzsche, echoing this. "A music in which music and accompaniment are not distinct I can henceforth tolerate only as an interlude, as an ideal noise that makes us long for the return of the song."[131]

Even if Stendhal's enthusiasm for Rossini, and that of the Abbé Galiani for Puccini, set his nerves on edge a bit, Nietzsche agrees with their defense of Italian music and the illustrations they drew upon. In 1887, pointing out that Gluck and Galiani had died just a century ago, the evil Nietzsche is preparing to denounce in *The Case of Wagner* is clear to him: "Thus we are celebrating the centenary of a great problem and of a fateful, probably *wrong* solution of the same," he writes to Gast.[132]

The history of music was punctuated by the opposition between French and Italian music, Germans "lending their ear—sometimes to the French side, sometimes to the Italian."[133] With Gluck, the French taste, "noble, pompous, rationalist," carried the day, and, once again, it is "his preponderance that Wagner established over the Italianizing taste, that is, over Mozart, Haydn, Rossini, Bellini, Mendelssohn; but it is the taste of France in 1830: literature having become master over music as over painting: 'program music,' the *'subject'* comes first!"[134]

Gast replies to the reflections that Nietzsche had sent him toward the end of 1887, particularly about the birth of French opera, by speaking of Monteverdi, who "through his dramatic conceptions [Gast could not have known much more about him] was close to Gluck and Wagner."[135] If he could have heard *Orfeo* and *Le Couronnement*—rediscovered, fifteen years later, in Paris—Nietzsche would almost surely have identified in these works the common source of both Italian and French tastes whose opposition so preoccupied him. He would also have pointed to a similarity in conception not just dramatic, but also musical between Monteverdi and Wagner: use of the *arioso,* halfway between the recitative and the aria, and in *Orfeo,* for the first time, the use of the leitmotiv, charged, as in Wagnerian drama, with both an emotional and a structural role. Perhaps Nietzsche would have withdrawn from this confrontation with the origin of evil, saying, like the hero of d'Annunzio's *Il Fuoco* (which was first published in Italian in 1900), that Monteverdi "with the simplest of means had attained the peak of beauty that Wagner only rarely reached, in his confused aspiration to rediscover the world of Sophocles."[136] Be that as it may, after having early on diverged, Italian and French tastes were later to become, despite polemics and quarrels, combined in differing proportions—more so, in any case, than Nietzsche, given to antinomies by nature and partly blinded by his struggle against Wagner, would have been likely to admit.

"The fact that Rousseau was among the first admirers of Gluck makes one think," he commented, "to me, at least, everything that Rousseau valued is a little questionable, likewise everyone who has valued *him*."[137] Not having looked back earlier in eighteenth century, to the Querelle des Bouffons (1752–54), Nietzsche spared himself a painful surprise, namely, finding himself on the same side as his detested alter ego, who at the time was the principal instigator of the opponents to French music. Against Rameau's lyrical tragedies overloaded with "complicated, tiring harmonies," Rousseau held up as a model of melodic simplicity *La servante maîtresse* by Pergolesi, a diverting entertainment that, compared with Rameau, revealed as much genius as did Offenbach's operettas and Gast's music in comparison with Wagner's operas. The situation would have been all the more painful for Nietzsche in that, beyond Rameau, Rousseau, "that masked plebian," had launched himself, in fact, against the king, the court, and the nobility, who were defending French music. Caught between his love-hate relation with Wagner and his aversion for Rousseau, which concealed a number of affinities between them, Nietzsche would probably have ended up against Rousseau. But if he could have heard a work such as *Hyppolite et Aricie*—performed again in Paris in 1908 after a century and a half of being forgotten—he would have surely perceived the kinship between their respective old idols without letting himself be misled by the anti-Wagnerian and anti-German declarations and slogans ("Down with Gluck! Up with Rameau!") that accompanied the composer's resurrection.

Almost twenty years after *The Birth of Tragedy*, therefore, Nietzsche had completely reversed his positions. Against the triumphant Wagnerian drama, he now defends operas that he had once condemned as the product of a "nonaesthetic need," an "idyllic tendency," of a nostalgia for a time of "primordial existence of the artistic and good man," and in which music was "completely alienated from its true dignity as the Dionysian mirror of the world."[138]

"Music should be Mediterrananized"

Even though it was not "heroic," it was to the idyllic that Nietzsche now aspires, with often, since he has to defend himself against himself and against his illnesses, "that sort of forced gaiety" so much his own.[139] "The *genius of gaiety* must be set in opposition to parochial 'German seriousness'

in music," he recommends to Gast, asking him to look for scores of works by
Puccini in Venice.[140]

> Leaving behind suffocating German noise
> For Mozart, Rossini, and Chopin
> I see your boat, German Orpheus,
> Turn toward Greek lands.
>
> Oh, do not hesitate to turn the heading of your desire
> Toward southern lands,
> Isles of the Blessed, the play of Greek nymphs
> No boat has ever had a lovelier goal—
> This is what is henceforth given me.[141]

As is evident, the dichotomy with a psychophysiological origin that
Nietzsche makes use of between "sick" music and music that entices one
toward life is intersected by another, geographical one, a dichotomy of
North and South.

The North: "The gray of dawn. First yawnings of reason. Cockcrow of
positivism"; "the idea grown sublime, pale, northerly, Königsbergian";[142]
Wagnerian fogs; "an absence of Northern unnaturalness: . . . one must first
come artificially upon the feeling of well-being, art there is a kind of self-
avoidance. Ah, this October light on every joy!"[143] There Protestantism en-
dures—"that spiritually impure, boring form of *décadence*"[144]—allied with
Wotan, the god of bad weather and his "muggy recitatif":

> I do not have enough strength for the North: there uncouth, artificial
> souls rule who work as assiduously and necessarily at their measures of
> prudence as does the beaver on his dam. And to think it is among them
> that I passed my whole youth! This struck me when for the first time I
> saw the evening with its velvet red and gray rise in the sky over
> Naples—like a shudder of sympathy with myself that I should have be-
> gun my life by being old, and tears and the feeling of being saved just at
> the last moment.
>
> I do have enough spirit for the South.[145]

The South of pure melody and "good animal conscience," where like
Wagner, Nietzsche, liberated by his illness from the servitude of teaching,
passes the most crystal clear of the last years of his conscious life, moving
between Genoa, Nice, Venice, and Turin. There sings "that popular tongue

of music, tender, mad, turn by turn too sweet and too burning, with its mis-chievous indulgence toward everything, and even toward 'vulgarity.'"[146] Whereas, on the contrary, "a vulgar turn in Northern works . . . in German music, for example, offends me unspeakably. Here there is a sense of shame; the artist has lowered himself in his own eyes and could not even help blush-ing: we are ashamed with him and feel so offended because we sense that he considered it necessary to lower himself for our sake."[147] Since Strauss, who did not blush about seasoning with a touch of vulgarity the finale of his *Impressions of Italy*, a work whose orchestration, moreover, owes more to Berlioz than to Wagner, maybe this work, which Nietzsche could have heard, since it was composed in 1887, might have overcome the prejudices against German music he gave vent to a year earlier in *Beyond Good and Evil*:

> Against German music all kinds of precautions seem to me to be indi-cated. Suppose somebody loves the south as I love it, as a great school of convalescence, in the most spiritual as well as the most sensuous sense, as an uncontainable abundance of sun and transfiguration by the sun that suffuses an existence that believes and glories in itself: well, such a person will learn to be somewhat on his guard against German music, because in corrupting his taste again it also corrupts his health again.
>
> If such a southerner, not by descent but by *faith*, should dream of the future of music, he must also dream of the redemption of music from the north, and in his ears he must have the prelude of a more profound, more powerful, perhaps more evil and mysterious music, a supra-German music that does not fade away at the sight of the voluptuous blue sea and the brightness of the Mediterranean sky, nor does it turn yellow and then pale as all German music does.[148]

More than Strauss's *Impressions of Italy*, Nietzsche would have appreci-ated the genuinely Mediterranean inspiration the very Wagnerian Hugo Wolf would reveal in his two great lieder cycles, one Spanish and one Ital-ian, but above all in his short *Italian Serenade*, filled with a joyful yet pro-found grace, and his *giocoso* opera *El Corregidor* (1895), drawn from Alarcon's short story, which was also to inspire Manuel de Falla's ballet *The Three-Cornered Hat*.

Worn out, tired of its nocturnal torments, dying Romanticism aspired for light. "Il faut méditerraniser la musique," Nietzsche said in *The Case of Wagner*.[149] This formula brought smiles in Germany, where it was interpreted retroactively as a symptom of the madness that carried off its author. Yet it exactly describes the brilliant renaissance that French music of the day underwent: from *Carmen* (1875) to Chabrier's *España* (1883) and Ravel's *Rapsodie espagnole* (1907) to Debussy's *Iberia* (1910), it resisted the pressure of Wagnerianism by turning joyfully toward Spain, whose best musicians all spent time in Paris, at the same time it concluded a fruitful alliance from the rear with the young Russian school.[150]

That an anti-German provocation (very German in itself) plays a large part in the passion Nietzsche proclaims for the South is undeniable. But both his works and his correspondence bear witness to the deep happiness he often experienced *there*, across the Alps. Whereas in 1872, during a first trip toward the South, having just arrived in Bergamo, "a complete and sudden revulsion against Italy (especially paintings!)" had quickly made him "reverse course,"[151] after his first stay there, in September 1876, following the disappointment of Bayreuth, he did more than simply acclimate himself to it. If, apart from Lorrain and Poussin, references to paintings remain rare from his pen, Apollonian images and visual metaphors become more and more frequent. Nietzsche, we might say, was no longer content just to think what was real; despite his myopia and his eye troubles, we find him looking, contemplating, open to the forms that the light reveals to him against an azure background or sharp shadows. (The climate in Italy is "the greatest of artists," Stendhal had said.) His style gains in breadth and alacrity; its tempo is livelier, communicating to the reader a euphoria that is both at once physical and intellectual. *Daybreak* or *The Gay Science*, where the "tender, multicolored epidermis" of the sea shimmers, that "lovely monster," along with certain of his "halcyon," luminous poems, may make us think of Valéry's *Cimetière marin* or Debussy's *La Mer*, for which Nietzsche would have been an ideal audience.

> That way is my *will*: I trust
> In my mind and in my grip.
> Without plan, into the vast
> Open sea I head my ship.
>
> All is shining, new and newer,
> upon space and time sleeps noon;
> Only *your* eye—monstrously,
> Stares at me, infinity![152]

At least *Iberia*, along with *La Mer*, would have filled the need for light and rhythm that Nietzsche felt at this time. In Debussy—although surely not the Debussy of *Pelléas*, for Cocteau will say that it is still like Wagner and that "Wagner is typically music listened to head in hands"[153]—Ravel, Chabrier, Albeniz, Turina, and Falla, Nietzsche would have found "what we others, *we halcyons*, miss in Wagner—*la gaya scienza*, light feet, wit, fire, grace; the great logic, the dance of the stars; the exuberant spirituality, the southern shivers of light; the smooth sea—perfection."[154] These were all things that constitute "precisely the perfection and ultimate maturity of every culture and art," and for that reason "we men of the 'historical sense'" (i.e., we Germans, sick, proud of always becoming . . .), "find [it] most difficult to grasp, to feel, to taste once more, to love once more . . ."[155]

Madness prevented Nietzsche from hearing the music that would, no doubt, have best met his expectations. It was in the theater in the end, despite all he said against it, that he discovered what came closest to it: *Carmen*. Praise for this opens the *allegro con fuoco* of *The Case of Wagner* like the clash of a cymbal:

> This music seems perfect to me. It approaches lightly, supplely, politely. It is pleasant, it does not *sweat*. . . . Have more painful tragic accents ever been heard on the stage? How are they achieved? Without grimaces. Without counterfeit. Without the *lie* of the great style.
>
> Finally, this music treats the listener as intelligent, as if himself a musician—and is in this respect, too, the counterpart of Wagner, who was, whatever else he was, at any rate the most *impolite* genius of the world. . . .
>
> This work, too, redeems; Wagner is not the only "redeemer." With this work one takes leave of the damp north, of all the steam of the Wagnerian ideal. . . . From Mérimée it still has the logic in passion, the shortest line, the *harsh* necessity; above all, it has what goes with the torrid zone: the dryness of the air, the *limpidezza* in the air. . . . Its cheerfulness is African; fate hangs over it; its happiness is brief, sudden, without pardon. . . .
>
> Finally, love—love translated back into nature. Not the love of a "higher virgin"! No Senta-sentimentality! But love as *fatum*, as fatality, cynical, innocent, cruel—and precisely in this a piece of nature. That love which is war in its means, and at bottom the deadly hatred of the sexes!—I know no case where the tragic joke that constitutes the essence of love is expressed so strictly, translated with equal terror into a formula, as in Don José's last cry, which concludes the work:
>
> *"Yes. I have killed her,*
> *I—my adored Carmen!"*[156]

"The more French music learns to form itself in accordance with the actual needs of the *âme moderne,* the more it will 'Wagnerize,'" he had predicted two years earlier in *Beyond Good and Evil.*[157] The concerts he attended in Monte Carlo often confirmed this for him. Guiraud and Massenet sounded like *"bad Wagner"*: "A picturesque music, empty of ideas, lacking naïveté and veracity. Nervous, brutal, insupportably tiresome and swaggering—and so made up!! . . . *[D]écadence.*"[158] Still, among what Nietzsche considered the reasons for the superiority that the French could aspire to, "in spite of all voluntary and involuntary Germanization and vulgarization of their taste," their temperament, being "a halfway successful synthesis of north and south," preserved them from the "gruesome northern gray on gray and the sunless concept-spooking and anemia—the disease of *German* taste," for they "periodically turned toward and away from the south, in which from time to time Provençal and Ligurian blood foams over." Thus "it was for them that *Bizet* made music, this last genius to see a new beauty and seduction—who discovered a piece of *the south of music.*"[159] "His stroke of genius" had been "to give resonance" to a new and at the same time old sensibility "which up to then had not found a language in the *cultivated* music of Europe, a more southern, browner, more suntanned sensibility," incomprehensible to the "humid idealism of the north."

Nietzsche heard *Carmen* (which had premiered in Paris in March 1875) for the first time at the Politeana Theater in Genoa on 27 November 1881. His enthusiasm is evident, the next day, in a letter to Gast:

> Hurray! Friend! Have again come to know something good, an opera of François Bizet (who is he?!): *Carmen.* Sounded like a short story by Mérimée, witty, strong, here and there shocking. A genuinely French talent for *opéra-comique,* in no way disoriented by Wagner, on the contrary, a real student of Hector Berlioz. I had no idea something like this was possible! It seems that the French are on a better path in the domain of dramatic music, and they have a big lead over the Germans on one essential point: for them passion is not so *far-fetched* (as, for example, *all* Wagner's passions).[160]

A week later, his enthusiasm was still high, and will remain so:

> It came as a great shock to hear that Bizet was dead. I heard *Carmen* for a second time—and had once more the impression of a first-rate novella, like one by Mérimée. Such a passionate and graceful soul! For me this

work is worth a journey to Spain—an extremely *southern* work! Do not laugh at this, old friend, my "taste" is not so easily led astray.[161]

His taste could err: in placing, for lack of a better choice, Offenbach, Audran, and even Gast on the same level as Wagner. But here, Nietzsche is not mistaken, nor is he, three days later, when he writes again to Gast: "I am not far from believing that *Carmen* is the best opera there is; and for as long as we shall live, it will figure in every repertory in Europe."[162] The rapid worldwide success of Bizet's masterpiece would more than confirm this judgment.

If Nietzsche forces things a bit in seeing in Bizet a "student" of Berlioz, at least he did not commit the error, which a number of Parisian critics made, of aligning Bizet with Wagner. To the "harmonic fog" of the Wagnerian orchestra, Bizet opposes "the absolute transparency of his woven counterpoint, the utilization of each instrument in terms of its specific coloration, in the voice that is most natural and fitting to it (Wagner does violence to every instrument), his most *economic* use, *délicatesse* instead of a dark, subterranean stimulation of our instincts."[163] One page of *Carmen* recalled the Old Enchanter for Nietzsche: the duet between Don José and Micaela ("Parle-moi de ma mère"). "A touch beneath my taste, too sentimental, too *Tannhäuserian*," he wrote in the margin of his copy of the score.[164] This is new proof of his insightfulness, since this is the part that Wagner liked best: What does Kundry do to seduce Parsifal? She talks about his mother. But, apart from this detail, Bizet belongs to "the enormous domain of art that is anti-German and will remain so, and from which once and for all young Germans, horned Siegfrieds and other Wagnerians, are excluded."[165] Anti-German are the *buffo*, the *habenera,* and the *séguedilla*, which plunge Nietzsche into "bliss," particularly the second of these, "a seductive, irresistible, demonic, provocative, jesting game. This is how the ancients conceived of Eros. I know nothing like it. To be sung in Italian, not German."[166] In no way upset by the toreador's aria, which offended more "delicate" souls, he judged that "it couldn't be more characteristic." He adds to this that "I have often heard it sung in the streets. It has entered the blood of the Genevese and mine, too." The card game trio seems to him to have "Mozart's grace," and the major chord that comes with the "unpitying card" is "thoroughly frightening." In the overture—that "magnificent circus din"—the second theme strikes like "an epigram about passion, the best one to be written since Stendhal's pages *sur l'amour*," while he is "moved to tears" by the abrupt modulation to F-major with the fortissimo entry of the brass in the interlude preceding the fourth act. As for the final scene, it is "a masterpiece, something to study, as regards gradation, contrasts, logic," and, after the reply by Don José, "*Ansi le salut de mon âme . . . ,*" a "true music of tragedy."

Carmen had "an electrifying effect" on Nietzsche, reports Resa von Schirnhofer, who often spent time with him during the last years of his life and with him attended a corrida in Nice (without horses and where the bull was not killed) that was accompanied by extracts from the opera. "He lent an ear, as though transfigured, enthusiastically drawing my attention to the power of the rhythm, the elementary vitality, the picturesque color of the music." Anyone who would claim after Nietzsche's death that his enthusiasm was "planned and artificial," would seem to her, when she remembered this episode, to be uttering a complete untruth:

> What is more, it seems to me that this music flogged his nerves like an invigorating storm, that it engulfed him, to the very depths of his psychopathic personality, filling his being with a feeling of happiness similar to the one that invaded him when the mistral blew. The love he bore for this music was, for me, sincere; what it had to do with calculations and second thoughts was the way in which he afterward made use of it as an artistic touchstone against Wagner.[167]

Indeed, hardly had he made a few sparkling references to *Carmen* in *The Case of Wagner* when, a few pages further on, with his habitual duplicity, Nietzsche stresses that he has declared "war on Wagner," and having "harsh words for the cretinism of Bayreuth, the last thing I want to do is start a celebration for any *other* musician. *Other* musicians don't count compared to Wagner."[168] A few days before his collapse, he will repeat this to Carl Fuchs: as an "ironic antithesis to Wagner," and nothing more, Bizet produces "a lot of effect!" "It would be an incomparable lapse of taste if I were to have limited myself to praise for Beethoven. What is more, Wagner was mad with jealousy over Bizet." Yet as his correspondence and that of Schirnhofer attests, Bizet represented more than this to him. Of the music Nietzsche dreamt of, *Carmen,* again, was the most successful approximation to it he had heard.[169] But he did not disown Bizet as he had done, at least in words, with others who he had previously admired. It is just that a year earlier in Monte Carlo, we know he had heard the prelude to *Parsifal* ("Has Wagner ever done better?") and, ever since, he was taken again with *Tristan:* "The central work without equal not only in music but in all the arts."[170] "You will find in *Ecce Homo* an astonishing page about *Tristan,* about my whole relationship with Wagner," he writes on 31 December 1888 to Gast. "Wagner is altogether the foremost name in *E. H.* Wherever I admit no doubts, here too

I had the courage to go the whole way."[171] It was because *Tristan* was the "central work" and because Wagner had dominated his life that Nietzsche had to attack them. "I am in a state of *chronic vulnerability* because of which I try, in those moments when I am well, to take revenge, and not a pretty one, that is, through an excess of *hardness*," he had confided just a few months before to his "faithful Kurwenal."[172] But this "excess of hardness" did not extend to the publication of *Nietzsche contra Wagner*, which Nietzsche broke off work on prior to his collapse.

> I think I know better than anyone else of what tremendous things Wagner is capable—the fifty worlds of alien ecstasies for which no one besides him had wings; and given the way I am, strong enough to turn even what is most questionable and dangerous to my advantage and thus to become stronger, I call Wagner the great benefactor of my life. That in which we are related—that we have suffered more profoundly, also from each other, than men of this century are capable of suffering— will link our names again and again, eternally.[173]

"Judge me presumptuous, mad with pride," Wagner had once written to Liszt, "if I dare tell you this: those I have touched, those I have really moved, even if only for an instant, they are marked for their whole lives." If Wagner only belonged to his "illnesses" as Nietzsche said, this was one he could not cure himself of, comments Schaeffner. But by "illness," Nietzsche surely meant life itself, which throughout unending suffering, he wanted to affirm in its plenitude and innocence. "Life *shall* inspire confidence," he notes in 1888. "The task thereby defined is enormous. To resolve it, the human being must already be by nature a liar: more than anything else he must be an *artist*."[174] Every human being was to be this artist that Nietzsche dreamed of becoming, he who, in Valéry's words, "was all that he did not want to be and nothing that he wanted to be"[175]—At least, he wanted it . . .

Return to the "Original Homeland"

"Art is the great stimulus to life," we read in *Twilight of the Idols*.[176] Even the art of Wagner? Several weeks after having denounced its deleterious effects, Nietzsche could not explicitly acknowledge this. But in his notebooks, three years earlier, he did confess it: "An artist of this type, for all his will to deny the world, ultimately sings the praises of something that is, after all, *possible in this world; art can be nothing other than world-affirmation*."[177] While it might make one ill (as Nietzsche already was), this "physiological objection" only concerned "the consumer's point of view," which, following Schopenhauer, Nietzsche had made his own by overly assigning to Wagner's music the same morbid origin as its effects. But if one adopts the artist's point of view (as Nietzsche more and more did at the end of the 1880s) or becomes an artist oneself, it then becomes obvious that all creation, "the torture of the duty of creating," proceeds from the "Dionysian instinct."

In closing in on itself, Nietzsche's destiny thus seems to follow a circle, like the eternal return—or rather, a spiral. Indeed, even when, like Wagner, he proclaims the salvific character of art, albeit against the background of the will to power, Nietzsche, despite his apology for instinct, nonetheless means to preserve in an extreme tension the best from his "positivist" period: the intellectual freedom extolled in *Human, All Too Human* and, above all, in *Daybreak* and *The Gay Science,* his books that he most preferred at this time.

The ideal was "the Socrates who practices music," to whom he had meant to devote the last chapter of *The Birth of Tragedy.* One might say as well "something contradictory in itself," "an incarnate dissonance"—such as he himself never ceased to be. For "one is an artist only on the condition of experiencing what nonartists call form as content, the thing itself."[178] And nowhere is the identity of form and content more manifest than in music. Music, without which life would be an "error, exhausting toil, an exile," and which returns with pressing insistence in Nietzsche's last writings and his last letters, while he is more and more intensely feeling its effects.[179]

> Has it been noticed that music liberates the spirit? Gives wing to thought? That one becomes more of a philosopher the more one becomes a musician?—The gray sky of abstraction rent as if by lightning; the light strong enough for the filigree of things; the great problems near enough to grasp; the world surveyed as from a mountain.—I have just defined the pathos of philosophy.—And unexpectedly answers drop into my lap, a little hail of ice and wisdom, of *solved* problems.—Where am I?[180]

"*Music* is by far the best thing: now at present more than ever I would have liked to be a musician," he wrote to Gast in 1884.[181] And three years later: "Beyond a doubt, in the very depths of my being I would have liked *to have been able* to compose the music that you yourself compose—and my own music (books included) was only done *faute de mieux.*"[182] For lack of being able truly to master that art of sounds thanks to which, as he imagined it in *The Gay Science,* his thoughts would have better penetrated "men's ears and hearts better. With music one can seduce men to every error and every truth: who could refute a tone?"[183]

In the train that returned him to Germany the day after his fatal crisis of 6 January 1889, in the company of Franz Overbeck, Nietzsche was dozing because of the effect of chloral, but waking up a number of times, sometimes he sang, and among these songs was a marvelous barcarole of "a wholly peculiar melody": the gondolier's song, written in Venice. "When I seek a synonym for 'music,' I find it only in Venice." Venice, where, as Nietzsche knew, Wagner had composed the shepherd's tune in *Tristan* from a gondolier's song, the tune that Nietzsche in *The Birth of Tragedy* calls "the shepherd's melody of metaphysics."[184]

While madness had exiled him from life, and while his words, before they ran out, only revealed the disorder in his thoughts, music remained his ultimate recourse. A report from the hospital in Basel in January 1889 notes that "When one asks about his state, he responds that he feels well, but that he can only express his state in music."[185] In fact, he was able to do so, as in the days of his youth, with some astonishing improvisations—as though Dionysus survived for a moment the twilight of Apollo. "Not one absurdity," Gast will note at one point, "nothing but phrases of a Tristan-like inspiration, *pianissimo;* then fanfares of trombones and trumpets, a Beethovenlike furor, exultant songs, meditations, reveries—indescribable!"[186]

Nothing probably could calm the "unlimited regressive suspicion" that animated and devoured his thought, nothing except music—except that unconditioned, almost ungenerated chord whose echo he had perceived in *Tristan,* when after the tragic catastrophe the dissonances melt into the almost tacit unity that finally submerges all speech, and when the soul, impatient with all mediation, answers the call of its "original homeland."

FS   *Frühe Schriften,* ed. Hans Joachim Mette, Carl Koch, and Karl
Schlechta, 5 vols. (1933–40; reprint, Munich: Beck, 1994)

KGW BW   *Nietzsche Werke. Kritische Gesamtausgabe* [KGW]: *Briefwechsel,*
ed. Giorgio Colli, Mazzino Montinari et al., 4 vols. (Berlin:
de Gruyter, 1975–2000)

KSA   *Sämtliche Werke: Kritische Studienausgabe,* ed. Giorgio Colli
and Mazzino Montinari, 15 vols. (Munich: Deutscher
Taschenbuch, 1980)

SB   *Sämtliche Briefe: Kritische Studienausgabe,* ed. Giorgio Colli
and Mazzino Montinari, 8 vols. (Munich: Deutscher
Taschenbuch, 1986)

SL   *Selected Letters of Friedrich Nietzsche,* ed. and trans.
Christopher Middleton (Chicago: University of Chicago
Press, 1969; reprint, Indianapolis: Hackett, 1996)

$\mathcal{N}$OTES

FOREWORD

1. Letter to Peter Gast, 27 October 1887, in Friedrich Nietzsche, *Sämtliche Briefe: Kritische Studientausgabe,* ed. Giorgio Colli and Mazzino Montinari, 8 vols. (Munich: Deutscher Taschenbuch, and Berlin: de Gruyter, 1986), 8: 179. For an English-language translation, see *Selected Letters of Friedrich Nietzsche,* ed. and trans. Christopher Middleton (Chicago: University of Chicago Press, 1969; Indianapolis: Hackett, 1996), letter no. 156, 273.

2. Friedrich Nietzsche, *Der musicalische Nachlass* (B), ed. Curt Paul Janz, with a preface by Karl Schlecta (Basel: Bärenreiter, 1976). A chronology of Nietzsche's compositions can be found in the third volume of Janz's biography, *Nietzsche: Biographie,* trans. Marc B. de Launay, Violette Queuniet, Pierre Rusch, and Marcel Ulubeyan, 3 vols. (Paris: Gallimard, 1984–85).

3. Friedrich Nietzsche, *Piano Music,* performed by John Bell Young and Constance Keene, pianists (Newport Premier, MPP 85513 [1992]); *The Music of Friedrich Nietzsche,* John Bell Young and Thomas Coote, pianos, Nicholas Eanet, violin, John Aler, tenor (Newport Classic Premier, NDP 85535 [1993]); *The Compositions of Friedrich Nietzsche,* documentary recordings of forty-three works for voice, violin, choir, piano, and piano duet, supervised and presented by Wolfgang Bottenberg (Montreal: Concordia Publications [Concordia University Department of Music, 7141 Sherbrooke Street West, Montreal, Quebec H4B 1R6, Canada]); *Friedrich Nietzsche: Lieder, Piano Works, Melodrama,* Dietrich Fischer-Dieskau, baritone, Aribert Reimann and Elmar Budde, piano (Phillips Classics 426 863-2 [1995], Musical Heritage Society 514837M).

4. Friedrich Nietzsche, *"The Birth of Tragedy" and "The Case of Wagner,"* trans. Walter Kaufmann (New York: Vintage Books, 1967), 192.

CHAPTER ONE

1. In his insightful introduction to a multivolume work that I will refer a great deal to below, Friedrich Nietzsche, *Lettres à Peter Gast*, 2 vols., trans. Louise Servicen (Monaco: Éd. du Rocher, 1957), 1: 44.

2. Friedrich Nietzsche, *Human, All Too Human: A Book for Free Spirits*, trans. R. J. Hollingdale (New York: Cambridge University Press, 1996), vol. 2, part 1, § 186, 259; and Arthur Schopenhauer, *The World as Will and Representation*, trans. E. F. J. Payne (New York: Dover, 1969), 235–36. The discussion in Schopenhauer gives an exact musical representation of Wagner's prelude to *The Rhinegold*—even though Wagner did not know of this book at the time. The aphorism "The Cult of Culture" is prefigured by this note from 1873: "Definition of culture—as a tempering and attuning of many initially antagonistic forces that are now made to play a melody." *Sämtliche Werke: Kritische Studienausgabe*, ed. Giorgio Colli and Mazzino Montinari, 15 vols. (Munich: Deutscher Taschenbuch, 1980), 7: 713 (hereafter cited as *KSA*).

3. *Human, All Too Human*, vol. 1, § 626, 197.

4. Friedrich Nietzsche, *The Gay Science, with a Prelude in Rhymes and an Appendix of Songs*, trans. Walter Kaufmann (New York: Vintage Books, 1974), § 354, 299. Already in his preparatory notes for *Wagner in Bayreuth* (*Unfashionable Observations*, trans. and with an afterword by Richard T. Gray [Stanford: Stanford University Press, 1995], hereafter cited as *Richard Wagner in Bayreuth*), Nietzsche had written: "Now language thinks for everyone, everyone is its slave and no one any longer has individuality under this enormous constraint. Yet when uplifted by music, one must feel sufficiently distanced to perceive this typical conformity in all that is said and written." *KSA*, 8: 260.

5. Friedrich Nietzsche, *Twilight of the Idols*, in *"Twilight of the Idols" and "The Antichrist,"* trans. R. J. Hollingdale (Baltimore: Penguin, 1968), § 26, 82–83.

6. *KSA*, 12: 493.

7. Marcel Proust, *In Search of Lost Time*, trans. C. K. Scott Moncrieff and Terence Kilmartin, rev. by D. J. Enright, 6 vols. (New York: Modern Library, 1993), 5: 344.

8. Jean-Jacques Rousseau, *Essay on the Origin of Languages and Writings Related to Music*, trans. and ed. by John T. Scott, The Collected Writings of Rousseau, vol. 7 (Hanover and London: University Press of New England, 1992). Regarding Rousseau and Nietzsche, see the section titled "L'alter ego," in the postscript by Jean Lacoste, "Le rêve parisien de Nietzsche," in Nietzsche, *Oeuvres* (Paris: Éd. Robert Laffont, 1993), 1: 342–45.

9. Friedrich Nietzsche, *The Birth of Tragedy*, in *"The Birth of Tragedy" and "The Case of Wagner,"* trans. Walter Kaufmann (New York: Vintage Books, 1967), § 3, 20.

10. Quoted in Curt Paul Janz, *Nietzsche: Biographie*, trans. Marc B. de Launay, Violette Queuniet, Pierre Rusch, and Marcel Ulubeyanm, 3 vols. (Paris: Gallimard, 1985), 3: 18. Nietzsche was unable to reject his need for music, "and often he listened to tones at a time when he wanted to listen to thoughts," noted Lou Andreas-Salomé in the very insightful book she devoted to him, *Nietzsche*, ed., trans., and with an intro. by Sigfried Mandel (Redding Ridge, CT: Black Swan Books, 1988), 33.

11. Nietzsche closed his letter to Peter Gast dated 25 May 1888 with the words, "The unlucky musicaster greets you." *Sämtliche Briefe: Kritische Studienausgabe,* ed. Giorgio Colli and Mazzino Montinari, 8 vols. (Munich: Deutscher Taschenbuch, 1986), 8: 32 (hereafter cited as *SB*).

12. From a letter to Guy de Pourtalès dated 16 November 1929, printed in "Paul Valéry: Lettres et notes sur Nietzsche," in Michel Jarrety, *Valéry, pour quoi?* (Paris: Les Impressions Nouvelles, 1987), 26. Nietzsche's "musical sense," writes Charles Andler, "drew from the German language sonorities that the most melodious of prose writers, even including Goethe, or the bellowing organs of Schiller and Hölderlin, never were able to produce." *Nietzsche, sa vie et sa pensée,* 6 vols. (Paris: Bossard, 1920–31), 1: 259–60. Andler even speaks of "the prose most impregnated by melody that Germans have ever written."

13. According to the memory of Louis Kelterborn, one of Nietzsche's students at Basel, quoted by Janz, *Nietzsche: Biographie,* 1: 475. See also Friedrich Nietzsche, *Beyond Good and Evil: Prelude to a Philosophy of the Future,* trans. Walter Kaufmann (New York: Vintage Books, 1966), § 247, 183–84.

14. Letter to Elisabeth Nietzsche dated 20 May 1885, *SB,* 7: 53. Around the same time he wrote in his notebooks, "I prefer my dashes [literally, thought-strokes] to those thoughts I have communicated." *KSA,* 11: 469.

15. *KSA,* 9: 519.

16. Friedrich Nietzsche, *Ecce Homo,* in *"On the Genealogy of Morals" and "Ecce Homo,"* trans. Walter Kaufmann (New York: Vintage Books, 1967), "Thus Spoke Zarathustra," § 1, 295.

17. *KSA,* 9: 320.

18. Richard Wagner, "About Conducting" (1869), in *Richard Wagner's Prose Works,* trans. William Ashton Ellis, 8 vols. (London, 1892; reprint, New York: Broude Brothers, 1966), 4: 304. The Wagnerian obsession for *tempo*—for the "proper" tempo—was taken over by Nietzsche, under whose pen the word often recurs. For example, in *Ecce Homo,* he speaks of the "tempo of signs" and the "tempo of organic exchanges."

19. *Beyond Good and Evil,* § 246, 182.

20. *KSA,* 9: 117.

21. *KSA,* 8: 530.

22. *Twilight of the Idols,* "'Reason' in Philosophy," § 3, 36.

23. *KSA,* 8: 261. This fragment is meant to distance Nietzsche from book 3 of Plato's *Republic,* on music as the "key part of education," which precedes the section devoted to gymnastics.

24. Foreword, *Twilight of the Idols,* 21.

25. Friedrich Nietzsche, *Daybreak: Thoughts on the Prejudices of Morality,* ed. Maudemarie Clark and Brian Leiter, trans. R. J. Hollingdale (New York: Cambridge University Press, 1997), § 327, 324.

26. We have to make exception as regards Nietzsche; Pierre Lasserre, *Les idées de Nietzsche sur la musique* (Paris: Mercure de France, 1907); André Schaeffner; and

Clément Rosset, in particular, in his book *La force majeure* (Paris: Minuit, 1983), to which the following discussion owes much.

27. "Life without music is nothing but an error, exhausting toil, an exile," he writes to Peter Gast on 15 January 1888 (*SB*, 8: 232). See also *Twilight of the Idols,* "Maxims and Arrows," § 33.

28. *The Gay Science,* § 334, 262. "Is art a consequence of a *dissatisfaction with what is actual?* Or an expression of *gratitude for happiness one has enjoyed?*" *KSA,* 12: 119.

29. In *Nietzsche,* Eric Blondel speaks of a "psychophysiophilology." See also Michel Haar, "La physiologie de l'art: Nietzsche vu par Heidegger," in *Nouvelles lectures de Nietzsche,* ed. Dominique Janicaud, Cahiers L'Age d'Homme, 1(Lausanne: L'Age d'Homme, 1985), 70–80.

30. *KSA,* 9: 170.

31. *The Gay Science,* § 372, 332.

32. *Twilight of the Idols,* § 3, 26.

33. "After theology, there is no art equal to music. The prophets practiced no other, nor does geometry, or arithmetic, or astronomy, it is as though they believed music and the divinity were almost close relatives," said Luther. Letter to Ludwig Senfl, 4 October 1530.

34. J. Marquet de Norvins, *Souvenirs d'un historien de Napoléon: Mémorial de J. de Norvins,* vol. 1, ed. L. de Lanzac de Laborie (Paris: Plon, 1986), 300.

35. Here I refer the reader to Paul Benichou's seminal book, *The Consecration of the Writer, 1750–1830,* trans. Mark K. Jensen (Lincoln: University of Nebraska Press, 1999).

36. Luigi Magnani, *Les cahiers de conversation de Beethoven* (Neuchâtel: Éd. de la Baconnière, 1971), 144 f.

37. Schopenhauer, *The World as Will and Representation,* 1: 264.

38. Marcel Beaufils, *Comment l'Allemagne est devenue musicienne* (Paris: R. Laffont, 1983), 378.

39. *KSA,* 8: 107.

40. See the posthumous fragment from July–August 1879 in *KSA,* 8: 610, and in *Ecce Homo,* "Twilight of the Idols," 316. In "The Wanderer and His Shadow," § 295, he associates this "heroic idyll" with Poussin. See also Nietzsche's letter to Peter Gast dated 30 October 1888, *SB,* 8: 461 (for an English translation, see *Selected Letters of Friedrich Nietzsche,* ed. and trans. Christopher Middleton [Chicago: University of Chicago Press, 1969; Indianapolis: Hackett, 1996], no. 182, 318 (hereafter cited as *SL*). "Knowing by itself is joyless, just as seeing is joyless," he writes in his notebooks from 1872–73. *KSA,* 7: 525.

41. See Jean Philippon, "Nietzsche et Raphaël," in *Nouvelles lectures de Nietzsche,* ed. Dominique Janicaud, Cahiers L'Age d'Homme, 1 (Lausanne: L'Age d'Homme, 1985), 92–107.

42. Note by Cosima Wagner in her diary for 18 March 1880, *Cosima Wagner's Diaries,* 2 vols., ed. and annotated by Martin Gregor-Dellin and Dietrich Mack, trans. Geoffrey Skelton (New York: Harcourt Brace Jovanovich, 1978–80), 2: 453. And in

Religion and Art (1881) we find: Painting says "'this signifies.' But music tells us 'that is'—for she stops all strife between reason and feeling, and that by a tone-shape completely removed from the world of appearances, not to be compared with any thing physical, but usurping our heart by act of Grace." *Richard Wagner's Prose Works,* 6: 224.

43. Posthumous fragment from 1871, *KSA,* 7: 307.

44. Ernst Bertram, *Nietzsche: Essai de mythologie* (Paris: Reider, 1932), 63.

CHAPTER TWO

1. Friedrich Nietzsche, *Frühe Schriften,* ed. Hans Joachim Mette, Carl Koch, and Karl Schlechta, 5 vols. (1933–40; reprint, Munich: Beck, 1994)), 1: 27 (hereafter cited as *FS*).

2. *FS,* 1: 1–2.

3. *FS,* 1: 18.

4. *FS,* 1: 18.

5. Friedrich Nietzsche, *Human, All Too Human: A Book for Free Spirits,* vol. 1, § 145, 80.

6. Posthumous fragment (7 [60]) from spring 1887 in *KSA,* 12: 315. And we read in *The Gay Science,* "the world has become 'infinite' for us all over again, inasmuch as we cannot reject the possibility that *it may include infinite interpretations*" (§ 374, 336)— just like a musical score.

7. We could say the same for the theater. Yet, beyond the fact that, in general, one does not read a piece of music as one can a script, without the aid of the scenery, the virtual character of the former is more pronounced, inasmuch as music, unlike language, always to a greater or lesser extent escapes the grasp of meaning. For other reasons (as we shall see), Nietzsche does not think of theater when he speaks of interpretation—in the first place, because there is no theater without actors and an audience, whereas the ideal interpreter, for him, is the solitary musician-philosopher he himself was.

8. *Human, All Too Human,* vol. 2, part 1, § 126, 242.

9. Nietzsche's perspectivism, of course, equally has a philosophical-political dimension, which Philippe Raynaud has well laid out. There is no truth, for if there were, this would indicate that human beings were equal. This is why *"science and democracy* belong together . . . as surely as do art and 'good society'" (*KSA,* 12: 347). Leftist Nietzscheanism, like that Foucaultianism which has been all the rage on U.S. campuses for some time now, would surely have provoked Zarathustra's "strident laughter." See the article on Nietzsche by Philippe Raynaud in *Dictionnaire de philosophie politique,* ed. Phillipe Raynaud and Stépane Rials (Paris: Presses Universitaires de France, 1996), 430–35.

10. "Über Stimmungen" [On Moods], in *FS,* 2: 407–8.

11. *KSA,* 13: 597.

12. The formula cited at the beginning of this sentence is taken from *The Gay Science,* § 291, 234, devoted to Genoa, where Nietzsche celebrates those "bold and au-

tocratic human beings" who built this city: "each rebelled against each at home, too, and found a way to express his superiority and to lay between himself and his neighbor his personal infinity."

13. Paul Deussen, who reported this anecdote in his *Souvenirs de Nietzsche* (1901); see also Geneviève Bianquis, ed., *Nietzsche devant ses contemporains* (Paris: Éd. du Rocher, 1959), 42; and Janz, *Nietzsche: Biographie,* 1: 17.

14. From a letter addressed to his mother and sister dated 10 July 1865. *SB,* 2: 74.

15. *Conversations of Goethe with Johann Peter Eckermann,* trans. John Oxenford (New York: Da Capo, 1998), 394. Since Goethe, German has distinguished between *teufflisch,* diabolic, inspired by Satan, and *dämonisch,* "demonic," inspired by a "daimon," like that of Socrates, for example. "A musician, when he is composing, truly falls into a sort of insane somnambulistic state," Wagner confided to Cosima. "How different from a literary work—words are the gods living within a convention, but tones are the daemons." Entry for 25 February 1870, *Cosima Wagner's Diaries,* 1: 193.

16. *KSA,* 13: 235–36.

17. *Ecce Homo,* "Thus Spoke Zarathustra," 300.

18. See the chapter "Nietzsche ou la métaphysique de la psychophysiologie," in Marcel Gauchet, *L'inconscient cérébral* (Paris: Seuil, 1992), 127–52.

19. *The Birth of Tragedy,* § 2, 40.

20. Letter to Carl von Gersdorff dated 7 April 1866, in *SB,* 2: 122. See also Janz, *Nietzsche: Biographie,* 1: 83–85. "I owe my most lovely impressions to storms," he noted in 1858 in his first attempt at autobiography before writing, six years later, an invocation to the storm that announces *Zarathustra. FS,* 1: 8.

21. *The Gay Science,* § 84, 139. See also Plato, *Timaeus,* 47c.

22. *SB,* 4: 77. "At times I sink into the perilous domain of the lunatic," he says in the previous sentence, characterizing "this musical excitation" as "semi-psychiatric."

23. Janz, *Nietzsche: Biographie,* 3: 424.

24. A posthumous fragment from 1876–1878. *KSA,* 8: 465.

25. *Conversations of Goethe with Johann Peter Eckermann,* 327, see also 324.

26. *FS,* 1: 5.

27. *FS,* 1: 18.

28. *FS,* 1: 26–27.

29. Letter to Gustav Krug and Wilhelm Pinder, his friends in Germania, dated 14 January 1861, *SB,* 1: 137–38.

30. Letter to Gustav Krug and Wilhelm Pinder dated 27 April 1862, *SB,* 1: 202. See also his essay from 1862, *"Fatum* and History," in which he presents himself as having a will to negation and destruction, announcing the works to come. *FS,* 2: 54–62.

31. *KSA,* 8: 463.

32. *KSA,* 11: 455.

33. *KSA,* 12: 444–45. See also *Human, All Too Human,* vol. 2, part 1, §§ 150, 171, and 298, where he praises "Handel's inflexible manliness and freedom under the law" (§ 298, 281).

34. *SB*, 3: 120.

35. Cited in Janz, *Nietzsche: Biographie*, 1: 83.

36. Letter to Gustav Krug and Wilhelm Pinder dated 12 June 1864, *SB*, 1: 283.

37. *KSA*, 8: 423.

38. *Human, All Too Human*, vol. 1, § 155, 83. Beethoven's notebooks had been published for the first time by the musicologist Martin Gustav Nottebohm in 1865 and 1872. Nietzsche's comment irritated Wagner: "R . . . talks with disgust about Nietzsche's denial of inspiration as shown by the Beethoven sketchbooks; it would be better, he says, if such sketches were not published—as if the search for a form for a particular inspiration were the denial of its existence!" Entry from 27 July 1878, *Cosima Wagner's Diaries*, 2: 123.

39. *Human, All Too Human*, vol. 1, § 145, 80.

40. *The Birth of Tragedy*, § 1, 35.

41. Perhaps Nietzsche also owed this feeling of an always near and threatening chaos to his hallucinatory crises, as this odd autobiographical note, written between autumn 1868 and spring 1869, bears witness: "What I dread is not the horrifying form standing behind my chair but its voice: not its words but the appallingly inarticulate, inhuman sounds of that form. If only it would speak as men do!" *Friedrich Nietzsche: Werke*, ed. Karl Schlechta (Munich: Hanser, 1956), 3: 148. See also Janz, *Nietzsche: Biographie*, 1: 232–33. This note should be compared with what Nietzsche will say about Socrates (one of his "masks") in *Twilight of the Idols*: "It is not only the admitted dissoluteness and anarchy of his instincts which indicates *décadence* in Socrates: the superfetation of the logical and that *barbed malice* which distinguishes him also point in that direction. And let us not forget those auditory hallucinations which, as 'Socrates' demon,' have been interpreted in a religious sense" (§ 4, 31). Perhaps it was to such hallucinations that Nietzsche compared that "surprising ground of terror" that also characterizes the Dionysian in *The Birth of Tragedy*.

42. *Écrits autobiographiques, 1856–1869*, trans. Marc Marcuzzi and Max Marcuzzi (Paris: Presses Universitaires de France, 1994), 113.

43. *KSA*, 13: 246.

44. *SB*, 2: 209 (*SL*, no. 7, 22).

45. *FS*, 1: 18

46. *The Birth of Tragedy*, § 19, 119.

47. Janz, *Nietzsche: Biographie*, 1: 78.

48. This comes from a fragment on "the essence of music." *FS*, 2: 114. Already considered overly conservative in his own day, the Austrian composer and theoretician Johann Georg Albrechtsberger (1736–1809) taught Beethoven counterpoint in 1794 and 1795. He was the author of *Elementary Method of Composition*, on which his fame was based. This was the textbook Nietzsche used.

49. *SB*, 4: 77.

50. *KSA*, 11: 13.

51. *Daybreak*, § 239, 239.

52. *KSA*, 12: 543.

53. Nietzsche is talking about the Scandinavian *Edda* (*Premiers écrits*, 183–84).

54. *Premiers écrits*, 159–60; cf. Janz, *Nietzsche: Biographie*, 1: 81. Nietzsche's efforts at *Ermanarich* take up fifty pages of *Premiers écrits*.

55. *KSA*, 13: 249; *The Case of Wagner,* in *"The Birth of Tragedy"* and *"The Case of Wagner,"* trans. Walter Kaufmann (New York: Vintage Books, 1967), § 5, 166. Nietzsche is here using the word *idiotic* in the sense given it by Dostoevsky.

56. *The Gay Science*, § 369, 326.

57. *Beyond Good and Evil*, §§ 240, 174, and 173. *Die Meistersinger* was the Wagner work that was most preferred by Brahms and by his friend, the Viennese critic Eduard Hanslick (despite the caricature Wagner made of him in the character of Beckmesser).

58. Letter dated 6 September 1863, *SB*, 1: 253.

59. *The Birth of Tragedy*, § 21, 130.

60. *The Birth of Tragedy*, § 5, 49.

61. Letter dated 10 January 1883, *SB*, 6: 316–17. In his *Mémoirs, ou Essais sur la musique* [1789–97] (Liege: Éd. de Wallonia, 1914), André Ernest Modeste Gréty had proposed something similar (which he seems not to have applied), but for him, contrary to Nietzsche, music took on its full meaning only when it was based on a text.

62. *Nietzsche Werke. Kritische Gesamtausgabe* [KGW]*: Briefwechsel*, ed. Giorgio Colli, and Mazzino Montinari et al., 4 vols. (Berlin: de Gruyter, 1975–2000), vol. 1, pt. 1 (hereafter cited as *KGW BW*). In his chronology of Nietzsche's works and musical compositions, Janz has this note for the year 1860: "Beginning in August, isolated movements and drafts of a Christmas oratorio for soloists, mixed choir, and orchestra (until spring 1861). October: rough sketches of texts for the Christmas oratorio." *Nietzsche: Biographie*, 3: 608.

63. *KGW BW*, vol. 2, part 4, 53.

64. *The Birth of Tragedy*, § 5, 49. What Valéry called an "état chantant."

65. Quotation is from *Ecce Homo*, 106—*DP.*

66. Quotation is from *Thus Spoke Zarathustra*, 302—*DP.*

67. Marcel Beaufils, *Le lied romantique allemand* (Paris: Gallimard, 1982), 177.

CHAPTER THREE

1. See Alfred Einstein, *Music in the Romantic Era* (New York: W. W. Norton, 1947), 25–28.

2. Marcel Brion, *Schumann et l'âme romantique* (Paris: Albin Michel, 1954, 1986), 322. In December 1861, in an essay written for the members of Germania on Byron's dramatic poetry, Nietzsche had labeled Manfred an *Übermensch* and called the work itself *"ein übermenschliches Werk." FNJ*, 2: 10, 14.

3. Letter to Carl von Gersdorff, 4 August 1865, *SB*, 2: 75.

4. *Écrits autobiographiques*, 169.

5. Thomas Mann, *Reflections of a Nonpolitical Man*, trans. Walter D. Morris (New York: Frederick Ungar, 1983), 87.

6. "Retrospect on my two years at Leipzig from 17 October 1865 to 10 August

1867" (*FS*, 3: 298). "The need to know myself, to gnaw away at myself strongly seized me. . . . While I brought all my qualities and efforts before the tribunal of a gloomy self-contempt, I was bitter, unjust, and unrestrained in hatred toward myself. Nor did I neglect physical tortures. For two straight weeks, I forced myself not to go to bed before 2:00 A.M. and to get up again at exactly 6:00. A nervous excitation took hold of me and who knows what degree of madness I might have reached if the seductions of life, pride, and the constraint of regular studies had not opposed it." *FS*, 3: 298.

7. This sums up, broadly speaking, the traditional interpretation of Schopenhauer's theory of music, which we can find, in just about the same terms, in Nietzsche and Wagner. Clément Rosset, in his *Esthetique de Schopenhauer* (Paris: Presses Universitaires de France, 1989), has proposed an original interpretation that, even though it "diverges from Schopenhauer's explicit affirmations," has the merit of rendering his thought less obscure and more coherent. Moreover, as we shall see, it is close to some reflections that Nietzsche wrote in his notebooks while working on *The Birth of Tragedy* but which he did not make use of in the book itself. Cf. *KSA*, 7: 359–64.

8. Schopenhauer, *The World As Will and Representation*, 1: 264.

9. *The Birth of Tragedy* § 21, 127. "That *shepherd's melody*" refers to the English-horn solo at the beginning of the third act of *Tristan und Isolde*.

10. *Ecce Homo*, "Why I Am So Clever," § 6, 249.

11. Letter to Carl von Gersdorff dated 11 October, *SB*, 2: 174.

12. *SB*, 2: 332.

13. Letters to Erwin Rhode dated 22 and 28 February 1869, *SB*, 2: 379.

14. Letter to Wagner dated 17 February 1860, in Lois Boe Hyslop and Francis Edwin Hyslop, Jr., *Charles Baudelaire: A Self-Portrait. Selected Letters* (London: Oxford University Press, 1957), 156–57. See also Charles Baudelaire, "Richard Wagner and *Tannhäuser* in Paris," in *The Painter of Modern Life and Other Essays*, trans. Jonathan Mayne (London: Phaidon Press, 1964), 111–46.

15. Letter dated 9 December 1868, *SB*, 2: 352–53.

16. Letter dated July 20 1872, *SB*, 4: 26.

17. *Richard Wagner in Bayreuth*, 263.

18. *Richard Wagner in Bayreuth*, 274.

19. *Friedrich Nietzsche: Werke* (Schletchta), 3: 110.

20. Entry from 2 August 1878, *Cosima Wagner's Diaries*, 2: 128.

21. Karl Jaspers, *Nietzsche: An Introduction to the Understanding of His Philosophical Activity*, trans. Charles F. Wallraff and Frederick J. Schmitz (Chicago: Henry Regnery, 1965), 32. "Wagner had the courage of despair," Nietzsche noted in his notebook in the spring of 1888. "His position toward music was at bottom desperate. He lacked both things that make a *good* musician: nature and culture, the predestination to be a musician and the training and education in music" (*KSA*, 13: 349). In 1888, when the score of *Die Feen* was published, Peter Gast read it and praised it highly to Nietzsche, who was then in the course of finishing *The Case of Wagner*: "'Gracious' comic-opera music, marked by some audacious features." Cited by André Schaeffner in *Lettres à Peter Gast*, 1: 169.

22. See his letter to Paul Deussen dated February 1870, *SB*, 3: 98 (*SL*, no. 20, 64).

23. *SB*, 3: 95.

24. What is more, Nietzsche had foreseen the unfavorable reception his book would receive from university professors: "I always fear that the philologists because of the music, the musicians because of the philology, the philosophers because of the music and the philology, will *not* want to read the book, and so am anxious and sorry for my dear Fritzsch [his editor]," he wrote to Erwin Rohde on 23 November 1871. *SB*, 3: 248.

25. Posthumous fragment from the summer of 1876, *KSA*, 8: 307.

26. Posthumous fragment from 30 May 1876, *KSA*, 8: 287.

27. Nietzsche cites this formula in a letter to Malwida von Meysenberg from the middle of December 1882, adding, "There are a frightening number of things I have to *dominate* in myself." *SB*, 6: 303.

28. Lou Salomé, *Nietzsche*, 17. "To *have* to combat one's instincts—that is the formula for *décadence*: as long as life is *ascending*, happiness and instinct are one.—" *Twilight of the Idols*, § 11, 34.

29. Letter to Paul Rée from the end of August 1881, *SB*, 6: 124.

30. *KSA*, 12: 404. There is much melancholy in the portrait of Goethe in the *Twilight of the Idols*, and in which he ideally projects himself: "What he aspired to was *totality;* he strove against the separation of reason, sensuality, feeling, will . . . he disciplined himself to a whole, he *created* himself" (§ 49, 102).

31. *SL*, no. 93, 180.

32. "One must never forget that Wagner, in the second half of the nineteenth century, in his way—which is certainly not that of good and insightful men—reminded us that art is something important and magnificent," comments Nietzsche, during the summer of 1878 in his preparatory notes for *Human, All Too Human*. And, seven years later, he returns to this theme: "Richard Wagner has without a doubt has given the Germans of our era the most comprehensive premonition of what an artist *could* be: respect for the 'artist' suddenly increased considerably; everywhere he has awakened new evaluations, new desires, new hopes; and perhaps, above all, precisely because of the merely annunciatory, incomplete, imperfect nature of his artistic productions. Who has not *learned* from him!" *KSA*, 11: 554–55.

33. *SB*, 3: 36. See also the no less enthusiastic letter, from the next day, that he writes to his other friend, Gustav Krug, *SB*, 3: 37–39 (*SL*, no. 17, 56–57).

34. Letter to Erwin Rohde dated 29 May 1869, *SB*, 3: 13.

35. Letters to Erwin Rohde dated 9 November and 9 December 1868, *SB*, 3: 340–41, 352 (*SL*, no. 11, 35–42), and *Correspondance*, ed. Giorgio Colli and Mazzino Montinari, trans. Henri-Alexis Baatsch, Jean Bréjoux, and Maurice de Gandillac, 2 vols. (Paris: Gallimard, 1986), 1: 632. Similarly, a year later: "Believe me, Schopenhauer and Goethe, Aeschylus and Pindar are still alive" (*SB*, 3: 52). And to Wagner on 22 May 1869 (his birthday): "the best and loftiest moments of my life, are associated with in fact your name and I know only one other man, your great spiritual brother, Arthur

Schopenhauer, whom I regard with equal reverence, even *religione quadam.*" *SB*, 3: 8 (*SL*, no. 15, 53).

36. Letter dated 20 May 1873, addressed to Wagner for the celebration of his sixtieth birthday. It begins as follows:

> Beloved Master,
>
> It is now really two generations that the Germans have had you—and there are certainly many who, like my friends and me, will celebrate the next Ascension Day as the day of your descent to earth, wondering at the same time what will be the fate of every genius descending to earth, a fate that is truly more reminiscent of a descent to hell." (*SB*, 4: 153)

Nietzsche designates Wagner as "Pater Seraphicus" in another letter to him dated 21 May 1870. This character from the second part of Goethe's *Faust* announces in the final scene the arrival of "a young troop of spirits," those "happy young boys" "born at midnight, almost lost to their parents but won for the angels." In signing this letter "One of the happy young boys," Nietzsche suggested that Wagner helped him to be born to real life—as is confirmed in the letter dated 20 May 1873. Cf. *SB*, 3: 115–16 and 588.

37. Letter dated 19 June 1870, *SB*, 3: 125.

38. See his letter to Cosima dated 19 June 1870 and that to Wagner himself dated 24 January 1872.

39. *SB*, 6: 36. "I think of him with lasting gratitude, for I owe him some of the most forceful stimuli toward intellectual independence," he wrote in January of the same year to Malwida von Meysenbug. *SB*, 6: 5.

40. Andreas-Salomé, *Nietzsche*, 54.

41. Entry from 4 May 1870, *Cosima Wagner's Diaries*, 1: 216. "If I were locked up in prison, I should ask only for Greek literature and things about Greece. From these people derive joy; I am well aware that they did not dot all the i's, but from them we have learned happiness, they are without sin." 1: 196, 6 March 1870.

42. Richard Wagner, *My Life*, 2 vols. (New York: Dodd, Mead and Company, 1911), 1: 411.

43. Richard Wagner, "A Communication to My Friends" (1851), in *Richard Wagner's Prose Works*, 1: 334–35.

44. Wagner, *My Life*, 1: 415.

45. Richard Wagner, "Art and Revolution" (1849), in *Richard Wagner's Prose Works*, 1: 32, 33. When Charles Andler cites this essay, oddly he does not mention the explicit reference Wagner makes in it to Dionysus. *Nietzsche*, 1: 375.

46. "The Tragedy of the Greeks having evolved from a compromise between the Apollonian and the Dionysian elements," he writes in this essay ("The Destiny of Opera," *Richard Wagner's Prose Works*, 5: 138–39), something which Nietzsche may have seen as an indiscrete revelation of what he was going to say in *The Birth of Tragedy.*

47. This is a note from the fragment "The Artists of the Future" (1849), cited by Dieter Borchmeyer in *Richard Wagner, Theory and Theatre* (Oxford: Clarendon Press, 1991), 164.

48. Here we recognize an idea dear to Rousseau: the antecedence and primacy of the sung over the spoken voice. In the article "Voice" in his *Dictionary of Music*, he writes that "in a language which would be completely harmonious, as was the Greek at the beginning, the difference of the speaking and the singing voices is null: we should have the same voice for speaking and for singing." Jean-Jacques Rousseau, *A Complete Dictionary of Music*, 2d ed., trans. William Waring (London, 1779; reprint, New York: HMS, 1975), 464.

49. Wagner, *Opera and Drama*, in *Richard Wagner's Prose Works*, 2: 283–84.

50. Wagner, "Zukunft Musik" (a letter to a French friend, Fr. Villot), in *Richard Wagner's Prose Works*, 3: 338. To which Wagner adds: "Over against the orchestra and the importance it has assumed, the chorus . . . no longer is significant in the way the ancient chorus was, this is obvious. It is allowed only as an active character, and above all where it is not necessary in such a role, it can only now become an embarrassment and superfluous. For its ideal participation in the action has passed entirely over to the orchestra and is evident there in an always present form, one which is never embarrassing." This is why *The Ring* includes only a single chorus (in the second act of *Götterdämmerung*), which Wagner moreover did not take to be a "Greek chorus," reserving that title for the funeral march in the third act. "I have composed a Greek chorus . . . but a chorus which will be sung, so to speak, by the orchestra; after Siegfried's death, while the scene is being changed." Entry from 29 September 1871, *Cosima Wagner's Diaries*, 1: 417–18.

51. *The Birth of Tragedy*, § 21, 126.

52. "About Conducting," in *Richard Wagner's Prose Works*, 4: 342.

53. *The Birth of Tragedy*, § 17, 109.

54. *KSA*, 7: 351–52.

55. *Beyond Good and Evil*, § 248, 184.

56. Entry from 5 April 1871, *Cosima Wagner's Diaries*, 1: 354. The preceding December, when Nietzsche had offered her as a birthday gift a manuscript, "The Birth of the Tragic Concept," she wrote, "the depth and excellence of his survey, conveyed with a very concentrated brevity, is quite remarkable; we follow his thoughts with the greatest and liveliest interest. My greatest pleasure is in seeing how R.'s ideas can be extended in this field" (312–13, entry from 26 December 1870).

57. The phrase "strange collaboration" comes from Andler, *Nietzsche*, 1: 392.

58. *Twilight of the Idols*, § 4, 108.

59. Letter dated 26 November 1871, *KGW BW*, vol. 2, part 2, 464. "You know that for the 'Muses with Dionysus in Their Midst' I had in mind Genelli's watercolor, which Wagner had at Tribschen," Nietzsche wrote to Erwin Rhode on 16 July 1872 regarding *The Birth of Tragedy, SB*, 4: 25 (*SL*, no. 42, 98).

60. *SB*, 3: 63.

61. "The Utility and Liability of History for Life," in *Unfashionable Observations*,

trans. and with an afterword by Richard T. Gray (Stanford: Stanford University Press, 1995), 86. Let us further note that the concept of "monumental history" that Nietzsche uses here is borrowed from Wagner, who had presented it in "A Communication to My Friends." "The example of R. had revealed to him all the meaninglessness of the modern world," Cosima commented in her diary on reading this book.

62. *KSA*, 7: 375. In the same work, Nietzsche speaks of "the Herculean power of music" that "attained its supreme manifestation in tragedy." *The Birth of Tragedy*, § 10, 75.

63. Wagner, *Opera and Drama*, in *Richard Wagner's Prose Works*, 4: 240.

64. Wagner, "Zukunft Musik," *Richard Wagner's Prose Works*, 2: 313.

65. Wagner, "Beethoven," in *Richard Wagner's Prose Works*, 5: 121.

66. *The Birth of Tragedy*, § 2, 40. For the Greeks, *harmony* meant an ordered sequence of tones based on a modal scheme, not, as for us today, the simultaneous resonance of several different notes. Harmonic chords were unknown to Greek music, which was made up of a quite simple melody, that flowed within a narrow ambit, one that, when voice was added, was sustained by instruments whose structure and range were rudimentary in comparison to ours and as regards the effects they could produce. It was nothing at all like the Dionysian music Nietzsche conceived of starting from Wagner.

67. Wagner, "The Destiny of Opera," in *Richard Wagner's Prose Works*, 5: 151.

68. "Greek Musical Drama" was a lecture given at Basel on 18 January 1870 (see *KSA*, 1: 515–32, 531–32). The "current reformer of the arts" is, of course, Richard Wagner. "We can still hope for a reawakening of Greek antiquity of which our fathers could only have dreamed," Nietzsche wrote to Richard Meister in a letter dated 14 July 1871 (*SB*, 3: 210).

69. "Art and Revolution," in *Richard Wagner's Prose Works*, 1: 54, 50.

70. "Art and Revolution," in *Richard Wagner's Prose Works*, 1: 37. If during the Renaissance the Church had appropriated "the revival of art" to represent the things of religion in meaningful and lovely forms that were "a complete denial of the very essence of the Christian religion," it was because the "enthusiasm of belief" had gone out and, having become a mere "worldly despotism," it did not fear "trumpeting her own hypocrisy" (1: 40).

71. "For if we reach the right, then all our future social bearing cannot but be of a pure artistic nature, such as alone befits the noble faculties of man," "Art and Revolution," in *Richard Wagner's Prose Works*, 1: 65. "Existence and the world seem justified only as an aesthetic phenomenon," Nietzsche claimed in *The Birth of Tragedy*, § 24, 141.

72. "Art and Revolution," in *Richard Wagner's Prose Works*, 1: 65. In January 1849, six months before writing *Art and Revolution*, Wagner had outlined a play to be called *Jesus of Nazareth*. In this, Jesus came to abrogate human laws and, in particular, the law of property, having brought into the world scandal and sin and to abolish sin and preach the law of love. But men, hardened by evil, did not listen to him. And while Judas and Barabbas were thinking of a Jewish uprising against Rome, Jesus chose to die on Calvary, not out of any distaste for life but because death was the sole means of

protest that an isolated individual can oppose to the triumph of evil. This pessimistic conclusion resembles that of *Lohengrin*, in which, through the features of the swan knight, the misunderstood artist searched in vain among men the trustworthy love he needed.

73. *The Birth of Tragedy,* § 18, 111.

74. *KSA,* 7: 140. "Nietzsche set aside Wagner's evaluation [of slavery] as tainted by the humanitarianism of 1848," notes Charles Andler. "The superiority of the Greeks' pessimism was recognizable, according to him, by their indifference concerning slavery and by that cruelty that did not fear whipping a multitude so that an elite should have the consolation of a refined culture," Andler, *Nietzsche,* 1: 375. This idea that slavery was a necessity had already been expressed in his text "The Greek State," *KSA,* 1: 764–77. We find it again later in *Human, All Too Human:* "A higher culture can come into existence only where there are two different castes in society: that of the workers and that of the idle" (vol. 1, § 439, 162). And finally: "as if slavery were a counterargument and not instead a condition of every higher culture, every enhancement of culture." *Beyond Good and Evil,* § 239, 169.

75. First version of section 2 of *Ecce Homo,* "Why I Write Such Good Books." Three years earlier he had written in his notebooks: "Richard Wagner divined from the depth of that prophetic instinct, which was so much in contradiction with his deficient and foolhardy education, that he had encountered that fateful man who held in his hands the fate of Germans and not just of German culture" *KSA,* 11: 357. Wagner's letter dated 12 June 1872, "To Friedrich Nietzsche, Professor of Classical Philology at the University of Bâle" can be found in *Richard Wagner's Prose Works,* 5: 292–98.

76. Letter of 3 June 1869, *KGW BW,* vol. 2, part 2, 14.

77. Cited from *Considérations inactuelles, I et II,* "Dates et événements," 480. Nietzsche "is the only living person, apart from Constantin Frantz, who has provided me with something, a positive enrichment of my outlook," Wagner told Cosima. Entry from 5 January 1871, *Cosima Wagner's Diaries,* 1: 319.

78. Cited by E. F. Podach, *L'effondrement de Nietzsche* (1931; reprint, Paris: Gallimard, 1978), 69. To which Wagner added: "Before, my social sphere went no further than Pohl, Nohl, and Porgès"—the "idealists" of the *Bayreuther Blätter* that Nietzsche will make fun of in *Ecce Homo.*

79. *KSA,* 11: 615.

80. Cosima Wagner, in *KGW BW II₂* 140–41. She is referring to the scene with the Rhine maidens and Siegfried in the third act of *Götterdamerung.* "Nietzsche felt a personal attachment to it," Peter Gast will say to Franz Overbeck in a letter dated 26 March 1880, cited in Janz, *Nietzsche: Biographie,* 2: 256. "Music of the *Rhine Maidens*— autumnal beauty," is referred to in one of his notes from summer 1878. *KSA,* 8: 498.

81. Letter dated 10 January 1872, *KGW BW,* vol. 2, part 2, 504 In the same letter he also writes: "You have published a book without equal. The character of this work reduces to just about nothing any influence that by chance may have been exercised on you: what distinguishes your book among all others is the complete certitude with which an originality, deeply thought through, has come to the light of day. How else

could the dearest wish of my wife and I have been accomplished, one day to see coming from the outside something that would win our total adhesion?"

82. Letter to his mother and sister, from the end of December 1864, *SB*, 2: 34.

83. From an initial version of sect. 3 of *Ecce Homo*, "Why I Am So Wise," cited from *Le Cas Wagner; Crépuscule des Idoles; L'Antéchrist; Ecce Homo; Nietzsche contre Wagner*, trans. Jean-Claude Hémery, Oeuvres philosophiques complètes, 8, pt. 1 (Paris: Gallimard, 1974), 531.

84. Three months later, a physician at the clinic in Jena recorded in the patient register this phrase from his patient: "It was my wife, Cosima Wagner, who brought me here."

85. In March 1874, in a letter containing his comments on the second essay in *Unfashionable Observations*, Erwin Rhode reproached him for the abrupt way in which he connects ideas: "You *deduce* too little, and you leave overly much to the reader the task of finding the *bridges* between your thoughts and assertions," *KGW BW*, vol. 2, part 4, 421. Wagner had written to Mathilde Wesendonck, "My subtlest and deepest art I now might call the art of Transmutation, for my whole artistic woof consists of such transitions: I have taken a dislike to the abrupt and harsh; often it is unavoidable and needful, but even then it should not enter without the *Stimmung* being so definitively prepared for a sudden change, as of itself to summon it. My greatest masterpiece in this art of subtlest and most gradual transition is assuredly the big scene in the second act of *Tristan und Isolde*." Letter dated 29 October 1859, in *Richard Wagner to Mathilde Wesendonck*, trans. William Aston Ellis (London: H. Grevel & Co. 1911), 184–85.

86. Wagner had written to Nietzsche on 12 February 1870:"You know how poor I am when it comes to philology just as, in return, you find yourself in the same situation when it comes to music. If you had become a musician, you would be about what I should have become had I obstinately committed myself to philology. Now stay a philologist while allowing yourself, as such, to be directed by music. What I am telling you is to be taken with the utmost seriousness," *KGW BW*, vol. 2, part 2, 146.

87. Letter to Wagner dated 21 May 1870, *SB*, 3: 123 (*SL*, no. 22, 66).

CHAPTER FOUR

1. Cited in Geneviève Bianquis, ed., *Nietzsche devant ses contemporains* (Paris: Éd. du Rocher, 1959), 223.

2. Letter dated 20 July 1872, *SB*, 4: 26.

3. Letter dated 24 July 1872, *SB*, 2: 240. In 1867, at Meiningen, Nietzsche had heard an "orchestral fantasy" by Bülow, *Nirvana*, that he judged to be "frightful" (ibid., 1: 530). Before separating himself from Wagner, Hans von Bülow (1830–94) had been his preferred disciple and indefatigable factotum during the years 1850–60. When in 1854 von Bülow had showed Wagner the score of *Nirvana*—in which one could see a prefiguration of several measures of the prelude to *Tristan*—Wagner warmly complemented him but indicated certain reservations, which are worth recalling in light of the

reproaches von Bülow will address to Nietzsche: "Experience indeed has taught me that objects of musical representation exist that absolutely cannot be expressed in any other way than through revealing harmonies, of a kind that appear to cruelly wound the ears of philistines. When I occasionally recognized that in my own works, I was immediately led to hide as much as possible any harmonic harshness, so that finally they ceased to produce their effect by themselves, at least for my sensibility. Now I cannot get rid of the impression that the situation is absolutely the reverse for you, that is, for you the harshness is supposed to be heard for what it is; and that turns out to be the case most disagreeably for me in those passages where I see the whole invention is only made manifest by such harshness." Then, after having admitted that he sometimes had been able to accustom himself to such things, Wagner concluded: "But that does not last very long, and I fall back to my old weakness, which makes me believe that art consists precisely in communicating the most rare and most extraordinary impressions in such a way that the listener's attention will not be distracted in hearing them in the material sense but rather will obey the seduction of my appeals without resistance and will accept the most unusual ones." Richard Wagner, *Lettres à Hans de Bülow*, ed. Georges Khnopff (Paris: Éd. Georges Crès & Cie, 1928), 51–52.

4. Draft of a letter dated the end of October 1872, *SB*, 4: 77. And Nietzsche adds these significant remarks (already cited above): "With all this, I am infinitely far—believe me—from judging and appreciating Wagner's music starting from such musical excitement which half comes from psychiatry. . . . In Wagner what I appreciate is exactly that supreme necessity—and there where, as an imperfect musician I can only grasp it in a conceptual way, it is at the level of faith that I take it for granted. But in this last piece of music, what gave the most pleasure, with the maddest kind of exuberance, was precisely a kind of caricature of the necessity I have just referred to."

5. *KSA*, 11: 510.

6. *KSA*, 12: 60. "Cruelty can be the relief of tense, proud souls, of such as are accustomed to being hard toward themselves" (12: 83). See also *Human, All Too Human*, vol. 1, § 142, and *Beyond Good and Evil*, § 229. In *The Birth of Tragedy*, the mixture of cruelty and voluptuousness characterizes the "Dionysian barbarians" that Nietzsche opposes to Greeks disciplined by Apollo.

7. *SB*, 4: 79.

8. *Ecce Homo*, "Why I am So Clever," § 4, 245–46.

9. *Beyond Good and Evil*, § 245, 181–82.

10. *Human, All Too Human*, vol. 2, part 2, § 161, 347.

11. In August 1865, during a conversation with a professor from Geneva, Nietzsche qualified "the wholly German musical sensibility" of Schumann in this way. Cited in Janz, *Nietzsche: Biographie*, 3: 145. Two years later, after having heard Schumann's *Paradies und die Peri* (op. 50) at a concert, he wrote to Franz Overbeck: "Such a shameful enervating of feeling! And what a philistine, a shopkeeper swims in the middle of this gassy lemonade lake, I fled the hall!" (3: 261).

12. From a deleted passage of section 7 of *Ecce Homo*, "Why I Am So Wise," quoted from *Le Cas Wagner; Crépuscule des Idoles; L'Antéchrist; Ecce Homo; Nietzsche con-*

tre Wagner, trans. Jean-Claude Hémery, Oeuvres philosophiques complètes, 8, pt. 1 (Paris: Gallimard, 1974), 532.

13. *KSA*, 8: 308.

14. *The Gay Science,* § 98, 150. In this aphorism Nietzsche refers to Brutus's personal freedom, not that of Rome, which seems to him to be a disguise: "Could it really have been political freedom that led this poet to sympathize with Brutus—and turned him into Brutus's accomplice? Or was political freedom only a symbol of something inexpressible? Could it be that we confront some dark event and adventure in the poet's soul, which he only wants to speak of in signs?" (§ 98, 150). André Schaeffner notes, "It is atrocious to think that this aphorism justifying Brutus's act should have appeared while Wagner was still alive." *Lettres à Peter Gast*, 1: 140.

15. Preface, *The Case of Wagner,* Preface, 156.

16. For symptoms of anti-Semitism, see, for example, the first two volumes of his *Correspondence*. Heller is cited by Georges-Arthur Goldschmidt in his preface to Daniel Halévy, *Nietzsche* (Paris: Hachette-Pluriel, 2000).

17. *KSA*, 8: 500.

18. *KSA*, 12: 80.

19. *Ecce Homo,* "Why I Am So Clever," § 6, 249.

20. The quoted phrase comes from Baudelaire and is cited in "Richard Wagner and *Tannhäuser* in Paris," 137. In his excellent *Aspects of Wagner,* Bryan Magee comments that Wagner's music "makes possible a passionate warmth and fullness of emotion without personal relationships" (Oxford: Oxford University Press, 1988), 42.

21. "Freedom from *ressentiment,* enlightenment about *ressentiment*—who knows how much I am ultimately indebted, in this respect also, to my protracted sickness! This problem is far from simple: one must have experienced it from strength as well as from weakness," *Ecce Homo,* "Why I Am So Wise," § 6, 229.

22. On receiving the book, her initial reaction, recorded in her journal was: "It seems to me to contain much inner rage and sullenness, and R. [Richard] laughs heartily when I say that Voltaire, here so acclaimed, less than any other man would have understood *The Birth of Tragedy*." Entry for 25 April 1878, *Cosima Wagner's Diaries*, 2: 94.

23. *Human, All Too Human,* vol. 1, § 428, 158.

24. *Human, All Too Human,* vol. 1, § 430, 158. Nietzsche's sister would confirm to Cosima that it was indeed she who Nietzsche had in mind when he wrote these two aphorisms.

25. *Human, All Too Human,* vol. 1, § 162, 85. "In morally belittling the genius, they no longer feel blinded by his intellect, but closer to him," he wrote in his notebooks from 1870. *KSA*, 7: 51.

26. *Human, All Too Human,* vol. 1, § 164, 87–88.

27. Entry for 11 May 1871, *Cosima Wagner's Diaries*, 1: 365. She had learned from Wagner's nephew, Clement Brockhaus, that Nietzsche had presented his sister with the same essay on Homer he had given to her, and what is more, with the same dedicatory poem.

28. Entry for 11 May 1871, *Cosima Wagner's Diaries*, 1: 399. Nietzsche wrote in

his notebooks: "The iron hates the magnet when the magnet does not fully succeed in drawing it to itself—but continues to attract it nevertheless." *KSA,* 10: 47.

29. Cited in Bianquis, *Nietzsche devant ses contemporains,* 89. Before adopting silence, Wagner had replied to *Human, All Too Human* with several points directed against professors in his essay "Public and Popularity" (*Prose Works of Richard Wagner,* 6: 51–81), which appeared in the *Bayreuther Blätter* in August 1878. But it was, indeed, a deeply felt silence, as is shown by this entry from Cosima's diary from 1 October 1879: "I note [in Herr v. Hagen's book] the quotation from Nietzsche and I have to acknowledge in tears what we have lost in him" (2: 374).

30. *KSA,* 11: 15. "I need war," he confided to Erwin Rohde in May 1872, *SB,* 4: 4; see also Ernst Bertram, *Nietzsche,* "Judas," 189–205.

31. *Ecce Homo,* "Why I Am So Wise," § 7, 231.

32. "On Naive and Sentimental Poetry," in Friedrich Schiller, *Essays,* ed. Walter Hinderer, trans. Daniel O. Dahlstrom (New York: Continuum, 1998), 204–7.

33. *The Gay Science,* § 98, 151.

34. *Human, All To Human,* vol. 1, § 629, 198–99; see also 2, § 357, 143.

35. *Human, All To Human,* vol. 2, part 1, § 60, 227–28. "Virtues too can perish of jealousy. Surrounded by the flame of jealousy, one will in the end, like the scorpion, turn one's poisonous sting against oneself." *Thus Spoke Zarathustra: A Book for All and None,* trans. Walter Kaufmann (New York: Viking Press, 1966), "On Enjoying and Suffering the Passions," 37.

36. *Ecce Homo,* "Human, All-Too-Human," § 3, 286. And in the following section: "It was then that my instinct made its inexorable decision against any longer yielding, going along, and confounding myself" (§ 4, 287).

37. "Nietzsche's Philosophy in Light of Recent History" (1947), trans. Richard and Clara Winston, in Thomas Mann, *Last Essays* (New York: Alfred A. Knopf, 1966), 150.

38. *KSA,* 11: 461; see also *KSA,* 11: 576: "My judgment is *mine:* nor does another gain the right to it easily." Jean Cocteau will remember this: "The danger of *The Case of Wagner* is that it is an idiot who flings it in your face. There are truths which can only be said after one has acquired the right to say them." "Cock and Harlequin," in *A Call to Order,* trans. Rollo H. Myers (London: Faber and Gwyer, 1926), 30.

39. *KSA,* 11: 491.

40. Posthumous fragment from July 1879, *KSA,* 8: 591.

41. *KSA,* 8: 536.

42. The phrase quoted comes from Paul Claudel, "Richard Wagner, rêverie d'un poète français," in *Figures et paraboles* (Paris: Gallimard, 1936), 170.

CHAPTER FIVE

1. Preface to vol. 2, *Human, All Too Human,* § 1, 209–10.

2. *Richard Wagner in Bayreuth,* 277.

3. *Richard Wagner in Bayreuth,* 277–78.

4. *Schopenhauer as Educator,* in *Unfashionable Observations,* trans. and with an afterword by Richard T. Gray (Stanford: Stanford University Press, 1995). 197 (hereafter cited as *Schopenhauer as Educator*).

5. *KSA,* 7: 353–55.

6. From his 1886 preface to *The Birth of Tragedy,* titled "An Attempt at a Self-Criticism," § 6, 25.

7. *Schopenhauer as Educator,* 209–10. Nietzsche here is paraphrasing what his "educator" had written in *Parerga and Paralipomena,* 2.

8. *Schopenhauer as Educator,* 210.

9. *Richard Wagner in Bayreuth,* 284. In his preparatory notes we even find during the summer of 1875 a revolutionary accent that will not appear again, an echo, perhaps, of the compassion he felt in 1871 for the Communards. "There are still enough men who are the fruitful soil in which Wagner can sow—enough men who know at least how to fight and work: Bayreuth is the proof. And so for the coming days we have good work in wiping out the weeds with sickles and scythes. . . . Down with art that does not grow into social revolution and lead to the renovation and unification of the people!" *KSA,* 8: 218. It sounds like Wagner's *Art and Revolution* from 1849! See also in the posthumous writings from 1870–73, Nietzsche's "Call to the Germans," which he wrote in October 1873 intended for the Wagner societies, wherein he writes notably that "with the word 'Bayreuth' it is not just a certain number of men, a kind of party with specific musical tastes that is at issue, but rather the nation." *KSA,* 1: 896. This appeal was not used by the sponsors of the festival, despite its having Wagner's and Cosima's approval.

10. *Richard Wagner in Bayreuth,* 284.

11. *Richard Wagner in Bayreuth,* 282. If music was the "rediscovered language of right feeling," this was because, according to Nietzsche, who here links up with Rousseau, language was "sick," worn out with overuse, and having removed "itself as far as possible from the vivid emotion that at its origin it knew how to express in total simplicity," in order to "seize the domain of thought, which is the opposite of feeling," "its force was exhausted in this inordinate extension during the short span of modern civilization." Thus "in the decline of languages," man had become "the slave of words" and conventions.

12. *Ecce Homo,* "Human, All-Too-Human," § 2, 285.

13. This is the initial version of the passage cited in the preceding note no. 12.

14. After his descent into madness, Nietzsche himself was to be similarly consecrated. Already in the 1890s, encouraged by the Nietzsche archives under the direction of his formidable sister, there developed in Germany a commerce in images, portraits, and statues in *kleinplastik* representing the prophet and martyr with his long, emblematic moustache. Groups of pilgrims and tourists began to invade the Engadine and the mountain site of Sils Maria that had inspired *Thus Spoke Zarathustra.* The "experience of solitude [Einsamkeitserlebnis]" was transformed into a lucrative tourist industry. See Steven E. Ascheim, *The Nietzsche Legacy in Germany* (Berkeley: University of California Press, 1992), 32–35.

15. "God, Nietzsche! If only you had known him. He never laughed and always seemed taken aback by our jokes," Cosima will write to Richard Strauss in 1901. "He was shortsighted, too, to the point of weaksightedness; a poor night bird, blundering into things right and left—one who it is strangely touching to encounter as an advocate." Quoted by Martin Gregor-Dellin, *Richard Wagner: His Life, His Work, His Century,* trans. J. Maxwell Brownjohn (New York: Harcourt Brace Jovanovich, 1983), 394.

16. *Ecce Homo,* "Human, All-Too-Human," § 2, 284.

17. Edouard Schuré, *Précurseurs et révoltés* (Paris: Libraire académique Perrin, 1930), 143. The dedication to *The Birth of Tragedy* concludes with these words: "I am convinced that art represents the highest task and the truly metaphysical activity of this life, in the sense of that man to whom, as my sublime predecessor on this path, I wish to dedicate this essay" (31–32).

18. *KSA,* 7: 503. He had written to Wagner shortly thereafter, "Ah, most venerable Master, how happy I am today. I have escaped a great danger in my life: that of never having approached you, of not having seen either Tribschen or Bayreuth. Since I have been carrying with me the festive feeling of the laying of the foundation stone, I have been feeling so calm; the fate life has in store for me matters less" (letter dated 24 June 1872, *SB,* 4: 16). "The 'Hymn to Joy' (22 May 1872), one of my highest emotions," we read in his notebooks for June–July 1879 (*KSA,* 8: 580). "Now I finally feel on the way. 'Happy as the stars in their course, follow, brothers, your route . . .' 1876, what a pitiful and failed festival! And now the *Bayreuther Blätter* is throwing up a smoke screen against the 'Hymn to Joy.'" *KSA,* 8: 380.

19. *KSA,* 8: 380.

20. Cf. *Human, All Too Human,* vol. 1, § 122, 68. "I loved and revered Richard Wagner more than anyone else," he will write in his notebooks in 1885, "and if he had not had the bad taste—or the unfortunate obligation—to make common cause with a kind of 'spirits' I found impossible, with his followers, the Wagnerians, I would have had no reason to bid farewell to him during his lifetime; to him, the most profound and most audacious, the most misunderstood too of those men so difficult to know today, to him with whom acquaintance allowed me to advance in knowledge more than any other." *KSA,* 12: 80.

21. *Ecce Homo,* "Human, All-Too-Human," § 2, 285–86.

22. Schuré, *Précurseurs et révoltés,* 143. Regarding Nietzsche's presence in Bayreuth in 1876, see Ernest Newman, *The Life of Richard Wagner* (New York: Cambridge University Press, 1976), vol. 4, chapters 25–27, which I have drawn upon in the preceding paragraphs. See also Andler, *Nietzsche, sa vie et sa pensée,* 1: 539–46.

23. "Need for a full work of art," he noted early in 1871 (*KSA,* 7: 154). Even ten years later, although disenchanted, he will still write: "Wagner, the first of our era to aspire to higher ends through the *unification* of the arts. He was the initiator of experimentation in this domain." Posthumous fragment from early 1881, *KSA,* 9: 434.

24. Posthumous fragment from fall 1869, *KSA,* 7: 27.

25. "Das griechische Musikdrama," *KSA,* 1: 518.

26. *The Art-Work of the Future*, in *Richard Wagner's Prose Works*, 1: 183–84.

27. "Opera and Drama" (1851), in *Richard Wagner's Prose Works*, 2: 356. In *The Art-Work of the Future* (1850), Wagner had already written that "each separate art can bare its utmost secret to their common public through a mutual parleying with the other arts; for the purpose of each separate branch of art can only be fully attained by their reciprocal agreement and co-operation of all the branches in their common message" (1: 184). Wagner's reflections stand in a German tradition that runs from Goethe, Schiller, and Novalis to Schlemmer and Brecht.

28. Posthumous fragment from early 1874, *KSA*, 7: 761.

29. *Richard Wagner in Bayreuth*, 293. In 1875, he had noted that "it required the eye of a genius to bring together again what had formed a whole at its origin, but that over the course of history had divided into several disciplines, and, today, to *try out a comprehension of the whole*." *KSA*, 8: 200.

30. *Richard Wagner in Bayreuth*, 312.

31. *KSA*, 8: 541–42. After being a great lover of opera, Eugène Delacroix, was led to the same kind of objection. In his diary for 1857 he writes: "The moderns have invented a type of art which brings together everything which should charm the mind and the senses. . . . Unfortunately all these operas are tiresome, because they hold you for too long a time in a situation which I shall call abusive. This performance, which holds the senses and the mind within its control, is the quicker to fatigue. You are promptly fatigued at the sight of a gallery of pictures: what then are we to say of an opera, uniting in a single frame the effects of all the arts together?" *The Journal of Eugene Delacroix*, trans. Walter Pach (New York: Crown Publishers, 1948), 587, entry for 16 May 1857.

32. "Das griechische Musikdrama," *KSA*, 1: 529.

33. *KSA*, 8: 544.

34. "Das griechische Musikdrama," *KSA*, 1: 530.

35. Posthumous fragment from the fall of 1869, *KSA*, 7: 24. The following citations are from the same fragment.

36. *The Birth of Tragedy*, § 19, 115. Nietzsche, like Wagner and their contemporaries, talked about the history of opera in complete ignorance of all the great masterpieces prior to Gluck. It was only at the beginning of the twentieth century that the operas of Monteverdi, Lully, Rameau, and others began to be rediscovered, a rediscovery that continues to our own day. The Florentine Camerata, at the end of the fifteenth century in reaction against the "artifice" of counterpoint and polyphony and drawing upon Plato (the melody ought to depend on the words), cultivated the "mondoy" from which emerged the *stile rappresentativo*, which was closer to rediscovering "the secret of ancient music" than was Nietzsche in *The Birth of Tragedy*. But we should add that after having denounced opera in *The Birth of Tragedy* as an almost antimusical genre, an offshoot of "theoretical man" (by opposing it to the "sublime" music of Palestrina), six years later, in *Human, All Too Human*, Nietzsche will adopt a position more in conformity with historical truth by presenting opera as a reaction to the excesses of polyphony: "for in opera the laity promulgated its protest against a cold

music grown too learned and sought to restore to Polyhymnia her soul" (vol. 1, § 219, 101).

37. "Das griechische Musikdrama," *KSA*, 1: 522.

38. *The Gay Science*, § 368, 325–27. The "enlightened Wagnerian" probably designates Cosima Wagner who, hurt by *Human, All Too Human*, had sent a long letter dated 1 March 1879, to Nietzsche's sister, in which, seeking to explain its author's change of heart, she writes notably: "I want once again to return to my physiological explanation; a subject worn down in its organism can no longer support the power of certain sensations and certain conceptions, and the disagreeable sensation he experiences leaves him no other way out than treason." Cited in Curt Paul Janz, *Nietzsche: Biographie*, 2: 270–71. Nietzsche's physiological objection to Wagner's music returns again in *The Case of Wagner* and can be found frequently in the posthumous fragments from 1888–189.

39. *The Gay Science*, § 80, 135. In this same aphorism, the author of *The Birth of Tragedy* carries his disavowal to the point of writing: "The Athenian went to the theater *in order to hear beautiful speeches*. And beautiful speeches were what concerned Sophocles: pardon this heresy!"

40. Jean-Jacques Rousseau, *Letter on French Music*, in *Essay on the Origin of Languages and Writings Related to Music*, 154.

41. This resemblance was first pointed out in an essay by the musicologist Paul-Marie Masson, "Rameau and Wagner," *Musical Review* 25 (1939): 466–78. Through Gluck, he notes, but also through the works of Mehul, Cherubini, Boeldieu, and Spontini, which he conducted in Dresden and which "preserve very clearly the distinctive features of French dramatic music," Wagner, "without knowing it, found a link with Rameau and French opera of the eighteenth century." The resemblance was further developed by Cuthbert Girdlestone in his important work, *Jean-Philippe Rameau. Sa vie, son œuvre* (Paris: Desclée de Brouwer, 1962, 1983). "It is impossible to forget the impression of Wagnerianism provoked by a first encounter with one of Rameau's operas" (132; see also 594–95).

CHAPTER SIX

1. Entry for 23 July 1878, *Cosima Wagner's Diaries*, 2: 119.

2. *KSA*, 8: 558.

3. From a posthumous fragment dating from 1871, *KSA*, 7: 276–77.

4. *The Birth of Tragedy*, § 16, 102–3, where Nietzsche quotes at length and comments on the following passage from *The World as Will and Representation*. "Such particular pictures of human life, set to the universal language of music, are never bound to it or correspond to it with stringent necessity; but they stand to it only in the relation of an example chosen at will to a general concept. . . . When now, in the particular case, such a relation is actually given, that is to say, when the composer has been able to express in the universal language of music the stirrings of will which constitute the heart of an event, then the melody of the song, the music of the opera, is expressive.

But the analogy discovered by the composer between the two must have proceeded from the direct knowledge of the nature of the world unknown to his reason, and must not be an imitation produced with conscious intention by means of concepts, otherwise the music does not express the inner nature, the will itself, but merely gives an inadequate imitation of its phenomenon. All truly imitative music does this."

5. Wagner, *Opera and Drama*, in *Richard Wagner's Prose Works*, 2: 102.

6. Wagner, *The Art-Work of the Future*, in *Richard Wagner's Prose Works*, 1: 153. The harsh judgment Wagner makes on Rossini's aesthetic—whose error was not "to have understood opera except from the angle of absolute melody"—did not prevent him from holding Rossini to be "a great artist" or from appreciating his works. As Carl Dalhaus observes, in accordance with the distinction established by Hegel, one can "subjectively" admire what one "objectively" condemns from a historical-philosophical point of view.

7. For each art, in effect, "evolves along a line of force which finally brings it to its limit, and it cannot overstep this limit without danger of losing itself in the unintelligible and absolutely fantastic, nay, absurd." Wagner, "Zukunft Musik," in *Richard Wagner's Prose Works*, 3: 308.

8. Richard Wagner, "Beethoven's Choral Symphony at Dresden," in *Richard Wagner's Prose Works*, 7: 239–55. In these program notes, Wagner writes, "With this opening of the last movement Beethoven's music takes on a more definitely *speaking* character: it quits the mould of purely instrument music, observed in all the three preceding movements, the mode of infinite, indefinite expression; the musical poem is urging toward a crisis, a crisis only to be voiced in human speech" (7: 251–52). See also the important work of Carl Dalhaus, *The Idea of Absolute Music* (Chicago: University of Chicago Press, 1989), to which the following pages owe much, and the insightful work of Thomas S. Grey, *Wagner's Musical Prose: Texts and Contexts* (Cambridge: Cambridge University Press, 1995), which appeared after the publication of the original French edition of this book.

9. E. T. A. Hoffmann, *E. T. A. Hoffmann's Musical Writings: Kreisleriana, The Poet and the Composer, Music Criticism*, ed. David Charlton, trans. Martyn Clarke (Cambridge: Cambridge University Press, 1989), 96–98.

10. In his *Complete Dictionary of Music*, for example, Rousseau writes in the article titled "Natural": "*Natural* music is that which the human voice forms by opposition to the artificial music which is executed with instruments" (269). See also the entry "Music," where after having offered praise for lyrical and theatrical music, he comments: "How much soever we may seek for moral effects in the physic of Sounds, only, we shall never find them, and our reasoning will be without understanding" (259).

11. The musical aesthetics of feeling developed in Germany at the end of the eighteenth century and during the first half of the nineteenth century. Heinichen, Mattheson, Marpug, and Quantz were its best-known exponents. "Everything that happens without praiseworthy feelings is nothing, does nothing, and means nothing," said Mattheson. However, this aesthetic did not exclude all rationality since the

expression of feelings was governed by a method borrowed from rhetoric. Edouard Hanslick gives a number of statements from these feeling-theorists in appendix B to his *On the Musically Beautiful*, trans. Geoffroy Payzant (Indianapolis: Hackett, 1986), 86–91.

12. Hanslick, *On the Musically Beautiful*, 28.

13. Wagner, *The Art-Work of the Future*, in *Richard Wagner's Prose Works*, 1: 126.

14. Wagner, "Beethoven," in *Richard Wagner's Prose Works*, 5: 106.

15. Wagner, "On the Name *Musikdrama*," in *Richard Wagner's Prose Works*, 5: 303.

16. Friedrich Nietzsche, *On the Genealogy of Morals*, in *On the Genealogy of Morals and Ecce Homo*, trans. Walter Kaufmann (New York: Vintage Books, 1967), § 5, 103.

17. In 1872, while correcting the proofs of *Opera and Drama* for the collected edition of his prose works, Wagner will say to Cosima: "I know what Nietzsche didn't like in it—it is the same thing which Kossak took up and which set Schopenhauer against me: what I said about words. At the time I didn't dare to say that it was music which produced drama, although inside myself I knew it." Entry for 11 February 1872, *Cosima Wagner's Diaries*, 1: 457. However, in returning to the question about how this all came about, some time later, Wagner will conclude that it was a "mystery" (1: 550, entry from 4 November 1872).

18. See Carl Dahlhaus, "The Twofold Truth in Wagner's Aesthetics: Nietzsche's Fragment 'On Music and Words,'" in *Between Romanticism and Modernism* (Berkeley: University of California Press, 1980), 19–39. As Thomas Grey puts it: "In his exposition of the changing accentuation of Wagner's position over time, Dahlhaus is acutely aware of [his] ambivalences and their origin in Wagner's divided loyalties to conflicting Romantic ideals of autonomy and synthesis. What he perhaps fails to stress, in an exposition of the larger historical picture, is the extent to which Wagner's ambivalences were in fact characteristic of the musical culture at large, while an unqualified valorization of musical autonomy remained exceptional. . . . Wagner may have been an extreme example of [the] divided resistance to musical autonomy, in his role as operatic reform-theorist, but (as in so many ways) he was also an epitome of the culture at large." Grey, *Wagner's Musical Prose*, 12 and 8.

19. As Dahlhaus notes, "It is uncertain whether by "causal nexus" he means only the historical provenance of "pure instrumental music" out of dance music (as such fulfilling a function) and usual music (which it imitated) or whether he also means the dependence of a dramatic score on the prescribed text and scenario; it is of no great importance to decide, since both meanings are open to the objection that the genesis of a musical form cannot be automatically equated with its aesthetic value. The banal fact that the text and scenario precede music . . . does not prevent the text and the stage action from appearing as a translation and simile of the music . . . when the work is completed." "The Twofold Truth in Wagner's Aesthetics," in *Between Romanticism and Modernism*, 36.

20. Richard Wagner, "On Franz Liszt's Symphonic Poems," in *Richard Wagner's*

Prose Works, 3: 246–47; see also his letter to Franz Liszt dated 14 October 1849, in *Correspondence of Richard Wagner and Franz Liszt* [1897], 2 vols., trans. Francis Heffer, rev. W. Aston Ellis (New York: Haskell House, 1969), 1: 45–46.

21. Entry for 24 April 1881, *Cosima Wagner's Diaries*, 2: 659.

22. Entry for 12 November 1878, *Cosima Wagner's Diaries,* 2: 198. See also the entry for 18 December 1877, in which Wagner tells how much he owes to the *Well-Tempered Clavier* (1: 1007). In his essay, "What Is German?" (1865–78), he designates Bach as the supreme incarnation of German genius. But it must be noted that Wagner refers exclusively to Bach's music for keyboard; he never speaks of the cantatas or the passions.

23. Schopenhauer in fact savored opera as a kind of absolute music. If he was keen on Rossini it was for the very reason behind Wagner's criticism of him in *Opera and Drama*. Rossini in his operas did not seek to make his music "stick closely to the words, and to mould itself to the events" through wanting to make it "speak a language not its own." "No one has kept so free from this mistake as Rossini; hence his music speaks its *own* language so distinctly and purely that it requires no words at all, and therefore produces its full effect even when rendered by instruments alone" (Schopenhauer, *The World as Will and Representation*, 1: 262). In 1854, Wagner had sent Schopenhauer (who died in 1860) the score of *The Ring*. He replied by way of a common acquaintance: "Thank your friend Wagner for me for having sent me his *Nibelungen,* but tell him to put his music in the bottom drawer and that he has more genius as a poet. As for me, Schopenhauer, I remain faithful to Rossini and Mozart!" See Edouard Sans, *Richard Wagner et la pensée schopenhauerienne* (Paris: Klincksieck, 1969).

24. This is what Liszt implies in his essay on *Tannhäuser* and *Lohengrin* when he writes: "Wagner would certainly have written the dedication for *Alceste,* if Gluck had not already done so."

25. "Experience proves," Wagner wrote in his *Beethoven,* that music "loses nothing of its character when all kinds of different texts are adapted for it. . . . Any alliance between music and poetry leaves the latter in a position of inferiority."

26. Wagner, "Beethoven," in *Richard Wagner's Prose Works*, 5: 112, 111. Here Wagner is largely inspired by Schopenhauer (cf. ibid., 5: 65–68). If in the most intense moments, we understand the action without seeing it, this is because in abolishing the world of appearances the music reveals to us the world's innermost essence: the drama of the Will, for which the action presented on stage is only an analogical substitute, more or less anecdotal depending on how much the composer-dramaturge has compressed and concentrated it.

27. On 23 September 1878, referring to *Parsifal*, he said to Cosima: "Oh, I hate the thought of all those costumes and grease-paint! When I think that characters like Kundry will now have to be dressed up. . . . Having created the invisible orchestra, I now feel like inventing the invisible theater." *Cosima Wagner's Diaries*, 2: 154.

28. In 1870 he had asked, "What is the thing written down as compared with the inspiration? What is notation in comparison with imagination? The former is governed by the specific laws of convention, the latter is free, boundless. That is the

tremendous thing about Beethoven, that in his last quartets he was able to remember and record improvisations, which could only be done through art of the highest, highest order. With me it is always the drama which flouts convention and opens up new possibilities." Entry for 4 December, *Cosima Wagner's Diaries*, 1: 302. Absolute music itself "is a kind of drama . . . a theme and a countertheme which combine in a dance," he will add in 1882 (2: 821, entry for 7 March). But while thinking of writing symphonies, he could also say that this was "obsolete, done with." Entry for 28 March 1878, *Cosima Wagner's Diaries*, 2: 51.

29. Entry for 22 September 1879, *Cosima Wagner's Diaries*, 2: 368.

30. Entry for 18 March 1870, *Cosima Wagner's Diaries*, 1: 200.

31. Entry for 16 August 1869, *Cosima Wagner's Diaries*,1: 137.

32. Marcel Beaufils, *Musique du son, musique du verbe* (Paris: Klincksieck, 1994), 190. "Sound and word form nothing more than a block of sonorous concepts. The sound thinks and proffers, and the word is only noise. Their frontier is wiped away" (191).

33. Letter to Richard Strauss dated 24 September 1913, in Richard Strauss, Hugo von Hofmannsthal, *Correspondance, 1900–1929* (Paris: Fayard, 1992), 226.

34. The expression "verbal instrumentation" comes from the symbolist poet René Ghil, *Traité du verbe* (Paris: Giraud, 1886). Influenced by both Wagner and Helmholtz's *On the Sensations of Tone as a Physiological Basis for the Theory of Music*, Ghil compares a poem to a piece of music by drawing on a "scientific" analysis of the relationships between the sounds in music and in language.

35. Letter to Karl Gaillard dated 30 January 1844, in *Selected Letters of Richard Wagner*, ed. and trans. by Stewart Spencer and Barry Millington (London: J. M. Dent and Sons, 1978), 118.

36. Letter dated 11 February 1853, in *Correspondence of Richard Wagner and Franz Liszt*, 1: 254. "It would be absolutely impossible for me simply to write music to another man's poems, not because I consider this beneath me, but because I know, and know by experience, that my music would be bad and meaningless," he had already written on 5 December 1849 (1: 56).

37. Richard Wagner, *Lettres à Otto Wesendonck, 1852–1870* (Paris: Calmann-Lévy, 1924), 88. "I can't get back to *Siegfried*, and my feelings wander far and wide and are ready to fall wherever my mind brings them. Really, everything has become insipid and superficial."

38. Letter to Princess Marie zu Sayn-Wittgenstein dated 19 December 1856, partially quoted by Robert Bailey in "The Method of Composition," in *The Wagner Companion*, ed. Peter Burbidge and Richard Sutton (London: Faber and Faber, 1979), 308. Bailey reproduces "the earliest dated sketches for *Tristan*," which Wagner had written by this date.

39. Entry for 28 September 1878, *Cosima Wagner's Diaries*, 1: 158.

40. Entry for 24 December 1879, *Cosima Wagner's Diaries*, 1: 416.

41. Entry for 1 October 1878, *Cosima Wagner's Diaries*, 1: 161, and for 11 December 1878, 1: 225.

42. Entry for 21 June 1869, *Cosima Wagner's Diaries*, 1: 111.

43. Entry for 15 September 1873, *Cosima Wagner's Diaries*, 1: 676.

44. Entry for 21 June 1869, *Cosima Wagner's Diaries*, 1: 111. See also the entry for 9 February 1881 (2: 618).

45. Wagner, "Zukunft Musik," in *Richard Wagner's Prose Works*, 3: 327.

46. *Richard Wagner in Bayreuth*, 303.

47. Posthumous fragment from 1871, *KSA*, 7: 323–24. "*Tristan* as a symphony, to which gets added myth," Nietzsche had also noted about the same time (*KSA*, 7: 229). And, four years later, in his preparatory notes for *Richard Wagner in Bayreuth*, referring to "the seduction that the symphonic form exercises over Wagner," he says: "Do you not feel how often Wagner submits with cruel resolve to the dramatic whole, which is unpitying like a fate, and how the musician does not come through to what he really desired?—This fidelity toward oneself or toward a higher self, of something feminine toward something masculine, is Wagner's innermost problem; it is from there that he understands the *world*" (*KSA*, 8: 215–16). In a word, Wagner is supposed to have been an absolute musician contradicted by himself—like Nietzsche, unable to compose except with some literary support.

48. "La mise en scène de *Tristan et Isolde*," from *La musique et la mise en scène* [1897], in Adolphe Appia, *Oeuvres complètes* (Paris: L'Age d'Homme, 1986), 2:, 176.

49. Posthumous fragment from winter 1872–1873, *KSA*, 7: 567. This is perhaps the one time where Nietzsche refers to the visual impressions he had from some spectacle.

50. *The Birth of Tragedy*, § 21, 127.

51. "Das griechische Musikdrama," lecture given by Nietzsche at Basel on 18 January 1870, *KSA*, 1: 529. Our purpose here, of course, is not to examine the historical truth of Nietzsche's analyses or arguments regarding the birth and development of Greek tragedy. The best work in this regard is M. S. Silk and J. P. Stern, *Nietzsche on Tragedy* (New York: Cambridge University Press, 1981).

52. *KSA*, 1: 530.

53. *KSA*, 7: 276–77.

54. "Richard Wagner, Revery of a French Poet" (1885), in *Mallarmé: Selected Prose Poems, Essays and Letters*, trans. Bradford Cook (Baltimore: Johns Hopkins University Press, 1956), 74.

55. "Une nouvelle forme dramatique: Les chanteurs dans la 'fosse'" (1924), reprinted in André Schaeffner, *Essais de musicologie et autres fantaisies* (Paris: Le Sycomore, 1980), 297–316, here quoting 313.

56. *KSA*, 8: 542.

57. Schaeffner, *Essais de musicologie*, 357.

58. Schaeffner, *Essais de musicologie*, 316. The quoted passage comes from *The Birth of Tragedy*, § 7, 59. Nietzsche's text continues: "this comfort appears in incarnate clarity in the chorus of satyrs, a chorus of natural beings who live ineradicably, as it were, behind all civilization and remain eternally the same, despite the changes of generations and of the history of nations." Stravinsky's *Sacre du printemps* obviously comes to mind.

59. "I would only believe in a god who could dance," says Zarathustra ("On Reading and Writing," 41), who sings two "dancing songs." In this book, "my style is a *dance*—a play of symmetries of every kind, and an overleaping and mockery of these symmetries," Nietzsche will write to his friend Erwin Rohde, 22 February 1884. *SB*, 6: 479 (*SL*, no. 121, 221).

60. *KSA*, 12: 111.

61. *The Gay Science*, § 347, 290; *Twilight of the Idols*, § 7, 65–66.

62. *The Birth of Tragedy*, § 2, 40. "Our most sacred convictions, our most unalterable faith in the matter of supreme values, are *judgments of our muscles*," he notes in the spring of 1888, *KSA*, 13: 169.

63. *Twilight of the Idols*, § 10, 73.

64. Cf. Martin Green, *Mountain of Truth: The Counterculture Begins: Ascona, 1900–1920* (Hanover: University Press of New England, 1986); see also Steven E. Aschheim, *The Nietzsche Legacy in Germany, 1890–1990* (Berkeley: University of California Press, 1992), chap. 3: "The Not-So-Discrete Nietzscheanism of the Avant-Garde." For a good short introduction to Laban, Wigman, and Duncan, see Paul Bourcier, *Histoire de la Danse en Occident* (Paris: Seuil, 1978).

65. In her autobiography, *My Life* (New York: Boni & Liveright, 1927), 341.

66. Duncan, *My Life*, 141. In the preface to *The Dance of the Future* (New York: Bowles-Goldsmith Co., 1903), Federn described Duncan as "the incarnation of Nietzsche's intuition."

67. Duncan was equally a Wagnerian. In 1904, Cosima Wagner asked her to arrange the Bacchanal for *Tannhäuser* in Bayreuth. She had discovered among the master's writings a small notebook containing a description of this scene that fit perfectly with the ideas of the dancer. Her choreography did not go unnoticed.

68. In a posthumous fragment from the fall of 1881 (*KSA*, 9: 587). Having attended the superb performances of Stravinsky's *Noces* in 1923, Jacques Copeau wrote that with this work had appeared probably the one "possibility for a renewal of tragedy." Quoted in Schaeffner, *Essais de musicologie*, 299.

69. *KSA*, 12: 90.

70. "Das griechische Musikdrama," *KSA*, 1: 530. Mallarmé, who preferred ballet to opera—"the theatrical form of poetry par excellence"—would also have applauded this renaissance. And that it, with its Russian origin, came to flower in Paris would certainly have pleased Nietzsche.

71. "Cock and Harlequin," 33.

72. *The Birth of Tragedy*, § 8, 65.

73. *The Case of Wagner*, § 9, 174.

74. *The Birth of Tragedy*, § 21, 126–27.

75. *The Birth of Tragedy*, § 21, 127.

76. *The Birth of Tragedy*, § 21, 127–29.

77. Posthumous fragment from spring-autumn 1871, *KSA*, 7: 372.

78. *The Birth of Tragedy*, § 3, 40.

79. "Out of the Dionysian root of the German spirit a power has arisen which,

having nothing in common with the primitive conditions of Socratic culture . . . *German music* as we must understand it, particularly in its vast solar orbit from Bach to Beethoven, from Beethoven to Wagner" (*The Birth of Tragedy*, § 19, 119). His condemnation of fugue and counterpoint follows shortly after this passage. Nietzsche no doubt is thinking of Wagner who, in his *Art-Work of the Future*, denounced in counterpoint the product of what absolute music had achieved: "Art's artificial playing-with-itself, the mathematics of feeling, the mechanical rhythm of egoistic Harmony . . . quite incapable of answering any *soul-needs*" (*Richard Wagner's Prose Works*, 1: 118). Nietzsche's criticism also recalls that of Rousseau, who reproached the "pedantic" form of the fugue for being too "written." See his "Letter on French Music," in *"Essay on the Origin of Languages" and Writings Related to Music*, ed. and trans. John T. Scott, Collected Works of Rousseau, vol. 7 (Hanover, NH: University Press of New England, 1998), 157–58.

80. Wagner, "Beethoven," in *Richard Wagner's Prose Works*, 5: 75–76. This must be compared with his autobiography, in which Wagner recounts how, on 5 September 1853, in a hotel room in La Spezia, he concluded the prelude to *Das Rhinegold*. "Returning, in the afternoon, I stretched myself, dead tired, on a hard couch, awaiting the long-desired hour of sleep. It did not come, but I fell only into a kind of somnolent state, in which I felt as though I were sinking into a swiftly flowing water. The rushing sound formed itself in my brain into a music sound, the chord of E flat major, which continually re-echoed in broken forms; these broken chords seemed to be melodic passages of increasing motion, yet the pure triad of E flat major never changed, but seemed by its continuance to impart infinite significance to the element in which I was sinking. I awoke in sudden terror from my doze, feeling as though the waves were rushing high above my head. I at once recognized that the orchestral overture to the *Rhinegold*, which must long have lain latent within me, though it had been unable to find definite form, had at last been revealed to me." *My Life*, 2: 603.

81. It is worth noting that Nietzsche characterizes the music that the Greeks practiced before coming to know Dionysus as the "wave beat of rhythm, whose formative power was developed for the representation of Apollinian states." *The Birth of Tragedy*, § 3, 40.

82. Posthumous fragment from 1871 cited in *KSA*, 7: 287.

83. *The Birth of Tragedy*, § 25, 143–44.

84. *The Birth of Tragedy*, § 2, 39.

85. Posthumous fragment, *KSA*, 7: 69.

86. *KSA*, 7: 187 ff.

87. Wagner, "Beethoven," in *Richard Wagner's Prose Works*, 5: 74–76. Before Nietzsche attended a performance of *Tristan* in 1872, Wagner had advised him to "put away his spectacles and only listen to the orchestra" ["Brille ab!—Nichts als das Orchester dürfen Sie hören], according to André Schaeffner. *Lettres à Peter Gast*, 1: 81.

88. Recall that in his letter to Peter Gast dated 10 January 1883, already cited in chapter 2, Nietzsche will recommend, with an eye to "a whole opera act in view of its symphonic unity," that "the whole scenic aspect must be *present* to him. But *not* the *word!*" *SB*, 6: 316.

89. *KSA*, 7: 185.

90. *KSA*, 7: 366.

91. *Richard Wagner in Bayreuth*, 309.

92. "Wagner unconsciously strives for a form of art in which the original problem of opera would be surmounted: namely, the *greatest possible symphony* in which the principal instruments sing a song that can be made perceptible through an action. It is not as language but as *music* that his music marks formidable progress," Nietzsche writes in his notebooks from 1871. *KSA*, 7: 323.

93. "Das griechische Musikdrama," *KSA*, 1: 529.

94. Posthumous fragment from the beginning of 1871, *KSA*, 7: 366.

95. *KSA*, 7: 369.

96. For example, in the posthumous fragment, *KSA*, 7: 762.

97. Yet in his notebooks he also acknowledges that this is not the case. For example: "Enjoyment of art depends on a certain knowledge; even the most popular art. There is no immediate effect on the listener, a reaching beyond the limits of the intellect." *KSA*, 8: 423–24.

98. Posthumous fragment from the spring of 1880, *KSA*, 9: 82. "The word affects first the world and only after that the feelings, and often the path is so long that the goal is not attained," he wrote in 1869. "Music, on the contrary, touches the heart immediately, for it is the truly universal language, understood everywhere." *KSA*, 1: 528.

99. "Beethoven," in *Richard Wagner's Prose Works*, 5: 102. At bottom, Wagner is simply returning to what he had already said thirty years earlier in his "A Pilgrimage to Beethoven," where in speaking of the Ninth Symphony, the composer praises "the genius of the human voice," yet also complains to himself that "the poem must necessarily limp behind the music" (7: 42).

100. "The term [leitmotiv] and its methodology," notes Thomas S. Grey, "grew out of the impulse he had created: the impulse to endow music with determinate ideas, poetic intentions, substantial meanings. Or had he created it? The impulse was certainly one Wagner read in the musical culture of his time—the culture which, according to Liszt, was ever more in search of an 'Ariadne's thread' through the mazes of modern music with all its complex harmonies, labyrinthine forms, and portentous motivic signs. Listeners listened for threads of discursive meaning even in symphonies and quartets, as well as operas. The claim that the symphony had been sublated within music drama was perhaps not pure hubris, since Wagner's music can be said to have subsumed widespread listening practices and offered them a new, richer, more suitable ground for cultivation (so he maintained)." Grey, *Wagner's Musical Prose*, 373.

101. Entry for 22 January 1871, *Cosima Wagner's Diaries*, 1: 325. In Paris in 1860, Wagner discovered that a lack of German in no way prevented his French admirers from appreciating his operas (none of which had yet been translated into French). Wagner reports in *My Life* that one of these admirers, Frédéric Villot, curator of paint-

ings at the Louvre, told him "with great insight that the music had precisely made clear the subject" of his works.

102. *The Case of Wagner,* § 8, 172–73.

103. "Das griechische Musikdrama," *KSA,* 1: 528. He even says, "as for the relation of music to ancient drama, the opinion expressed by Gluck in the well-known foreword to his *Alceste* is perfectly correct."

104. Posthumous fragment from the fall of 1869, *KSA,* 7: 17.

105. *KSA,* 7: 366.

106. Posthumous fragment from the beginning of 1874, *KSA,* 7: 770.

107. *KSA,* 8: 541.

108. *KSA,* 8: 542.

109. *The Birth of Tragedy,* § 21, 126.

CHAPTER SEVEN

1. *Richard Wagner in Bayreuth,* 308–9.

2. *Human, All Too Human,* vol. 2, part 1, § 139, 245.

3. *Beyond Good and Evil,* § 256, 197.

4. A fragment from the summer of 1878, *KSA,* 8: 535.

5. A fragment from the summer of 1875, *KSA,* 8: 235. "He creates his lyrical characters exclusively from his musical moods alone, and this is why they come together as *a whole,*" he had already noted in 1871, no doubt alluding to *Tristan. KSA,* 8: 330.

6. *The Case of Wagner,* § 8, 173.

7. Fragments from the summer of 1875, *KSA,* 8: 196.

8. *Richard Wagner in Bayreuth,* 317. He continues: "Wagner's ingenuity in things small and large, the omnipresence of his spirit and his diligence, is of a sort that, upon looking at a Wagnerian score, one is tempted to believe that no real effort and labor went into it."

9. Fragments from January–February 1874, *KSA,* 7: 788. Most commentators on Nietzsche, taking him at his word, read the fourth *Unfashionable Observation* as a concealed farewell to Wagner imposed on Nietzsche by his gratitude toward him, whereas his true thoughts would be found in his preparatory notes. But these same notes often contain sharper praise of the musician than does the published text; as for his criticisms, they have to do above all with Wagner's early works (*The Flying Dutchman, Tannhäuser,* and *Lohengrin*), which Nietzsche, in fact, did not really know very well.

10. A fragment from the summer of 1875, *KSA,* 8: 211. "Wagner demonstrates his *power* above all in the way he conquers the recalcitrant. There is no longer a single musician who does not listen to him attentively from deep within himself and who does not find him more worthy of being heard than all the rest of music. . . . When one speaks of art, whether this be in Japan or on the prairies of America, one takes just one

position into account, the one one holds regarding Wagner. And perhaps the whole modern history of art, of the last centuries as well as of those to come, will be centered on *this one name.*" *KSA,* 8: 211–12.

11. *The Case of Wagner,* § 10, 177.

12. *The Case of Wagner,* § 7, 170–71.

13. *Ecce Homo,* "The Birth of Tragedy," § 4, 274; "The Untimely Ones," § 3, 280.

14. *The Case of Wagner,* § 7, 170–71.

15. Letter dated 5 October 1879, *SB,* 5: 450–51 (*SL,* no. 82, 169).

16. Letter dated 5 November 1879, *SB,* 5: 461.

17. Paul Valéry, *Cahiers* (Paris: Gallimard, 1957), 2: 1021. This recalls Boileau, who said of Bruyère's *Caractères* that this work "only needed a sharp wit, since it freed one of the servitude of transitions, which is the stumbling block of most writers."

18. Letter dated 24 March 1872, Nietzsche, *Correspondance,* 2: 677.

19. *KSA,* 9: 520–21.

20. "We Germans are Hegelians even if there never had been any Hegel, insofar as we (unlike all Latins) instinctively attribute a deeper meaning and greater value to becoming and development than to what 'is'; we hardly believe in the justification of the concept of 'being.'" *The Gay Science,* § 357, 306. This instinctive predilection for becoming characterizes Wagner's music, as Nietzsche shows in aphorism § 240 of *Beyond Good and Evil,* devoted to the overture to *Die Meistersinger,* where moreover he pastiches with talent the "infinite melody": One finds in it "something German in the best and worst senses of the word, something manifold, formless, and inexhaustible in a German way. . . . This kind of music expresses best what I think of the Germans: they belong to the day before yesterday and the day after tomorrow—*as yet they have no today*" (173–74).

21. *Human, All Too Human,* vol. 2, part 1, § 113, 238–39, and § 134, 244.

22. *Human, All Too Human,* vol. 2, part 1, § 113, 238–39. See also vol. 1, § 199, where Nietzsche praises "the incomplete . . . which presents to the hearer's imagination the illusion of a dazzling sea and obscures the coast on the other side" (95).

23. "Music is a woman," Wagner said in *Opera and Drama* and as such lacks the will or motivation to shape itself. It is poetry that does this.

24. The same complaints are to be found again in the neo-classical Stravinsky of *The Poetics of Music in the Form of Six Lessons,* trans. Arthur Knodel and Inglof Dahl (Cambridge, MA: Harvard University Press, 1947), who accuses Wagner of having transgressed the natural laws of musical order: "Wagner's work corresponds to a tendency that is not, properly speaking, a disorder, but one which tries to compensate for a lack of order. The principle of endless melody perfectly illustrates this tendency. It is the perpetual becoming of a music that never had any reason for starting, any more than it has any reason for ending. Endless melody thus appears as an insult to the dignity and to the very function of melody which, as we said, is the musical intonation of a cadenced phrase. Under the influence of Wagner the laws that secure the life of song found themselves violated, and music lost its melodic smile" (62).

25. *The Case of Wagner,* §§ 1, 10; *KSA,* 9: 520. Let us also note that Wagner did not

seem to appreciate the aphoristic style. One day, having read some Lichtenberg, he said to Cosima "that he finds it difficult on the whole to read such isolated thoughts, strung together, the time comes when he no longer really knows what he was reading; one needs a context, a plan, a drama. 'In the end I watch them as if they were fleas, waiting for one of them to bite.'" Entry for 21 March 1878, *Cosima Wagner's Diaries*, 2: 46.

26. *KSA*, 8: 246. "One should not conceal or denature the *actual way* in which our thoughts have come to us," he notes in 1885, just before citing Pascal's *Pensées. KSA*, 11: 522.

27. *The Gay Science*, § 87, 142–43 (where Wagner is targeted without being named), and *Nietzsche contra Wagner*, "What I Admire," in *The Portable Nietzsche*, ed. and trans. Walter Kaufmann (New York: Penguin, 1968), 662, 663.

28. *The Gay Science*, § 87, 143.

29. *The Case of Wagner*, § 7, 172.

30. *KSA*, 8: 424 and 12: 60.

31. Postscript, *The Case of Wagner*, 183. But German critics, both conservative and Marxist, will see in the aphoristic and fragmentary technique adopted by Nietzsche a mode of exposition proper to an age of haste and confusion, well adapted to the modern public of newspaper readers, whose attention is intermittent, and thinking in slogans. See Aschheim, *The Nietzsche Legacy in Germany, 1890–1990*, 43.

32. *The Gay Science*, § 368, 325–26.

33. "The servile *submission* of the artist to his public (like that which J. S. Bach himself confessed to in forever humiliating words in the dedication of his great Mass) is perhaps more difficult to discern from music," notes Nietzsche in 1885, "for there it conceals itself more deeply and more radically. No one would put up with listening to me if I were to communicate my observations on this subject" (*KSA*, 11: 433). Three years later he will not hold back from communicating them as regards Wagner.

34. *The Case of Wagner*, § 11, 179.

35. *Beyond Good and Evil*, § 256, 197.

36. *KSA*, 11: 676–77.

37. *The Case of Wagner*, § 8, 173.

38. *The Case of Wagner*, § 10, 178.

39. *Ecce Homo*, "Thus Spoke Zarathustra," § 1, 295. And, of course, the four books of *Thus Spoke Zarathustra*, placed under the sign of the death of God, do correspond to the four dramas of *The Ring*, which ends with *Götterdämerung*.

40. Nietzsche, letter to Peter Gast dated 25 July 1884, *SB*, 6: 515.

41. Jean Starobinski, *Jean-Jacques Rousseau: Transparency and Obstruction*, trans. Arthur Goldhammer (Chicago: University of Chicago Press, 1988), 36.

42. *Thus Spoke Zarathustra*, "On Passing By," 177.

43. *KSA*, 12: 51. See also *Beyond Good and Evil*, § 290. "*Opera*, according to the most explicit documents, begins with *the demand by the listener to understand the words*," he noted in 1871. "What? The listener *demands*? The words have to be understood?" Posthumous fragment from early 1871, *KSA*, 7: 271.

44. *Richard Wagner in Bayreuth*, § 9, 313–14.

45. See *The Gay Science,* § 354, and *Beyond Good and Evil,* § 284; also *Human, All Too Human,* part 1, § 200. "We no longer have a sufficiently high estimate of ourselves when we communicate." *Twilight of the Idols,* § 26, 82.

46. *The Gay Science,* § 367, 324.

47. *Daybreak,* § 255, 258.

48. Posthumous fragment from 1871, *KSA,* 1: 577. "But if we imagine a hearer for these endemic outbursts, we could predict for him a fate similar to that of Pentheus, the indiscreet eavesdropper: that of being torn apart by the Maenads." *KSA,* 7: 368.

49. *KSA,* 11: 673.

50. "The intoxicated man as a work of art without a public," we read in the preparatory notes to *The Birth of Tragedy* (*KSA,* 7: 68). "I have always had in mind to write a small book and then to read it myself," he wrote in his diary at the age of fourteen. *FS,* 1: 11.

51. Roland Barthes, "Loving Schumann," in *The Responsibility of Forms: Critical Essays on Music, Art, and Representation,* trans. Richard Howard (New York: Hill and Wang, 1985), 293–95.

52. *KSA,* 11: 676.

53. *The Birth of Tragedy,* § 1, 37.

54. *The Art-Work of the Future,* in *Richard Wagner's Prose Works,* 1: 193.

55. *KSA,* 7: 761. During the same period, moreover, Nietzsche praised language, that "expression of a soul in common . . . broader than any individual" who is enriched by it through "an intimate, refined exchange." *KSA,* 7: 831–32.

56. *Thus Spoke Zarathustra,* "The Return Home," 183, *The Gay Science,* § 365, 321, *Beyond Good and Evil,* §§ 25, 44, 284.

57. Cf. Janz, *Nietzsche: Biographie,* 2: 73.

58. This letter to Overbeck is quoted in Erich Friedrich Podach, *L'effondrement de Nietzsche,* 41, as is the following sentence, which is followed by a passage from *Thus Spoke Zarathustra.* "I may say that this hidden element, the intimation of a taciturn solitude," says Lou Andreas-Salomé, "was the first, strong impression through which Nietzsche's appearance fascinated one" (Andreas-Salomé, *Nietzsche,* 9).

59. "I am addressing the most grotesque section of the public—a theater audience," he said one day to Cosima. Entry from 11 July 1871, *Cosima Wagner's Diaries,* 1: 510.

60. "If art is nothing other than the ability to communicate to others what one has experienced, then every work of art contradicts itself if it cannot make itself understood. Hence Wagner's greatness as artist must consist precisely in that demonic ability to *communicate* his nature, which speaks of itself in all languages, as it were, and allows his inner, most personal experience to be recognized with supreme clarity." *Richard Wagner in Bayreuth,* § 9, 308.

61. This appeal, let us recall, was not accepted by the board of the "Wagner Societies." *KSA,* 1: 896.

62. Again there is a comparison to be drawn with Rousseau who, in his *Politics*

and the Arts: Letter to d'Alembert on the Theatre, trans. Alan Bloom (Glencoe, Ill.: Free Press, 1960), after having condemned the theater, "that frivolous [and pernicious] amusement," gives an apology for the festival where one shows nothing if not the spectators themselves become actors, "so that each one sees and loves himself in the others so that all will be better united" (126). Rousseau and Nietzsche, in fact, had great difficulty in putting up with daily kinds of sociability: veiled, fragmented, warm or cold. They needed either solitude or (largely imaginary) fusion: egalitarian, sweet, gentle, Helvetic for the former; inegalitarian, intoxicating and terrifying for the latter. There is an exacerbated, German Rousseau in Nietzsche.

63. "Das griechische Musikdrama," *KSA,* 1: 522.

64. *The Birth of Tragedy,* § 8, 62–63. Here Nietzsche is projecting the darkness of the *Festspielhaus* at Bayreuth with its invisible orchestra on the Greek theater, which had inspired Wagner. "His seat once taken," Wagner wrote, "he finds himself in an actual 'theatron,' i.e., a room made ready for no other purpose than his looking in, and that for looking straight in front of him. Between him and the picture to be looked at there is nothing plainly visible, merely a floating atmosphere of distance, resulting from the architectural adjustment of two proscenia whereby the scene is removed as it were to the unapproachable world of dreams, while the spectral music sounding from the 'mystical gulf,' like vapours rising from the holy womb of Gaia beneath the Pythia's tripod, inspires him with that clairvoyance in which the scenic picture melts into the truest effigy of life itself." Richard Wagner, "The Festival-Playhouse at Bayreuth, with an Account of the Laying of Its Foundation Stone" (1872), in *Richard Wagner's Prose Works,* 5: 535.

65. *The Birth of Tragedy,* § 8, 64.

66. "Das griechische Musikdrama," *KSA,* 1: 521.

67. *The Birth of Tragedy,* § 8, 64.

68. Posthumous fragment from between the end of 1870 and April 1871, *KSA,* 7: 191. Let us recall that "the tragic chorus of the Greeks" was supposedly "older, more original and important than the 'action' proper. . . . Originally tragedy was only 'chorus' and not yet 'drama.'" *The Birth of Tragedy,* § 8, 65–66.

69. *The Birth of Tragedy,* § 7, 59–60.

70. "The Dionysiac World View" (1870), in Friedrich Nietzsche, *The Birth of Tragedy and Other Writings,* ed. Raymond Geuss and Ronald Speirs, trans. Ronald Spiers (New York: Cambridge University Press, 1999), 130.

71. "The Dionysiac World View," 130.

72. *The Birth of Tragedy,* § 8, 63.

73. "The Dionysiac World View," 130.

74. Nietzsche reports this fact, which does not appear in the book itself, in his preparatory notes for *The Birth of Tragedy.* We are to assume that Sophocles and Aeschylus were not fully "conscious" actors since Nietzsche, in his book and even more in his notes, designates Euripides as "the enemy of everything that is instinctive" and the first to make himself "above everything else the echo of conscious thought."

75. "Das griechische Musikdrama," *KSA*, 1: 531.

76. "Das griechische Musikdrama," *KSA*, 1: 525.

77. "This perplexity in regard to the chorus already manifests itself in Sophocles—an important indication that even with him the Dionysian basis of tragedy is beginning to break down. He no longer dares to entrust to the chorus the main share of the effect, but limits its sphere to such an extent that it now appears almost coordinate with the actors." *The Birth of Tragedy*, § 14, 92.

78. *The Birth of Tragedy*, § 15, 96.

79. *The Gay Science*, § 368, 325.

80. Posthumous fragment from the summer of 1880, *KSA*, 9: 132–33.

81. Letter to Baron von Seyditz dated 4 January 1878, *SB*, 9: 132–33 (*SL*, no. 79, 166).

82. Letter to Peter Gast dated 1 April 1887, *SB*, 8: 52.

83. Posthumous fragment from 1871, *KSA*, 7: 290. "What are the Fausts and Manfreds of the theater to anyone who is somewhat like Faust and Manfred? But it may give him something to think about that characters of that type should ever be brought upon the stage," he will exclaim ten years later in the *Gay Science*, § 86, 142. And to be sure, the profaner, the actor himself, is a creature to avoid: "It is sad but characteristic of the unspeakable poverty of German society that you find pleasure from actors. That has also happened to me," Nietzsche had written in February 1870 to his friend Paul Deussen. *SB*, 3: 100.

84. Letter to Erwin Rhode dated 3 September 1869, *SB*, 3: 52.

85. Posthumous fragment from the end of 1870 through April 1871, *KSA*, 7: 159.

86. In the letter cited above to Peter Gast dated 1 April 1887, in which he tells Gast that he has abstained from seeing *Carmen* performed, Nietzsche then adds, "Return to . . . the very *nature* of music—which in the end is the most ideal form of modern *honesty!*" *SB*, 8: 52.

87. *Richard Wagner in Bayreuth*, 292. As regards Goethe, Nietzsche, evidently, had in mind Wagner's essay on Beethoven, where he had written: "With *Goethe*, the conscious leaning toward plastic art was so strong that at a momentous epoch of his life he actually deemed himself intended for its practice, and, in a certain sense, his whole life through he preferred to regard his poetic labours as a kind of effort to make up for a missed career as painter" ("Beethoven," in *Richard Wagner's Prose Works*, 5: 64). As for Wagner's theatrical gifts, they were noted and admired by those who had seen him give lectures or heard him rehearse his works. This did not prevent him from having the same distaste for actors as did Nietzsche.

88. *Richard Wagner in Bayreuth*, 312.

89. Fragments from the beginning of 1874, *KSA*, 7: 762.

90. *KSA*, 7: 760, 758.

91. *KSA*, 7: 763.

92. *KSA*, 7: 777.

93. *The Case of Wagner*, § 11, 178–79.

94. *The Gay Science*, § 368, 325.

95. *KSA*, 11: 453.

96. *Thus Spoke Zarathustra*, "The Magician," 255–56.

97. Posthumous fragment from the summer of 1878, *KSA*, 8: 495. Similarly: "Insight into the *injustice of idealism*, in that I avenged myself on Wagner for my disappointed expectations" (*KSA*, 8: 543). As for knowing men as they are, the time had come: Nietzsche was thirty-three years old. Therefore it is not surprising that later he will reproach Germans for lacking a psychological education, for being completely "naïve," "innocents in this realm"—"which is none too distantly related to the tediousness of German company"—whereas the French had behind them "a few centuries of moralistic work" (*Beyond Good and Evil*, § 254, 193–94). Decidedly, it is difficult to recover from not having had a real courtly society, one that trains the elite "*in vulpatate psychologica*" (193).

98. *Beyond Good and Evil*, § 40, 50; see also § 278, 223–24. In § 270 we read: "There are free, insolent spirits who would like to conceal and deny that they are broken, proud, incurable hearts. . . . From which it follows that it is characteristic of more refined humanity to respect 'the mask' and not indulge in psychology and curiosity in the wrong place" (221). See also *Human, All Too Human*, vol. 2, part 1, § 232, 272.

99. *Beyond Good and Evil*, § 275, 223. In other words, there is no good psychology without a psychology of the psychologist.

100. Andreas-Salomé, *Nietzsche*, 10. Beneath a calm, reserved appearance, Nietzsche was (like Wagner) "subject to violent and abrupt changes of mood." Lou Andreas-Salomé in *Friedrich Nietzsche, Paul Rée, Lou von Salomé: Correspondance*, trans. Ole Hansen-Løve and Jean Lacoste (Paris: Presses Universitaires de France, 1979), 153.

101. *The Birth of Tragedy*, § 8, 65.

102. *Twilight of the Idols*, § 4 and § 5, 31. "*Socrates*, to be perfectly honest, is so close to me I am almost always struggling with him," he notes in 1875. Posthumous fragment, *KSA*, 8: 97.

103. *Ecce Homo*, "Why I Am a Destiny," § 1, 326.

104. *SB*, 8: 578 (*SL*, no. 206, 347). In his correspondence, Nietzsche often reveals his "lack of self-confidence."

105. Nietzsche cites this comment in his letter to Erwin Rohde dated 25 October 1872, *SB*, 4: 72 (*SL*, no. 45, 104).

106. *Ecce Homo*, "The Birth of Tragedy," § 1, 270.

107. *Ecce Homo*, "Why I Am So Clever," § 4, 247.

108. In his letter to Cosima Wagner dated 3 January 1889, "To Princess Ariadne, my beloved," Nietzsche adds: "I was . . . perhaps Richard Wagner. . . . But this time I come as the victorious Dionysus who will transform the earth into a festival. . . . Not that I would have much time. . . . The heavens rejoice that I am here. . . . I have also hung on the cross." *SB*, 8: 573.

109. *Daybreak*, § 421, 414. "I have always said decisive things about myself in such a way that anyone, feeling it to be about himself, will fall into almost the opposite of pleasure," he writes in 1888 in a version of "We the Antipodes" of *Nietzsche contra Wagner*, which he will set aside.

110. *Daybreak*, § 14, 16.

111. Quoted by Bianquis, *Nietzsche devant ses contemporains*, 213, 218.

112. *The Gay Science*, § 361, 316.

113. *KSA*, 12: 80–81.

114. *The Case of Wagner*, § 8, 173.

115. "Socrates and Tragedy" (1870), in *KSA*, 1: 539, 533. "What is art?" he had asked himself the preceding year. "Engendering what is without will by the will and *instinctively*. When there is consciousness, this is called craft." Posthumous fragment, fall 1869, *KSA*, 7: 23.

116. In the first place, Wagner, who did not share the post-Beethoven Romantic vision that he is often said to illustrate. If he could speak highly of "the lovely unconsciousness of artistic creation," it was in opposition to the difficulties he experienced when he turned to his theoretical labors. "Be on guard against underestimating the value of reflection," he wrote to Hanslick in January 1847. "The work of art produced unconsciously belongs to ages separated from our own by an immense interval. The work of art of a period of high culture can only be produced by a fully self-conscious artist. . . . It is only for a genius of extraordinary richness that that marvelous alliance of a conscious, reflective mind with immediate and spontaneous creative power can take place. This is why this alliance is so rarely realized. Yet if we can doubt that a genius of this order will soon appear, we must, on the other hand, admit that for every artist who really makes progress in his art, we can find, already, a more or less happy mixture of these two opposed gifts." Quoted in Henri Lichtenberger, *Richard Wagner, poète et penseur* (Paris: Félix Alcan, 1911), 177.

117. Writing of *Carmen*, he makes the following telling comment: "I am delighted by strokes of good fortune of which Bizet is innocent." *The Case of Wagner*, § 7, 157–58.

118. Second postscript, *The Case of Wagner*, 188. Pierre Klossowski notes that "Nietzsche's aphorisms . . . tend to give the *very act of thinking* the virtue of resistance to any 'conceptualization,' to keep it beyond the 'norms' of the understanding, and thus to substitute for 'concepts' what he calls *values*." *Nietzsche and the Vicious Circle*, trans. Daniel W. Smith (London: Athlone, 1997), 257. Because the aphorism generally affirms without arguing, it conforms to the instinct that dictates it. "An instinct is weakened when it rationalizes itself: for *by* rationalizing itself it weakens itself" (postcript, *The Case of Wagner*, 181. "A virtue that 'proves' itself by arguments" is no longer one: to remain one "it must never become conscious of its principles." Posthumous fragment from spring 1888, *KSA*, 13: 289.

119. Lou Andreas-Salomé says this letter was "written between the publication of *The Gay Science* and his mystical work, *Thus Spoke Zarathustra*." Andreas-Salomé, *Nietzsche*, 91.

120. *Thus Spoke Zarathustra*, "On The Three Metamorphoses," 27.

121. *The Antichrist*, § 57, 177, and §14, 125. "Everything *good* is instinct—and consequently easy, necessary, free" (*Twilight of the Idols*, § 2, 48). The reader will recognize here the Schopenhauerian theme of reason as weakening instinct. Cf. *The World*

as Will and Representation, § 27; see also Marcel Gauchet, *L'inconsient cérébral* (Paris: Seuil, 1992).

122. In his *Introduction aux études de philologie classique,* published with his "Introduction aux leçons sur l'Oedipe-Roi de Sophocle" (Éditions Encre Marine, 1994). "If one has the opportunity to question Nietzsche's students," Carl Albrecht Bernoulli reported in 1908, "they seem to agree in remembering with a kind of religious awe having received the teachings, not of a professional pedagogue but of a Greek ephor in the flesh, who had joined them in a leap through time and space to reveal to them Homer, Sophocles, Plato, and their gods. He impressed them as speaking from his memory of things that to him seemed completely natural and still alive." Bianquis, *Nietzsche devant ses contemporains,* 52.

123. "Music, as the art where the power of instinct predominates." Fragment from 1869–70, *KSA,* 7: 49.

124. See Alain Clément, *Nietzsche et son ombre: Essai* (Bourges: Éd. Amor-Fati, 1989), 28–29, the best short book on Nietzsche.

125. *Human, All Too Human,* vol. 1, § 624, 197.

126. *Thus Spoke Zarathustra,* "On Poets," 126. If they lie too much, this is because, of course, they do not believe in themselves. A few pages earlier, Zarathustra says, "Whoever does not believe in himself always lies" ("On Immaculate Perception," 123).

127. Fragment from spring 1888, *KSA,* 13: 398.

128. *KSA,* 13: 310.

129. Overbeck, cited in Janz, *Nietzsche: Biographie,* 2: 432.

130. Thomas Mann, "The Sorrows and Grandeur of Richard Wagner," in *Pro and contra Wagner,* trans. Allan Blunden (Chicago: University of Chicago Press, 1985), 120–21.

131. *Thus Spoke Zarathustra,* "The Magician," § 2, 255. But the deceitful song of the magician (§ 1) becomes truthful in the Dithyrambs of Dionysus where Nietzsche attributes these to Ariadne, who offers herself to the blows of her "unknown god," her "executioner-god," Dionysus.

132. "It is to the problem of the relation between art and truth that I devoted my first serious efforts," he noted in 1888. "Even now I feel a sacred horror in the face of this conflict." *KSA,* 13: 500.

CHAPTER EIGHT

1. The ribald farce that followed the tragedy in the festival of Dionysus. The leading characters were satyrs.

2. From *Nietzsche contra Wagner,* "Wagner as the Apostle of Chastity," § 3, 674–75, where Nietzsche takes up again and expands the charge made in *On the Genealogy of Morals,* at the end of "What Is the Meaning of Ascetic Ideals?" § 2, 98–99.

3. Posthumous fragment from the summer of 1880, *KSA,* 9: 129.

4. *KSA,* 12: 112. He continues: "This suspicion does more to harm him in my

eyes than does the disappointment of having placed my hopes in an aging Romantic whose knees were already weak enough to fall down before the cross."

5. Posthumous fragment from fall 1881, *KSA*, 9: 591.

6. Nietzsche does not mention this confidence in his notes until the fall of 1884 (*KSA*, 11: 250), then returns to it two more times in the two following years (see *KSA*, 11: 535–36, and 12: 111–12). He would never do so publicly. According to his sister, Elizabeth Förster-Nietzsche—whose testimony must always be taken with caution—it was at Sorrento, in November 1876, when the two men met for the last time, that Wagner had told Nietzsche this. "Had he had in mind the picturesque ritual of the Catholic church, which always creates a deep impression upon sensitive artistic natures, my brother would have had less reason to doubt his sincerity." *The Nietzsche-Wagner Correspondence*, ed. Elizabeth Förster-Nietzsche, trans. Caroline V. Kerr (New York: Boni & Liveright, 1921), 294. Nietzsche apparently "forgot" this important detail when in *Beyond Good and Evil* (§ 256) he will accuse Wagner of denying his "German nature" in preaching *"the way to Rome"* (198). For his sister—who also attributes this interpretation to him—Wagner's "conversion" was an act of hypocrisy, since in the light of the poor financial results of the first Bayreuth Festival he is supposed to have said in 1876 that "the Germans do not wish to hear anything about gods and goddesses at present, they are only interested in something of a religious character" (*The Nietzsche-Wagner Correspondence*, 294–95). Cosima Wagner does report Wagner having said something similar about Protestant communion. Entry from 13 December 1873, *Cosima Wagner's Diaries*, 1: 707–8.

7. *Thus Spoke Zarathustra*, "On the Flies of the Market Place," 52.

8. Posthumous fragment from summer 1875, *KSA*, 8: 203–4. Shortly thereafter, he adds: "Toward religion, he [Wagner] is as uninhibited toward religion as Aeschylus toward the various Zeuses. Essentially non-religious" (*KSA*, 8: 275). Artists are not religious, he will say in *Human, All Too Human* (vol. 1, § 125), but this time against Wagner, by invoking Homer, Aeschylus, Aristophanes, the great artists of the Renaissance, Shakespeare, and Goethe rather than referring to Wagner by name.

9. This reflection of Wagner from after 1880, is noted in "The Brown Book," a diary he kept from 1865 to 1882. See *The Diary of Richard Wagner, 1865–1882: The Brown Book*, annotated by Joachim Bergfeld, trans. George Bird (London: Victor Gollancz, 1980), 200. "Godhead is nature, the will that seeks salvation and, to quote Darwin, selects the strongest to bring this salvation about," he said another time to Cosima (entry from 24 January 1878, *Cosima Wagner's Diaries*, 2: 22). And a bit later, in a draft of *Art and Religion*: "Under God's features, man seeks to represent, strictly speaking, a being that is in no way submitted to the sufferings of life (of the world), and also who is placed above the world; it is Jesus (Buddha) who triumphs over the world; we have never believed in a creator God." Sans, *Richard Wagner et la pensée schopenhauerienne*, 115.

10. Christ's blood "could never flow in the interest of howsoever favoured a single race; no, it shed itself on all the human family, for noblest cleansing of Man's blood from every stain," writes Wagner in 1881. "Hence the sublime simplicity of the

pure Christian religion, whereas the Brahminic, for instance, applying its knowledge of the world to the ensurance of supremacy for one advantaged race, became lost in artificiality and sank to the extreme of the absurd" ("Hero-Dom and Christendom," in *Richard Wagner's Prose Works*, 6: 283). The sympathy Wagner felt at the end of his life for Gobineau did not lead him to adopt the latter's racial theory. "It is by no means impossible that humanity should cease to exist, but if one looks at things without regard to time and space, one knows that what really matters is something different from racial strength—see the Gospels," he tells Cosima on 14 February 1881 (*Cosima Wagner's Diaries*, 2: 622). And the following June, while dining with Gobineau, "he is downright explosive in favor of Christian theories in contrast to racial ones" (entry from 2 June 1881, 2: 672). Wagner was an anti-Semite but not a racist, otherwise he would not have asked (without success) Hermann Levi, the conductor who directed the premiere of *Parsifal*, to accept baptism, nor would he have expressed "great admiration" for the North during the American Civil War.

11. Mann, "To the Editor of *Common Sense*," in *Pro and contra Wagner*, 198–203.

12. Gregor-Dellin, *Richard Wagner: His Life, His Work, His Century*, 789.

13. Richard Wagner, *Religion and Art* (1881), in *Richard Wagner's Prose Works*, 6: 213. "There are certain things human beings have been able to express only in symbols," he confided to Cosima on 27 April 1880, "and the church has committed the crime of consolidating these and forcing them on us as realities through persecution; it is permissible for art to use these symbols, but in a free spirit and not in the rigid form imposed by the Church; since art is a profound form of play, it frees these symbols of the accretions the human craving for power has attached to them." *Cosima Wagner's Diaries*, 2: 470.

14. Entry from 20 October 1878, *Cosima Wagner's Diaries*, 2: 177.

15. *The Antichrist*, § 31, 143.

16. Entry from 26 September 1877, *Cosima Wagner's Diaries*, 1: 984. She emphasized this in a letter she wrote in February 1877 to Dr. Otto Eiser, Nietzsche's physician, who, using Nietzsche as an intermediary, had proposed an interpretation of the libretto of *Parsifal* to Wagner in which he compared the work to Calderón's *autosacramentales*: "Calderón used his genius to dramatize Church dogmas for the people, but *Parsifal* has nothing in common with any Church, nor indeed with any dogma, for here the blood turns into bread and wine, whereas it is the other way round in the Eucharist. *Parsifal* picks up where the Gospels leave off; and its poet continued to structure and create his material, heedless of all that already existed." Borchmeyer, *Richard Wagner: Theory and Theatre*, 401–2, n. 59. In *Human, All Too Human*, vol. 1, § 141, Nietzsche will denounce "the insupportable superlative Christianity of Calderón" (76).

17. Letter dated 28 September to King Ludwig II of Bavaria.

18. Wagner, *Religion and Art*, in *Richard Wagner's Prose Works*, 6: 248, 249. Eleven years earlier in his essay on Beethoven, Wagner rejecting what he had written in *Art and Revolution*, had said the same thing. Confronted with the "whole modern world of Appearance, which hems him in on every side to his despair," man experiences the need for a redemptive force; and "as Christianity stepped forth amid the Roman civil-

isation of the universe, so *Music* breaks forth from the chaos of modern civilisation. Both say aloud: 'our kingdom is not of this world'" ("Beethoven," 5: 120).

For interpretations of *Parsifal*, see Richard Wagner, *Parsifal*, trans. Marcel Beaufils (Paris: Aubier-Montaigne, 1964); Sans, *Richard Wagner et la pensée schopenhauerienne;* Lucy Beckett, *Richard Wagner: Parsifal* (Cambridge: Cambridge University Press, 1981); Dieter Borchmeyer, *Richard Wagner: Theory and Theatre.* See also Carl Dahlhaus, *Richard Wagner's Music Dramas* (Cambridge: Cambridge University Press, 1979).

19. Entries from 7 April 1879 and 29 April 1879, *Cosima Wagner's Diaries,* 2: 288, 2: 299). At one time Wagner did think of having Parsifal intervene during the third act of *Tristan und Isolde,* and he did consider the Grail as the spiritualization of the Nibelungen treasure.

20. Wagner, "A Communication to My Friends" (1851), in *Richard Wagner's Prose Works,* 1: 375.

21. Posthumous fragment from 1875–1876, *KSA,* 8: 273.

22. Letter to Liszt dated 16 December 1854, *Correspondence of Richard Wagner and Franz Liszt,* 2: 54.

23. Letter to Richard Wagner dated 15 October 1872, *SB,* 4: 62. Brunhilde sings the verse "Whoever wounds me awakens me" after Siegfried has awakened her by embracing her, a moment Nietzsche will say where "Wagner achieves such a loftiness and sanctity of mood that we cannot help but think of the glowing ice- and snow-covered peaks of the Alps." *Richard Wagner in Bayreuth,* 265. This verse is cited by Nietzsche in his posthumous fragments from the spring of 1878, *KSA,* 8: 507.

24. *The Gay Science,* § 370, 327–28, and *Nietzsche contra Wagner,* "We Antipodes," 669.

25. *Richard Wagner in Bayreuth,* 327. Announcing the revolution that German philosophy must one day produce, Heine underscores that "the most frightening" revolutionaries are "the philosophers of nature." "The philosopher of Nature will be terrible because he will appear in alliance with the primitive powers of Nature, able to evoke the demonic energies of old Germanic Pantheism—duing [*sic*] which there will awake in him that battle-madness which we find among the ancient Teutonics who fought neither to kill nor conquer, but for the very love of fighting itself. It is the fairest merit of Christianity that it somewhat mitigated that brutal German *gaudium certaminis* or joy in battle, but it could not destroy it. And should that subduing talisman, the Cross, break, then will come crashing and roaring forth the wild madness of the old champions, the insane rage, of which Northern poets say and sing. That talisman is brittle, and the day will come when it pitifully break. The old stone gods will rise from long-forgotten ruin, and rub the dust of a thousand years from their eyes, and Thor, leaping to life with his giant hammer, will crush the Gothic cathedrals! But when those days shall come, and ye hear the stamping and ring of arms, guard ye well, ye neighbours' children, ye French, and put not forth your hands into what we are doing in Germany, for verily evil will come upon you for that." *Germany,* The Works of Heinrich Heine, vol. 5, trans. Charles Godfrey Leland (London: William Heineman, 1906), 207–8.

26. *Beyond Good and Evil,* § 256, 197–98.

27. Poetic fragment from the fall of 1884, *KSA,* 11: 300; see also another poetic fragment from the same period, "To Richard Wagner," in *KSA,* 11: 319.

28. *On the Genealogy of Morals,* "What Is the Meaning of Aesthetic Ideals?" § 3, 100.

29. *Richard Wagner in Bayreuth,* § 1.

30. *Ecce Homo,* "Why I Am a Destiny," § 1, 326. "I shudder in thinking about those who, without being made for my ideas, will claim my authority," he wrote to his sister in June 1884.

31. First version of § 2 of the chapter "Why I Write Such Good Books."

32. *KSA,* 8: 533.

33. *KSA,* 11: 491.

34. *KSA,* 12: 55.

35. *KSA,* 12: 370.

36. *Ecce Homo,* "Human, All-Too-Human," § 5, 288.

37. "Afterward read *Parzival* with Prof. Nietzsche, renewed feelings of awe," notes Cosima (entry from 25 December 1869, *Cosima Wagner's Diaries,* 1: 176). No reference to *Parsifal* is to be found in Nietzsche's correspondence from this period. In referring to his Christmas vacation at Tribschen, he writes to his friend Rohde in January or February: "—a lovely and sublime memory! It is absolutely indispensable that you be, you too be initiated into this magic." *SB,* 3: 93.

38. Fragment from fall 1887–March 1888, *KSA,* 12: 354: "*Around 1876* I was terrified to see the whole of what I had wanted up to then *compromised,* when I understood what Wagner wanted to get to."

39. *KSA,* 12: 407, 13: 477: "Even the bravest of us rarely has the courage for what he really *knows* . . ." (which also appears in *Twilight of the Idols,* "Maxims and Arrows" 2, 23). The idea appears at least twice in his letters from this period. To Franz Overbeck in 1887: "If Only I had the courage to *think* all that I am"; and to Georg Brandes, in December of the same year: "What a human being takes already to be 'true' or not yet to be so depends, it seems to me, more on his courage, on the degree of strength of his courage . . . (I only rarely have the courage for what I really know)." *SB,* 8: 206.

40. "The danger of modesty," *KSA,* 12: 278. "What costs the most? One's modesty; not to have paid heed to one's most personal needs; to take oneself for another; to think oneself vile; to lose all subtlety in listening to one's instincts . . ." (*KSA,* 13: 464). In *Twilight of the Idols,* Nietzsche will speak "all the 'false modesties' that [at that time] turned [him] away from the *task* of [his] life."

41. See, e.g., Bianquis, *Nietzsche devant ses contemporains.* In August 1882, shortly after having met him and easily discerned the man behind the mask, Lou Salomé commented: "There is in Nietzsche's character, like in an old castle, a lot of dark dungeons and secret compartments that escape superficial observation, but that constitute his real nature." *Friedrich Nietzsche, Friedrich, Paul Rée, and Lou von Salomé: Correspondance,* 156.

42. Cited by Podach, *L'effondrement de Nietzsche*, 75. "Over the years I dealt with people and took renunciation and politeness to the point of never talking about things that were in my heart. Yes, this is almost the only way I lived with people," he writes in his notebooks from spring 1885. *KSA*, 11: 448.

43. *KSA*, 12: 354. "It was difficult, very difficult to have for six years to be an adversary to someone who one had admired and loved, as I loved Wagner," he wrote to Malwida von Meysenbug on 21 February 1883, shortly after the composer's death. "And it was very hard, as his adversary, to condemn myself to silence—for the sake of the respect that the man *as a whole* deserves." *SB*, 6: 335.

44. Quoted in Dietrich Fischer-Dieskau, *Wagner and Nietzsche*, trans. Joachim Neugroschel (New York: Seabury, 1976), 161.

45. Fischer-Dieskau, *Wagner and Nietzsche*, 162–63.

46. Nietzsche added this section titled "Sorrow Is Knowledge" to *Human, All Too Human*, vol. 1, § 109, 61, when he learned that Hans von Wolzogen had refused to publish three long essays on music by Peter Gast in the first issue of the *Bayreuther Blätter*, for which he was the editor. His irritation was all the greater since the idea for this journal first came from him. See Curt von Westernhagen, *Wagner: A Biography* (New York: Cambridge University Press, 1978), 2: 534.

47. For example, he wrote to her on 15 June 1882, "I've been thinking that, in a few weeks, I could accompany you to Bayreuth, were you not to find any better company," before going on to Tautenburg, a village in Thuringa near to Bayreuth. *SB*, 6: 204.

48. Quoted in Janz, *Nietzsche: Biographie*, 2: 37.

49. In *Ecce Homo*, "Why I Am So Wise," § 1, Nietzsche cites as his distinguishing features his "fingers for *nuances*" and his extralucid "psychology of 'looking around the corner'" (223).

50. *SB*, 6: 507–8. Heinrich von Stein, who was Wagner's son's tutor, had expressed to Nietzsche, in response to having received the third part of *Zarathustra*, the desire to see him at Bayreuth for the performance of *Parsifal*. Nietzsche's letter is dated 22 May—Wagner's birthday!

51. See his letter to Peter Gast of 19 February 1883, *SB*, 6: 334.

52. Letter dated 21 May 1884, *SB*, 6: 507 (*SL*, nos. 124, 226) and letter dated 27 October 1886, *SB*, 7: 273. "If I am not completely mistaken about my future," he wrote to Malwida von Meysenbug in March 1882, "the best part of the Wagnerian influence will live on in my own influence, it's almost comic to say." *SB*, 6: 185.

53. The words "offense" and "mortal wound" applied to Wagner's return to Christianity appear in the letter from Nietzsche to Malwida von Meysenbug dated 21 February 1883, referred to above, which was published for the first time in 1985 by Mazzino Montinari in *Nietzsche-Studien* 14 (1985): 13–21. "He offended me in a *mortal* way—I must tell you!—his slow, groveling return to Christianity and the Church I felt as a personal insult: my whole youth and its orientation seemed to me soiled by the fact I had rendered homage to a spirit capable of *such* a step" (*SB*, 6: 335). Prior to the publication of this letter, these two words, which were also used by Nietzsche but

with no commentary in a long-known letter to Overbeck from the same period, led Gregor-Dellin in his recent biography of Wagner to see in them a clear allusion to Wagner's well-intended slip to Nietzsche's physician regarding his health and sexual practices. See Martin Gregor-Dellin, *Richard Wagner,* 734–44; U. Müller and P. Wapnewski, eds., *Wagner Handbook* (Cambridge: Harvard University Press, 1992), 338.

54. Posthumous fragment from the summer of 1878, *KSA,* 8: 535.

55. *KSA,* 12: 349.

56. Curiously, when Nietzsche reproaches "aging Romantics" for having "fallen prostrate at the foot of the cross," he never mentions Schumann or Liszt, who had, however, in 1865 received the tonsure and the four minor orders. In January 1872, he had sent Liszt a copy of *The Birth of Tragedy* accompanied by a letter in which he said how much the book owed to him: "When I think of the small number of those who have instinctively grasped in an effective manner the phenomenon I describe and name "Dionysian"—it is always you that first comes to mind: the most secret mysteries of this phenomenon must be so familiar to you that I have never failed to consider you with the greatest theoretical interest as one of its most noteworthy exemplifications." To which Liszt replied: "In your book there simmers and blazes a powerful spirit that touched the very heart of me. I must confess that I lack the training and knowledge that would allow me completely to appreciate your work: the Greek world and the idolatry of it in which scholars indulge have remained largely foreign to me; I consider as the highest spiritual fact that the Athenians should have erected an altar to the "unknown god," an altar on which the whole of Olympus shattered once Saint Paul had proclaimed the identity of this *unknown god;* it is not around Parnassus and the Helicon that my gaze wanders, rather my soul is attached to Tabor and Golgatha" (*KGW* BW, vol. 2, part 1, 327, and vol. 2, part 2, 557). It would have been interesting to know Nietzsche's reaction to this letter.

57. Preface, *Human, All Too Human,* vol. 2, § 3, 211, "Assorted Opinions and Maxims" and "The Wanderer and His Shadow." Two years later, in *Nietzsche contra Wagner,* he will speak of an "unexpected catastrophe."

58. Letter to Peter Gast dated 19 February 1883, *SB,* 6: 333 (*SL,* nos. 111, 208). See also *Daybreak,* § 542, "The Philosopher and Age," 541–43.

59. Posthumous fragment dated 25 November 1887, *KSA,* 13: 16. In a draft of a letter to Cosima found among the final drafts for *The Case of Wagner,* Nietzsche wrote: "You are well aware how much I know the influence you have exercised over Wagner—you are even more aware to what point I despise that influence. . . . I turned my back on Wagner and you the moment the imposture began." See also Andler, *Nietzsche, sa vie et sa pensée,* 2: 333–34. In reality, Cosima had converted to Protestantism and did so ardently because she wanted to be genuinely German (as a reaction against the painful childhood she had in Paris, neglected by her parents). She was one who made the decision to have her children by Wagner baptized as Protestants. Nietzsche is projecting on Wagner what in fact happened to Liszt, who would return to the fervent Catholicism of his youth largely through the influence of Princess Sayn-Wittgenstein, which Wagner judged to be extremely harmful.

60. *The Case of Wagner*, § 3, 161.

61. Letter to Erwin Rohde dated 8 October 1868, *SB*, 2: 322 (*SL*, no. 10, 33).

62. Posthumous fragment from fall 1881, *KSA*, 9: 581. Nietzsche will return at least twice to this theme in 1887–88.

63. Posthumous fragment from spring 1888, *KSA*, 13: 41–42.

64. Letter dated 21 January 1887, *SB*, 8: 12–13 (*SL*, no. 149, 257–58).

65. Posthumous fragment from January 1887, *KSA*, 12: 198–99. Whereas during his "positivist" phase Nietzsche had found "too much of Christianity and the Middle Ages" in the music of Bach, it was with great pleasure that he learned in May 1888 that the Parisians "were madly enthusiastic about the *Saint Matthew Passion*." "*Le Figaro*, yes, *Le Figaro!*" he writes to Peter Gast, "devoted a whole page of its musical supplement to the melancholic aria 'Take pity on me, my God.'" *SB*, 8: 319.

66. Letter to Peter Gast dated 25 July 1882, *SB*, 6: 23 (*SL*, no. 100, 190). The casuist adds, for the usage of the profane: "You will understand, dear friend, that this does not mean I am praising *Parsifal*!! What sudden *décadence!* And what Cagliostroism!" There is nothing Wagnerian about Nietzsche's oratorio, notes Curt Paul Janz, who edited his musical works. "Yet it is the same demand that is found in this oratorio and in *Parsifal*: the will to put into a work of music the Christian experience of transcendence . . . as an emotional vehicle for the Christian mystery." Janz, *Nietzsche: Biographie*, 2: 421.

67. Postscript, *The Case of Wagner*, 184. Shortly thereafter he notes in a draft for *Ecce Homo*: "After the crime of *Parsifal*, Wagner should not have died in Venice, but in jail." First redaction of section 5 of *The Case of Wagner*, "Why I Write Such Good Books."

68. Postscript, *The Case of Wagner*, 183. See also *On the Genealogy of Morals*, "What Is the Meaning of Aesthetic Ideals?"

69. In a fragment from October 1888 that at first was to be part of *Twilight of the Idols*. *KSA*, 13: 601.

70. *KSA*, 13: 600–1. In the violent letter that he will write to Malwida von Meysenbug on 20 October 1888, Nietzsche speaks of his "deep hatred for the repugnant sexuality of Wagnerian music." Yet thirteen years earlier, in his preparatory notes for the fourth essay in *Unfashionable Observations*, he deplored the "repugnant character" of what was said or written about Wagner: "Here and there, there are real outbursts of fury, and they have gone so far as to indicate by the name 'Wagner' everything there is of the diabolic in the arts of seduction and intoxication."

71. *KSA*, 13: 601. Tristan and Isolde, "really experienced, are almost a debauchery," he also noted about the same time in his notebook. *KSA*, 13: 513.

72. *The Case of Wagner*, 161, 162. In his youth, the orchestra conductor Bruno Walter (born in 1876) had experienced this prudishness. In the eyes of the very conservative musical milieu in Berlin where he grew up, in the shadow of Joseph Joachim, a disciple of Mendelssohn and champion of Brahms, Wagner was considered to be a corrupting influence like the devil. He had "corrupted also the music, had abandoned all moderation and form." "It was added in a low voice—there was another wicked

and impure element in Wagner's music, tone that was still beyond me. I knew quite well that they were referring to sensuality, which I found rather interesting and by no means wicked." Bruno Walter, *Theme and Variations: An Autobiography*, trans. James Austin Galston (London: Hamish Hamilton, 1947), 42.

73. *Beyond Good and Evil*, § 264, 214. Nietzsche implicitly refers to his own parents and ancestors as well, who "at some point . . . sacrificed ancient prerogatives of birth and possessions in order to live entirely for their faith—their 'god'—as men of an inexorable and delicate conscience which blushes at every compromise."

74. Later, two or three times, when he will be attracted to a woman he hardly knew or had only recently met (Lou Salomé in particular), Nietzsche will make a proposal of marriage by way of a third party.

75. *The Nietzsche-Wagner Correspondence*, 65–66.

76. Preface, *Ecce Homo*, § 2, 217. "The satyr," he writes in *The Birth of Tragedy*, was "a symbol of the sexual omnipotence of nature which the Greeks used to contemplate with reverent wonder" (§ 8, 61). But let us also recall that in this book Nietzsche takes care to distinguish the "Dionysian Greek" who played a part in the spectacle of tragedy from the "Dionysian barbarian" whose festivals led to "extravagant sexual licentiousness" (§ 2, 39).

77. "Notes sur Nietzsche," in Jarrety, *Valéry, pour quoi?* 33.

78. Postscript, *The Case of Wagner*, 183.

79. *Twilight of the Idols*, § 9, 72.

80. *The Birth of Tragedy*, § 4, 45.

81. In "Beethoven" (1870).

82. *Human, All Too Human*, vol. 1, § 219, 101–2.

83. *The Birth of Tragedy*, § 5, 23.

84. *The Birth of Tragedy*, § 12, 86.

85. For example: "Apollo's Hellenic world was bit by bit internally dominated by Dionysian forces. Christianity is already to be found there." *KSA*, 7: 137; see also 243–57, 262, 274, and 304–5.

86. *The Birth of Tragedy*, §§ 17, 106, and 11.

87. *Ecce Homo*, "The Case of Wagner," § 2, 320.

88. *The Birth of Tragedy*, § 23, 136–37; see also § 19 where Nietzsche opposes "the vaulted structure of Palestrina harmonies" to the "thoroughly externalized operatic music" of that period (114).

89. This is how Nietzsche talks about Kundry in a letter dated 4 January 1878 to his friend Reinhart von Seyditz, *SB*, 5: 300 (*SL*, no. 165, 165–66), and in *The Case of Wagner*.

90. *Nietzsche contra Wagner*, "Wagner as the Apostle of Chastity," § 3, 675.

91. Fragment from October 1888 (23 [2]), which was first found in his copy of *Twilight of the Idols, KSA*, 13: 295.

92. Fragment from spring 1888 (14 [117]) (ibid., 86).

93. *Twilight of the Idols*, § 2, 43.

94. Mann, "Nietzsche's Philosophy in the Light of Recent History," 145.

95. Preface (1886), in *Human, All Too Human*, vol. 2, § 4, 211. "A searching out of what it is in truth that hurts *me*, a sacrificing of everything, an extreme tension," he writes in his notebooks from 1882–83. *KSA*, 10: 174.

96. Preface for the second edition, *The Gay Science*, 36.

97. *Beyond Good and Evil*, § 270, 220.

98. "My 'philosophy,' if I have any right to so name what mistreats me to the very roots of my being, is no longer communicable," he wrote to Franz Overbeck, 2 July 1885 (*SB*, 7: 62). And five years earlier he had written to Malwida von Meysenbug, not without a touch of pride: "As regards torments and renunciations, my life, these past years, can be compared to that of any ascetic, at any time." *SB*, 6: 5

99. *Thus Spoke Zarathustra*, "On the Famous Wise Men," 2, 104.

100. Quoted by André Schaeffner in *Lettres à Peter Gast*, 1: 262. Nietzsche, "that sado-masochist unto himself," Lou Andreas-Salomé will later say. *The Freud Journal of Lou-Andreas-Salomé*, trans. Stanley H. Levy (New York: Basic Books, 1964), 143.

101. Letter to Peter Gast dated 13 July 1882, *SB*, 6: 222 (*SL*, no. 97, 186).

102. Letter to Peter Gast dated 1 September 1882, *SB*, 6: 249.

103. Fully quoted by Nietzsche in his letter to Peter Gast dated 1 September 1882 (*SB*, 2, 110). Lou Salomé reports that, having shown this poem to Freud, he read it, then "folded the poem and tapped it on the arm of his chair: 'No, you know! I can't really go along with that! Just one persistent cold dragging on would be enough to cure me of such wishes!'" Lou Andreas Salomé, *Looking Back: Memoirs*, ed. Ernst Pfeiffer, trans. Breon Mitchell (New York: Paragon House, 1991), 105.

104. Letter quoted in *Lettres à Peter Gast*, 1: 266; and in Charles Andler, *Nietzsche, sa vie et sa pensée*, 2: 447.

105. Reported by André Schaeffner in *Lettres à Peter Gast*, 1: 183, and also by Ernst Bertram, *Nietzsche*, 158.

106. In a letter to Gast dated 10 November 1887, Nietzsche even calls his composition "*Hymnus ecclesiasticus*." *SB*, 8: 191 (*SL*, no. 156, 273).

107. Letter to Peter Gast dated 27 October 1887, *SB*, 8: 179 (*SL*, no. 156, 272–73). The same month, in a letter addressed to the conductor Felix Motll, which was never posted, Nietzsche writes: "I wish this piece of music may serve as amplification, where the *words* of the philosopher must, as is the case with words, remain by necessity unclear. The *affect* of my philosophy finds its expression in this hymn." *SB*, 8: 172–73.

108. *Ecce Homo*, "Thus Spoke Zarathustra," § 1, 296–97.

109. *Ecce Homo*, "Why I Am So Clever," § 10, 258.

110. Posthumous fragment from summer 1878, *KSA*, 8: 500.

111. *Daybreak*, § 113, 69.

112. *On the Genealogy of Morals*, "What Is the Meaning of Ascetic Ideals?" § 10, 115. Nietzsche also refers to this legend in *Daybreak*, § 113. Earlier in section 2 of *On the Genealogy of Morals* (§ 18, 87–88), which is a sadomasochistic history of morals, Nietzsche shows how ideals, moral beauty and even aesthetic beauty could have not seen

the light of day without the pleasure human beings take in mistreating themselves. On asceticism, see also *Human, All Too Human*, vol. 1, §§ 136–37.

113. *Ecce Homo*, "Why I Am So Wise," § 4, 228. "If I must pity, at least I do not want it known; and if I do pity, it is preferably from a distance" (*Thus Spoke Zarathustra*, "On the Pitying," 88). See also *Daybreak*, § 143, 108–9.

114. *The Antichrist*, § 7, 118.

115. *Twilight of the Idols*, § 35, 87.

116. *The Antichrist*, § 2, 116. As Theodor Adorno will write in his Frankfurt School idiom: "It might well be asked whether Nietzsche's criterion of health is of greater benefit than the critical consciousness that Wagner's grandiose weakness acquires with the unconscious forces responsible for his own decadence." *In Search of Wagner*, trans. Rodney Livingstone (London: Verso, 1981), 154–55.

117. Fragment 14 [140d] from spring 1888, *KSA*, 13: 323–24. *"The weak have more spirit,"* "strength turns one into a moron," he points out in *Twilight of the Idols*. And a year before, in *On the Genealogy of Morals*: "The history of humanity would certainly be something inept apart from the spirit with which the unpowerful have animated it."

118. According to Meta von Salis who was staying at Sils-Maria at the same time as Nietzsche, during the summer of 1887. Janz, *Nietzsche: Biographie*, 3: 267.

119. Letter to Peter Gast dated 21 July 1881, *SB*, 6: 109.

120. Epilogue, *The Case of Wagner*, 191.

121. "To *overcome* all that is Christian through something over-Christian, not simply to jettison it," is what he recommends in one of his notes from the fall of 1885. *KSA*, 11: 682.

122. Preface, *Daybreak*, § 4, 4.

123. I borrow this metaphor from Erich Heller, *The Importance of Nietzsche* (Chicago: University of Chicago Press, 1968), 7. "For me, Nietzsche is, above all, contradictory," Paul Valéry wrote to Gide. "For example, he wipes out A by method B, then he demolishes B; and hangs on to both of them just the same." Jarrety, *Valéry, pour quoi?* 16.

124. "Über Stimmungen" [On Moods] (April 1864), in *FS*, 2: 406–8.

125. Quoted by Thomas Mann (*Etudes*, 81). "Speaking to Nietzsche about the changes that already lay behind him," reports Lou Andreas-Salomé, "elicited from him remarks he made half in jest: things taken their course and continue to develop, but where to? When everything has taken its course—where does one run to? When all possible combinations have been exhausted, what happens then? How could one then not arrive again in belief? Perhaps in a *Catholic* belief? And from the background hiding place of these assertions emerged the added, serious words: 'In any case, the circle could be more possible than a standing still.'" *Nietzsche*, 32. In his "jottings" titled "*Fatum* und Geschichte [Fate and History]," which he wrote at Pforta in 1864, in evoking the enterprise of negation—of the existence of God and of Christianity—into which he had thrown himself, Nietzsche described it as "a battle with no certain out-

come, to the point at last when painful experiences and sad events lead our heart back to the old faith of our childhood." *FS*, 4: 55–56.

CHAPTER NINE

1. *The Gay Science*, § 370, 327–28.
2. *Nietzsche contra Wagner*, "We Antipodes," 669.
3. *The Birth of Tragedy*, § 7, 59.
4. *The Birth of Tragedy*, § 19, 119.
5. *Ecce Homo*, "The Birth of Tragedy," § 4, 274.
6. *KSA*, 12: 118.
7. *The Case of Wagner*, § 4, 163–64.
8. Dahlhaus, *Wagner's Music Drama*, 141. And even though, with a Puritan's sarcasm George Bernard Shaw objects to the idea of redemption through love, in *The Perfect Wagnerite: A Commentary on the Nibelung's Ring* (1898) (New York: Dover, 1967), he gave a more faithful interpretation, in light of the socialist ideals of 1848, than the fable concocted by Nietzsche in *The Case of Wagner*.
9. Letter dated 16 (?) December 1854, *Correspondence of Richard Wagner and Franz Liszt*, 2: 53.
10. "It does not say much for Schopenhauer that he did not pay more attention to my *Ring des Nibelungen*," he will tell Cosima on 29 March 1878. "I know of no other work in which the breaking of will . . . is shown as being accomplished—through the individual strength of a proud nature *without the intervention of a higher grace*, as in Wotan. I'm convinced that Sch. would have been annoyed that I discovered this before I knew about his philosophy—I, a political refugee, the indefensibility of whose theories had been proved by his disciple Kossak on the basis of his philosophy, since my music is supposed to have no melody." *Cosima Wagner's Diaries*, 2: 52.
11. Letter dated 16 May 1855, *Correspondence of Richard Wagner and Franz Liszt*, 2: 86.
12. Richard Wagner, "What Boots This Knowledge?" supplement to *Religion and Art*, in *Richard Wagner's Prose Works*, 6: 262.
13. Entry from 2 June 1879, *Cosima Wagner's Diaries*, 2: 316–17.
14. Ibid., 677, entry for 17 June 1881.
15. Wagner, *Religion and Art*, in *Richard Wagner's Prose Works*, 6: 239–40, 252.
16. *Nietzsche contra Wagner*, "Where Wagner Belongs," 672. "A Capitulation" (*Richard Wagner's Prose Works*, 5: 3–33) was a ponderous "comedy in the ancient manner" that Wagner unsuccessfully proposed to Hans Richter to set to music in the style of Offenbach. He set this aside after being turned down by a Berlin theater.
17. Entries for 7 October and 18 October 1878, *Cosima Wagner's Diaries*, 2: 174, 165. "Much talk about the French, R. says he is ashamed that their instincts about the Germans in 1870 had proved correct (Schuré, for example)." Entry for 11 January 1879, *Cosima Wagner's Diaries*, 2: 251.
18. Entry for 9 May 1879, *Cosima Wagner's Diaries*, 2: 305.

19. *The Birth of Tragedy,* "Attempt at a Self-Criticism," 17.

20. As reported by Cosima Wagner. Entry from 14 January 1882, *Cosima Wagner's Diaries,* 2: 790.

21. Letter dated 28 September 1869, *SB,* 3: 58 (*SL,* no. 18, 58–59).

22. *The Case of Wagner,* § 5, 165–66.

23. *Human, All Too Human,* vol. 1, § 473, 173.

24. Posthumous fragment from June–July 1885, *KSA,* 11: 587. He adds: "In fact, I would wish that it could be demonstrated by a few great experiments that in a socialist society life negates itself, cuts off its roots. Earth is big enough and humanity still has enough resources for me not to deprive myself of wishing for this practical lesson and demonstration *ad absurdum,* even if it should be won and paid for by an enormous cost in lives."

25. Wagner was a resolute adversary of vivisection, against which he wrote a pamphlet in 1879 that concludes: "Human dignity begins to assert itself only at the point where man is distinguishable from the Beast by pity for it, since pity of man we ourselves may learn from the animals when treated reasonably and as becomes a human being. If we are to be marked for this, disclaimed by our National Intelligence, and Vivisection is to continue to flourish in public and private as before, at least there is one good thing for which we might thank its defenders: that a world in which 'no dog would longer care to live' we can gladly leave as Men, though no 'German Requiem' [alluding to Brahms] be played to our ashes!" "Against Vivisection," in *Richard Wagner's Prose Works,* 6: 210.

26. Fragment from August–September 1885, *KSA,* 11: 675–76. Nietzsche, who denounced the "abominable dragon's seed of nationalism," was no less hostile than was Wagner to the "madness of armaments." In his "last observation," written when he was on the threshold of madness, in early January 1889, he will say: "If we can dispense with wars, so much the better. I can think of better uses for the 12 billion that armed peace costs Europe every year. There are other ways of paying homage to physiology than military hospitals . . ." *KSA,* 13: 643–44.

27. For a detailed discussion, cf. Sans, *Richard Wagner et la pensée schopenhauerienne,* 313–34.

28. *Richard Wagner to Mathilde Wesendonck,* 75. "The first manifestation of transcending oneself is sexual love," he had already written in the draft for his *Jesus of Nazareth* in 1849.

29. *KSA,* 8: 191. Similarly, in *The Gay Science,* where he denies Wagner standing as Schopenhauer's disciple, Nietzsche emphasizes that "nothing could be more contrary to the spirit of Schopenhauer than what is distinctively Wagnerian in Wagner's heroes: I mean the innocence of the utmost selfishness, the faith in great passion as the good in itself—in one word, what is Siegfried-like in the countenance of his heroes." *The Gay Science,* § 9, 154.

30. From the third act of *Tristan,* quoted by Nietzsche in *The Birth of Tragedy,* § 21, 127.

31. *Correspondence of Richard Wagner and Franz Liszt,* 2: 53–54.

32. Schopenhauer, *The World as Will and Representation*, vol. 2: "Supplements to the Fourth Book," 41, "On Death and Its Relation to the Indestructibility of Our Inner Nature," 508.

33. *Tristan und Isolde*, act 3. One thinks also of the duet in act 2, "O sink hernieder, Nacht der Liebe." "It is in death that love is sweetest: for the man who loves, death is a nuptial night, a secret of sweet mysteries," Novalis wrote in his *Hymns to the Night* (1800). See also Thomas Mann, "The Sorrows and Grandeur of Richard Wagner," 124–30.

34. *Richard Wagner in Bayreuth*, 303.

35. Letter dated 21 December 1871, *SB*, 3: 257 (*SL*, no. 33, 85). Three years earlier, let us recall, in a letter to the same friend, Nietzsche compared Wagner's music to "a Schopenhauerian sea of sounds where the most secret waves" provoke a "shock" that he felt resonate to his very depths.

36. *The Birth of Tragedy*, § 7, 59–60.

37. *Richard Wagner to Mathilde Wesendonck*, 118.

38. Ricardo Viñes, *Journal intime, 1897*, cited in Marcel Marnat, *Maurice Ravel* (Paris: Fayard, 1986), 37.

39. *Ecce Homo*, "Why I Am So Clever," § 6, 250. "No one is free to become a Christian or not to do so: one is not 'converted' to Christianity—one must be sufficiently sick for it," he comments at almost the same time in *The Antichrist* (§ 51, 168).

40. *The Gay Science*, § 370, 328.

41. *The Case of Wagner*, § 5, 166.

42. Entry for 5 November 1878, *Cosima Wagner's Diaries*, 1: 190.

43. See Dominique Jameux, "Politique des *Maîtres chanteurs*," *L'Avant-Scène Opéra* nos. 116–117, 172–81. "Except here, Wagner was never a democrat," he notes. Instead of democrat (since he believed in equality among human beings), it might be more correct to say that Wagner was never a liberal in the classic sense.

44. Mann, "The Sorrows and Grandeur of Richard Wagner," 130.

45. *KSA*, 12: 118.

46. *KSA*, 8: 487

47. Posthumous fragment from early 1871, *KSA*, 7: 359.

48. *The Birth of Tragedy*, § 12, 82.

49. Posthumous fragment from summer 1878, *KSA*, 8: 520. For the profound lassitude and even distaste Nietzsche experienced very quickly toward teaching and philology, see his letters to his friends from early 1871 (*SB*, vol. 3). His professor's chair at Basel, he will say in *Ecce Homo*, was like his commitment to Wagner, "a total aberration of my instincts" and he became aware of this at the same time. "It was then, too, that I first guessed how an activity chosen in defiance of one's instincts, a so-called 'vocation' for which one does not have the least vocation, is related to the need for *deadening* the feeling of desolation and hunger by means of a narcotic art—for example, Wagnerian art. Looking about me cautiously, I have discovered that a large number of young men experience the same distress: one antinatural step virtually compels the second. In Germany, in the *Reich*—to speak unambiguously—all too

many are condemned to choose vocations too early, and then to waste away under the burden they can no longer shake off.—These people require Wagner as an *opiate:* they forget themselves, they are rid of themselves for a moment.—What am I saying? For *five or six hours!*" *Ecce Homo*, "Human, All-Too-Human," § 3, 286–87.

50. *KSA*, 8: 549–50.

51. *The Gay Science*, § 87, 143, a passage used again in *Nietzsche contra Wagner* in a section tellingly titled "Where I Admire."

52. Posthumous fragment from fall 1885, *KSA*, 12: 118.

53. Preface to volume 2, *Human, All Too Human*, § 3, 211.

54. Letter from Cosima Wagner, *KGW BW* II₄ 66.

55. "At the Lamoureux Concert in 1893," an allocution given 4 January 1931 on the occasion of the fiftieth anniversary of the Concerts Lamoureux, in Paul Valéry, *Occasions*, trans. Roger Shattuck and Frederick Brown, Collected Works, vol. 2 (Princeton: Princeton University Press, 1970), 198–99.

56. Paul Valéry, *Analects*, trans. Stuart Gilbert, Collected Works, vol. 14 (Princeton: Princeton University Press, 1970), 219. Valéry's ambivalent attitude toward music has the same principal object—Wagner—as does Nietzsche's, whose arguments he sometimes literally reproduces. One example is when he reproaches music for producing "effects without a cause." Let us also recall Tolstoy, who, after having loved music for many years, denounced it in his book *What Is Art?*—particularly that of Beethoven, Schumann, Berlioz, Liszt, and Wagner "dedicated to the expression of unhealthy emotions."

57. "*The energy of healthiness* reveals itself in the sick by *sudden resistance* to the elements that *make one sick* . . . by an instinctive reaction, for example, in me, against music." *KSA*, 13: 389.

58. *Human, All Too Human*, vol. 1, § 215, 99. "Music does *not* reveal the essence of the world and its will as Schopenhauer claimed," he will note in 1885. "Music only reveals the musicians! And they don't know it themselves! And good thing, too, perhaps, that they don't!" (*KSA*, 12: 77–78). As Swann will put it more drolly in *À l'ombre des jeunes filles en fleur* [Within a Budding Grove]: "What music shows—to me, at least—is not the 'triumph of the Will' or 'In Tune with the Infinite,' but, shall we say, old Verdurin in his frock coat in the palmhouse in the Zoological Gardens." Marcel Proust, *In Search of Lost Time*, trans. G. K. Scott-Moncrieff and Terence Kilmartin, rev. by D. J. Enright, 6 vols. (New York: Modern Library, 1993), 2: 146.

59. *On the Genealogy of Morals*, "On Ascetic Ideals," § 6, 103.

60. *Human, All Too Human*, vol. 1, § 219, 101.

61. *Human, All Too Human*, vol. 1, § 150, 81–82.

62. *Human, All Too Human*, vol. 1, § 153, 82.

63. Paul Bourget, *Études et portraits* (Paris: A. Lemmerre, 1889), 248.

64. Stéphane Mallarmé, *Oeuvres complètes* (Paris: Gallimard, 1945), 388–89.

65. Camille Mauclair, *La Religion de la musique* (Paris: Librairie Fischbacher, 1909).

66. Mauclair, *La Religion de la musique*, 26–27.

67. *Nietzsche contra Wagner,* "Where Wagner Belongs," 672. See also *Beyond Good and Evil,* §§ 254, 256.

68. *Human, All Too Human,* vol. 2, part 1, § 319, 285.

69. *Human, All Too Human,* vol. 2, pt. 2, § 85, 334, and § 87, 332.

70. Posthumous fragment from fall 1889, *KSA,* 9: 203.

71. See the posthumous fragments from summer 1875, *KSA,* 8: 259–61.

72. *Twilight of the Idols,* § 2, 61. In *Daybreak* (§ 207, "The German attitude to morality," 128) he had said that the danger to Germans "lies in everything that suppresses the reasoning faculties and unchains the emotions (as, for example, the immoderate use of music and spirituous drinks): for, in a German, emotion is directed against his own advantage and is self-destructive like that of a drunkard."

73. "Slavery is everywhere visible, although it does not admit this to itself," he notes in fall 1881 (*KSA,* 9: 527). This is a theme that recurs often in his notebooks. And with it, he again links up with Rousseau. "You peoples of the modern world, you have no slaves, but you are slaves yourselves; you pay for their liberty with your own. It is in vain that you boast of this preference; I see more cowardice than humanity in it." Jean-Jacques Rousseau, *The Social Contract,* trans. Maurice Cranston (New York: Penguin, 1968), 143. If Nietzsche had read these lines from book 2, chapter 15 of the *Social Contract,* he would surely have made them his own even though they came from his detested alter ego.

74. *Human, All Too Human,* vol. 2, pt. 1, § 170, 251; § 169, 250; vol. 1, § 282, 131–32; § 283, 132; § 285, 132; *KSA,* 9: 664; *Twilight of the Idols,* § 30, "The right to stupidity," 13: 429.

75. *Human, All Too Human,* vol. 2, pt. 2, § 168, 349; vol. 2, pt. 1, § 171, 252–54; vol. 1, § 147, 80.

76. *Daybreak,* § 197, "German hostility to the Enlightenment," 117.

77. *KSA,* 8: 190. A short time before Nietzsche had written: "When he gives life to Christian and Nordic myth, he does so without expressing anything dogmatic or being old-fashioned in this customary manner of the poet" (*KSA,* 8: 189). Also: "The apparently *reactionary-romantic* element. His opposition to *civilization*" (*KSA,* 8: 266). "Feeling, premonition, unconsciousness, instinct [Nietzsche would later become a vehement advocate for all of this].—But all this is to be taken merely as *appearance:* its *character is progressive.*" *KSA,* 8: 266.

78. *Human, All Too Human,* vol. 2, pt. 1, § 171, 253. "To the height of the Enlightenment corresponds the height of the counter-Enlightenment in Schopenhauer and Wagner," Nietzsche wrote in his notebook in spring 1877. *KSA,* 8: 382.

79. Fragment from spring 1888, *KSA,* 13: 248. "Music and its dangers—its exhilaration, its art of arousing Christian states, and above all that melange of transposed sensuality and the frenzy of prayer (Francis of Assisi)—goes hand in hand with uncleanliness of head and exaltation of heart: break the *will,* overexcite the senses, musicians are lechers." *KSA,* 12: 319; see also 12: 522–23.

80. Posthumous fragment from fall 1880, *KSA,* 9: 95. Shortly thereafter he will note: "For Milton and Luther, for whom music was part of life, the defective and fa-

natical development of the understanding and the unleashing of hate and abuse were perhaps provoked in part by the indiscipline of music" (*KSA*, 9: 426). He will even bring himself to cite approvingly Kant's harsh judgments about music: "Music possesses a certain lack of urbanity"; "in a way it imposes itself," "it is harmful to freedom." *KSA*, 12: 267.

81. *Human, All Too Human*, vol. 2, pt. 2, § 167, 348.

82. *Human, All Too Human*, vol. 2, pt. 2, § 86, 332.

83. *Daybreak*, § 197, 118.

84. *Human, All Too Human*, vol. 1, § 244, 116–17.

85. Posthumous fragment from summer 1878 (*KSA*, 8: 552). In *Human, All Too Human* (vol. 2, pt. 1, § 213), Nietzsche, who we know had eye trouble, goes so far as to recommend "the artistic education of the eye from childhood on" in preference to "the artistic cultivation of the ear," for the former, he says, has "the invaluable attendant benefit of rendering the eye *sharp, tranquil and persevering* in the observation of men and situations" (263).

86. *KSA*, 8: 516.

87. *Human, All Too Human*, vol. 1, § 222, 105.

88. *Human, All Too Human*, vol. 1, § 223, 105–6. "We are experiencing the decline of the LAST *art*—Bayreuth convinced me of this," he notes during the summer of 1878. *KSA*, 8: 547.

89. "Music is in full bloom. How infinitely superior Beethoven is to Goethe." Posthumous fragment from the beginning of 1874, *KSA*, 7: 785.

90. *KSA*, 9: 241. In a letter to Heinrich von Stein dated 15 October 1885, he writes of "the real German devil, the genius or *daimon* of obscurity." *SB*, 7: 110 (*SL*, no. 138, 248).

91. Hermann Hesse, *Steppenwolf* [1927], trans. Basil Creighton, updated by Joseph Mileck (New York: Holt, Rinehart and Winston, 1963), 135–36.

92. See my preface to Thomas Mann, *Wagner et notre temps* (Paris: Hachette-Pluriel, 1978).

93. Thomas Mann, "Nietzsche and Music," 144. The following year (23 June 1925), in seeking to explain to the composer Hans Pfitzner his "recent intellectual orientation" (that is, his support for the Republic), Mann wrote to him: "Our drama, maestro, is in the history of the spirit, in its great representative lines, unfolding over time; we others, today, are only a replay, at the current journalistic level, of *Nietzsche contra Wagner*." *Lettres de Thomas Mann*, vol. I: 1889–1936 (Paris: Gallimard, 1970), 296–98.

94. Thomas Mann, *The Story of a Novel: The Genesis of Doctor Faustus*, trans. Richard and Clara Winston (New York: Alfred A. Knopf, 1961), 228.

95. Mann, *The Story of a Novel*, 205–6. In *The Closing of the American Mind*, Allan Bloom presents a reflection similar to Nietzsche's and Mann's regarding romantic music. Highly critical of Nietzsche, on this topic Bloom nonetheless only cites *The Birth of Tragedy*, even though he could have found further supporting arguments from the works of Nietzsche's "positivist" phase. See the chapter titled "Music" in Allan Bloom,

The Closing of the American Mind: How Higher Education Has Failed Democracy and Impoverished the Souls of Today's Students (New York: Simon and Schuster, 1987), 68–81.

CHAPTER TEN

1. Posthumous fragment from September–October 1888, *KSA*, 13: 596.

2. *KSA*, 9: 183.

3. Letter from Nietzsche to Dr. Otto Eiser from early 1880, *SB*, 6: 3.

4. See *The Birth of Tragedy*, § 18, and the posthumous fragments from 1869–71.

5. Rosset, *La Force Majeur*, 69.

6. Nietzsche uses this expression in a fragment from April–June 1885, *KSA*, 11: 490. It recurs in *Beyond Good and Evil*, where he refers to the ideal he opposes to Schopenhauer' philosophy: "the ideal of the most high-spirited, alive, and world-affirming human being who has not only come to terms and learned to get along with whatever was and is, but who wants to have *what was and is* repeated into all eternity, shouting insatiably *da capo*" (§ 56, 68). "The musical rubbish of the eternal return," Paul Valéry will say. "Notes sur Nietzsche," in Jarrety, *Valéry, pour quoi?* 34.

7. Posthumous fragment from spring–fall 1881, *KSA*, 9: 505.

8. *KSA*, 11: 610–11.

9. *Twilight of the Idols*, "Expeditions of an Untimely Man," § 49, 102–3, and "What I Owe to the Ancients," § 4, 109.

10. "Preface for the second edition (1886)," *The Gay Science*, 38.

11. *The Birth of Tragedy*, § 19, 121.

12. *The Birth of Tragedy*, § 3, 41.

13. *The Birth of Tragedy*, § 25, 143–44.

14. Fragment from August–September 1885, *KSA*, 11: 649.

15. Fragment from spring 1888, *KSA*, 13: 246–47.

16. Fragment from fall 1887, *KSA*, 12: 433, and another from spring 1888, *KSA*, 13: 297. "Classic taste: is the will to simplify, to strengthen, to the manifestation of happiness, to fecundity, to courage for psychological *nakedness*," he also notes in 1888. "In order to extricate oneself from chaos, by a hard-fought struggle, to reach this degree of *structuration*—some CONSTRAINT is needed: one must have the choice either to perish or *assert oneself*. A sovereign race cannot develop to this level except starting from a terrible and violent beginning. Problem: where are the *Barbarians* of the 20th century? They will show themselves and consolidate their position only after enormous socialistic crises—these will be the elements capable of *the greatest hardness toward themselves*, guarantors of the *longest will . . .*" *KSA*, 13: 17.

17. "Beethoven as dependent on Rousseauean feeling—for which he became the echo," he notes in spring 1884 (*KSA*, 11: 121). But then a year later: "*Beethoven* belongs to Rousseau and to that humanitarian current that in part anticipated the Revolution, in part succeeded it and transfigured it, but he belongs even more to the capital event of the last millenium, the appearance of Napoleon" (*KSA*, 11: 539). See also *Beyond Good and Evil*, § 245, 180–82.

18. Fragment from spring 1888, *KSA*, 13: 489–91. Nietzsche, it is clear, overlooks or underestimates the unaltered classical ground of French Romanticism.

19. Nietzsche's praise also encompasses the high Christian spirituality that was then blooming in France. His target is Christianity as impregnated with Germanness and the "simple-mindedness" of *Parsifal*. The well-known aphorism no. 192 from *Daybreak* in which Nietzsche describes Christian France of the seventeenth century is indicative of this: it is titled "The desire for perfect opponents." See Jean Lacoste's postscript to the first volume of Nietzsche's *Oeuvres:* "Nietzsche et la civilization française" (Paris: R. Laffont, 1993), 1301–65.

20. *The Case of Wagner,* § 9, 175.

21. *Human, All Too Human*, vol. 1, § 221, 103. The passage continues: "One only has to read Voltaire's *Mahomet* from time to time to bring clearly before one's soul what European culture has lost once and for all through this breach with tradition." And when we read *Ecce Homo,* we think of the Voltaire of the *Letters from England* who admired Shakespeare yet was disconcerted by his "odd sentences" and lack of good taste: "My artist's taste vindicates the names of Molière, Corneille, and Racine, not without fury, against a wild genius like Shakespeare" (*Ecce Homo,* "Why I Am So Clever," § 3, 243). Regarding Voltaire, recall Cosima Wagner's comment on reading *Human, All Too Human,* see p. 223, n. 22.

22. *Human, All Too Human*, vol. 1, § 221, 102.

23. *Human, All Too Human*, vol. 1, §221, 103.

24. *KSA*, 11: 441.

25. *Human, All Too Human*, vol. 2, part 2, § 140, 343.

26. "A hyperclassicism of difference" is how Luc Ferry sums up Nietzsche's final aesthetic in *Homo aestheticus: The Invention of Taste in the Democratic Age,* trans. Robert de Loaiza (Chicago: University of Chicago Press, 1993), 182–87. "If one needs to make a tyrant of *reason* . . . then there must exist no little danger of something else playing the tyrant." *Twilight of the Idols,* "The Problem of Socrates," § 10, 33.

27. *Human, All Too Human*, vol. 2, part 2, § 168, 349, and a fragment from 1878–79, *KSA*, 8: 579–80.

28. Fragment from fall 1887, *KSA*, 12: 523.

29. Fragment from early 1871—already referred to above (*KSA*, 7: 359). Schopenhauer's phrase about music, the "language of the heart," which Nietzsche cites in this fragment, comes from his *Parega.* I am drawing here on Dahlhaus's *Between Romanticism and Modernism.* As already indicated, the interpretation that Nietzsche gives in this fragment of Schopenhauer's conception of the will and his metaphysics is close to that proposed by Clément Rosset in his *Esthétique de Schopenhauer.*

30. Letter to Rudolf Buddensieg dated 12 July 1864, *SB*, 1: 293. Buddensieg was a fellow student at Pforta who had questioned Nietzsche about the relationship between the emotion experienced by the hearer of a musical work and the intrinsic quality of such a work.

31. Hanslick, *On the Musically Beautiful,* xxiii. Hanslick's name is mentioned once by Nietzsche in his preparatory notes for *The Birth of Tragedy:* "Music 'the most

subjective art': in what really is it not an art? In its 'subjectivity,' that is, it is purely pathological insofar as it is not a purely nonpathological *form*. This is Hanslick's point of view." *KSA*, 7: 310.

32. Hanslick, *On the Musically Beautiful*, chap. 5, 59; see also Einstein, *Music in the Romantic Era*, 349–52.

33. Hanslick, *On the Musically Beautiful*, 60, 30.

34. *Human, All Too Human*, vol. 1, § 215, 99.

35. *The Birth of Tragedy*, § 19, 120.

36. *Twilight of the Idols*, "Expeditions of an Untimely Man," § 24, 81.

37. *KSA*, 13: 300.

38. *KSA*, 13: 465.

39. *The Case of Wagner*, § 5, 166, 164.

40. Julien Gracq, *Lettrines* (Paris: José Corti, 1967), 178.

41. Plato, *Republic*, 398b–400c. "Plato, the greatest enemy of art Europe has yet produced." *On the Genealogy of Morals*, part 3, § 25, 154.

42. *KSA*, 12: 285. At one time during this period, Nietzsche had the intention to include a long chapter "on the physiology of art" in the "principal work" he was working on, which never saw the light of day.

43. *KSA*, 8: 388.

44. See Blondel, *Nietzsche, le corps et la culture*, 298.

45. *Daybreak*, § 461, "Hic Rhodus, hic salta," 462. Among his fragments from spring and summer 1888, Nietzsche notes regarding music: "Has it not lost all more spiritual beauty, all high and exuberant perfection, which in its audacity still embraces grace, the irresistible leap and dance of logic . . ." *KSA*, 13: 491.

46. Quoted in Henry-Louis de La Grange, *Gustav Mahler*, vol. 2, *Vienna: The Years of Challenge, 1897–1904* (New York: Oxford University Press, 1995), 403.

47. Cf. *Thus Spoke Zarathustra*, 227–28. For a time, Mahler thought about naming this symphony "The Gay Science" or "My Gay Science." Some of its movements were written separately in 1896 and 1897. It was not performed as a single work until June 1902.

48. Richard Strauss, *Recollections and Reflections*, ed. Willi Schuh, trans. L. J. Lawrence (Westport, CT: Greenwood, 1974), 155. When *Thus Spake Zarathustra* was performed for the first time on 27 November 1896 in Frankfurt under the composer's direction, Peter Gast complained about the spirit of the work, which he maintained betrayed the original.

49. As he told Jean Marnold, the musical critic for *Mercure de France*, according to Romain Rolland, in his *Journal* for 22 March 1907. "Richard Strauss et Romain Rolland," in *Richard Strauss and Romain Rolland: Correspondance, fragments de journal*, Cahiers Romain Rolland, 3 (Paris: Albin Michel, 1951), 163–64.

50. Claude Debussy, from an article that appeared in *Gil Blas*, 30 March 1903, "Monsieur Croche the Dilettante Hater," trans. B. N. Langdon Davis, in *Three Classics in the Aesthetic of Music* (New York: Dover, 1962), 46. This article ends with the well-known phrase, "I say again that it is not possible to withstand his irresistible domination."

51. "Richard Strauss et Romain Rolland," 138.

52. Strauss, *Recollections and Reflections*, 156.

53. This is what he hinted more than once to an uncomprehending Hofmannsthal. See *A Working Friendship: The Correspondence between Richard Strauss and Hugo von Hofmannsthal*, 250, 258, 262.

54. *Human, All Too Human*, vol. 1, § 217, 100. Wagner, we have seen, thought something similar. See also *Daybreak*, § 239, where having begun by saying that "our composers have made a great discovery: *interesting ugliness* too is possible in their art!" Nietzsche adds, "But you will have to hurry! Every art which has made this discovery has turned out to have only a short time to live" (239).

55. Second postscript, *The Case of Wagner*, 187.

56. The first French translation of *The Case of Wagner* appeared in 1893. According to René Peter, Debussy read it "with a passionate amusement." *Claude Debussy* (Paris: Gallimard, 1944), 63–64.

57. "Cock and Harlequin," 13.

58. Igor Stravinsky, *Chronicle of My Life* (London: Victor Gollancz, 1936), 68–69.

59. Charles Baudelaire, *Eugene Delacroix: His Life and Work*, trans. Joseph M. Berstein (New York: Lear Publishers, 1947), 42.

60. Speaking of this piece for piano, which was then titled "Hymn to Friendship," Nietzsche wrote to Malwida von Meysenbug, on 2 January 1875: "Furthermore, I have revised and put into order the compositions from my youth. It is eternally a wonder to me how, the immutability of character reveals itself in music. What a boy expresses in music is so clearly the language of his deepest nature as a whole, that even the man does not wish anything in it to be changed—apart of course from its imperfections of technique etc." *SB*, 5: 7.

61. The composer replied to these two gifts with a polite, ambiguously worded note (without mentioning the musical score), which Nietzsche took as a sign of profound recognition: "Johannes Brahms takes the liberty of thanking you most sincerely for what you have sent him—he regards it as a signal honor, and he is grateful for the considerable stimulus he has derived from it. Most respectfully" (quoted by Nietzsche in a letter to Peter Gast dated 20 December 1887, *SB*, 8: 212). Brahms had read with interest *Beyond Good and Evil*, but as he wrote in 1888 to his friend Elizabeth von Herzogenberg, Nietzsche was reputed to be "a fitting illustration of his book." "Don't waste the precious daylight too often by reading such things and remember the saying 'the reverse may be true.'" See David S. Thatcher, "Nietzsche and Brahms: A Forgotten Relationship," *Music and Letters* 54, no. 3 (July 1973): 261–80.

62. Letter dated 14 June 1874, *SB*, 4: 236.

63. The *Triumphlied*, op. 55, was based on a text from Revelation 19 that refers to the massacre of the Beast and the triumph of the Kingdom of God. As Claude Rostand, Brahms's biographer, indicates, it was written in a state of "patriotic and warlike delirium." *Brahms* (Paris: Fayard, 1978), 470. Obsessed by Wagner, the French seem to forget or to be unaware that Brahms was undoubtedly of all the German composers the most nationalistic and the most Francophobic.

64. See Wagner, "About Conducting," in *Richard Wagner's Prose Works*, 4: 348, 349, 363.

65. Entry from 6 August 1874, *Cosima Wagner's Diaries*, 1: 779.

66. Entry from 6 August 1874, *Cosima Wagner's Diaries*, 1: 780.

67. Entry from 8 August 1874, *Cosima Wagner's Diaries*, 1: 780.

68. *KSA*, 7: 765.

69. *Richard Wagner in Bayreuth*, 319. Schaeffner's comment comes from *Lettres à Peter Gast*, 1: 71.

70. Posthumous fragment from summer 1878, *KSA*, 8: 535.

71. On 8 June 1887 he wrote to Peter Gast that Brahms was thinking of composing a "romantic opera," with a text by J. V. Widmann adapted from a comedy by Gozzi, "The Public Secret" (*SB*, 8: 87). Two years before this, Tchaikovsky had written to one of his correspondents: "To abstain from composing operas is the work of a hero, and we have only one such hero in our time—Brahms." Cited by Herbert Weinstock, *Tchaikovsky* (New York: Alfred A. Knopf, 1966), 266.

72. Second postscript, *The Case of Wagner*, 188.

73. Second postscript, *The Case of Wagner*, 187–88. There is something surprising about such praise for female followers of Wagner. Perhaps Nietzsche is here thinking of Madame Louis Ott, a charming Parisian, gifted with a lovely voice, whom he met at Bayreuth in 1876 ("a charming Parisienne tried to console me," he says in *Ecce Homo*) and with whom he maintained until 1872 "one of his most tender and most fervent epistolary relationships" (Janz, *Nietzsche: Biographie*, 2: 177). Otherwise, Nietzsche thought no higher of female Wagnerians than of female Brahmsians. If he is somewhat discrete in *The Case of Wagner*, where he attributes the composer's success to his effect on "the nervous system and therefore on women," in his notebooks, on the contrary, he lets fly with his physiologist's perspective: "As regards the true 'Maenads' who worship Wagner, we can without hesitation conclude hysteria and sickness: something is not right within their sexuality; or there is a lack of children or, in the most tolerable case, lack of men" (*KSA*, 11: 674). Prior to the first postscript to *The Case of Wagner*, Nietzsche had written in his notes in 1885: "How much middle-class German mediocrity feels at ease today in the music of its Brahms, to which it feels itself related" (*KSA*, 12: 46). "In the evening alone with our friends; conversation about Herr Brahms and his damaging and bigoted influence on the educated middle classes," Cosima Wagner reports in her diary entry for 1 August 1874 (1: 778). That Nietzsche had pronounced a "death sentence" on the composer (as he wrote to Gast on 9 August 1888, *SB*, 8: 382) did not stop his sister Elizabeth Förster-Nietzsche and Gast from having a piece by Brahms (*Klänge*) performed at the funeral service for Nietzsche held in Weimar on 27 August 1900.

74. Second postscript, *The Case of Wagner*, 188.

75. See Wagner, "On the Application of Music to the Drama," in *Richard Wagner's Prose Works*, 6: 182.

76. *Twilight of the Idols*, "Expeditions of an Untimely Man," § 43, 96–97.

77. *KSA*, 12: 240.

78. *Lettres à Peter Gast*, 1: 162. "The best German opera is that by my friend Heinrich Köselitz [Peter Gast], the only one who is free from Wagnerian Germany: a new composition of *Matrimonio segreto*. The second best is Bizet's *Carmen*—which is almost as free; the third best, Wagner's *Die Meistersinger:* a masterpiece of musical dilettantism," wrote Nietzsche in his notebooks from the spring of 1888 (*KSA*, 13: 463). Regarding Gast, cf. Schaeffner's comments in *Lettres à Peter Gast*, 1: 153–83. The conductor Herman Levi, whom Nietzsche respected, thought Gast "an utter incompetent" (according to Gregor-Dellin, *Wagner*, 518). What Nietzsche heard in Gast's music was undoubtedly the music to which he aspired more than what Gast actually wrote. As he would say to Franz Overbeck in 1885: "the need he had for it was such that it made him less capable of really evaluating it."

79. *Human, All Too Human*, vol. 2, part 2, § 157, 346.

80. *Human, All Too Human*, vol. 1, § 164, 88.

81. *Human, All Too Human*, vol. 1, § 165, 88.

82. Initial version of § 7 of *The Case of Wagner*.

83. In his letter of invitation, Karl Mendelssohn added, after having said that he held Bach's preludes and fugues in the highest regard, "but this does not stop me from holding Wagner's music for the greatest thing this century has produced and I would confess to anyone the gripping effect it has produced on me. I do not know Wagner personally, but I do not doubt that if I were to make his acquaintance and he were to welcome me as a friend, we should get on well. That in his writings he judges the influence of Jews to be deleterious to the development of modern music, and that he takes my father to be a Jew, is a point for debate; I believe we could examine the pros and cons while navigating the blue waves of the Ionian Sea." *KGW BW*, vol. 2, part 2, 546.

84. Letter to Hugo von Senger dated 23 September 1872, *SB*, 4: 50.

85. See "About Conducting," in *Richard Wagner's Prose Works*, 4: 180.

86. Richard Wagner, "Judaism in Music," in *Richard Wagner's Prose Works*, 3: 75–122. It is interesting to compare to this portrait the judgment of Heine, who, contrary to Nietzsche, did not see an art of lying in dramatic music. "Mendelssohn always gives us occasion to reflect on the highest problems in aesthetics. He constantly recalls, for example, the great question, What is the difference between Art and the Falsehood? We admire in this master, most of all, his great talent for form, for style, his gift for appropriating whatever is most remarkable, his delightfully beautiful summary or plan [*Faktur*], his fine lizard-like ear, his delicate antennae or snail-horns of perception, and his serious or earnest—I may say passionate—indifference. Should we seek in a sister art for a similar instance, we may find it in poetry, and it is called Louis Tieck. This master, also, knew well how to reproduce that which was most excellent, be it in writing or by declamation. He could even affect the natural and unaffected, yet he never created anything which conquered masses and remained alive in their hearts. . . . The more gifted Mendelssohn may sooner succeed in creating something which may endure, but not on the ground where, above all things, truth and passion are required—on stage; for Ludwig Tieck, not withstanding his most ardent

yearning, never achieved a theatrical success." "The Musical Season of 1844," in *Lutèce* [1855], in *The Works of Heinrich Heine*, vol. 4: *The Salon*, trans. Charles Godfrey Leland (London: William Heinemann, 1893), 408–9.

87. Whence, too, the note to his postscript to *The Case of Wagner* which, like killing two birds with one stone, hints that Wagner was the son of a Jewish actor, his stepfather, Ludwig Geyer. But, even though Wagner may have believed this, it seems well established that this was not the case; and, in any case, Ludwig Geyer was not a Jew.

88. *KSA*, 8: 545–46.

89. *KSA*, 12: 90. We find a brief comparison to Brahms as well in this same volume: "—the forms borrowed, by Brahms for example, as the typical 'epigone,' similarly Mendelssohn's cultivated Protestantism (one recreates after the fact an earlier 'soul' . . .)" *KSA*, 12: 285.

90. *Beyond Good and Evil*, § 245, 181, 182.

91. Fragment from the summer of 1882, *KSA*, 9: 682.

92. *Human, All Too Human*, vol. 2, part 2, § 159, 347.

93. *Human, All Too Human*, vol. 2, pt. 2, § 160, 347.

94. Bianquis, *Nietzsche devant ses contemporains*, 97–98.

95. Fragment from 1882, *KSA*, 9: 682. "Poor, sick France, sick in its will," he will say in *Twilight of the Idols*, something his compatriots also will have come to believe, particularly the Imperial general staff in August 1914.

96. *KSA*, 8: 545.

97. Fragment from 17 December 1888, *KSA*, 13: 642). Today Nicolo Jomelli (1714–74) has been largely forgotten—only one of his works, *Passione*, is available. He had been a pupil of Leo and of Prata at Naples and was the first Italian composer to react against the sclerosis that threatened *opera seria*. As such, he represents an important step between Pergolosi and Mozart.

98. Entry for 25 March 1880, *Cosima Wagner's Diaries*, 2: 457–58. The "impersonal" character Wagner saw in Leo's *Miserere* is also what he admired in Bach's keyboard works. A short time thereafter, Wagner also heard *La Bataille de Marignan* by Clément Jannequin, as performed by the pupils of the Conservatory in Naples, but the work apparently did not please him. See Cosima's comment from 21 April 1880 (2: 468). In March 1886, at Monte Carlo, Nietzsche will listen "with a lively curiosity to some old things by Rameau" (fragments from *Castor et Pollux*), according to a letter to Peter Gast, *SB*, 7: 165. Regarding this rediscovery of older and Baroque music, see Ivan Alexandre's preface, "Le printemps des Anciens," in *Guide de la musique ancienne et baroque* (Paris: R. Laffont, 1993), vi–xlviii.

99. *Human, All Too Human*, vol. 2, pt. 2, § 165, 348. Throughout most of the nineteenth century, *Don Giovanni*, one of the few operas by Mozart to stay in the repertoire, did so at the price of various transformations and mutilations since it was treated as another Romantic grand opera. Thought to be incongruous, the final sextet was cut, and the scene with the Commandatore was usually the excuse for some large-scale spectacle where the macabre was mixed with the infernal. See my "Mozart, 1798–1985,"

in the new edition of *Mozart* (Paris: Hachette, 1985), 213–63, which I have drawn upon in the following pages. See also his preface to Nietzsche's *Lettres à Peter Gast* (132–34), in which Schaeffner was the first to analyze the "lesson in interpretation" Nietzsche gave of this work in this passage from *Human, All Too Human*.

100. *The Case of Wagner,* § 9, 174.

101. *Human, All Too Human,* vol. 2, pt. 2, § 165, 348.

102. *Beyond Good and Evil,* § 245, 180.

103. "A la veille de *Pelléas et Mélisande,*" *Revue d'histoire et de critique musicale* (1902), reprinted in Debussy, *Monsieur Croche et autres écrits* (Paris: Gallimard, 1971), 267.

104. Paul Dukas, "Mozart et Rameau," *La Revue hebdomadiare* (May 1901), reprinted in *Les écrits de Paul Dukas sur la musique* (Paris: Société d'Éditions françaises et internationales, 1948), 540–43.

105. Entry from 6 July 1869, *Cosima Wagner's Diaries,* 1:120–21. "We are too apt to vent our bad humour on Wagner. But we ought to have the courage to go back as far as Beethoven. It is there that the drama, or rather the melodrama, begins," Cocteau will write in "Cock and Harlequin" (72).

106. *The Case of Wagner,* § 3, 169.

107. *KSA,* 12: 344.

108. *KSA,* 12: 361. Nietzsche's admiration for Offenbach also extended to his librettists, Meilhac and Haléy, "the best poets to whom my taste promises immortality," he writes in his notebooks in October 1888 (*KSA,* 13: 619). "The texts of Offenbach have something captivating about them and are probably the only case so far where opera has worked in *favor* of poetry," he had written to Gast a few months earlier (*SB,* 8: 275). What a pleasant surprise it must have been for him to learn that *The Case of Wagner*—that "operetta music" he had first of all meant for Parisians—was his first book to be translated into French, and this by Halévy's son, Daniel, in collaboration with Robert Dreyfus. See my "Daniel Halévy et Nietzsche," in the catalog for the exhibition *La Famille Halévy, 1760–1960,* presented at the Musée d'Orsay in 1996 (Paris: Fayard, 1996).

109. *KSA,* 12: 41–42.

110. *SB,* 8: 275 and 8: 204.

111. In 1867—the year that he heard *La Belle Hélène* for the first time, with enthusiasm, in Leipzig—Nietzsche thought about spending a year in Paris along with his friends Rohde and Gersdorff. See *SB,* 2: 205, 212, 254, 264, 274, 276. See also Jean Lacoste, "Le rêve parisien de Nietzsche," postscript to *Oeuvres,* 1: 1304–8.

112. *Ecce Homo,* "Why I Am So Clever," § 5, 248.

113. Entry for 21 April 1913, Stefan Zweig, *Journaux, 1912–1940* (Paris: Belfond, 1986).

114. *KSA,* 8: 367. Perhaps Nietzsche would have been surprised, and touched, by the anecdote that Jean Cocteau recounts in his *Portraits-souvenir* (1900–14): "One night, several years ago, at Offenbach's *La Belle Hélène,* a friend pointed out an old lady crying in the shadows of a neighboring box. It was Cosima Wagner. Switzerland!

Tribschen! Paul Rée! Nietzsche's words: 'We will go to see them dancing the cancan in Paris,' the joyous youth, the arguments, the brawls. . . . Cosima Wagner might perhaps have borne the *Ride of the Valkyries* courageously. She was crying during the *Royal March.*" *Souvenir Portraits: Paris in the Belle Epoque,* trans. Jesse Browner (New York: Paragon House, 1990), 36–37.

115. *SB*, 8: 444. This, the most successful of the operettas created by Edmond Audran (1840–1901), premiered in Paris on 28 December 1880, then was performed in Vienna and Berlin the following year and in Milan in 1886.

116. *SB*, 8: 478–79.

117. "As regards the elementary conditions of genius, Offenbach was more of a genius than Wagner." *KSA*, 12: 522.

118. Marcel Proust, *In Search of Lost Time,* vol. 5: *The Captive,* 205. *Le Postillon de Longjumeau* was a well-known comic opera by Adolphe Adam (1803–1856), first presented at the Opera-Comique in 1836.

119. Letter dated 16 December 1888, *SB*, 8: 526–27 (*SL*, no. 191, 333–35).

120. *Ecce Homo,* "Why I Am So Clever," § 7, 251.

121. The following rare fragment from his notes from fall 1881 bears witness to this: "Verdi is weak in inventions with any lovely sensuality and he even lets us see that he has to treat them very sparingly. But he holds his public by means of his few inspirations—they are as impoverished as he is, notwithstanding the fact that they want nothing more, any more than he himself does—hence he is their man and their master. W[agner] too has an impoverished sensuality and relative to melody he has an obstinacy for such poverty to the point of madness—but how has been able to build out of this a bridge to the ideal!" *KSA*, 9: 600.

122. Second postscript, *The Case of Wagner,* 188, and *The Gay Science,* § 80, 135.

123. Letter to Peter Gast dated 4 March 1882, *SB*, 6: 174.

124. Letter to Peter Gast dated 16 September 1882, *SB*, 6: 262. Bellini was born in Catania.

125. Fragments from fall 1881, *KSA*, 5: 595. "The fiotura and cadences of music are like a soothing ice in summer" (5: 593).

126. Entry from 7 March 1878, *Cosima Wagner's Diaries,* 2: 35.

127. The following year, for another performance of this work, given for his benefit, Wagner even wrote an aria for bass and chorus, "Norma il predesse."

128. "Autobiographical Sketch" (1842), in *Richard Wagner's Prose Works,* 1: 9.

129. He had send a copy of his "Hymn to Life" to the orchestra conductor Felix Mottl, who replied with an "extremely polite" letter, Nietzsche writes to Peter Gast, although "he would have preferred a composition richer in melody—ah, how right he is!" *SB*, 8: 184.

130. Letter dated 17 November 1880, *SB*, 6: 47–48.

131. Fragment from fall 1881, *KSA*, 9: 630.

132. Letter dated 10 November 1887, *SB*, 8: 190 (*SL*, no. 157, 274).

133. Posthumous fragment from May–July 1885, *KSA*, 11: 538. "A properly *German* taste in music still does not exist even today," he adds.

134. *KSA*, 11: 538. In the letter to Gast just cited (n. 133 above), Nietzsche correctly comments that it is a question of an "opposition between styles": where the composers come from is of no account here. Thus Handel is an Italian, Gluck a Frenchman. . . . There are native-born Italians who honor the French style, there are native-born Frenchmen who write Italian music." Regarding this "great stylistic opposition," Nietzsche recommends that Gast read "the *Mémoires* of Président de Brosses (his *Italian Journey*, 1739), in which this problem is continuously touched on, and with passion."

135. Quoted by Schaeffner in *Letters à Peter Gast*, 1: 331. This is also what Paul Dukas will conclude in 1905, after having studied the scores for *Orfeo* and the *Couronnement de Poppée* "reconstituted" by Vincent d'Indy, who was also to direct their performance at the Schola Cantorum: "At bottom and in form Monteverdi's innovations stand in a direct relation to those of Lulli, Rameau, Gluck, and Wagner. The musician from Cremona was the first in this great line and the equal of his brothers in genius. His conception of drama is grandiose, almost austere." "Claudio Monteverdi," *Chronique des arts et de la curiosité* (March 1905), reprinted in *Les écrits de Paul Dukas sur la musique*, 619. Nietzsche, Wagner, and Gast could have known *Orfeo* since the score of this work, unlike that of *Le Couronnement*, had been published in 1609 and then again in 1615. Several copies of these editions still exist, two of them in Germany. The first modern German edition was by Robert Heitner in 1881. Nietzsche had sent Peter Gast the book by Arthur Pougin, *Les vrais créateurs de l'opéra français* (Paris: Charavay, 1881). "The most interesting passage is made up of a long letter written in 1659 by Perrin, that original mind to whom we owe French opera. In it, he methodically enumerates, under nine headings, the reasons for French repugnance for Italian opera of the time, and *in response to which* innovation was tried for. This letter, reproduced for the first time in this book, is a capital fact for the history of culture." *SB*, 8: 211–12.

136. Gabriele D'Annunzio, *Le Feu*, trans. Georges Hérelle (Paris: Calmann-Lévy, 1924), 285.

137. Letter to Peter Gast dated 24 November 1887, *SB*, 8: 203 (*SL*, no. 159, 277).

138. *The Birth of Tragedy*, § 19, 115, 117, 119.

139. Cf. his letter to Franz Overbeck dated 18 October 1888, *SB*, 8: 453 (*SL*, no. 180, 314–16).

140. Letter dated 10 November 1887, *SB*, 8: 190 (*SL*, no. 157, 275).

141. A poem that Nietzsche perhaps dedicated to Peter Gast, *KSA*, 11: 302–3. Mozart is annexed to the south, he whose "genius was not German" and who "was always dreaming of Italy when he was not there. *Human, All Too Human*," vol. 2, pt. 2, § 152, 345.

142. *Twilight of the Idols*, "How the 'Real World' at last Became a Myth," § 3, 40. Königsberg was Kant's hometown.

143. *KSA*, 12: 37.

144. Fragment from fall 1887, *KSA*, 12: 484.

145. Fragment from fall 1881, *KSA*, 9: 607. Shortly before this, he had written: "'How could I bear to live up to now!' on the Posilippo, traveling in a carriage—Light

of evening" (*KSA*, 9: 600). Wagner, whom the "permanent gray of the winter sky over Bayreuth" wore out, too had spent time in Naples the preceding year, from 4 January until 7 August. Cosima's diary carries many reminders of the pleasure this climate and countryside gave him, in particular, the view they discovered from the Posilippo. "If I lived in Naples or in Andalusia, or even in one of the Antilles, I should write a great deal more poetry and music than in our grey, misty climate, which disposes one only to abstraction," he wrote to Liszt on 13 April 1852 (*Correspondence of Richard Wagner and Franz Lizst*, 1: 197). It was in Palermo that he had completed the orchestration of *Parsifal* in 1881.

146. "One's masks fall away on hearing Italian music," he writes to himself in the fall of 1881. *KSA*, 9: 588.

147. *The Gay Science*, § 77, 132.

148. *Beyond Good and Evil*, § 255, 195.

149. *The Case of Wagner*, § 3, 159.

150. Nor should we overlook Edouard Lalo's *Symphonie espagnole* (1873). Nietzsche would no doubt have been highly amused to learn that in July 1889, during the Bayreuth Festival, Emmanuel Chabrier, who had been invited by Cosima to dine at the Villa Wahnfried, played *España* on the master's piano. Nietzsche seems not at this time to have heard anything Russian, other than a performance in Nice in 1886 by a chorus whose European tour was causing a great splash. But not for him: "*tours de force* of choral singing, the *pianissimi*, the acceleration of *tempo*, and a certain virginal purity of voice evidently merit great praise. But most of it was not sufficiently Russian . . . or as Russian only uniquely in the vulgar, instinctive sense (with a melancholic submission impregnating even the gayest tune). The virile note, the mark of the ruling classes and their pride, was completely lacking." *SB*, 7: 166, 27 March 1886.

151. According to a letter dated 7 November 1872 to Malwida von Meysenbug, *SB*, 4: 80 (*SL*, no. 47, 108). "If I were to have gone to Florence, it would have been *exclusively* to see you (and not for a few paintings)," he wrote to her a few months later, *SB*, 4: 141. See Guy de Pourtalès, *Nietzsche en Italie* (Paris: L'Age d'Homme, 1993).

152. "Toward New Seas," one of six "Songs of Prince Vogelfrei" that Nietzsche published as an appendix to *The Gay Science* (371). In the same book, see also the quite lovely aphorisms: § 60, "Women and their action at a distance" (123–24) and § 310, "Will and Wave" (247–48) as well as *Daybreak*, § 423, "In the great silence." Let us also recall that in *Doctor Faustus*, one of the first works composed by Adrian Leverkühn (Nietzsche's novelistic double) is a *Meerleuchten* ("Mirror-Like" or "Sea Phosphorences") symphonic reverie "of a sparkling, nocturnal impressionism."

153. Cocteau, "Cock and Harlequin," 33.

154. *The Case of Wagner*, § 10, 178.

155. *Beyond Good and Evil*, § 224, 152.

156. *The Case of Wagner*, §§ 1–2, 157–59.

157. *Beyond Good and Evil*, § 254, 193.

158. Letter to Peter Gast dated 6 January 1888, *SB*, 8: 227. Nietzsche had heard the evening previously, among other things, the *Chasse fantastique*, a symphonic poem

by Ernest Guiraud, as well as selections drawn from Massenet's score for Leconte de Lisle's *Erynnies* (according to *Lettres à Peter Gast*, 1: 333). Two years before this, extracts from Massenet's *Scènes alsaciennes* had already displeased him: "thoroughly modern, orchestrated in a frightfully polychromatic fashion. I had not thought one could prostitute orchestration this way," he wrote to Gast on 27 March 1886. *SB*, 7: 165.

159. *Beyond Good and Evil*, § 254, 194–95.

160. *SB*, 6: 144. At the time, *Carmen* was a huge success throughout Europe and often over works by Verdi and Wagner. It had been in the repertory of the Vienna opera for six years. Wagner attended two performances there shortly after its premiere on 6 November 1875. As for Berlioz, Nietzsche seems to have much appreciated him during his youth, and even afterward. "This evening I knew a quarter-hour of real happiness: I heard Berlioz's *Roman Carnival*," Nietzsche wrote, for example, to Erwin Rohde on 15 November 1874, following a concert given by the Basel Concert Society. *SB*, 4: 276.

161. Letter dated 5 December 1881, *SB*, 6: 145 (*SL*, no. 92, 180). In reply to his earlier letter, Gast had written on 29 November that Bizet had been dead for six years and that he had been a pupil of Fromenthal-Halévy.

162. Letter to Peter Gast, 8 December 1881, *SB*, 6: 147.

163. From two versions of the chapter on *Human, All Too Human* in *Ecce Homo*, *KSA*, 13: 23.

164. Nietzsche wrote seventy comments in pencil in the margins of a score of *Carmen* that he sent to Peter Gast in January 1882. A copy of this annotated score exists in the Bibliothèque nationale in Paris.

165. *KSA*, 13: 23.

166. "For us fatalists of today the lascivious melancholy of a Moorish dance is more likely to move our hearts than is the Viennese sensuality of a German waltz— too blond, too stupid a sensuality," *KSA*, 12: 473. Something of this Moorish (gypsy, really) dance carried over into the "Among the Daughters of the Wilderness" episode of *Thus Spoke Zarthustra*.

167. Quoted by Janz, *Nietzsche: Biographie*, 3: 35. Having attended a new performance of *Carmen* in Genoa, Nietzsche wrote to Peter Gast on 22 March 1883: "This music touches something very deep in me, and I promise myself I shall always bear this and expel my most extreme malice rather than perish from it. During these days, I have been composing Dionysian songs wherein I take the liberty of saying horrible things in a horrible way, leading to laughter. This is the most recent form of my madnesss" (*SB*, 6: 347). As for the mistral, to which Resa von Schirnhofer alludes, let us note that Nietzsche wrote in 1884 a "dance song" titled "To the Mistral," which he sent to Peter Gast, hoping that it would awaken "that great *Orchester-Tanz*, with a sublime abandon" that lay dormant within him, "a dance for *large* orchestra capable of roaring and rumbling." *SB*, 6: 558.

168. Second postscript, *The Case of Wagner*, 186.

169. Nietzsche heard not just *Carmen* by Bizet, but also with great pleasure his *Roma* suite from *Arlésienne* ("the adagietto gives a wholly sublime sound," he told

Gast on 8 October 1884, *SB*, 6: 540) and the overture *Patrie*. As for *Les Pêcheurs de perles*, he dared not listen to more than one act (in December 1887), for as he told Peter Gast, "The work has not yet found its equilibrium, the influence of models (Gounod, Fel. David, Wagner's *Lohengrin*) is too directly evident in it and has not been assimilated" (*SB*, 8: 212). A good judgment on his part.

170. Letter to Carl Fuchs dated 27 December 1888, *SB*, 8: 554 (*SL*, no. 196, 341). Cf. the portion of *Ecce Homo* devoted to *Tristan* ("Why I Am So Clever," § 6, 249–51), which we have already referred to.

171. In his penultimate letter to Gast, *SB*, 8: 567 (*SL*, no. 199, 344).

172. Letter of 1 February 1888, *SB*, 8: 239.

173. *Ecce Homo*, "Why I Am So Clever," § 6, 250–51. "I feel proud that I have now marked myself out and that people will now always link my name with yours," he had written to Wagner sixteen years previously, shortly after the appearance of *The Birth of Tragedy*. Letter dated 2 January 1872, *SB*, 3: 272 (*SL*, no. 38, 91).

174. Fragment from March 1888, *KSA*, 13: 520. Shortly after this, he writes: "It is unworthy of a philosopher to declare: the beautiful and the good are one; if, furthermore, he adds '"the true equally so,' he deserves a beating. Truth is ugly: *we have art* so that we do not perish from the truth." *KSA*, 13: 500.

175. "Notes sur Nietzsche," in Jarrety, *Valéry, pour quoi?* 35.

176. *Twilight of the Idols*, "Expeditions of an Untimely Man," § 24, 81.

177. *KSA*, 11: 661. "Every good book, even one written against life, is an incitement to live," Thomas Mann will say.

178. *KSA*, 13: 533.

179. As can be seen, for example, in his letter to Peter Gast dated 2 December 1888: "Just returned from a big concert, which really made on me the strongest impression of any concert I have been to—my face kept making grimaces, in order to get over a feeling of extreme pleasure, including, for ten minutes, the grimace of tears." *SB*, 8: 498 (*SL*, no. 188, 327).

180. *The Case of Wagner*, § 1, 158.

181. Letter dated 25 February 1884, *SB*, 6: 480.

182. Letter dated 22 June 1887, *SB*, 8: 95.

183. *The Gay Science*, § 106, 162. In the notes contemporaneous with the writing of this book we find: "Music is my, our *precursor*—to speak personally and well and nobly! Unspeakably much has not yet found words or thoughts—as our music *proves*—*not* that no word or no thought might be found." *KSA*, 9: 582.

184. Franz Overbeck's account of the voyage from Turin to Basel can be found in *Nietzsche devant ses contemporains*, 150–53; and epilogue, *SL*, 351–55. André Malraux made use of this account in his *The Walnut Trees of Altenburg* (New York: Howard Fertig, 1989), 77. The "Gondolier's Song" (sometimes called "Venice") is included in the "Intermezzo" of *Nietzsche contra Wagner*, from which I took the sentence about Venice and music. "The last night I passed near the Pont du Rialto brought me an unbelievable music, an adagio from earlier times, that moved me to tears as though there had never been an adagio until then," Nietzsche wrote to Peter Gast on 2 July 1885 (*Lettres*

à Peter Gast, 2: 188). He stayed in Venice from 10 April until 6 June and occupied a room opening on the Grand Canal near the Pont Rialto.

From Wagner's "Beethoven" (in 1858): "Sleepless one night in Venice, I stepped upon the balcony of my window overlooking the Grand Canal: like a deep dream the fairy city of lagoons stretched in shade before me. From out the breathless silence arose, the strident cry of a gondolier just woken on his barque; again and again his voice went forth into the night, till from remotest distances its fellow-cry came answering down the midnight length of the Canal: dreary melodic phrase, to which the well-known lines of Tasso were also wedded in his day, but which in itself is certainly as old as Venice's canals and people. After many a solemn pause, the ringing dialogue took quicker life, and seemed at least to melt into unison; till finally from far and near died softly back to new-won slumber." "Beethoven," in *Richard Wagner's Prose Works*, 5: 173–74.

185. Bianquis, *Nietzsche devant ses contemporains*, 158.

186. "Would that someone would bring me a phonograph!" he concludes in the letter he writes to Widemann on 1 February 1890. Bianquis, *Nietzsche devant ses contemporains*, 172.

ᛒIBLIOGRAPHY

WORKS BY NIETZSCHE

Nietzsche, Friedrich. *Ainsi parlait Zarathoustra: Un livre que est pour tous et qui n'est pour personne*. Trans. Maurice de Gandillac. Oeuvres philosophiques complètes. Paris: Gallimard, 1971.

———. *Aurore: Pensées sur les préjugés moraux. Fragments posthumes, début 1880–printemps 1881*. Trans Julien Hervier. Oeuvres Philosophiques Complètes, 4. Paris: Gallimard, 1970.

———. *Beyond Good and Evil: Prelude to a Philosophy of the Future*. Trans. Walter Kaufmann. New York: Vintage Books, 1966.

———. *"The Birth of Tragedy" and "The Case of Wagner."* Trans. Walter Kaufmann. New York: Vintage Books, 1967.

———. *Le Cas Wagner; Crépuscule des Idoles; L'Antéchrist; Ecce Homo; Nietzsche contre Wagner*. Trans. Jean-Claude Hémery. Oeuvres Philosophiques Complètes, 8, pt. 1. Paris: Gallimard, 1974.

———.*Considérations inactuelles, I et II: David Strauss, l'apôtre et l'écrivain. De l'utilité et des inconvénients de l'histoire pour la vie. Fragments posthumes, eté 1872– hiver 1873–1874*. Trans. Pierre Rusch. Oeuvres Philosophiques Complètes, 2, pts. 1–2. Paris: Gallimard, 1990.

———. *Considérations inactuelles, III et IV: Schopenhauer éducateur. Richard Wagner à Bayreuth. Fragments posthumes, début 1874—printemps 1876*. Trans. Henri-Alexis Baatsch, Pascal David, Cornélius Heim, Philippe Lacoue-Labarthe, and Jean-Luc Nancy. Oeuvres Philosophiques Complètes, 2, pts. 3–4. Paris: Gallimard, 1988.

———. *Correspondance*. Ed. Giorgio Colli and Mazzino Montinari. Trans. Henri-Alexis Baatsch, Jean Bréjoux, and Maurice de Gandillac. 2 vols. Paris: Gallimard, 1986.

———. *Daybreak: Thoughts on the Prejudices of Morality.* Ed. Maudemarie Clark and Brian Leiter. Trans. R. J. Hollingdale. Cambridge: Cambridge University Press, 1997.

———. *Dernières lettres.* Trans. Catherine Perret, with a preface by Jean-Michel Rey. Paris: Petite Bibliothèque Rivages, 1989.

———. "The Dionysiac World View." In *The Birth of Tragedy and Other Writings.* Ed. Raymond Geuss and Ronald Speirs. Cambridge: Cambridge University Press, 1999.

———. *Dithyrambes de Dionysos: Poèmes et fragments poétiques posthumes, 1882–1888.* Trans. Jean-Claude Hémery. Oeuvres Philosophiques Complètes, 8, pt. 2. Paris: Gallimard, 1974.

———. *Écrits autobiographiques, 1856–1869.* Trans. Marc Marcuzzi and Max Marcuzzi. Paris: Presses Universitaires de France, 1994.

———. *Fragments posthumes, automne 1884–automne 1885.* Trans. Michel Haar and Marc B. de Launay. Oeuvres Philosophiques Complètes, 11. Paris: Gallimard, 1982.

———. *Fragments posthumes, automne 1885–automne 1887.* Trans. Julien Hervier. Oeuvres Philosophiques Complètes, 12. Paris: Gallimard, 1978.

———. *Fragments posthumes, automne 1887–mars 1888.* Trans. Pierre Klossowski and Henri-Alexis Baatsch. Oeuvres Philosophiques Complètes, 13. Paris: Gallimard, 1976.

———. *Fragments posthumes, début 1888–début janvier 1889.* Trans. Jean-Claude Hémery. Oeuvres Philosophiques Complètes, 14. Paris: Gallimard, 1977.

———. *Fragments posthumes, eté 1882–printemps 1884.* Trans. Anne-Sophie Astrup and Marc de Launay. Oeuvres Philosophiques Complètes, 9. Paris: Gallimard, 1997.

———. *Fragments posthumes, printemps–automne 1884.* Trans. Jean Launay. Oeuvres Philosophiques Complètes, 10. Paris: Gallimard, 1982.

———. *Friedrich Nietzsche, Paul Rée, Lou von Salomé: Correspondance.* Trans. Ole Hansen-Løve and Jean Lacoste. Paris: Presses Universitaires de France, 1979.

———. *Frühe Schriften.* Ed. Hans Joachim Mette, Carl Koch, and Karl Schlechta. 5 vols. 1933–40. Reprint, Munich: Beck,1994.

———. *Le Gai savoir; Fragments posthumes, 1881–1882.* Trans. Pierre Klossowski, rev. by Marc. B. de Launay. Oeuvres Philosophiques Complètes, 5. Paris: Gallimard, 1967.

———. *The Gay Science.* Trans. Walter Kaufmann. New York: Vintage Books, 1974.

———. *Humain, trop humain: Un livre pour esprits libres. I, Fragments posthumes, 1876–1878.* Trans. Robert Rovini. Oeuvres Philosophiques Complètes, 3, pt. 1. Paris: Gallimard, 1968.

———. *Humain, trop humain, Un livre pour esprits libres. II, Fragments posthumes, 1878–1879.* Oeuvres Philosophiques Complètes, 3, pt. 2. Paris: Gallimard, Trans. Robert Rovini. Paris: Gallimard, 1968.

———. *Human, All Too Human: A Book for Free Spirits.* Trans. R. J. Hollingdale. New York: Cambridge University Press, 1986.

———. *Lettres à Peter Gast*. Trans. Louise Servicen, with an intro. by André Schaeffner. 2 vols. Monaco: Éd. du Rocher, 1957.

———. *Der musikalische Nachlass* (B). Ed. Curt Paul Janz, with a preface by Karl Schlecta. Basel: Bärenreiter, 1976.

———. *La naissance de la tragédie. Fragments posthumes, automne 1869–printemps 1872*. Trans. Michel Haar, Philippe Lacoue-Labarthe, and Jean-Luc Nancy. Oeuvres Philosophiques Complètes, 1, pt. 1. Paris: Gallimard, 1977.

———. *The Nietzsche-Wagner Correspondence*. Ed. Elizabeth Förster-Nietzsche. Trans. Caroline V. Kerr. New York: Boni & Liveright, 1921.

———. *Nietzsche Werke. Kritische Gesamtausgabe: Briefwechsel*. Ed. Giorgio Colli, Mazzino Montinari, et al. 4 vols. Berlin: de Gruyter, 1975–2000.

———. *Oeuvres*. Ed. Jean Lacoste and Jacques Le Rider. 2 vols. Paris: R. Laffont, 1993.

———. *"On the Genealogy of Morals" and "Ecce Homo."* Trans. Walter Kaufmann. New York: Vintage Books, 1967.

———. *Par-delà bien et mal. [Suivi de] La généalogie de la morale*. Trans. Cornélius Heim, Isabelle Hildenbrand, and Jean Gratien. Oeuvres Philosophiques Complètes, 7. Paris: Gallimard, 1971.

———. *The Portable Nietzsche*. Ed. and trans. Walter Kaufmann. New York: Penguin, 1968.

———. *Sämtliche Briefe: Kritische Studienausgabe*. Ed. Giorgio Colli and Mazzino Montinari. 8 vols. Munich: Deutscher Taschenbuch, and Berlin: de Gruyter, 1986.

———. *Sämtliche Werke: Kritische Studienausgabe*. Ed. Giorgio Colli and Mazzino Montinari. 15 vols. Munich: de Gruyter, 1980.

———. *Selected Letters of Friedrich Nietzsche*. Ed. and trans. Christopher Middleton. Chicago: University of Chicago Press, 1969. Reprint, Indianapolis: Hackett, 1996.

———. *Sur l'avenir de nos établissements d'enseignement; La Philosophie à l'époque tragique des Grecs; Vérité et mensonge au sens extra-moral; et autres écrits posthumes, 1870–1873*. Trans. Jean-Louis Backes, Michel Haar, and Marc B. De Launay. Oeuvres Philosophiques Complètes, n.s., 1, pt. 2. Paris: Gallimard, 1975.

———. *"Twilight of the Idols" and "The Antichrist."* Trans. R. J. Hollingdale. Harmondsworth: Penguin, 1968.

———. *Thus Spoke Zarathustra: A Book for All and None*. Trans. Walter Kaufmann. New York: Viking Press, 1966.

———. *Unfashionable Observations*. Trans. with an afterword by Richard T. Gray. Stanford: Stanford University Press, 1995.

———. *Werke in drei Bänden*. Ed. Karl Schlechta. Munich: Hanser, 1956.

SECONDARY SOURCES

Adorno, Theodor. *In Search of Wagner*. Trans. Rodney Livingston. London: Verso, 1981.

Alexandre, Ivan. Preface to *Guide de la musique ancienne et baroque*. Paris: R. Laffont, 1993.

Andler, Charles. *Nietzsche, sa vie et sa pensée.* 6 vols. New ed. 3 vols. Paris: NRF, 1958.

Andreas-Salomé, Lou. *The Freud Journal of Lou Andreas-Salomé.* Trans. Stanley H. Levy. New York: Basic Books, 1964.

———. *Nietzsche.* Ed., trans., and with an intro. by Siegfried Mandel. Redding Ridge, CT: Black Swan Books, 1988.

———. *Looking Back: Memoirs.* Ed. Ernst Pfeiffer. Trans. Breon Mitchell. New York: Paragon House, 1991.

Appia, Adolphe. *Oeuvres completes.* 10 vols. Paris: L'Age d'Homme, 1986.

Aschheim, Steven E. *The Nietzsche Legacy in Germany, 1890–1990.* Berkeley: University of California Press, 1992.

Bailey, Robert. "The Method of Composition." In *The Wagner Companion.* Ed. Peter Burbidge and Richard Sutton. London: Faber and Faber, 1979.

Barthes, Roland. "Loving Schumann." In *The Responsibility of Forms: Critical Essays on Music, Art, and Representation.* Trans. Richard Howard. New York: Hill and Wang, 1985.

Baudelaire, Charles. *Eugene Delacroix: His Life and Work.* Trans. Joseph M. Bernstein. New York: Lear Publishers, 1947.

———. *The Painter of Modern Life and Other Essays.* Trans. Jonathan Mayne. London: Phaidon Press, 1995.

Beckett, Lucy. *Richard Wagner: Parsifal.* Cambridge: Cambridge University Press, 1981.

Bertram, Ernst. *Nietzsche. Essai de mythologie.* Paris: Rieder, 1932.

Beaufils, Marcel. *Le lied romantique allemand.* Paris: Gallimard, 1982.

———. *Comment l'Allemagne est devenue musicienne.* Paris: R. Laffont, 1983.

———. *Musique du son, musique du verbe.* Paris: Klincksieck, 1994.

Bianquis, Geneviève, ed. *Nietzsche devant ses contemporains.* Monaco: Éd. du Rocher, 1959.

Blondel, Eric. *Nietzsche, le corps et la culture: La philosophie comme généalogie philologique.* Paris: Presses Universitaires de France, 1986.

Bloom, Allan. *The Closing of the American Mind: How Higher Education Has Failed Democracy and Impoverished the Souls of Today's Students.* New York: Simon and Schuster, 1987.

Borchmeyer, Dieter. *Richard Wagner: Theory and Theatre.* Oxford: Clarendon Press, 1991.

Bourcier, Paul. *Histoire de la danse en Occident.* Paris: Seuil, 1978.

Bourget, Paul. *Études et portraits.* Paris: A. Lemmerre, 1889.

Brion, Marcel. *Schumann et l'âme romantique.* Paris: Albin Michel, 1986.

Burbidge, Peter, and Richard Sutton, eds. *The Wagner Companion.* London: Faber and Faber, 1979.

Claudel, Paul. "Richard Wagner, reverie d'un poète." In *Figures et paraboles.* Paris: Gallimard, 1936.

Clément, Alain. *Nietzsche et son ombre: Essai.* Bourges: Amor Fati, 1989.

Closson, Ernest. "Nietzsche et Bizet." *Revue musicale* (1 May 1922): 147–54.

Cocteau, Jean. "Cock and Harlequin." In *A Call to Order.* Trans. Rollo H. Myers. London: Faber and Gwyer, 1926.

————. *Souvenir Portraits: Paris in the Belle Époque*. Trans. Jesse Browner. New York: Paragon House, 1990.

Correspondence of Wagner and Liszt. Trans. Francis Hueffer. Rev. by W. Aston Ellis. 2 vols. New York: Haskell House, 1969.

Dahlhaus, Carl. *Richard Wagner's Musical Dramas*. New York: Cambridge University Press, 1979.

————. *Between Romanticism and Modernism: Four Studies in the Music of the Later Nineteenth Century*. Berkeley: University of California Press, 1980.

————. *The Idea of Absolute Music*. Chicago: University of Chicago Press, 1989.

D'Annunzio, Gabriele. *Le feu*. Trans. Georges Hérelle. Paris: Calmann-Lévy, 1924.

Debussy, Claude. *Three Classics in the Aesthetic of Music: Monsieur Croche the Dilettante Hater*. Trans. B. N. Langdon Davis. New York: Dover, 1962.

————. *Monsieur Croche et autres écrits*. Paris: Gallimard, 1971.

Delacroix, Eugène. *The Journal of Eugéne Delacroix*. Trans. Walter Pach. New York: Crown, 1948.

Deussen, Paul. *Erinnerungen an Friedrich Nietzsche*. Leipzig: Brockhaus, 1901.

Dukas, Paul. *Les écrits de Paul Dukas sur la musique*. Paris: Société d'Éditions Françaises et Internationales, 1948.

Duncan, Isadora. *The Dance of the Future*. New York: Bowles-Goldsmith Co., 1908.

————. *My Life*. New York: Boni and Liveright, 1927.

Einstein, Alfred. *Music in the Romantic Era*. New York: W. W. Norton, 1947.

Ferry, Luc. *Homo aestheticus: The Invention of Taste in the Democratic Age*. Trans. Robert de Loaiza. Chicago: University of Chicago Press, 1993.

Fischer-Dieskau, Dietrich. *Nietzsche and Wagner*. Trans. Joachim Neugroschel. New York: Seabury, 1976.

Gauchet, Marcel. *L'inconscient cérébral*. Paris: Seuil, 1992.

Ghil, René. *Traité du verbe*. Paris: Giraud, 1886.

Girdlestone, Cuthbert. *Jean-Philippe Rameau: Sa vie, son œuvre*. Paris: Desclée de Brouwer, 1983.

Goldschmidt, Georges-Arthur. Preface to Daniel Halévy, *Nietzsche*. Paris: Hachette, 1977.

Gracq, Julien. *Lettrines*. Paris: José Corti, 1967.

Green, Martin. *Mountain of Truth. The Counterculture Begins: Ascona, 1900–1920*. Hanover: University Press of New England, 1986.

Gregor-Dellin, Martin. *Richard Wagner: His Life, His Work, His Century*. Trans. J. Maxwell Brownjohn. San Diego: Harcourt Brace Jovanovich, 1983.

Grérty, André Ernest Modeste. *Mémoires; ou, Essais sur la musique*. Liège: Éditions de Wallnia, 1914.

Grey, Thomas S. *Wagner's Musical Prose: Texts and Contexts*. Cambridge: Cambridge University Press, 1995.

Haar, Michel. "La physiologie de l'art: Nietzsche vu par Heidegger." In *Nouvelles lectures de Nietzsche*, ed. Dominique Janicaud, 70–80. Cahiers L'Age d'Homme, 1. Lausanne: L'Age d'Homme, 1985.

Hanslick, Eduard. *On the Musically Beautiful: A Contribution towards the Revision of the Aesthetics of Music.* Trans. Geoffrey Payzant. Indianapolis: Hackett, 1986.

Heine, Heinrich. "The Musical Season of 1844." In vol. 9 of *The Works of Heinrich Heine.* Trans. Charles Godfrey Leland. London: William Heinemann, 1893.

———. *Germany.* Vols. 5–6 of *The Works of Heinrich Heine.* Trans Charles Godfrey Leland. London: William Heinemann, 1906.

Heller, Erich. *The Importance of Nietzsche: Ten Essays.* Chicago: University of Chicago Press, 1988.

Helmholtz, Hermann von. *On the Sensations of Tone as a Physiological Basis for the Theory of Music.* Trans. Alexander J. Ellis. New York: Dover, 1954.

Hesse, Hermann. *Steppenwolf.* Trans. Basil Creighton, updated by Joseph Mileck. New York: Holt, Rinehart and Winston, 1963.

Hoffmann, E. T. A. *E. T. A. Hoffmann's Musical Writings: Kreisleriana, the Poet and the Composer, Music Criticism.* Ed. David Charlton. Trans. Martyn Clarke. Cambridge: Cambridge University Press, 1989.

Hyslop, Lois Boe, and Francis Edwin Hyslop, Jr., eds. *Charles Baudelaire: A Self-Portrait. Selected Letters.* London: Oxford University Press, 1957.

Janz, Curt Paul. *Nietzsche: Biographie.* Trans. Marc B. de Launay, Violette Queuniet, Pierre Rusch, and Marcel Ulubeyan. 3 vols. Paris: Gallimard, 1984–85.

Jameux, Dominique. "Politique des *Maîtres chanteurs.*" *L'Avant-Scène Opéra* no. 116–117: 172–81.

Jarrety, Michel. *Valéry, pour quoi?* Paris: Les Impressions Nouvelles, 1987.

Jaspers, Karl. *Nietzsche: An Introduction to the Understanding of His Philosophical Activity.* Trans. Charles F. Wallraff and Frederick J. Schmitz. Chicago: Henry Regnery, 1965.

Klossowski, Pierre. *Nietzsche and the Vicious Circle.* Trans. Daniel W. Smith. London: Athlone, 1997.

Lacoste, Jean. "Le rêve parisien de Nietzsche." Postscript to Nietzsche, *Oeuvres,* 1: 1301–65. Paris: R. Laffont, 1993

La Grange, Henry-Louis de. *Gustav Mahler.* Vol. 2, *Vienna: The Years of Challenge, 1897–1914.* New York: Oxford University Press, 1983.

Lasserre, Pierre. *Les idées de Nietzsche sur la musique.* Paris: Mercure de France, 1907.

Lichtenberger, Henri. *Richard Wagner, poète et penseur.* Paris: Félix Alcan, 1911.

Liébert, Georges. Preface to *Wagner et notre temps.* Paris: Hachette, 1978.

———. "Mozart, 1798–1985." In *Mozart.* Paris: Hachette, 1985.

———. "Daniel Halévy et Nietzsche." In *La Famille Halévy, 1760–1960.* Exhibition catalog. Paris: Fayard, 1996.

Lockspeiser, Edward. *Debussy: His Life and Work.* New York: Macmillan, 1965.

Magee, Bryan. *Aspects of Wagner.* Oxford York: Oxford University Press, 1988.

Magnani, Luigi. *Les cahiers de conversation de Beethoven.* Neuchâtel: Éd. de la Baconnière, 1971.

Mallarmé, Stéphane. *Oeuvres complètes.* Paris: Gallimard, 1945.

———. "Richard Wagner, Revery of a French Poet." In *Mallarmé: Selected Prose Poems,*

Essays and Letters. Trans. Bradford Cook. Baltimore: Johns Hopkins University Press, 1956.

Malraux, André. *The Walnut Trees of Altenburg.* New York: Howard Fertig, 1989.

Mann, Thomas. "Nietzsche and Music." In *Past Masters and Other Papers.* Trans. H. T. Lowe-Porter. New York: Alfred A. Knopf, 1933.

———. *Études. Goethe, Nietzsche, Joseph et ses frères.* Trans. Philippe Jaccottet. [Lausanne]: Mermod, 1949.

———. *The Story of a Novel: The Genesis of Doctor Faustus.* Trans. Richard and Clara Winston. New York: Alfred A. Knopf, 1961.

———. "Nietzsche's Philosophy in the Light of Recent History." In *Last Essays.* Trans. Richard and Clara Winston. New York: Alfred A. Knopf, 1966.

———. *Lettres de Thomas Mann.* Vol. 1: 1896–1936. Paris: Gallimard, 1970.

———. *Reflections of a Nonpolitical Man.* Trans. Walter D. Morris. New York: Frederick Ungar, 1983.

———. "The Sorrows and Grandeur of Richard Wagner." In *Pro and contra Wagner.* Trans. Allan Blunden. Chicago: University of Chicago Press, 1985.

Marnat, Marcel. *Maurice Ravel.* Paris: Fayard, 1986.

Massohn, Paul-Marie. "Rameau and Wagner." *Musical Review* 25 (1939): 466–78.

Mauclair, Camille. *La Religion de la musique.* Paris: Librairie Fischbacher, 1909.

Montinari, Mazzino. "Nietzsche-Wagner im sommer 1875." *Nietzsche-Studien* 14 (1985): 13–21.

Moorhead, J. K., ed. *Conversations of Goethe with Johann Peter Eckermann.* Trans. John Oxenford. New York: Da Capo, 1998.

Müller, Ulrich, and Peter Wapnewski, eds. *Wagner Handbook.* Cambridge, MA: Harvard University Press, 1992.

Newman, Ernest. *The Life of Richard Wagner.* Cambridge: Cambridge University Press, 1976.

Norvins, Jacques Marquet de. *Souvenirs d'un historien de Napoléon: Mémorial de J. de Norvins.* Vol. 1. Ed. L. de Lanzac de Laborie. Paris: Plon, 1986.

Peter, René. *Claude Debussy.* Paris: Gallimard, 1944.

Pfeiffer, Ernst, Karl Schlechta, and Erhart Thierbach, eds. *Friedrich Nietzsche, Paul Rée, and Lou von Salomé: Correspondance.* Trans. Ole Hansen-Løve et Jean Lacoste. Paris: Presses Universitaires de France, 1979.

Philippon, Jean. "Nietzsche et Raphaël." In *Nouvelles lectures de Nietzsche,* ed. Dominique Janicaud, 92–107. Cahiers L'Age d'Homme, 1. Lausanne: L'Age d'Homme, 1985.

Podach, Erich Friedrich. *L'effondrement de Nietzsche.* Paris: Gallimard, 1931, 1978.

Pougin, Arthur. *Les vrais créateurs de l'opéra français, Perrin et Cambert.* Paris: Charavay Frères, 1881.

Pourtalès, Guy de, comte. *Nietzsche en Italie.* Lausanne: Éditions L'Age d'Homme, 1993.

Proust, Marcel. *In Search of Lost Time.* Trans. G. K. Scott-Moncrieff and Terence Kilmartin, rev. by D. J. Enright. 6 vols. New York: Modern Library, 1993.

Raynaud, Phillipe. "Nietzsche." In *Dictionaire de philosophie politique*. Ed. Phillipe Raynaud and Stéphane Rials. Paris: Presses Universitaires de France, 1996.

Richard Strauss and Romain Rolland: Correspondance, fragments de journal. Cahiers Romain Rolland, 3. Paris: Albin Michel, 1951.

Richard Wagner to Mathilde Wesendonck. 3d ed. Trans. William Aston Ellis. London: H. Grevel & Co., 1911.

Rosset, Clément. *La force majeure*. Paris: Minuit, 1983.

———. *Esthétique de Schopenhauer*. Paris: Presses Universitaires de France, 1989.

Rostand, Claude. *Brahms*. Paris: Fayard, 1990.

Rousseau, Jean-Jacques. *Politics and the Arts: Letter to d'Alembert on the Theatre*. Trans. Alan Bloom. Glencoe, Ill.: Free Press, 1960.

———. *The Social Contract*. Trans. Maurice Cranston. New York: Penguin, 1968.

———. *A Complete Dictionary of Music*. 2d ed. Trans. William Waring. London, 1779. Reprint, New York: AMS, 1975.

———. *"Essay on the Origin of Languages" and Writings Related to Music*. Ed. and trans. John T. Scott. Collected Works of Rousseau, 7. Hanover, NH: University Press of New England, 1998.

Sans, Edouard. *Richard Wagner et la pensée schopenhauerienne*. Paris: Klincksieck, 1969.

Schaeffner, André. *Essais de musicologie et autres fantaisies*. Paris: Le Sycomore, 1980.

Schiller, Friedrich. "On Naïve and Sentimental Poetry." In *Essays*. Ed. Walter Hinderer. Trans. Daniel O. Dahlstrom. New York: Continuum, 1998.

Schopenhauer, Arthur. *Pararega and Parilpomena: Short Philosophical Essays*. 2 vols. Trans. E. F. J. Payne. Oxford: Clarendon Press, 1974.

———. *The World as Will and Representation*. Trans. E. F. J. Payne. 2 vols. New York: Dover, 1969.

Schuré, Edouard. *Précurseurs et révoltés*. Paris: Perrin, 1930.

Shaw, Bernard. *The Perfect Wagnerite: A Commentary on the Niblung's Ring*. New York: Dover, 1967.

Silk, M. S., and J. P. Stern. *Nietzsche on Tragedy*. Cambridge: Cambridge University Press, 1981.

Starobinski, Jean. *Jean-Jacques Rousseau: Transparency and Obstruction*. Trans. Arthur Goldhammer. Chicago: University of Chicago Press, 1988.

Strauss, Richard. *Recollections and Reflections*. Ed. Willi Schuh. Trans. L. J. Lawrence. Westport, CT: Greenwood, 1974.

Stravinsky, Igor. *Chronicle of My Life*. London: Victor Gollancz, 1936.

———. *Poetics of Music in the Form of Six Lessons*. Trans. Arthur Knodel and Inglof Dahl. Cambridge, MA: Harvard University Press, 1947.

A Working Friendship: The Correspondence between Richard Strauss and Hugo von Hofmannsthal. Trans. Hanns Hammelmann and Ewald Osers, with an intro. by Edward Sackville-West. New York: Random House, 1961.

Thatcher, David. "Nietzsche and Brahms: A Forgotten Relationship." *Music and Letters* 54, no. 3 (July 1973): 261–80.

Valéry, Paul. *Cahiers*. 29 vols. Paris: Centre national de la recherche scientifique, 1957.

———. *Analects*. Trans. Stuart Gilbert. Valéry Collected Works, 14. Princeton: Princeton University Press, 1970.

———. "At the Lamoureux Concert in 1893." In *Occasions*. Trans. Roger Shattuck and Frederick Brown. Valéry Collected Works, 2. Princeton: Princeton University Press, 1970.

Wagner, Cosima. *Cosima Wagner's Diaries*. Ed. and annotated by Martin Gregor-Dellin and Dietrich Mack. Trans. Geoffrey Skelton. 2 vols. New York: Harcourt Brace Jovanovich, 1978–80.

Wagner, Richard. *My Life*. 2 vols. New York: Dodd, Mead and Co., 1911.

———. *Lettres à Otto Wesendonck, 1852–1870*. Paris: Calmann-Lévy, 1924.

———. *Lettres à Hans de Bülow*. Ed. Georges Khnopff. Paris: G. Crès & Cie, 1928.

———. *Parsifal*. Trans. and with a preface by Marcel Beaufils. Paris: Aubier, 1964.

———. *Richard Wagner's Prose Works*. Trans. William Ashton Ellis. 8 vols. London, 1892. Reprint, New York: Broude Brothers, 1966.

———. *The Diary of Richard Wagner, 1865–1882: The Brown Book*. Annotated by Joachim Bergfeld. Trans. George Bird. London: Victor Gollancz, 1980.

———. *Selected Letters of Richard Wagner*. Ed. and trans. Stewart Spencer and Barry Millington. London: Dent, 1987.

Walter, Bruno. *Theme and Variations: An Autobiography*. Trans. James Austin Galston. London: Hamish Hamilton, 1947.

Weinstock, Herbert. *Tchaikovsky*. New York: Alfred A. Knopf, 1966.

Westernhagen, Curt von. *Wagner: A Biography*. Cambridge: Cambridge University Press, 1978.

Zweig, Stefan. *Journaux, 1912–1940*. Ed. Knut Beck. Trans. Jacques Legrand. Paris: Belfond, 1986.